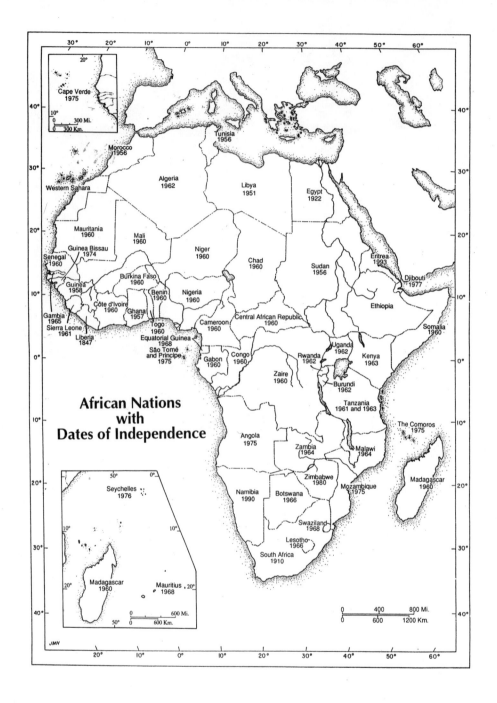

**African Nations with Dates of Independence**

Cape Verde 1975

Morocco 1956

Tunisia 1956

Algeria 1962

Libya 1951

Egypt 1922

Western Sahara

Mauritania 1960

Mali 1960

Niger 1960

Chad 1960

Sudan 1956

Eritrea 1993

Djibouti 1977

Senegal 1960

Guinea Bissau 1974

Guinea 1958

Burkina Faso 1960

Benin 1960

Nigeria 1960

Ethiopia

Somalia 1960

Côte d'Ivoire 1960

Ghana 1957

Togo 1960

Equatorial Guinea 1968

São Tomé and Principe 1975

Gambia 1965

Sierra Leone 1961

Liberia 1847

Cameroon 1960

Central African Republic 1960

Gabon 1960

Congo 1960

Zaire 1960

Rwanda 1962

Burundi 1962

Uganda 1962

Kenya 1963

Tanzania 1961 and 1963

The Comoros 1975

Angola 1975

Zambia 1964

Malawi 1964

Zimbabwe 1980

Mozambique 1975

Madagascar 1960

Namibia 1990

Botswana 1966

Swaziland 1968

Lesotho 1966

South Africa 1910

Seychelles 1976

Madagascar 1960

Mauritius 1968

JMH

*Africa Now*

# Africa Now

## PEOPLE • POLICIES & INSTITUTIONS

*Edited by*

STEPHEN ELLIS

*Editorial Advisory Board*
Chris Atim • Jean-François Bayart • Fifi Benaboud
Henrietta Moore • Washington Okumu

*Ministry of Foreign Affairs (DGIS)*
*The Hague*
*in association with*
JAMES CURREY
*London*
HEINEMANN
*Portsmouth (N.H.)*

796410420

Ministry of Foreign Affairs (DGIS)
The Hague
The Netherlands

in association with
James Currey Ltd
54b Thornhill Square, Islington,
London N1 1BE
England

Heinemann
A Division of Reed Publishing (USA) Inc
361 Hanover Street, Portsmouth
New Hampshire 03801–3912
USA

First published 1996

1 2 3 4 5 00 99 98 97 96

**British Library Cataloguing in Publication Data**

Africa Now: People, Policies and Institutions
I. Ellis, Stephen
960.329

ISBN 0–85255–231–9 Paper (James Currey)
ISBN 0–85255–232–7 Cloth (James Currey)

ISBN 0–435–08987–0 Cloth (Heinemann)
ISBN 0–435–08989–7 Paper (Heinemann)

Chapter head based on a design in
Rebecca Jewell *African Designs*
(British Museum Publications London 1994)

Endpapers. Hand-spun indigo-cotton textile, woven in
4-inch-wide strips, aso-oke, Yoruba, Nigeria.
Collection Horniman Museum. Photograph John Picton.

Jacket and cover. Machine-spun cotton, hand-woven in
4-inch-wide strips, Mali.
Collection Sarah Scott. Photograph John Picton.

Typeset in 10½/11½ pt Bembo by Colset Pte Ltd, Singapore
Printed in Great Britain by Villiers Publications, London N3

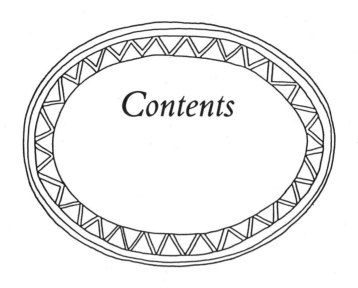

# Contents

# I

## *States & Citizens*

# II
# *Institutions & Policies*

# III
# *Africa in the World*

# List of Contributors

**Janine Aron** is an ESRC Research Fellow at the Centre for the Study of African Economies in the Institute of Economics and Statistics, University of Oxford, Great Britain. She also teaches at the University of the Witwatersrand, South Africa.

**Ernest Aryeetey** is a fellow of the Institute of Statistical, Social and Economic Research, University of Legon, Ghana.

**Chris Atim**, an economist, is a consultant living in London, Great Britain. He was formerly a member of the government of Ghana.

**Jean-Paul Azam** is Professor of Economics at CERDI (Centre d'étude et de recherche sur le développement international), University of Auvergne, Clermont-Ferrand, France.

**Jean-François Bayart** is director of the Centre d'études et de recherches internationales, Paris, France.

**Fifi Benaboud** is a staff member of the North–South Centre of the Council of Europe in Lisbon, Portugal.

**Chaloka Beyani** is Crown Prince Hassan Fellow of the Refugee Studies Programme at Queen Elizabeth House, Oxford, and a fellow of Wolfson College, Oxford, Great Britain. He was formerly a lecturer in law at the University of Zambia.

**Deborah Fahy Bryceson** is a researcher at the Afrika-studiecentrum, Leiden, Netherlands.

**Tiébilé Dramé** is the publisher of *Le Républicain* newspaper, Bamako, Mali. He was Minister of Foreign Affairs of Mali from 1991 to 1992, and research director of the United Nations' Mission in Haïti in 1993–4.

**Ali El-Kenz** teaches sociology at the University of Tunis, Tunisia. He taught previously at the University of Algiers.

**Stephen Ellis** is a researcher at the Afrika-studiecentrum, Leiden, Netherlands.

**Toyin Falola** is Professor of History at the University of Texas at Austin, Texas, USA.

**John Howe** is head of the Infrastructure Department at the International Institute for Infrastructure, Hydraulics and Environmental Engineering, Delft, Netherlands.

**Lilia Labidi** is Professor of Anthropology and Psychology at the University of Tunis, Tunisia.

**Colin McCarthy** is Professor of Economics at the University of Stellenbosch, South Africa.

**Henrietta Moore** is Reader in Anthropology at the London School of Economics, Great Britain.

**Lindani Ndlovu** is head of the Department of Rural and Urban Planning at the University of Zimbabwe, Harare.

**Washington Okumu**, a former international civil servant, is a consultant. He lives in Nairobi, Kenya.

**Solofo Randrianja** is head of the Department of History at the University of Tamatave, Madagascar.

**Mohamed Tozy** is head of the Department of Political Science at Hassan II University, Casablanca, Morocco.

**Nicolas van de Walle** is a research fellow at the Overseas Development Council, Washington DC, USA.

# FOREWORD

## JAN P. PRONK
*Minister for Development Co-operation*
*of the Netherlands*
*Co-Chairman of the*
*Global Coalition for Africa*

We are entering a new era. This applies equally to Africa and to the world. Africa is not merely undergoing a process of political and economic change, what we see is a transformation of societies, of a whole continent. The changes in Africa take place in an international environment that is also changing drastically. These developments seem to have accelerated over the first five years of the 1990s. They have led to new insights, new priorities and an intensified debate on fundamental issues all focusing on the main question: why has real development not taken off in many African countries?

Both Africans and their partners in development agree that the basic answers will have to be given by Africans themselves. Africans will have to decide in which direction and to what extent their countries should review their national and international policies and adjust them to the changed circumstances of the 1990s which offer both challenges and opportunities for Africa.

Despite this African responsibility, it is sometimes felt, and regretted, that Africa's partners show a tendency towards losing interest in Africa. They seem to become increasingly inward-looking and to concentrate their attention (and flow of funds) on themselves or other parts of the world.

This does not mean that the dialogue with Africa has halted. For example, as a result of the 1990 Maastricht Conference on Africa, the Global Coalition for Africa was established. In this forum, representatives of African governments, bilateral donors, regional and multinational agencies and other development partners examine in an informal, frank and open way the full range of long-term development issues. They aim at reaching a consensus on Africa's development objectives and strategies beyond the mere adjustment to factors from outside which was the main theme of the 1980s. Ever since its inception the GCA has tried to play a catalytic role in Africa's development debate and has at times been able to give a new impetus to discussions that had reached deadlock elsewhere.

In this respect I would like to mention specifically the issues of good governance and of the relationship between economic reform and political transformation. Many recent discussions have centred around this dual process and have led to an increased consensus on the necessity of wide participation in policy-making to deepen both political and economic reform and to increase ownership of the processes.

As soon as the Global Coalition partners accepted the offer of the Netherlands Government to host, in Maastricht, the 1995 GCA Plenary meeting on 'Africa's Future and the World' I immediately thought of a book, a collection of essays, as an appropriate gift for the participants. I take enormous pleasure in now being able to offer this book to those coming to Maastricht. I hope that its stimulating and thought-provoking chapters on political, economic and cultural aspects of African development will influence and enrich the urgently needed continued dialogue and partnership between Africa and the world.

The Hague, June 1995

INTRODUCTION

# *Africa Now*

## STEPHEN ELLIS

This book is intended as a review of some of the main trends in Africa in recent years in a wide variety of fields, including politics, economics and society at large. It is specifically intended to stimulate discussion. There is no precise historical starting-point for the analysis, and indeed one of the ideas underlying this project from its inception is the proposition that Africa's current situation, the nature of its public institutions and of the state's attitude towards the citizen and vice versa, are deeply rooted in history. It is commonplace to say that a continent's present is rooted in its past; such a statement would pass for an obvious cliché if it were applied to Europe, say, or Asia. Nevertheless, African problems are sometimes treated as if their roots lay no more than a few years in the past, rather than decades or centuries.

The last few years have seen very rapid changes in Africa, and in the world as a whole, which provide food for thought and discussion for people interested in international affairs. South Africa has abolished apartheid. One-party states have disappeared all over Africa, and virtually all countries have instituted a free press and some sort of multi-party system. Africa's population, growing more quickly than that of any other continent, has increased by perhaps 75 million since 1990. The Soviet Union, one of the two super-powers whose competition had such a massive bearing on the international order, has ceased to exist. Indeed the whole international system, which emerged in the world after 1945 and which witnessed the establishment of modern Africa's independent states, has changed profoundly. Global money transfers, instant communication and rapid airtravel have brought people, and countries, closer together. African capitals are in touch with other world capitals by phone, fax and electronic mail, and yet parts of rural Africa are in some respects more isolated from the rich world than at any time this century. African elites are as mobile as any other world citizens, but governments in developed countries take steps to exclude the poor. How are we to understand these things? What implications might they have for the years ahead?

It is clearly impossible to sketch an answer to these questions by compiling in a single volume a comprehensive survey of developments in 53 sovereign states at a particularly turbulent period. In practice, the only method of approaching the task of reviewing at least some significant developments, in a collection of essays such as the present one, is to identify a number of themes of general interest or relevance and to invite suitably qualified authors to address them. What exactly these themes should be is difficult to say, since it is necessary to encompass trends which will have a resonance over the whole of a large and varied continent. There is little that can be said about one African country which is not at once qualified by the experience of another. Some subjects of undoubted significance may be thought to merit a study of their own; others may merit only a section. What each reader might identify as the right balance will inevitably be a highly personal matter. Even with 14 separate thematic chapters there are vitally important subjects which do not form the subject of a specific essay in the present collection. For example, there is no essay on conflict and its mediation, despite the importance of the subject for many countries and the proliferation of wars. In part this is because of lack of space but it is also because of the great variety of situations in which conflict can arise, which means that armed conflict is better treated in various contexts: in relation to changes in local or national politics and economics, in relation to international relations, and so on. Similarly such major themes as debt, the environment, foreign policy, gender and others are not the subject of special chapters but are covered in passing, not because they are judged unimportant but because they are best understood in a variety of contexts. By the same token, although this study is based on themes rather than specific countries or regions, various countries are discussed in several chapters while others are not mentioned at all, or only barely.

In making a strategic choice of topics for discussion, there is a vast literature to consult, far too large for anyone to master in its entirety. Constant attempts are made by scholars and officials to draw parts of this literature into a coherent whole with a view to providing a basis for discussion and policy-making. For example, perhaps the first attempt to write a thorough survey of contemporary issues in Africa was that undertaken by the British civil servant Lord Hailey almost 60 years ago, which ran to a massive 1,837 pages and which, moreover, limited itself to Africa south of the Sahara rather than to the continent as a whole.[1] The number of such surveys has undoubtedly increased since 1945 and more especially since the majority of African countries became independent sovereign states in the 1950s and 1960s. To cite only a small number of examples among many, one London publisher has since 1971 produced an annual survey of Africa south of the Sahara to accompany the volume it has published on North Africa since 1954,[2] while a French publisher produces an annual survey of African politics.[3] A great variety of yearbooks and reference works concerning Africa is produced by official bodies of various sorts. On economic matters, the World Bank in particular has produced in recent years a series of important surveys and reports on Africa which not only constitute an

---

[1] Lord Hailey, *An African Survey* (Oxford University Press, London, first edition, 1938; second edition, 1945).
[2] *Africa South of the Sahara* and *The Middle East and North Africa* (annual publications, Europa, London).
[3] *L'année africaine* (edited annually by the Centre d'Etude d'Afrique Noire, Bordeaux, since 1963, and published by A. Pedone, Paris, since 1965).

essential corpus of documentation, but which have had a massive influence on the policies adopted by African governments and their international partners due to the World Bank's role as a money-lender. Some individuals have produced general treatments of their own in the form of essays.[4] Quite recently, the French government, the inheritor of the most durable of all European national relationships with Africa, commissioned a wide-ranging survey of African development and of the French contribution to it.[5]

If there has been a key theme of the literature on modern Africa since 1945, it has been that of 'development', a concept used to justify policies said to favour national political integration and economic growth, as well as the motive for massive transfers of funds and other forms of assistance from rich countries to Africa. In recent years there has been widespread agreement that Africa's development, however it is defined exactly, has run into serious problems. There are many different explanations possible for this, but most commentators would agree in attributing part of the reason to the changes in international economic and political relations after the mid-1970s which, even before the spectacular collapse of the Soviet-dominated political system in eastern Europe, marked a faltering of the post-1945 world system.[6] Some scholars have attributed a part of the explanation for the widespread problems encountered by many African countries to the state system which they inherited at independence.[7] For over a decade now some of the most thoughtful African writers have declared categorically that at least some African countries suffer from 'simply and squarely a failure of leadership'.[8] The most influential economists during this period, and most particularly the Bretton Woods institutions – the World Bank and the International Monetary Fund (IMF) – have concentrated their attention on the economic policies applied by those African governments which have called upon the international financial institutions to provide them with loans or other financial assistance. In considering how to act, the IMF and the World Bank believed that improved policies would halt and even reverse Africa's relative economic decline. But the evidence of success has been mixed, to say the least. The World Bank's own claims that the countries which have followed its advice most fully are now seeing improvements are not altogether convincing. The cutting of social security expenditure by many African governments (often, it appears, in preference to cutting expenditure on the armed forces or other sectors) raises questions of whether the social consequences of structural adjustment do not require more attention from international donors. Increasingly, commentators, and the Bretton Woods institutions themselves, are considering other options.[9]

A symptom of this was the World Bank's path-breaking 1989 report on sub-Saharan Africa, sub-titled *From Crisis to Sustainable Growth*.[10] Since its publication the Bretton Woods institutions, and, following their lead, the donor countries as a whole, have increasingly identified the quality of governance as a key factor in determining the success

---

[4] e.g. Guy Hunter, *The Best of Both Worlds? A challenge on development policies in Africa* (Oxford University Press, London, 1967).

[5] Serge Michailof (ed.), *La France et l'Afrique: vade-mecum pour un nouveau voyage* (Karthala, Paris, 1993).

[6] Eric Hobsbawm, *Age of Extremes: the short twentieth century, 1914–1991* (Michael Joseph, London, 1994), p. 6.

[7] Basil Davidson, *Black Man's Burden: the curse of the nation-state in Africa* (James Currey, London, 1992).

[8] Chinua Achebe, *The Trouble with Nigeria* (Kenyan edition, Heinemann Kenya, Nairobi, 1983), p. 1.

[9] World Bank, *Adjustment in Africa: Reforms, results and the road ahead* (Policy Research Report, Oxford University Press, New York, 1994); for a summary of trends in thinking by the international financial institutions, Thomas M. Callaghy & John Ravenhill, 'Vision, politics and structure: Afro-optimism, Afro-pessimism, or realism?', in Callaghy & Ravenhill (eds), *Hemmed In: Responses to Africa's economic decline* (Columbia University Press, New York, 1993), pp. 1–17.

[10] World Bank, *Sub-Saharan Africa: from crisis to sustainable growth* (World Bank, Washington DC, 1989).

or failure of Africa's economic development. Moreover, a number of writers on both economics and political science in recent years have come to identify the quality of public institutions and the civic culture which underpins them as vital factors determining the development of states and nations in general, sometimes described as 'the rules of the game in a society'.[11] This may be attributed in part to the success of some East Asian economies, which has caused theorists and practitioners to think again about exactly what factors lead to economic development. Some important studies have come to the conclusion that at the root of the culture which can generate economic growth are social attitudes developed over very long periods of time, many centuries.[12] One of the most influential works specifically on the state in sub-Saharan Africa in recent years has similarly drawn attention to patterns of political behaviour which are the product of decades or even centuries of evolution.[13] This is an important and timely modification of the view which dominated much of the literature on economic development in earlier decades and which tended to take a more narrowly technical approach to the question of how economic growth could be stimulated and of its relationship to politics. It may be added that some of the most stimulating and influential insights among those mentioned here are the result of work in a variety of academic disciplines, including political science, economics, history and anthropology.

In view of these trends, the present collection of essays is concerned rather less with identifying technical factors hindering or encouraging economic development, which dominated the literature on Africa for so long, than with a discussion of the relationship between individual Africans, the institutions which govern them at national or local level and which to some extent shape their lives, and the international context which has a bearing on both individuals and institutions. Policy, including economic policy, is important, of course, but it is misleading to consider it outside the context in which it is applied and the people who apply it.

## Organization

All of the essays in this collection are intended to be as broad as possible in orientation. However, for the sake of convenience the study is divided into three sections. The first part, consisting of five essays, is entitled 'States and citizens'. It begins with a wide-ranging survey of African history by Toyin Falola, which is intended as an introduction to some of the main themes of the collection as a whole. The other chapters in the first section describe some of the principal techniques which people use to organize or express themselves *en masse* and to structure the relations of power in African societies, or in other human societies for that matter, such as nationality, ethnicity and democracy, analysed by the historian Solofo Randrianja. On the larger scale collective identities involve the creation of 'imagined communities',[14] collections of individuals too numerous for each to have personal knowledge of the other, and which therefore depend for their coherence on an act of the imagination, expressed in symbols of allegiance or

[11] Douglass C. North, *Institutions, Institutional Change and Economic Performance* (Cambridge University Press, Cambridge, 1990), p. 3. cf. Robert D. Putnam, *Making Democracy Work: Civic traditions in modern Italy* (Princeton University Press, Princeton, NJ, 1993).
[12] Putnam, *Making Democracy Work*, esp. pp. 121–62.
[13] Jean-François Bayart, *L'Etat en Afrique: la politique du ventre* (Fayard, Paris, 1989). An English translation was published by Longman, London, in 1993.
[14] Benedict Anderson, *Imagined Communities: Reflections on the origin and spread of nationalism* (Verso, London, 1983).

belief. Precisely because these structures consist, ultimately, of millions of people, each with her or his own character, soul, hopes and fears, discussion of them as abstract categories inevitably carries the risk of losing sight of the individuals who constitute nations, states and other collectivities. These individuals are, in theory if not in practice, the beneficiaries of various public institutions and of the policies implemented by states, aid agencies and other actors in the public arena. Several authors were asked to qualify the generalized and necessarily impressionist nature of general essays on politics and society by demonstrating what these can mean for individuals. Ali El-Kenz examines the problems faced by youth in many parts of Africa and of their role in situations of conflict from the Algiers *casbah* to the townships of Cape Town. In every African country young people form an exceptionally high proportion of the total population as a result of the very high birth rates of recent decades. One of the most obvious areas in which the young in cities especially are searching for new forms of identity and cohesion is through religion, discussed by the political scientist Mohamed Tozy. Lilia Labidi considers what has happened to the social security networks which are available to the very poor, promised the benefits of modern health care and the welfare state at the time of independence, but finding these increasingly difficult to attain. Beyond her study of the dreadful plight of people who sell their own body organs for money, she identifies fundamental debates about the nature of public morality and of the relationship between the individual and the state.

At the heart of all social structures is the notion of belonging and of possessing, or of inclusion and exclusion. In the political world these same qualities, codified in law, constitute citizenship. In any state which models itself on what is now the mainstream international tradition, all holders of a given nationality are equal before the law and have equal civil and political rights, no matter what their disparities of wealth or other attributes. In the case of Africa, partial exceptions exist in formal monarchies, such as Morocco and Swaziland, where the notion of hereditary monarchy holds slightly different implications for the nature of the citizen's relationship to public authority. We may detect another formal difference in the case of states calling themselves Islamic, such as Mauritania and Sudan, where non-Muslims stand in a different relationship to public power from Muslims, inasmuch as they do not subscribe to the state religion. In almost all other cases, formal impediments to this general notion of citizenship have disappeared, notably since the abolition of apartheid in South Africa.

Needless to say, the formal existence of liberal constitutions or comprehensive legal codes does not in itself guarantee the existence of a real active citizenship or the rule of law. In fact the notion of citizenship implied in most African constitutions is at odds with the routine abuse of citizens' rights which is known to exist in some parts of the African continent. If, as several chapters in the present study suggest, African states are faced with profound problems which stem from the authoritarian nature of the state even when there is a multi-party constitution, then the solution will come about only in a redefinition of the relationship between governors and governed and the institutional arrangements they make for its expression, or in other words a redefinition of citizenship.

In this regard, one of the most striking developments in Africa since 1990 has been the shift in formal and institutional arrangements which express the relations of people to their governments. Some of the consequences of this in the economic field are dealt with in the second part of this book, entitled 'Institutions and policies'. Almost every country in Africa has now adopted one of the great symbols of active citizenship, namely the institution of regular, direct elections for senior executive and legislative office in which candidates from a variety of political parties may present themselves. Advocates of democracy argue that this is not only the fairest system, but also one which makes public power more responsive to people's economic needs and which is therefore more likely to encourage economic prosperity. Many of the political problems facing Africa would no doubt become easier to solve in conditions of material prosperity. Conversely, political stability or at least the rule of law is generally believed to favour investment and economic growth. Janine Aron, in an essay of historical depth as well as broad scope, considers the relationship between institutions and economic growth. Governments have adopted not only liberal political forms but also economic ones, with market mechanisms introduced into most areas to a greater degree than in the 1980s. These were designed in order to encourage the emergence of a vibrant private business sector by removing various constraints. Among other things, it was believed that this might cause the informal-sector economic activity which had grown rapidly from the late 1970s to be channelled instead into formal firms, which could operate officially and contribute through taxation to state revenue. However, as Ernest Aryeetey shows, the informal sector has continued to exist and even to expand, and has responded more rapidly to liberalization than the formal sector. The economist Jean-Paul Azam considers some of the effects of structural adjustment in the field of agriculture, where he finds the record to be mixed and to vary greatly from one country to another. He identifies some cases where a liberalized system of agricultural marketing has led to an improvement in market efficiency and even, in Morocco for example, has enabled agriculture to lead a process of economic growth, not through exports but by producing in the first place for the home market. The record is less positive in regard to manufacturing industry, studied by Lindani Ndlovu. He suggests that the rapid application of liberal policies has been devastating to industry in most of Africa, but suggests sectors in which there is promise of growth. Finally, Deborah Fahy Bryceson and John Howe, respectively an economic geographer and a civil engineer, look at some effects of structural adjustment on people in rural areas especially. They suggest that it has created new markets in rural land and labour but has also had complex effects within households, sometimes acting to the detriment of women deprived of older usufruct rights.

It is relevant to recall that all of Africa, with the exceptions of Ethiopia and Liberia, was colonized in some form or other by European powers and that the current political boundaries are essentially those drawn up at the Conference of Berlin in 1884–5.[15] The final part of the book, entitled 'Africa in the world', examines some of the factors governing some aspects of international affairs both within Africa and linking individual African countries to external actors. The political arrangements established in colonial times, and the way in which markets were structured, were intended in the first instance for the convenience of the metropolitan powers rather than for those of their African subjects. The current state system which is under such strain still bears traces of this, as Tiébilé Dramé, himself a former foreign minister of Mali, reminds us. There have been numerous attempts at enhancing regional cooperation or integration in Africa, a subject discussed by Colin McCarthy. In spite of the lack of success of most such attempts, regional trade is likely to be a key factor in forthcoming years, particularly in view of developments in trade policy in other parts of the world. One of the most striking features of African countries is that they have all, to varying degrees, been regarded as potential recipients of aid intended to enhance their economic development. How effective this aid has been

---

[15] Even Ethiopia and Liberia are only partial exceptions. Ethiopia was occupied illegally by Italian troops from 1935 to 1941. Thereafter a British force remained in parts of the country until 1948. Liberia was founded by settlers of African-American origin.

is a matter discussed by Nicolas van de Walle. Foreign aid, whatever other effects it may have had, has served to support the state system which emerged at the time of independence. This same system has proved to be a formidable producer of refugees and in many respects creates problems for economic migrants. International legislation, even where it is enforced, restricts such movements, and is increasingly ignored in practice, as Chaloka Beyani describes. The problems of refugees or other individuals in adversity can be understood only by reference to larger structures, even national or international affairs. All of these subjects overlap and impinge one upon another.

The present collection is intended in the first instance to stimulate discussion for a meeting of decision-makers from Africa and elsewhere and for non-governmental organizations. The concluding chapter, 'Africa's future and the world' is intended to be read as an interpretative essay which bases itself on the division of subjects within the book and on the points made by all the contributors, with a view to underlining some issues worthy of consideration by politicians, decision-makers and others concerned with Africa on the verge of the twenty-first century. We hope that readers of the book and the various contributors will regard it in this light.

## Acknowledgements

Any book to a large extent represents a joint effort, but particularly a collective one such as this. In the first instance, I am grateful to all of the individual authors as well as the five members of the Editorial Advisory Board whose advice was sought on the organization of the book and on the subjects covered. The people who generously agreed to serve as advisers to this project are all people with a broad knowledge of Africa and a suitable mix of professional backgrounds and regional affiliations. They are: Chris Atim, an economist and a former member of the government of Ghana; Jean-François Bayart, director of the Centre d'études et de recherches internationales in Paris; Fifi Benaboud, a staff member of the North-South Centre of the Council of Europe; Henrietta Moore, reader in anthropology at the London School of Economics; and Washington Okumu, a consultant on international affairs and former international civil servant. Their advice has been invaluable, but it should be said that they bear none of the responsibility for any mistakes or flaws which may be detected in the book, which are the responsiblity of the editor and the authors of the individual chapters alone.

I am also indebted to Jan Pronk, the Minister for Development Cooperation in the Netherlands Ministry of Foreign Affairs, for initiating and financing this project. There are few governments in the world which would be prepared to invest in a general study of this sort and, what is more, to leave the editor complete freedom as to the contents of the book. I am also grateful to a number of officials of the Directorate General for International Cooperation who have helped enormously in the preparation of the study, including notably Bernard Berendsen and Frédérique de Man; I would equally wish to record my thanks to the adviser to the Minister on the Global Coalition for Africa, Michel van Hulten, and his assistant Monica Schuerman. I wish to record my thanks to the Governing Body of the Afrika-studiecentrum, Leiden, for allowing me leave of absence from my regular functions in order to undertake the editing of this book.

Summary

## I *States & Citizens*

**Toyin Falola**: 'Africa in perspective'. This general historical introduction covers several centuries of history and the whole of the African continent. The author looks at the main events of the past, including the development of pre-colonial states and systems of political economy, the growth of Islam, the growth of European influence, the colonial period, the post-independence period, and the end of the Cold War.

**Solofo Randrianja**: 'Nationalism, ethnicity and democracy'. The author traces the origins of African nationalism during the colonial period and shows how it was a popular mass movement at the time of independence. Subsequently, however, nationalism became an ideology used in the defence of undemocratic states. The author discusses the relationship between this and ethnic identity, which is both an authentic expression of the culture of small communities and also a larger unit used by politicians in the pursuit of factional interests. The common element in many cases has been the role of the political and economic elites of Africa which have used the state as a means of acquiring wealth and power. In many places democratic movements are dominated by the same elites: there are genuine popular democratic movements in Africa, but these evolve only slowly.

**Ali El-Kenz**: 'Youth and violence'. In numerous cases, sustained violence such as in Algeria or spontaneous riots such as in Senegal in 1994 are carried out by young males especially. They are often motivated more by frustration, poverty and lack of economic prospects than by anything else. They can also be recruited to more organized movements of violence, including those claiming to be Islamic. In the cities where the problem of youth violence is most acute, the young are often victims of profound social dislocation. The great numbers of such young people are a consequence of Africa's high birth rate, which shows no signs of abating and which will certainly lead to further pressures as future generations reach adolescence, as well as of other economic problems.

**Mohamed Tozy**: 'Movements of religious renewal'. The author examines the religious renewal movements, both Christian and Muslim, which are to be found in all parts of Africa. These respond to deeply felt popular needs, both spiritual and social. Looking in more detail at a number of cases including Senegal, Algeria, Morocco and Nigeria, the author believes that renewal movements are more likely to be modern and forward-looking than archaic. They are having a major impact on civil society. Contrary to what is sometimes believed, young women in Morocco, for example, are prominent as supporters of new religious movements which they see as offering them greater access to public space than in the past.

**Lilia Labidi**: 'Building public morality'. Extreme experiences, such as the commerce in body parts and infant malnutrition, reveal the difficulties faced in Egypt and Tunisia by certain social groups which have not been able to benefit from the advantages offered by newly independent states. Focusing on violence directed against the self, the author asks whether there may be an organic tie between these phenomena and the underlying political culture and assesses the means these states have available to combat the nostalgia for models of identity suggested by the religious code.

## II  *Institutions & Policies*

**Janine Aron**: 'The institutional foundations of growth'. The author reviews African macro-economic policies since 1945, and demonstrates that economic outcomes are subject to 'path-dependence' or 'hysteresis', meaning that initial economic conditions pose a strong constraint while the impact of shocks and policy changes on economic capacity and capability is long-lasting. The chapter examines new thinking on the importance of the role of state and private institutions in economic growth and concludes that sustainable reform of debilitated African institutions will probably be only gradual, though cumulative. At root effective constitutions will be needed to provide accountability of government economic policy to its populace, and signal the credibility of African governments in a world now far more open to international competition than in the past.

**Ernest Aryeetey**, 'Formal and informal economic activities'. It was generally expected that, after structural adjustment reforms, informal economic activities would decrease in importance as formal economic activity was freed from various constraints. This does not seem to have happened in most cases. The author examines a number of factors relevant to this phenomenon, including the relative lack of private investment in much of sub-Saharan Africa and the actual mechanics of much informal-sector activity.

**Jean-Paul Azam**: 'The diversity of adjustment in agriculture'. Agricultural sectors were for several decades heavily taxed by both direct and indirect means by governments. Much of the inspiration for structural adjustment programmes introduced in the 1980s came from a belief that the elimination of state intervention would increase prices paid to producers and hence would stimulate the agricultural sector. The author analyses a range of examples including from Morocco, Côte d'Ivoire, Angola, Ethiopia and Madagascar to examine factors which lead to success or failure, and includes a study of the role of private traders who mediate between farmers and markets.

**Lindani Ndlovu**, 'Constraints to manufacturing production'. The author surveys some of the tendencies in African manufacturing industry, which has generally encountered serious problems, in part as a result of the implementation of liberal macro-economic policies which leave industry vulnerable to international competition and high interest rates. Although few observers would see manufacturing playing a leading role in African economic development in the short or medium term, there are examples of sectors in which some African countries have clear manufacturing potential which requires nurturing if it is to thrive.

**Deborah Fahy Bryceson** and **John Howe**: 'An agrarian continent in transition'. The authors examine recent changes in the fields of rural-urban migration and employment patterns. Policies of liberalization have had a marked effect in changing these patterns and in creating new markets in land and labour. They have profoundly altered the relationship between capital, land and labour. In many cases this has tended to have had an adverse affect on the position of women. Often, there is a troubling phenomenon of rural unemployment. In many parts of the continent, agricultural production for export is unlikely to lead to any substantial or general rise in prosperity, and the service sector may well have a more important role to play. Possible measures to combat this could include labour-intensive infrastructure programmes, which at present tend to be used restrictively by relief agencies in the wake of disasters such as famines. There are solid examples of road construction projects making extensive use of labour which are both cost-efficient and bring employment and other benefits.

## III *Africa in the World*

**Tiébilé Dramé**, 'The crisis of the state'. The author argues that many states in Africa now face a deep crisis. Examining the origins of this, the author points to the legacy of the authoritarian states established during the colonial period and rapidly transferred to African control at the time of independence. He asserts that the collapse of one-party regimes in the late 1980s and early 1990s was in fact a symptom of a deeper problem of the state itself in many cases. He examines the international context in which Africa now finds itself.

**Colin McCarthy**: 'Regional integration'. Africa has seen a great number of regional integration or cooperation schemes, few of which have been real successes. The author discusses some of these, and considers reasons for their failure, not least in the light of similar arrangements made in other continents. Much of the problem is political. He concludes that there are good reasons to encourage regional cooperation, at least in particular sectors or areas of activity, but that such cooperation should precede more ambitious efforts at formal integration.

**Nicolas van de Walle**: 'The politics of aid effectiveness'. The end of the Cold War and economic recession have led Western donors to reconsider past levels of support to developing countries. Although it is difficult to state with confidence how effective aid has been, it seems clear that it has been less effective in Africa than in other parts of the developing world, for reasons which the author examines.

**Chaloka Beyani**: 'Some legal aspects of migration'. Patterns of migration in many parts of Africa, in response to economic demands or political pressures, were altered by administrative controls introduced in colonial times. Both internal and external controls have been widely used by governments since independence to restrict movements of people. International legislation governing movements of migrants and refugees is becoming more restrictive or is not respected, and great problems are faced as a result by migrants and displaced people both inside and outside Africa.

# List of Acronyms

| | |
|---|---|
| AIS | *Armée islamique de salut* |
| AMC | Agricultural Marketing Corporation |
| AMU | Arab Maghreb Union |
| ASEAN | Association of South-East Asian Nations |
| BLNS | Botswana, Lesotho, Namibia, Swaziland |
| CEAO | *Communauté économique de l'Afrique de l'ouest* |
| CEMAC | *Communauté économique et monétaire de l'Afrique centrale* |
| CFA | *Communauté financière africaine* |
| CMA | Common Monetary Area |
| COMECON | Council for Mutual Economic Assistance |
| COMESA | Common Market for Eastern and Southern Africa |
| CSSPPA | *Caisse de stabilisation et de soutien des prix des produits agricoles* |
| DAC | Development Assistance Committee |
| ECA | Economic Commission for Africa |
| ECCAS | Economic Community of Central African States |
| ECOWAS | Economic Community of West African States |
| EFTA | European Free Trade Area |
| EU | European Union |
| FAO | Food and Agriculture Organization |

| | |
|---|---|
| FIS | *Front islamique de salut* |
| GATT | General Agreement on Tariffs and Trade |
| GCA | Global Coalition for Africa |
| GDP | Gross Domestic Product |
| GIA | *Groupe islamique armé* |
| GNP | Gross National Product |
| IFI | International financial institutions |
| IMF | International Monetary Fund |
| LDC | Least Developed Countries |
| MERCOSUR | *Mercado Común del Sur* |
| MMA | Multilateral Monetary Agreement |
| NAFTA | North American Free Trade Agreement |
| NGO | Non-governmental organization |
| OAU | Organization of African Unity |
| ODA | Overseas Development Assistance |
| OECD | Organization for Economic Cooperation and Development |
| ONCAD | *Office national de coopération et d'assistance au développement* |
| OPEC | Organization of Petroleum-Exporting Countries |
| PAMSCAD | Programme of Actions to Mitigate the Social Costs of Adjustment |
| PECC | *Programa de Emergencia para Commercilizaçäo no Campo* |
| PTA | Preferential Trade Area |
| RPED | Regional Programme on Enterprise Development in Africa |
| SACU | Southern African Customs Union |
| SADC | Southern African Development Community |
| SADCC | Southern African Development Coordination Conference |
| SAP | Structural adjustment programme |
| UDEAC | *Union douanière et économique de l'Afrique centrale* |
| UDEAO | *Union douanière et économique de l'Afrique occidentale* |
| UEMOA | *Union économique et monétaire ouest-africaine* |
| UMOA | *Union monétaire ouest-africaine* |
| UN | United Nations |
| UNDP | United Nations Development Programme |
| UNESCO | United Nations Educational, Scientific and Cultural Organization |
| UNFPA | United Nations Population Fund |
| UNHCR | United Nations High Commissioner for Refugees |
| UNICEF | United Nations Children's Fund |
| UNIDO | United Nations Industrial Development Organization |
| USA | United States of America |
| USAID | United States Agency for International Development |
| USSR | Union of Soviet Socialist Republics |
| VAT | Value-Added Tax |
| WHO | World Health Organization |

# I

# *States & Citizens*

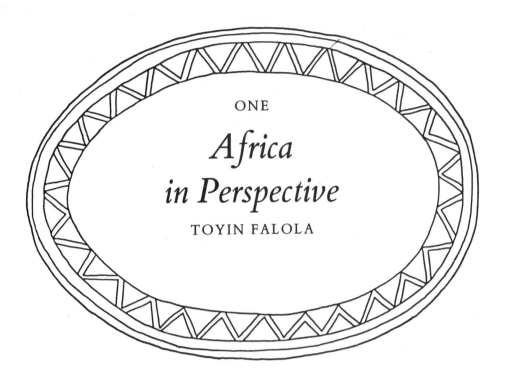

# ONE

# *Africa in Perspective*

## TOYIN FALOLA

Some people will blame our colonial oppressors. Well in some cases part of it is true but a whole lot of the blame should be put squarely on our own shoulders . . . Independence was thought to be the beginning of the golden era where political freedom and expression, freedom of association, free enterprise, economic prosperity, less ethnocentricism, responsibility and accountability of each and every one prevailed. These lofty ideals never happened because we replaced white imperialism with the black one.
*Ghana Drum*, March, 1992

The aim of this essay is to provide the historical context in which to situate a number of contemporary issues that are discussed in other chapters. My assumption is that the past influences the present in a variety of ways that explain the roots of contemporary problems, the continuity and resilience of aspects of indigenous institutions, some limitations to initiating new changes, and the rhetoric of where Africa stands in world politics and how its people define themselves. The essay is organized around six major themes, selected on the basis of their relevance to the current conditions in the continent.

## Pre-Colonial State Systems

Africa has been inhabited for more than three million years. By the first century A.D., many states had evolved; some were large and many were small. The state system continued to change until the nineteenth century, either by way of expansion or contraction. Political, social and economic institutions were adjusted to suit various times and needs, to adapt to the environment, and to respond creatively to new ideas from within and abroad.

There were regional differences, based on ecology, the degree of contact with outsiders, and the ability to use technology, notably iron. In North Africa, the early use of metals, camels and interactions within the Mediterranean world enabled civilizations to flourish and ideas to spread over a wider region. The same could be said of the northeast of the continent, with influences from North Africa and Arabia. The Sahara desert, once fertile, entered into recent history as the world's biggest desert. In this place, habitation was possible only around the oases. In West Africa, many large kingdoms emerged, and agriculture reached a high level of sophistication. In Central Africa, the forest and rivers sustained the economy, a religious complex emerged, and people lived in big villages. In East Africa, there were notable kingdoms, in addition to coastal cities that derived their rise and glory from the Indian Ocean trade. In Southern Africa, Bantu-speaking peoples lived in villages, built several large states, and depended considerably on cattle.

There were no people without a state, if we define a state to mean a sovereign government with defined boundaries. A government could have a small jurisdiction, no more than a village or clan, as in a number of Bantu-speaking groups in South Africa or the Berbers in North Africa. Many governments were of course big, like those in the kingdoms of Songhai in West Africa or Kilwa in East Africa. Patterns of authority varied from one place to another. In some areas, power was diffused among the elders, priests, and age-grade organizations. Yet in some others, power was centralized in the hands of powerful kings and high-ranking chiefs, like the rulers of Asante or Oyo, both in West Africa.

No people lived without a recognized authority which protected land, performed rituals, negotiated peace and resolved conflicts. In most of the continent, especially in village-based societies, the government rested on consensus rather than coercion. Religion served as the basis of power: authority was legitimated in religious sanctions, kings represented gods on earth, and many rulers combined political power with priestly duties. There were rules to remove bad leaders, and the emphasis of politics was on building social cohesion and maintaining the integrity of territorial sovereignty. Agriculture and trade were the major economic basis of power: rulers collected tribute and taxed commerce, in addition to having access to labour to engage in extensive production. In the big states, the control of regional markets and trade routes boosted the economy, enabled greater political centralization, and financed ambitious expansion.

While these states were different, they had a number of things in common: affinity in language groups, cosmologies, and art forms. Descent groups were unilineal, and the lineage constituted an economic unit and a basis of power. Farming and pastoralism were the most common occupations. Resources for survival and living were generated from within, tools were made from local materials, and the majority of the population were gainfully employed, adequately sheltered and fed.

The states also interacted with one another, both at the sub-regional and pan-regional levels, through trade, diplomacy, marriage, migrations, and warfare. Ecological differences promoted the exchange of goods and ideas. Lines of communication emerged to link the different regions. Population movements transcended ethnic boundaries, necessitated by factors such as nomadism, state expansion, drought, and pestilence. Such movements were possible because the infrastructure existed (for example, routes, rivers and pack animals) and the states created no human barriers to communication. So extensive was the interaction pattern that international trade such as that across the Sahara developed to connect West Africa with the north. The continent was linked by extensive regional trade networks. In the north, there was the age-old network with the Mediterranean. The Indian Ocean coastal systems connected the area of East Africa with the north and Asia. After the fifteenth century an 'Atlantic system' integrated the areas of Angola, Zaïre and the modern Republic of Congo. All these three systems were interlocked during the nineteenth century by traders who overlapped them and by local markets that fed them. Some parts of East and North Africa were equally connected with an international economy, bringing substantial economic benefits to the political class. Extensive trade promoted cultural interchanges; for instance, the Swahili language spread over East Africa and from there to eastern Zaïre and parts of modern Zambia, the Zande-Mangbetu culture emerged and spread in Equatorial Africa, and the Lingala creole language gained a wide currency in the modern Congo and Zaïre.

While the pre-colonial states have collapsed and been replaced by new countries, the history of the period continues to be relevant up until this very moment. To start with, the current concept of regionalism and projects of continental unity like the Organization of African Unity (OAU) and pan-African congresses and festivals rest partly on a cultural foundation with roots located in history. Ethnic linkages across borders and recent colonial history have justified the reference to Africa as a cultural entity. The very identity of Africa as a continent and of Africans as a people is formulated by criteria that draw from pre-colonial history and cultures. Shared values and traditions are added to a common history to define this African identity.[1]

There is hardly an African country where the issue of cultural policy has not been either discussed or formulated. Every cultural policy is about choosing from the past, creating an image fashioned out of history, using culture for national cohesion, and seeking consensus among diverse people. Tanzania under Nyerere attempted to draw on the values of the lineage to organize the modern state. Many countries changed their names, adopting instead those of older kingdoms like Ghana, Mali, and Benin. Such names as Zambia, Tanzania, Malawi, Azania and Zaïre replaced older ones, in the attempts to use culture as the source of symbols to galvanize contemporary society. Personal Christian names have also been devalued in such places as Togo and Zaïre, in preference for local names. While enjoying the luxuries of their Western-style palaces, cars, and aeroplanes, many leaders still look for objects from the past to create symbols. Thus, Kaunda designed 'African suits', Kenyatta used to carry a fly-whisk or walking stick, Mobutu wears a leopard-skin hat, and Obasanjo used his fingers to eat pounded yam and drank palm wine in State House.

Two very difficult aspects of the past to cope with are in the area of language and religion. With regard to language, the desire for a *lingua franca* based on a local language has not been fulfilled in most countries outside North Africa because of the difficulty of choosing one out of many. With respect to religion, many continue to look for ways to seek a compromise between creating a secular state and satisfying the wishes of powerful religious groups.

The criticism of the West, attacks on foreign models and the search for the liberation of the continent are often expressed as a cultural agenda. Many aspects of indigenous institutions are presented as alternatives to Western institutions. At different moments there have been African intellectuals who look to the past to recommend indigenous

---

[1] See for instance, W.E. Abraham, *The Mind of Africa* (University of Chicago Press, Chicago, IL, 1962); and V.C. Uchendu, 'The challenge of cultural transition in sub-Saharan Africa', *The Annals of the American Academy of Political Science and Sociology*, No. 432 (July 1977), pp. 70–9.

religion rather than Christianity, local dress instead of foreign suits, and African kingship and chiefs-in-council instead of European-type assemblies. In moments of crisis or hardship, leaders are known to have called upon their people to abandon assimilation to Western values, to go 'authentic' by returning to indigenous ways of life. The extraction of elements from the past has been a major tool in the hands of the political class to justify the mobilization of their people or simply to engage in propaganda.

It should be stressed that contemporary problems have cultural and historical contents. Current patterns of migration often reflect old cross-border ethnic links. New theatres of war are in part a revival of previous hostilities between groups and reflections of the troubled relations of the colonial period. The modern-day movements of pastoralists and refugees also resemble older migration patterns. The deliberate refusal of people to see trans-border trade as smuggling is based on the belief that they are transacting business with one another and members of their own groups who just happen to be partitioned into separate countries.

While we can talk of modern Africa with institutions that replicate those of the West, the continuity and resilience of indigenous cultures must be noted as a limit to the definition of the 'modern' and as a way of explaining the persistence of alternative and parallel institutions in most of Africa. Food habits, architecture, beliefs, dress, music, worldview, and so on continue in one form or another.

Adaptation and innovation are two common elements of pre-colonial history that have survived until modern times. People had to adapt to the environment and survive crises, wars, and foreign invasions. During this century, the African experience cannot be described solely as one of unconditional surrender to the forces of Westernization. Rather, the experience is one of innovation reflecting change and continuity with the past.

Finally, the past has been used by contemporary leaders to legitimate their behaviour and leadership style. Those leaders who refuse to leave power liken themselves to pre-colonial kings who died on the throne and whose word was law. Military dictators wrongly assert that democracy is alien to Africa. Socialist states like Tanzania likened the old lineage to socialism and communism. To be sure, some of these connections are attempts to justify policies, sometimes in ways that are dubious, but the very task of relating the present to the past is both valid and intellectually challenging.[2] Recently, Basil Davidson has argued in a major work that the failure of Africa is the acceptance of alien models and systems of values which contradict its own history and culture.[3]

## The Impact of Islam

The rise of Islam in the seventh century and its spread in the subsequent centuries was a revolution whose impact has endured until this day. The spread of Islam went hand in hand with Arab civilization. From the ninth to the eleventh centuries, a large number of Arab populations migrated to settle in such places as the Sahara, North Africa and the Nile valley. Here and in several other places, Arab culture spread rapidly, displacing previous languages and cultures. Thus, North Africa passed under a dominant Islamic and Arab influence which is retained to this day. It was through North Africa that Islam penetrated West Africa, beginning from the eighth century, and reached different

[2] One attempt is by A.A. Mazrui, *Cultural Forces in World Politics* (James Currey and Heinemann, London and Portsmouth, NH, 1990).
[3] B. Davidson, *Black Man's Burden: Africa and the curse of the nation-state* (James Currey, London, 1992).

parts at various times. During the nineteenth century, three great *jihads* reformed the religion and produced thousands of new converts. Further consolidation occurred during the present century. In the case of the eastern Sudan and the Horn of Africa, Islam spread from Egypt, principally along the Nile and also from direct contacts with Arabian Islam across the Red Sea. The spread of Islam was remarkable, recording a failure only in Ethiopia because of the resistance of the Amhara Christians. In East and Central Africa, Islamic penetration was a result of the long history of trade links with Arabia and Egypt. By the tenth century, there were Muslim settlements on the Somali and Sudanese coasts; further settlements were established between then and the sixteenth century in Kilwa and Mogadishu. Muslim culture spread along the East African coast. From the fourteenth to the fifteenth centuries an African-Arab culture emerged, giving rise to the Swahili language, an admixture of Arab and Bantu, now widely spoken in East Africa and parts of Central Africa. Central Africa's contacts with Islam came from Zanzibari and Swahili merchants who penetrated the Congo region.

The adoption of Islam had a number of far-reaching consequences. There are Arabic-speaking peoples in northern Sudan, and some black groups (like some Somali-speaking people) who define themselves as Arabs. Institutions associated with Islam – Koranic schools, the Arabic language, mosques and books – are parts of the features of African life. Islam affected politics by promoting centralization and large bureaucracies which employed the services of literate people. The *shari'a* (Muslim code of law) is important in many countries. Islam has been a source of unity, promoting bonds among followers and their countries.

Islam remains connected to the present and future of Africa. It provides the justification for the creation of a Muslim world or the smaller one of the Arab world. The Arab League and the Organization of the Islamic Conference are two examples of multilateral institutions that unite Muslim countries. Through them, financial aid circulates, common positions are taken on global issues, and the interests of Muslims are defended.

Contemporary politics and rivalry for power in such places as North Africa, Sudan, Nigeria, and Senegal, to mention but a few, cannot be fully comprehended without the Islamic factor. The role of Islam in modern politics does vary from place to place, but some generalizations can be made. In some places, as in Algeria and Sudan, there are those who want to make Islam the very centre of politics, rejecting Western secular constitutions. Yet, in some other places, like Nigeria, there is concern by some Muslims to minimize the power of a Christian intelligentsia. Third, there are countries (e.g. the Gambia, Mauritania, Burkina Faso, Senegal, Nigeria, Guinea, Niger, Mali, Somalia, Sudan) where, because Muslims constitute the majority of the population, policies and politics try to bear the imprint of this religion to avoid civil unrest. Fourth, Islam is used as a radicalizing ideology to fight for change, as in South Africa during the apartheid regime or in countries like Egypt. Finally, many Muslims are calling for a return to the first *Umma*, when the Prophet Mohammad ruled with regard for morality, faith, justice and fairness. In some places like Libya, Algeria and Sudan, demands for political reform have taken a violent form.

On religious and cultural grounds, there remains the old problem of confrontation with other religions. Islam is opposed to the revival or resurgence of traditional religion. Islam and Christianity struggle for converts in rough ways, engage in occasional conflicts, and struggle for the control of state power. Islam continues to challenge the ascendancy of Western culture in Africa. Islam is not opposed to many aspects of Westernization like schools, architecture and roads, but it is resolute in attacking what are perceived as the corrosive consequences of contacts with the West.

## The European Factor, Fifteenth-Nineteenth Centuries

If the principal achievement of Islam was to create new identities, that of the European incursion after the fifteenth century was to traumatize Africans. An international trade developed, which settled primarily for transaction in African slaves. The trade integrated Africa into the world economy; it began an established pattern of exporting African agricultural and extractive resources. This pattern was to influence the nature of Africa's political economy for a long time; the political elite profited from the trade and the continent was exposed to exploitation and external contacts of various sorts.[4]

Africa became the biggest slave pool in world history, supplying over twelve million people. As the victims were of productive age, the loss did incalculable damage to the economy and society. Africans were devalued in self-worth. The culture and history of slaves were dismissed: to the West, Africans were people without historical roots or culture, and nothing good was associated with them.

Could it be argued, as some people are inclined to do, that because the slave trade occurred a long time ago, its consequences are no longer with us? No, and any attempt to do so is to dismiss its continued relevance in African history and world politics. In the first place, the trade affirmed and spread a notion of black inferiority, a powerful negative notion that has stubbornly persisted. Today, there are people who attribute Africa's problems to intellectual inferiority, thus re-echoing those notions of the slave-trade era. The mythology remains that incompetent people can only destroy rather than build, and that Africans have always lacked the capability to govern themselves. Second, the trade was associated with racism. Then and now, racism tends to mark blacks outside of their continent. Third, in places like the United States, the emotions associated with the trade continue to affect how African-Americans interpret contemporary events, defend Africa (including its bad leaders) and promote an Afrocentric version of history, a sanitization of the past. Without understanding slavery, one would not appreciate how African-Americans relate to Africa and even to domestic American politics. To them, the stigmatization of inferiority has to be corrected, and racism confronted at all costs. Fourth, slavery re-enacts itself in modern times, in places like Sudan and Mauritania where people were bought in the 1980s. Descendants of slaves are still around, with implications for micro-level politics. The kidnapping of people, especially children, and cases of young girls on pilgrimage enticed into harems are sad reminders of this trade.[5]

Fifth, there are scholars who continue to link current underdevelopment to the slave trade. Such scholars point to the decline in the African population between 1650 and 1850, to socio-political conflicts among Africans during the same period, to the decline of states, and diminished productivity. In the words of J.E. Inikori, one of the leading analysts of the linkage between slavery and underdevelopment, 'export demand for captives chained tropical African societies and prevented them from moving forward economically over the period.' According to him, while the West witnessed immense developments in capitalism, the slave trade held back Africa:

> The demographic effects of the trade kept the ratio of population to agricultural land in tropical Africa extremely low, and so held back the development of the division of labour within and between sub-regions . . . the trade aborted the development of large-scale commodity production for export in tropical Africa that in the end gave all the advantages to the New World . . . The great inequality in economic power arising from this situation made it relatively easy for Europe to conquer and

[4] See the influential work of I. Wallerstein, *Africa and the Modern World* (Africa World Press, Trenton, NJ, 1986).
[5] See for instance, J. Derrick, *Africa's Slaves Today* (George Allen & Unwin, London, 1975).

impose colonial domination on tropical Africa from the late 19th century. The socio-political and economic processes that followed this conquest and colonial domination further worsened the disparity in economic and political power between Europe and North America on the one hand, and tropical Africa, on the other. The unequal relations between tropical Africa and the capitalist West that developed out of this situation and persist to the present day have acted as effective chains on African societies, making it impossible for them to adequately utilise their abundant and varied natural and human resources for their socio-political and economic development.[6]

Finally, the issue of reparations has reached the table of the United Nations, with demands by African leaders, supported by the OAU, for compensation amounting to $130 trillion. Reparations have led to the re-interpretation of the history of the slave trade and the roles of the West and the Arabs in it. Its main advocate used to be Chief M.K.O. Abiola, the celebrated rich man and politician cheated by the military from becoming the elected president of Nigeria in 1993. His argument, which has been repeated in many speeches, is that the West owes Africa reparations to apologize for slavery: 'Africa has been the greatest victim of slavery, colonialism, neo-colonialism, and apartheid. While the German genocide against the Jews lasted five years, the genocide of Europe against the African peoples lasted five hundred years, and still continues through apartheid, debt burden and unequal exchange.'[7]

During the heyday of trans-Atlantic commerce, European explorers worked to know more about Africa, a knowledge that was to serve the interests of capitalism and colonial conquest. Missionaries spread Christianity, with remarkable achievements after the mid-nineteenth century. Christianity was more than a religion: together with Western formal education, it created a new elite which was to inherit power in the twentieth century. Christianity was a veritable companion of colonial rule. Christianity and Islam offered a combined assault on indigenous religion. Many of the Christian teachings, especially by the foreign missions, conflicted with a number of aspects of indigenous culture, like polygamy for instance, and succeeded in producing converts with a different outlook on life.

## The Colonial Factor

The European partition of the late nineteenth century was a continuation of a tradition of incursion that began in the fifteenth century, but this now involved the complete takeover of the continent. The conquest was fast, sudden and successful, thanks largely to superior technology which crushed the African resistance forces. Only Liberia and Ethiopia retained their independence.

The pre-colonial states lost their freedom, and the new European powers determined how society would be governed and ordered. This loss has generally been interpreted by many African scholars and Marxist historians in tragic terms, one that connected with slavery to retard Africa, to counter a pro-colonial interpretation which glorified the period as a creative, powerful engine of positive transformation. In the celebrated UNESCO volume on the period[8] and a work of synthesis on the same subject, Adu

[6] J.E. Inikori, *The Chaining of a Continent. Export demand for captives and the history of Africa South of the Sahara, 1450–1870* (Institute of Social and Economic Research, University of the West Indies, Mona, Jamaica, 1992), pp. 54–6.

[7] Chief M.K.O. Abiola, 'Reparation for Africans in the motherland and diaspora'. Paper presented at the Reparation for African-Americans Workshops, Washington, DC, September 1990, reprinted in *Reparations: a collection of speeches by M.K.O. Abiola* (Linguist Service, Lomé, Togo, 1992), p. 234.

[8] A. Adu Boahen (ed.), *General History of Africa*, Vol. 7 (Heinemann and UNESCO, London, 1985).

Boahen maintains that, on the eve of the conquest, Africa had gone through some revolutions and changes – for example, the slave trade was abolished, there was a greater process of centralization, the military was modernized, constitutional reforms were embarked upon, a steady increase in population occurred, Islam and Christianity spread, and a new Christian elite was born. With these changes, the continent was 'poised for a major breakthrough on all fronts . . . Africans were full of optimism and felt quite ready to face any challenge that was thrown to them.'[9]

Whether there would have been a leap forward without the intrusive colonial intervention is in the realm of speculation. What is clear, however, is that this intervention was so decisive that many things have never been the same since then. Modern Africa, with new countries, secularized political institutions and new economies, owes certain things to European colonial rule. Each colony acquired an identity: a name, boundaries, a capital city, a central government, an official language, and other things that define what is 'modern'. Most of the changes of the period have become permanent legacies in such areas as language, economic and political institutions, culture, and the nature of international politics.

Peoples and groups were partitioned by competing European countries. New countries were formed, with new boundaries to replace the pre-colonial states. At the end of it all, some 48 countries emerged south of the Sahara, to replace thousands of pre-colonial states. The map looks tidier, but the problems are gargantuan, including the management of the new states and rivalries among them. Most of the boundaries were arbitrary. One consequence of this is that previous groups were disrupted, through a forced partition that allocated the same ethnic group to two or more countries.[10] Strained relations continue to characterize interactions among countries because of competing claims to territories or people. Examples include the tension between Nigeria and Cameroon over a number of groups on the southern frontier, South Africa and Botswana over the Tswana, Ghana and Togo over the Ewe, Nigeria and the Republic of Benin over the Yoruba, Senegal and Gambia over the Wolof, Kenya, Ethiopia and Somalia over the Somali. It is too late to reunify divided groups, but frontier tensions will continue as long as different countries pursue policies that disregard the fact that these groups were previous members of the same 'nations'. Competing imperialisms added to the gulfs created by the partition.

New models were gradually superimposed upon indigenous ones, including such institutions as the army, police and civil service. The colonial system was both paternalistic and authoritarian. Where it was possible, indigenous systems were manipulated to serve colonial needs. In some others, they were simply set aside. By independence, the chieftaincy system that sustained indigenous Africa had either lost its significance or its role was severely weakened. The system also thrived on discrimination and racism, with limited appreciation for Africans and their culture.

Power shifted to those with education, with the knowledge to understand the new Western political models. But this transfer should not be confused with democracy: colonial rule was by a handful of officers, lacking in any rigorous system of checks and balances and insensitive to opposition. The elite had to grapple with the transfer of power in the 1950s and 1960s, within the constraint of the colonial heritage.

Colonialism was exploitative, taking as much as possible away from the people, orienting their economy to serve external interests, and manipulating their labour for selfish

---

[9] A. Adu Boahen, *African Perspectives on Colonialism* (Johns Hopkins University Press, Baltimore, MD, 1987), p. 3.
[10] For details, see A.I. Asiwaju (ed.), *Partitioned Africans* (University of Lagos Press, Lagos, 1984).

ends. A modern economy was created: peasants produced cash crops for external markets; transportation rested on harbours, roads and railways; new financial houses and currency were introduced. The colonies depended on a few crops or minerals, thus creating the basis of mono-crop economies, foreign interests reaped substantial profits, little effort was made at real development, and in some areas like East Africa white settlers were allowed to take land to establish large plantations. The colonial system revealed its brutal self in the task to exploit: labour was coerced or underpaid.

Social and cultural changes accompanied colonial rule. One was the spread of Western education, although this was slow in the beginning. Yet another was the arrogant view that civilization was being introduced, promoting a belief in the superiority of a Western way of life. Other important changes included the emergence of new towns, different from the older ones in the sense that they were more ethnically heterogeneous, the emergence of a working population dependent on wages, and the greater monetization of society, land commercialization, the rise of nuclear families, the introduction of Western medicine, electricity, and piped water.

The combination of economic and social changes led to population increase, greater urbanization, enhanced mobility of goods and people, and deeper knowledge of the outside world. The continent was further integrated into the international economic and political system as a junior partner.

The continuity with pre-colonial history and the African ability to innovate limited the changes of the era. In some aspects of life, these checks were so strong that the imprint of the colonial era became quite small. In most parts of Africa, a colonial culture did not displace the pre-colonial culture. There were continuities in cultural practices, while creative changes were made to integrate new ideas with the old ones. Nowhere is continuity reflected more than in religion. The combined assault of Christianity and colonialism failed to destroy beliefs in spirits, witchcraft, masquerades and folk-tales. Nowhere was ethnicity and allegiance to previous 'nations' destroyed. Rather, colonialism promoted ethnicity, which was in turn carried over into the present. The colonial powers did not aim at creating strong national unity or loyalty. Indeed, in some colonies the effort was to weaken the move towards national unity in order to prevent nationalism.

Nevertheless, colonialism gave birth to a nationalism that destroyed it. Africans resisted many aspects of colonial rule and struggled for their freedom. By the mid-1960s, many had become independent. Others like the Portuguese colonies and Namibia followed later. Almost everywhere, independence was greeted with euphoria and the expectation of freedom and development. In most of these countries, the inheritors of power became like new lords presiding over feudal estates with reckless abandon and without regard for accountability or respect for their 'tenants'. Independence did not become a revolution, only a change of rulers: the colonial machinery of government was inherited and its symbols of power and authority were retained in most countries. But the new rulers faced a set of new problems: they had to preserve national unity, meet economic expectations, and mobilize their people for development.

## The Post-Independence Era

The various independent sovereign countries began to seek solutions to the problems of economic development and political instability. They accepted the colonial boundaries, assumed that European models would sustain them, and that they would function and acquire respect in the international community. However, from the very beginning, independence was severely limited: the continent was tied to a world economic system; colonial ideas in culture and education were carried over; ex-masters devised the means to retain control; and there were old ethnic divisions in society.

Economic development was the central issue. The struggle for independence was at the same time a struggle for economic development. New leaders had to be judged by their performance in liberating people from poverty. Economists had a field day, using Africa as the laboratory to test theories and models of development. These theories are the forerunners of the modern-day market-based, liberal-oriented reforms of structural adjustment programmes.[11] There was a consensus before 1939 that with the international division of labour and comparative advantage, Africa would witness substantial growth by selling its raw materials in exchange for imports. With the transition to an independent status, it was quickly realized that this theory did not hold. Modernization theorists argued that Africa should reform its institutions to aspire to become like the West, through a process of 'modernization' that would replace indigenous ways of life with Western models. Modernization theories failed. They were severely attacked in the 1960s and 1970s by the Marxists who argued that international trade, dependency and capitalism were the primary constraints to development. Marxism held great promise in those years, although it is now scorned in the 1990s.

The theoretical fluidity was played out on the ground. The new states had to fulfil the rising expectations of their populace by providing jobs, education, and social services. Trade had to be improved upon, and economies diversified. The domestic political scene had to be stabilized, and international affairs conducted in a beneficial manner. Africa has yet to overcome all these initial concerns. Changes are expressed in elaborate documents of development plans, reflections of economic theories of change. Programmes and their outcomes were grossly exaggerated in these plans. The constraint was always resources, and the early plans hoped that foreign resources would be obtained.

Essentially two models of planning were common. Many countries like Nigeria, Liberia, Kenya and Côte d'Ivoire adopted a capitalist path of private ownership and private management of the economy, allowing the state to interfere in those areas that required financial commitments beyond the reach of the private sector. Other countries such as Tanzania, Guinea, and for a while Egypt and Mali took a socialist path of state control and ownership of industries. In both models, results were disappointing, and by the 1970s there was a need for re-assessment. In the capitalist countries, indigenous private companies collaborated with external forces to milk the state. In the socialist ones, the state was a poor economic manager, never to be trusted. The countries saw economic stagnation, a worsening balance of payments, deteriorating terms of trade, wealth transfer, mass poverty, and decline in agricultural production. By the 1980s, the conclusion was that past policies had failed, and ideologies were seriously questioned. The need for economic diversification and foreign investments became the two paramount solutions in all countries, even in the few that still claimed to be socialist.[12]

Politics is central to development. Here, the failure is gross, without a solution even in sight. The basis of solidarity is still not the modern state (except occasionally) but the pre-colonial ethnic groups. New languages, laws, etc. continue to operate side by

[11] For an extensive discussion, see Toyin Falola, *Development Planning and Decolonization in Nigeria* (University of Florida Press, Gainesville, FL, 1995).
[12] See for instance J. Voss (ed.), *Development Policy in Africa* (Verlag Neue Gesellschaft GmbH, Bonn-Bad Godesberg, 1973), p. 10.

side with the old. Previous political institutions survive in various ways. Modern secular leaders still seek the means to manipulate 'traditional' ones. In places with military regimes, government has been stabilized by using the traditional chiefs as channels of communication to the people. In most countries, secular leaders lack credibility, with the result that alternative power centres, drawing from the geography and values of older pre-colonial nations, exist.

The political integration of component units has been a problem that defies solution. Rwanda is the most current example, where the state has failed to integrate its two major ethnic groups. Yet, Rwanda is not peculiar, and there are similar problems in neighbouring Burundi and on-going conflict in Sudan, Angola, Somalia and Liberia. Nigeria survived a civil war in the 1960s, but its recent politics have degenerated into an intense ethnic division whose consequences are still unfolding. Recent conflicts include those in Ethiopia, Mozambique, and Uganda. Problems relating to ethnic tensions have an old history, exacerbated by the colonial policy of divide and rule and competition for scarce resources.

The modern African state has exhibited other lapses and failings. In the first place, government and leadership have failed to acquire credibility, and in most cases the basis of power legitimation lies in violence. Most of the governments began with huge support in the first few years of independence, but the promise of mass-based political parties quickly degenerated to one-party authoritarian states.

Second, power has been used primarily to steal from the state. Political leadership is characterized by corruption and mismanagement. Built strongly on clientelism, political leaders reward their supporters with positions and money. Corruption on such a large scale compromises the management of the state, destroys morale, and wrecks the fabric of society. Because the private gains to be made from state power are enormous, competition to control the state is fierce and brutal. The end justifies the means, the winner takes all, and does everything to perpetuate himself.

Third, there is no effective way of changing regimes. Rulers refuse to relinquish power and the military uses violence to perpetuate itself. Political coercion and repression replace democracy. Life presidents have emerged, with a notion that a leader should 'possess' a state and government.[13] Less than ten countries have given their people the right to change leaders through the ballot box. Only six leaders are known to have voluntarily relinquished power until the 1990s and with the exception of Olusegun Obasanjo of Nigeria and Abdul al Dahab of Sudan, the rest did so after spending many years in office (Siaka Stevens of Sierra Leone, Leopold Senghor of Senegal, Julius Nyerere of Tanzania, and Ahmadou Ahidjo of Cameroon).

The major block to democracy has been the military. Usually self-motivated and greedy, the military has justified itself by accusing civilians of corruption and inability to manage the state. By 1970, half of the continent was governed by the military, a tradition that is currently sustained. Now totally discredited in many countries, the military rides into power by offering a better government and an improved economy. The military is, however, no different from the rest, and its performance is shoddy and unimpressive, to say the least. With the control of the means of violence, it violates human rights, spends a huge proportion of national revenues on arms, destroys democratic institutions, and promotes an anti-intellectual culture.

Fourth, military leadership is above reproach: alternative opinions are discouraged or

---

[13] For the most trenchant criticism of African leadership, see George B. Ayittey, *Africa Betrayed* (St Martins Press, New York, 1992).

punished, the press is restrained in most countries under military rule, and real opposition is not tolerated. A culture of silence is enforced, to allow arrogant dictators to govern as they wish. Critics are known to have been killed or jailed, and the lucky ones live in exile outside their countries. Some African rulers struggled for many years to retain power at any cost, and they denied civil liberties. Even peasants, without voice or power, are suppressed and destroyed, to prevent their being mobilized to demand reforms.

Fifth, there is no commitment to the rule of law. Where the military does not rule by decree, the judiciary is ignored. Thus, the modern state has failed to move beyond the imperial doctrine of exploitation. The legacy of African leadership is brutalizing and chaotic: fear, poverty, drought, warfare, theft, refugees and human rights abuse are commonplace.

While most events occur at the domestic level, there are regional and international dimensions to the management of the post-colonial states. At the regional level, the various countries thought that they could overcome the barriers of the colonial partition by forming inter-regional and international organizations. There was also a belief that regional organizations would create bigger markets, reduce dependence, and enhance resource flow. There was great optimism in the 1970s that West Africa would do well under the leadership of oil-rich Nigeria. Thus, the Economic Community of West African States (ECOWAS) emerged as an imitation of similar organizations in the continent. The aims of ECOWAS are shared by most others. Essentially, they are intended to alleviate and eliminate poverty and ensure success 'in the struggle against economic domination and subjugation by external forces'. This success would come if small states could cooperate to resist domination: 'a strong regional economic base will no doubt be an effective weapon in making such resistance possible'. The diagnosis of the problem is the failure to unite: 'the pattern of development in the sub-region was isolationist, based as it was on small national markets in several cases'. The solution was to unite: 'It is hoped that a large community market comprising 150 million consumers should be a big boost to production. It should encourage the expansion of the existing industries and the creation of new ones. This should make possible the reaping of economies of scale.'[14]

The rationale is brilliant and the solution intelligent enough. ECOWAS as an idea is not dead, and there are activities to point to, but the gap between advertised objectives and concrete achievement is very wide indeed. While a few accomplishments have been recorded, regionalism has yet to fulfil its mission partly for lack of political commitment, political instability, resource scarcity, a poor economic base, a lingering dependence on the West, and technological backwardness. Even among the cooperating countries, there are cases where members have been castigated as aliens and expelled, and refugees are never welcome. While the enthusiasm has dampened, regionalism is not dead.

The OAU was intended as a body to promote continental interests, such as the resolution of conflicts and the promotion of social and economic development. Formed in 1963, the OAU is to work for 'the unity and solidarity of African States'. It has worked to improve inter-state interactions, promote relations with a wider world, and seek answers to underdevelopment. Some successes have been recorded, but the constraints are overwhelming: as a voluntary association, it does not possess the force to assert itself; and its component members weaken its ability to speak with one voice. The pursuit of the goals of individual countries is more important than the continental one, sometimes leading to competition among countries and lack of enthusiasm. In spite of frontier

[14] 'A Decade of ECOWAS', *West Africa*, 27 May 1985.

tensions, policies to promote peaceful inter-group relations are not sufficiently creative or genuinely pursued to minimize conflicts and encourage the mobility of people and goods. Instead, they have been militarized, thus adding to the violence. Transactions in small goods by poor farmers and traders have been criminalized as smuggling, further embittering people and creating distance between the state and its people. To compound the problems, a number of countries have engaged in conflicts caused by ideological differences, personality clashes among leaders, territorial disputes, refugee problems, and external instigations.

The presence of the former European powers and superpower interest during the Cold War are essential to the understanding of post-colonial Africa. Africa could not escape membership of the international community or seek immunity from world politics. The trouble is that it is unable to interact with this community on its own terms. The international actors are stronger and the ability of the continent to exert influence on international politics is weak. In the early 1960s, expectations were rather high: foreign aid was expected, in addition to a sympathetic understanding of its problems. The United Nations, the Commonwealth and many foreign countries did meet some of these expectations.[15] But most African countries were unsatisfied: the support was too small, and not without strings. For those who made aid the corner-stone of their development efforts, they were to be sorely disappointed. There were two bigger troubles on the international scene.

The first was that the ex-colonial powers struggled successfully to retain their domination, thus ensuring wealth transfer in various forms. As during the colonial period, trade relations remain largely unequal, with Africa supplying raw materials at prices and quantities determined by the buyers. France never gave up a paternalistic view that its former African colonies are an extension of its influence and area of control. To retain their loyalty, it provided aid, stabilized their currencies, and offered advice. There are treaties on cultural cooperation. To support diplomatic efforts, there are military agreements which allow France to use the army to defend its African allies. France has propped up unpopular regimes. Britain, too, uses the Commonwealth to forge an alliance with its ex-colonies, and concentrates on measures that will continue to profit it economically. For other Western countries, getting the raw materials of the continent is more important than working towards its rapid progress. Indeed, an authoritarian strong man in charge is more desirable than a democratic government in negotiating commerce. Thus, at one time or the other, such countries as Kenya, Cameroon, Côte d'Ivoire, Liberia, Malawi, Uganda, and Ethiopia have had their dictatorial leaders toasted and supported by Western countries. Most of the aid the West offered to buy political support was misdirected, used for grandiose projects, or grossly mismanaged.

The second trouble was that the rivalry among the superpowers spilled over into Africa, generating tensions and conflicts. African countries sought all forms of assistance, but in the process they had to risk being drawn into superpower politics and losing their own sovereignty. Many thought that a policy of non-alignment would work, but it did not. Some were able to walk the tight-rope, and some could not. The United States did not have colonies, but it had commercial and economic interests in many countries, and wanted to halt the expansion of Soviet influence. Thus, it was hostile to socialist regimes and supported such so-called pro-West countries as Zaïre, South Africa, Liberia

---

[15] See for instance, L.B. Pearson, *Partners in Development: Report of the Commission on International Development* (Praeger, New York, 1969); and Commonwealth Economic Committee, *Special Commonwealth African Assistance Plan: Report for the year ending 31st March, 1962* (HMSO, London, 1963).

and Kenya. The Soviet Union, too, had no colonies, but was interested in the spread of its ideology. In order to contain communism, the United States and its allies had to prevent the emergence of so-called socialist policies or states, to neutralize the influence of the Soviet Union, and to interfere in the political process to ensure victories for anti-socialists. When it suited their interests, foreign powers supported authoritarian regimes in Africa with money, ideas, intelligence, and arms. African leaders were also able to manipulate East-West rivalry to advantage, selling their allegiance to the highest bidder, and playing one power off against the other. In the case of the Soviet Union, efforts were made to obtain sympathizers in many countries within the universities and political parties, and it succeeded in creating a number of client-states like Benin, Angola, Ethiopia and Mozambique. Substantial money was devoted to training young Africans, and by 1981 34,805 students had benefited from this arrangement. The Soviet concern was to find ways for Africa to break its links with the West and accept a socialist ideology. All sorts of assistance were offered, and its anti-imperialist propaganda succeeded in radicalizing a large number of Africans. Nevertheless, the political gains were small, and by the mid-1980s, it was already clear that most countries would not be persuaded to the Soviet side.

In the 1970s and 1980s, various practical and theoretical attempts were made to seek the means to overcome the grip of the West on the continent. African leaders called for more interaction among their countries and models of South-South cooperation were formulated to benefit from a so-called New International Economic Order.[16] Frustrated by the outcome of North-South relations, a strategy of delinking was proposed to create self-reliance for the South. Rather than tie their economies to the industrialized North which offered no promise of serving as a growth engine, they should rely on one another. South-South relations were to be built on financial cooperation, complementarity in trade, promotion of joint ventures, and other means that would do away with exploitation of one country by another. Africa, as part of an integrated Third World market, would benefit from economies of scale, enhance its bargaining power by reducing its dependence on the West, and increase its productive capacity. The great dream of the period included a possible alliance between Africa and Brazil. In the final analysis, South-South relations appeared more elegant on paper, far different in reality.

Still in response to the domination of the North and worsening economic performance, African countries sought solutions within a pan-regional approach. Many meetings and proposals culminated in the 1979 Monrovia Strategy for the Economic Development of Africa (the Monrovia Strategy, for short) which insisted that self-reliance and self-sustainment must underpin every planning effort. Realizing that the New International Economic Order of the 1970s had brought little progress, the Monrovia Strategy warned that Africa should not look forward or hope to benefit from any so-called restructuring of the international economic system. In 1980, the OAU convened a meeting to implement the Monrovia Strategy, leading to the well-advertised Lagos Plan of Action.[17] The Lagos Plan expected a miracle by the year 2000, through regionalism, better

---

[16] See for instance J. Carlsson, (ed.), *South-South Relations in a Changing World Order* (Scandinavian Institute, Uppsala, 1982) and E. Laszlo (ed.), *Cooperation for Development: Strategies for the 1980s* (Tycooly International Publishing Ltd., Dublin, 1984).

[17] *The Lagos Plan of Action for the Implementation of the Monrovia Strategy for the Economic Development of Africa adopted by the Second Extraordinary Assembly of the OAU Heads of State and Government, Devoted to Economic Matters* (Lagos, Nigeria, 28-9 April 1980).

management of resources, and a de-emphasis on foreign assistance.[18] This was the document of the 1980s, endorsed by the United Nations and the World Bank. The Lagos Plan gathered dust, and by the end of the decade conditions had deteriorated beyond the imagination of even the worst pessimist.

## Africa since the End of the Cold War

In the heyday of the nationalist struggles after World War II and the early years of independence, the mission of the African states was to transform and create a new positive image. The preface to most political and economic manifestoes revolved around a continent exploited since the fifteenth century. The leaders and their followers looked forward, and the most optimistic ones believed that, by 1995, the continent would be quite different.

Indeed, there is a difference by 1995, but it is not a positive one.[19] By this date, many of the gains of independence have been lost. Debt, drought, the fall in living standards, and wars are now the major issues. Poverty is on the rise, political dictatorship and military rule have become commonplace, and talented intellectuals and skilled professionals migrate to the West. Capital income falls dramatically, annual growth of the Gross National Product fell below zero during the 1980s, agriculture is declining, famine is reported in many places, and expenditure on welfare and social services has declined to the lowest level. Twenty-four of the thirty-six poorest countries in the world are in Africa and the projection is that Africa will end the century as the poorest continent. Africa now owes over $300 billion, with little to show for it. The people, too, have resorted to older forms of survival and resistance: armed robbery, corruption, prostitution, poverty-induced violence, etc.

Scholars are beginning to talk of disorder, chaos, environmental degradation, and dependence on the West. Building a viable nation-state has become more difficult than was expected: in many countries, the cohesion of the different groups has not been realized, and there is a limited mechanism to build consensus and resolve conflicts. A few states have collapsed, some are badly weakened, and many are grossly mismanaged. The debt burden, at a time of economic decline, jeopardizes development and mortgages the future of Africans. Attempts to break free of dependence on the West have ended in fiasco. Now, the wish is to attain an inflow of foreign finance at any cost. Two countries, Nigeria and Algeria, are compromising their leadership role because of complicated internal politics. Thus, the internal balance of power within the continent remains fluid, with the result that very few leaders and countries have the clout successfully to mediate in conflicts.

Strategies of attaining self-reliance are unsuccessful. Since the 1980s and particularly in the 1990s, the universal strategy is that of structural adjustment programmes. Although a few countries like Ghana have been used as examples of success, structural adjustment has been a colossal failure, and the expected gains have not accrued to the majority of the population.[20]

---

[18] A. Adedeji, 'The Monrovia Strategy and the Lagos Plan of Action: Five years after', in A. Adedeji and T. Shaw (eds), *Economic Crisis in Africa* (Lynne Rienner, Boulder, CO., 1985), p. 15.

[19] See A. Adedeji, 'The African challenges in the 1990s: New perspectives for development', *Indian Journal of Social Science*, 3 (1990), pp. 255–69.

[20] For details on structural adjustment and its severe limitations, see M.B. Brown and P. Tiffen, *Short Changed: Africa and world trade* (Pluto with the Transnational Institute, London, 1992); and R. van der Hoeven & F. van der Kraaij (eds)., *Structural Adjustment and Beyond in Sub-Saharan Africa* (Netherlands Ministry of Foreign Affairs, James Currey and Heinemann, The Hague, London and Portsmouth, NH, 1994).

There are some good developments. Reforms are swift in South Africa in the 1990s, leading to the dismantling of apartheid, and the historic election of 1994 with the emergence of Nelson Mandela as the country's first black president. If South Africa is able to stabilize its politics and turn its economy around, there are prospects that other African countries will derive some benefits in increased trade and political leadership. The changes in Eastern Europe since 1989 had consequences that reached Africa. Almost everywhere, demands for political change that have always been expressed in African history are widely reported and recognized internationally. Democracy in a multi-party framework has become the major desire. Civil society is becoming more and more radicalized. There is no longer confidence in the ability of the government or the state to work for progress, and the alienated populace is seeking new ways to survive. There are still problems: the intellectual justification of authoritarianism is very much alive; mass protest is still incapable of leading to the fall of military regimes; and opposition groups are fractionalized.

The international community is retreating from Africa, motivated by the strategic irrelevance of the continent to post-Cold War political calculations, frustration with African leaders, and the devotion of greater attention to Eastern Europe. Africa's raw materials and markets will continue to ensure inter-action, but, as in the past, the continent will be underpaid. The *Communauté financière africaine* (CFA) currency zone created by France to stabilize the currency of French-speaking Africa has weakened. Enthusiasm is declining for projects of cultural assimilation, and the French public is questioning the wisdom of military pacts with Africa. The Soviet Union has collapsed and the component states are too preoccupied with their own survival to worry about Africa. China, which had organized its interest in Africa on the assumption that the Soviet Union was an enemy, is certainly less interested in the continent. Pulling itself outside of the Third World is its main concern, while still using this same bloc to seek international recognition and obtain votes at the United Nations. Japan is aloof, the United States is lukewarm, and the European countries are re-assessing their role. Such countries as Brazil and South Korea, the middle-ranking powers, are preoccupied with promoting deeper relations with the West.[21] Africa and the rest of the Third World is now presented as a burden, both in the media and conservative intellectual circles: its aspiration for change is derided; Islam is replacing the Soviet Union as the new enemy; anti-Western movements are demonized; and Africa is regarded as a threat to global peace and security. Some problems in the West like immigration, drug addiction, and AIDS are being attributed to the Third World.[22] To deal with this burden, an influential writer recently suggested the creation of a league of civilized countries to police the Third World.[23]

## Conclusion

In the peak days of the dependency theory in the 1970s, the most respectable explanation of the African crisis was the external factor: the slave trade, colonial rule and the domination of the continent. No one must ever discount this factor. However, it is grossly

[21] See for instance, C. Stevens, *Europe and the Third World since Decolonization* (Macmillan, London, 1992); and Z. Laidi, *The Superpowers and Africa: The constraints of a rivalry, 1960–1990* (University of Chicago Press, Chicago, IL, 1990).
[22] For a devastating critique of anti-Third World positions, see Frank Furedi, *The New Ideology of Imperialism: Renewing the moral imperative* (Pluto, London, 1994).
[23] F. Fukuyama, *The End of History and the Last Man* (The Free Press, New York, 1992).

misleading to ignore or understate the internal factor: for instance, the troubles within the continent, generated by a leadership that victimizes its own people, takes positions that cannot bring credit to the continent, and squanders and mismanages collective resources. As other chapters in this book will point out, there is virtually no aspect of African society that does not require reform: politics must move away from dictatorship to mass participation; the role of the state as a predator must change to that of an agency to serve people; the international community must back off from supporting illegitimate and brutal political leaders to assist the people to gain freedom and enhance their living standards. The poverty of the people contrasts with the richness of the continent. The empowerment of the people, to allow mass participation in politics and to take charge of their own lives, has become more necessary than ever before.

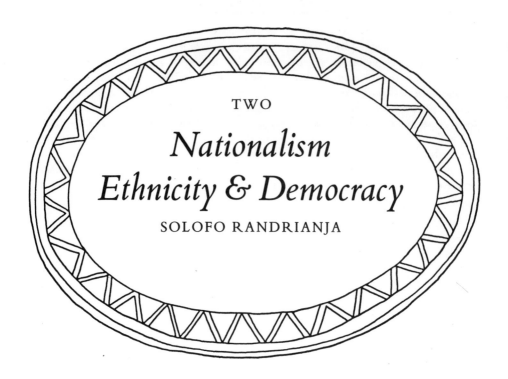

TWO

# Nationalism
# Ethnicity & Democracy

SOLOFO RANDRIANJA

The election of Nelson Mandela as head of the South African state in 1994 concluded
the process of African independence after nearly forty years. During this time, nationalism
inspired struggles for African independence only to transform itself in many cases into
an ideology in the service of the state. From a historical point of view, as is the case
with all living phenomena, nationalism has undergone variations and fluctuations in both
essence and form, but also, and primarily, in its function. Therefore, perhaps, it would
be more accurate to speak of African nationalisms.

After World War I and the failures of rural rebellion against European conquest,
African nationalism initially adopted an organizational form in order to confront European expansion. It subsequently resurfaced in an ideological form after World War II
with the development of African anti-colonialism which was to assimilate some of the
colonizers' own political traditions. Africa's political and intellectual elites[2] played a
significant part during this period.

A period of decline and disillusion followed. The nationalism which had originated
as an anti-colonialist ideology extolling national unity against the foreign oppressor, was
progressively transformed into an ideology of the newly independent states, most of

[1] The research for this chapter was made possible by my tenure of the Jill Natrass Visiting Research Fellowship
at the Centre for Social and Development Studies at the University of Natal. Whilst I acknowledge that I alone
am responsible for the ideas expressed in this text, I am particularly grateful to Professors S. Bekker and W. Freund.
[2] In this chapter, the term 'elite' refers to those groups which hold the combined control of political and economic
power. In the same perspective I shall use the expression 'political entrepreneurs' as well as the expressions 'culture
brokers' and 'cultural entrepreneurs' which are borrowed from other authors.

which were controlled by an oligarchy. The reality of the power enjoyed by the new leaders was hidden behind an anti-imperialist discourse, this new form being endorsed by nationalism from the end of the 1950s. The cycle of economic crises which began towards the mid-1970s, and the end of the Cold War, revealed the nature and function of this type of nationalism. The progressive restriction of the resources available to African states, the major source of wealth and social advancement and thus the object of elite rivalry, exacerbated internal rivalry within this group for the control of power. These rivalries increasingly led to ethnic mobilization and, more generally, to the manipulation of the cultural identities of groups. In the face of the colonizer, the nationalism of the 1950s which had advocated national unity proved increasingly incapable of containing its internal ethno-nationalisms. There was a multiplication of ethno-nationalist demands which attempted to mobilize groups of cultural origin. The attention of the media has focused primarily on these conflicts which are actually caused by economic and political rivalries, but which are interpreted as though they were ethnic conflicts.

Ethnic groups may also be perceived as a means adopted by African rural societies for defending themselves against globalizing systems such as states. At the same time, at the heart of these ethnic groups there exist conflicts of interest which are, in fact, their very essence. For how does one explain the continued existence of ethnic identities other than by their ability to adapt to change? One of the most recent of such changes is democratization.

## Nationalisms in Africa

### The origins of nationalism

According to the generally accepted classification,[3] two categories of anti-colonial movements succeeded one another: the primary resistance movements which lasted until some time around World War I, and the mass movements which were to lead African countries to independence. The former were often rural movements which were extremely backward-looking. They drew their inspiration mainly from the pre-colonial past and, in cases where they adopted a political programme, their aim was the restoration of an old order.

The second wave of movements of resistance to colonialism, the nationalist mass movements, was principally generated by educated town-dwellers. Their emergence after World War I was facilitated by the opening up of Africa to the world, largely as a result of the War. The African soldiers who had fought in Europe in the War brought back not only new diseases but also a new vision of the world.

Even if there were no direct links between the two types of movement (those of primary resistance and mass nationalism), and notwithstanding the fact that in certain places the two movements coexisted in time, it is nevertheless true that there is a kind of continuity in the management of power in Africa which, to a greater or lesser degree, managed to survive the rupture with the past represented by colonialism, both in terms of political personnel and in practice. Thus, in numerous colonial territories the concern for efficiency and the need for economy led colonizers to confirm in power the traditional authorities, one way or another, by conferring administrative duties upon them.

This relative continuity in the management of power via elites is a crucial factor which

---

[3] Terence O. Ranger, 'Connexions between primary resistance movements and modern mass nationalism,' *Journal of African History*, IX, iii and iv (1968), pp. 437–54 and 631–42.

has been largely neglected in the study of contemporary nationalism in Africa. In a broader sense too it has been neglected in the study of subsequent systems – such as socialism or, more recently, democracy – derived from the Western political tradition and assimilated by Africa via its elites.[4]

The partition of Africa between the different colonial powers fostered the development of struggles for independence and the growth of nationalism within territorial frameworks which, with certain exceptions, did not correspond to those in which pre-colonial African history had evolved. Notable exceptions include Madagascar, on account of its island status, and Ethiopia until World War II. Apart from these exceptions, the continent was almost entirely dismembered; so much so that in 1952 Lord Hailey, a leading strategist of British imperialism, commented:

> For the most part [territories] represent only geographical units and not communities with any such natural ties or affinities as can form the basis for nationhood . . . people who are brought together by fate into one governmental unit – generally as a result of outside action – can of course be welded into something like nationality by the force of circumstances . . . But it is an historical process . . . a matter of time, often of very considerable time.[5]

Colonialism represents an important break in this sense. Nationalism in Africa was elaborated in political struggles for emancipation and often as a reaction to the racist and disparaging views of colonial ideology. As such it is above all a product of the colonial situation in so far as it represents the actualization of 'Africanness' for the entire African continent. In this case, 'Africanness' represents a politicized supra-ethnicity and the African nation a myth[6] or, more accurately, an artifact of recent creation.

### Elites, nationalism and ideology

It is difficult to give a precise definition of African nationalism other than by considering the fluctuations in its usage in different periods and places. Originally, African nationalism was chiefly an organizational rather than a theoretical phenomenon. In the inter-War period associations of town-dwellers connected with Christianity, trade unions, and political parties were instrumental in struggles in favour of the emancipation of the elites. These elite groups subsequently declared themselves to be the voice of the people, transforming these organizations into breeding grounds for nationalism.[7]

As a tributary of eighteenth and nineteenth-century mainstream European nationalism, African nationalism is a particular type of 'cultural artifact', to use Benedict Anderson's[8] expression. It did not awaken African nations so much as create them. The demarcation of these nations is difficult to trace except for idiosyncratic cases such as Madagascar –

---

[4] Robert Archer, *Madagascar depuis 1972: la marche d'une révolution* (l'Harmattan, Paris, 1976) proposed, in the case of Madagascar, to trace the ancestry of those Malagasy who led the country from the 1970s. This sort of study would have unearthed roots dating at least as far back as the era of the monarchy in the nineteenth century. This is not a unique case.

[5] Quoted by Crawford Young, 'Evolving modes of consciousness and ideology: nationalism and ethnicity', in D. Apter & C. Rosberg (eds), *Political Development and the New Realism in Sub-Saharan Africa* (University Press of Virginia, Charlottesville, VA, 1994), p. 62.

[6] As John Degenaar maintains in referring to the case of South Africa, 'Nationalism is a politicised ethnicity, nationalism is the enemy of a democratic society'. John Degenaar, '*No sizwe*: the myth of the nation', *Indicator S.A.*, 10/3 (1993), p. 16.

[7] Solofo Randrianja, *Le Parti communiste de la région de Madagascar, 1930–1939: aux origines du socialisme malgache* (Foi et Justice, Antananarivo, 1990).

[8] Benedict Anderson, *Imagined Communities: Reflections on the origin and spread of nationalism* (Verso, London and New York, 1983).

favoured by its insularity – or other relatively stable state entities which were able to maintain their integrity in the face of European conquest, as in Ethiopia. In fact the entity nationalism sought to create could have assumed a pan-African form, a pan-cultural form (such as the Maghreb), that of a micro-state built on ethnic identity, and so on. In the event, history records that what was actually created was federations of territories sharing a common colonial past.

As a rule, nationalism was confined to each of the territories which had formerly been colonized, splintering into a multitude of variants. However, what the various nationalisms have in common – as pan-Africanism demonstrates – is their European origin. Nationalism in nineteenth-century Europe bred negative elements culminating in two world wars and the holocaust, the consequence of chauvinism, fascism and militarism. Pan-Africanism promoted and continues to promote solidarity based upon racial principles. However, these aspects of African nationalism escaped the attention of the historical actors of the time, who saw only the anti-colonialist aspect of nationalism, giving it the benefit of the doubt.

These theoretical and tactical differences have encouraged the existence of numerous regional variants of nationalism, as have other factors such as pre-colonial history, the role of the colonial powers in the formation of national elites, and the methods used to gain independence. In South Africa, which has the most developed capitalist economy of the continent, and where the working class is organized in powerful trade unions dominated by the left, nationalism is certainly very different from the nationalism of a country like Mali.

In any event, this splitting of nationalisms into many regional variants has been in the interests of the elites who originally promoted nationalism. The concept of the nation which results from this fragmentation actually turns the nation into the sphere of influence of a specific elite rather than a historically and culturally homogeneous entity. Seen in this light, elites should not be perceived only as a simple creation of colonization, or the transmission belt of colonial interests. They are also cultural intermediaries, cultural entrepreneurs or culture brokers, who have managed to reconcile collaboration with, and resistance to, colonial power in the management of their own interests. They succeeded in gaining recognition not only as the spokesmen for their compatriots, but also as agents of the colonial state in such a way as to reap the benefits of independence.

Africa's elites are its window on the outside world, not the agents of acculturation as has been suggested in the past. While revitalizing certain traditions, by means of nationalism they also created the opportunity in Africa for a type of open society where social status is acquired and not prescribed. Philibert Tsiranana, the first president of the first Republic of Madagascar, was fond of recalling his peasant origins.

One of the factors behind the triumph of African nationalism was not so much the promise of a return to the past, but rather the use of the past to introduce new elements. To achieve this, the elites succeeded in mobilizing in the struggle for independence kings and traditional authorities, women, and religions such as Islam, thus creating an internal dynamic within African societies in order to meet the challenge, imposed by colonization, of opening up to the contemporary world.

In the early phase, the modern elites played on their modernity, their Westernization, distancing themselves from African cultures. Later they returned to African cultures, 'objectifying them as an ancestral heritage which could be ideologized, in other words, used and reformulated for specific aims'.[9] In this way, these modern and 'national' elites

---

[9] S. Randrianja quoted by Françoise Raison-Jourde, 'Two contrasting Malagasy representations of democracy: the period of legalist means of resistance based on colonial French laws (1925–1945), the myth of democracy at work in rural communities during precolonial times (1955–1972)' History Workshop, University of the Witwatersrand, 1994.

undermined the foundations of the legitimacy of the traditional elites – elites which had acquired status in their regions and villages – and subjected them to their own authority. Furthermore, the prestige of the traditional elites was considerably reduced as a result of their own status (old, rural and therefore having a low level of education, often poor, provincial, etc.) but also because they are rooted in the ethnic systems in which they play a significant role. One of the main reasons for their weakened position was also the degree of cooperation which existed between colonial administrations and those so-called 'traditional' authorities which were integrated into the colonial system of administration.

However, even within the modern elites, differences in the level of education, together with economic differences, generated conflicts in the competition for power even after it had become increasingly evident that the political evolution was leading to independence. These conflicts were eventually to become institutionalized in violence and civil war as a mode of gaining access to power.

Thus, even though there is no doubt of the fact that it was the elites who benefited most from independence, the nature and success of independence depended entirely on the alliances and contradictions existing between the various elements of the elites. For, despite the various elections and other forms of popular consultation which had no historical precedent (that is, which were not rooted in any pre-existing democratic tradition), independence was negotiated mainly between African elites and the colonizing powers. The African populace was largely excluded from participation in this process, except in those areas where there was armed conflict and where, in most cases, it was a victim. We should not overlook the fact that, where it does not have the backing of the people, independence has often been artificial, such as in the South African homelands under apartheid. Once independence had been acquired, from being an ideology mobilized to seize power from the hands of the colonizers, nationalism was rapidly transformed into an ideology employed in the service of the newly independent states.

### Nationalism, state ideology and power: towards the failure of the nation-state?

When Africa was partitioned at the end of the nineteenth century, and again at the time of independence, the colonial powers attached little importance to the cultural homogeneity of human groups in constituting those territories, which, from the 1950s onwards, were to become independent nation-states. As one illustration amongst countless others, the peoples speaking the Kongo language were dispersed over three states, Congo, Zaïre and Angola, occupying territories which belonged to three different colonial powers, whereas in former times these peoples had constituted a powerful kingdom which lasted much longer than the colonial presence. Few homogeneous cultural groups escaped this process of dismemberment.

Independent African countries like Nigeria comprise heterogeneous groups subject to the imposition of a state-controlled structure. It is undoubtedly in this context that the concept of the nation as an 'imagined community' actually operates.[10] Each individual member of such a community feels an affinity which generates a sense of belonging even if this individual will never be able to know the other members of the community. Most of the time this affinity is associated with symbols which make the nation something

---

[10] Anderson, *Imagined Communities*.

visible, even if only partially (clothing, language, etc.). These symbols are usually cultural. The sense of belonging is often in the domain of *pathos* or emotion. Nationalism has built the *ethos*, the administrative framework capable of providing the individual with a universe which is familiar and which provides a sense of security.

The practical and tangible aspect of nations is the states controlled by elites. Hence it is not surprising that these states have adopted as one of the fundamental principles governing their relations in the framework of the OAU, respect for the frontiers inherited from colonization. It is thus control over people rather than the restoration of a defunct pre-colonial entity which motivated the nationalism enunciated by the elites. No doubt it is in this way that the democratic aspirations contained in most of the nationalist mass movements following World War II came to be stifled.

The elites were, for example, in the name of African primordialism, the main promoters of the idea that social classes do not exist in Africa, which was used as a justification for the one-party system at the time of independence.[11] Gradually, independence itself would reveal the true nature of the new authorities: a ruling class concerned to mobilize resources to its own advantage and preoccupied with its own reproduction. The nationalist discourse lost its primary function in order to readjust to the new situation. From its anti-colonialist origins preaching national unity, it became anti-imperialist, denouncing real and imaginary enemies of the nation represented by the incumbent political power. Post-independence nationalism thus became the ideology of the state serving to legitimize the power of a particular group.

> [Nationalism], in the form that it took, was at bottom a mystification which arose from the delusions of its ideologues: delusions transformed into realities which, when examined, transform themselves into delusions . . . The idea of nationalism changed from icon of liberation to captive doctrine of an African nation-state which has become a lifeless shell of bureaucratic or personal tyranny, corruption and defeat.[12]

The economic weakness of the newly independent states and the progressive drying-up of resources served to accelerate the metamorphosis of the state into an oppressive machine for extracting wealth and protecting a ruling group which proved incapable of resolving ethnic differences. Moreover, political rivalries within the ranks of the elite turned into violent conflicts often leading to military coups. Up until the beginning of the 1990s, with few exceptions, such transfers of power as did occur were almost always marked by violence tinged by ethnic conflicts.[13] These conflicts have certainly contributed to the present economic distress of the great majority of the states of the African continent.

The failure of the majority of African post-colonial nation-states no longer requires any demonstration, despite regional variants of greater or lesser significance and individual cases such as South Africa. But does the failure of the nation-state – which also represents the failure of the nationalism of elites, as is clearly shown by the paralysis and deterioration of African states – also herald the progressive disappearance of the nation, and, with it, the calling into question of its territory? Is there a decline of both nationality and nation in Africa? Can it be said that the sense of belonging even to a conceptual community is being superseded by other identities and other allegiances?

---

[11] Cf. Julius K. Nyerere, *Ujamaa: Essays on Socialism* (Oxford University Press, Dar es Salaam, 1968).

[12] Basil Davidson, 'The challenge of comparative analysis: anti-imperialist nationalism in Europe and Africa', paper presented to conference on state crisis in Eastern Europe and Africa, Bellagio, Italy, 1990, p. 13.

[13] But corruption is not the prerogative of civilians alone. In thirty years, the military budgets in Tropical Africa have increased forty-fold (not including South Africa and Rhodesia). C. Coquery-Vidrovitch, '30 années perdues ou étapes d'une longue évolution?', *Afrique contemporaine*, special edition, 4th quarter, (1992), p. 6.

The awareness of nationality has undeniably taken hold much more quickly in Africa than elsewhere in the world. This is especially true in the cities, places of ethnic inter-mixing, the places where power resides. In less than one generation, half of the African population will be urban-dwellers. 'People are now Senegalese, Kenyan or Ivorian or even Gabonese before being Serer, Wolof, Kikuyu, Bété or Fang'.[14] The reluctance of many multi-ethnic countries to adopt a federal constitution in the wake of the recent waves of political liberalization exemplifies this in more ways than one. The almost total rejection of a federal constitution as a means of consecrating the 'ethnicization' of the state, and the campaign for the reincorporation of the homelands in a new South Africa, can be compared with the comprehensive defeat of the supporters of Madagascar's second republic under President Didier Ratsiraka who, when he had his back to the wall, encouraged a secessionist movement under the federalist label.

In fact the content of the imagined community, the nation, is the problem posed by urbanization and the population explosion, and their political and economic conse-quences, a problem the post-colonial nationalist regimes have not managed to resolve. At regular intervals, this problem threatens the integrity of the nation-states far more than migratory patterns or inter-ethnic conflicts. And a problem of this nature cannot be solved simply by reorganizing the form of the state.

In 1994 in South Africa, for example, illegal migrants flooding across the border from countries like Mozambique were denounced in chauvinist terms equal to anything witnessed in countries such as France – and this was by the government authorities themselves. As a general rule, migratory movements by people seeking opportunities in the major South African industrial and mining centres, and previously in the plantations, have brought about significant shifts in the population without threatening the integrity of the nation.

However, it is also true that the distribution of ethnic groups in the various contem-porary states is a factor which exacerbates the problem posed by political and economic refugees, a factor which produces national destabilization. The movements of rapidly growing populations are largely due to the instability of their countries of origin. But despite the importance of the presence of refugees, host countries, with the cooperation of international organizations, tend to avoid absorbing refugees who are usually poor, illiterate and unqualified farmers. They are parked in temporary camps which are heavily guarded. Thus, not a single new trans-state ethnic confederation has even begun to take form as yet. Certain states have even used refugees as an instrument of their foreign policy, like apartheid South Africa in the case of Mozambique.

In general, refugees without professional qualifications are ruthlessly persecuted, whereas refugees with professional skills are not. The South-South brain drain works in favour of South Africa where, in the former homeland of Transkei, 20 per cent of doctors are Ugandan.[15] All of these policies are moving towards the reinforcement of existing nations, often to the benefit of the powerful nation-state.

On the other hand, the last two decades have witnessed an increasing emphasis on the internationalization of the economy which has fostered phenomena such as major population shifts and a greater fluidity of information thanks to new communication technology. It has become a serious question whether, in the long term, a process of this nature is not eventually going to lead to the disappearance of the nation-state in Africa, even if such a phenomenon seems far less evident in Europe.

---

[14] ibid., p. 6.
[15] Hussein Solomon, 'Migration in Southern Africa: a comparative perspective', *Africa Insight*, 24 (1994), pp. 60–71.

Another factor sometimes held to prefigure the more or less imminent disappearance of African nations is an implosion resulting from their own internal tensions, notably of an ethnic form. Usually ethnic demands are simply a manifestation of the struggle for power among elites or, at lower social levels, a form of resistance against a predatory and overbearing state. From this perspective, ethnic irredentism is more an expression of a crisis of citizenship than of the nation itself.[16] Examples of the secession of African nation-states on the basis of ethnicity, as in Yugoslavia or the republics of the former USSR, are rare. The preservation of the frontiers inherited from colonization has been a constant factor in state policies.[17]

However, society remains a site of political conflict and ethnicity in its politicized form is simply one means among many others at the disposition of political entrepreneurs. Although it is going too far to refer to ethnicity as a 'theatre of shadows',[18] it is nevertheless both a political tool in the rivalry between factions of elites in the struggle for power and a form of expression adopted by societies (particularly peasant societies) which have been divided into small units of this type by cultural entrepreneurs. This is one of a number of modes of expression that rub shoulders with each other in African society. Indeed, in the space of only some fifty years, African societies have, broadly speaking, developed from having a relatively small degree of inequality between top and bottom into a complex of competing hierarchies and fractions, including social classes.[19] These developments constitute a process of consolidation of the nation from below, which will lead in time to as many different methods of confronting the autocratic state inherited from the past, pre-colonial, colonial and post-colonial.

On the eve of the twenty-first century, distinct national cultures of politics and trade unionism have emerged to take their place alongside other original forms of association to demand democracy and emancipation. The various approaches to democratic transition illustrate this fact. In some cases the movement has come up against a strong personalization of power as in Zaïre; elsewhere, the transition has been smooth, as in Zambia.

Thus, if it is legitimate to speak of a crisis, it is a crisis of citizenship rather than of the nation, and a crisis of the state rather than a symptom of apathy among societies which, in their struggle to survive, demonstrate an inventiveness which has been a subject of debate in academic literature since the end of the 1980s. In the search by societies to take revenge against the state, will citizens call into question the existence of the nation? It is without doubt in this regard that the problem of ethnicity is best considered.

## Ethnicity: The Dancer and His Shadow

During the colonial period nationalist discourse emphasized national unity even if, in the daily activity of political organizations and political entrepreneurs, considerable concessions were made to ethnicity. But, after all, politics involves seizing opportunities. On the whole, anti-colonial nationalism aimed to transcend ethnic differences. The nationalists presented themselves as instruments of dynamic change which rejected

---

[16] René Lemarchand, 'Political clientelism and ethnicity in tropical Africa: competing solidarities in nation-building', *American Political Science Review*, LXVI, i (1972), pp. 68–90.
[17] Eritrea represents less the dismemberment of Ethiopia than the return to independence of a region annexed by the ruling dynasty in 1962.
[18] Jean-François Bayart, *The State in Africa: the politics of the belly* (Longman, London, New York, 1993), p. 41. This is a translation of the original French version, published by Fayard in 1989.
[19] Bill Freund, *The African Worker* (Cambridge University Press, Cambridge, 1988).

ethnicity as the retrograde element in opposed sets of values: nationalism and progress versus tribalism and anarchy. This type of social Darwinism in nationalist thought and discourse during the period of anti-colonial struggle represented ethnicity and ethnic groups as anachronisms which would disappear with progress. But during the first decades of independence, various political conflicts existing at the heart of the newly independent nations revealed that, in the competition for power, elites did not hesitate to make use of ethnicity. Without accurately defining this complex phenomenon, from the 1960s onwards the newly-invented term 'tribalism' was commonly used in reference to these conflicts. Above all, such conflicts mobilized partisan factions rather than nations, as the media of the time believed.

However, alongside this ethnicity which generates conflict, there exists also a form of social organization which is characteristic of many rural African communities: small units linked by kinship or by geography and which are conscious of their own existence.

Just like the shadow cast by a dancer which has its own existence, two sorts of ethnicity co-exist throughout history, competing but also dependent on each other. One is that ethnicity which divides people into categories in order to divide and rule; the second is that ethnicity which consists of the domestication of such politics and of the act of categorization by the rural masses which constitute the majority of the population of Africa. In reality these two strains of ethnicity correspond to two different sorts of ethnic group: those broad categories which usually draw their terms of reference from pre-colonial and/or colonial state-controlled structures, and, second, more restricted groups which take the form of a community small enough to perceive its identity in terms of ancestry and in bonds of mutual obligation. Between these two extremes of small groups and larger bodies, there exist many variants representing successive layers of historical creations which form an endless supply of material for reworking by individuals, groups and political entrepreneurs. Thus, if we concentrate on the areas in which conflict can arise, we can identify three areas of conflict involving ethnicity: internal conflicts within ethnic groups, which rarely attract major public attention; conflicts between ethnic groups which attract frequent public attention; and conflicts of ethnic groups against globalizing entities such as states. An important theoretical question constitutes a necessary prerequisite for further discussion of ethnicity: namely, the historical nature of ethnic groups.

## The historical nature of ethnic groups

If ethnicity may be defined as the process of forming a group identity explained and experienced in terms of kinship, it should be said that such a process is profoundly rooted in history and is far more universal than might be imagined.[20] In other words, ethnicity is an important part of the mechanism of political power. The politics of divide and rule, whose corollary is the ascription of ethnic groups, is one of the methods of government favoured by despotisms African and Oriental.[21] In order to understand this phenomenon, we have to adopt a long-term perspective (*la longue durée*), the perspective

---

[20] According to Anthony Smith for example, 'while national identity is mainly a modern phenomenon, pre-modern ethnic communities and identities are widespread and processes of national formation and representation are found in all epochs'. A. Smith, 'The problem of national identity, ancient, medieval and modern?' *Ethnic and Racial Studies*, 17, 3, (July 1994), pp. 375–99.

[21] J.-L. Amselle, 'La corruption et le clientélisme au Mali et en Europe de l'Est: quelques points de comparaison', *Cahiers d'études africaines*, 128, XXXII, 4 (1992), p. 640.

of those structures 'that time erodes only slowly and transmits over long periods'.[22]

Most studies of ethnicity emphasize the artificial character of ethnic groups created by colonization or in response to European aggression.[23] This viewpoint represents those who have been placed by governments into defined categories[24] as pawns, passive subjects of the march of history.

Both a historical and a comparative perspective enable ethnicity to be considered as a process of negotiating identity within groups as well as between groups within a much larger body which transcends, but simultaneously maintains, ethnic differences. This multiplies the number of possible identities an individual can assume depending on circumstances. In fact, without subscribing to fantasies about a timeless Africa, we may note that authors who are rightly opposed to practices of divide and rule describe a phenomenon which is as old as power itself. Africa is not primordially communalist as opposed to a resolutely individualist West. The gap between Europe and Africa was undoubtedly caused by the industrial and social revolutions of the eighteenth and nineteenth centuries which atomized the individual in Western society. Indeed, there are numerous points of convergence between Africa and Europe before the nationalist period.[25]

In any event, it would be to attribute to the colonizers a genius they did not have, if one were to grant them the exclusive paternity of the sin of tribalism, as is current practice in the field of politics; a glimpse into history as far back as the great pre-colonial states and empires of Africa shows this. The European colonizers simply reorganized to their own advantage the existing protocols of ties between groups.

The first step towards an understanding of the process of forming identity which is defined as ethnicity, is to investigate the actual content of the particular ethnic group in question. Historians are far from reaching consensus in this respect. However, the crystallization of kinship ties is often seen as being at the inception of ethnic groups in conditions of insecurity caused by large expansionist bodies such as the slave-trading states of the seventeenth and eighteenth centuries, or, for that matter, the colonial state and the predatory states created at the time of independence.[26] In such cases, the members of a group are conscious and active players. In the central highlands of Madagascar during the period of construction of the monarchy (sixteenth-eighteenth centuries) 'the self-sufficiency of the *foko*,[27] their geographical isolation, their extremely marked, if not absolute, endogamy . . . seem to be a typical peasant reaction to insecurity: threatened from all sides, often brought together in one place through the hazards of war rather than by a community of ancestors, farmers spontaneously seem to have sought to multiply mutual bonds of kinship . . . The constitution of closed groups, united by extremely complex networks of alliances, capable of incorporating refugees from elsewhere, was a protection against the outside, but it was also a guarantee against an overlord who, in theory, was their protector: whom do you single out for punishment

---

[22] Fernand Braudel, 'Histoire et sciences sociales. La longue durée', *Annales*, 4 (1958), pp. 725–53.

[23] Leroy Vail (ed.), *The Creation of Tribalism in Southern Africa* (James Currey, London, 1989).

[24] Gerhard Maré, *Brothers Born of Warrior Blood: Politics and ethnicity in South Africa* (Ravan Press, Johannesburg, 1992), p. 6.

[25] cf. for example Eugen Weber, *La fin des terroirs: la modernisation de la France rurale, 1870–1914* (Fayard, Paris, 1983).

[26] P. Ekeh, quoted by Crawford Young, 'Evolving modes of consciousness', p. 80.

[27] There is little agreement on this Malagasy term. Maurice Bloch proposes to translate it by the word 'deme', drawn from ancient Greece, which has the advantage of implying that this type of organization is universal. Maurice Bloch, *Placing the Dead: Tombs, ancestral villages and kinship organisation in Madagascar* (Seminar Press, London, 1971).

in a group where authority is totally diluted?'[28] However, for such groups to be functional, their size must correspond with the capacity of their members to control them. Such groups are thus of limited size.

In a context of this sort, ethnicity is a socially creative act which conditions the political organization of a group, its language, its culture, and so on, in an awareness of a common identity. At some point, this awareness achieves a degree of self-perpetuation at the group level, which means there are a number of possibilities for each individual, for whom the ethnic group becomes 'a palate of inclusion and exclusion'.[29] An entity constructed in this way is more social and cultural than political, unless politics is defined in the very broadest terms.

Ethnic groups of a much larger size, which can be considered to be political units, are an echo of these small groups. Large ethnic groups of the second type crystallize around leaders, or political entrepreneurs. Their contours are generally vague. The term Zulu, for example, initially referred only to the royal family of the Nguni group immediately prior to the accession to power of Shaka (1816–28) in the Natal region. Historical studies of the Zulus as well as of other similar groups often reveal a process of unification, which presupposes the existence of disparate groups at the outset. These groups are united solely by their being subject to an expansionist power whose role is ambiguous, since it unifies while maintaining elements of division. These are the very conditions which allow such a power to endure. The elements of such a system are mutually dependent, at the same time as they define themselves by their differences, both in complementing one another and in situations of competition. The two extremes which may be adopted within the context of a globalizing power are assimilation and genocide. Thus, the ethnic group, considered as a political unit, under the influence of cultural entrepreneurs, endures through its collective consciousness. The empire of Shaka has disappeared but the Zulu ethnic group survived by assuming new attributes. 'Most historical identities have been adapted numerous times in order to serve as the basis for contemporary nationalities', Turner remarks.[30]

This historical perspective shows ethnicity to be seen as an operation involving both dominators and dominated, because the two types of ethnicity are interdependent as well as competing or even antagonististic, depending on the circumstances. This process implies a never-ending process of negotiation and questioning which is the reason for the indefinite and fluid character of ethnic groups. Often, its most tangible element is the name applied to the whole.

An ethnic group, then, is not always a unit defined by reference to a fixed territory and culture, nor is it as permanent as colonial ethnographers and their later followers would have us believe.

The relations between dominators and dominated which lie at the heart of an ethnic group are played out in the control of the process of forming identity, which thus becomes an area of conflict and negotiation.[31] The control of the production of historical knowledge becomes strategically important because it permits the fixing of the process of forming identities at a certain period. The metaphor of kinship plays an important part in obscuring certain historical facts and in connecting current identity to a

---

[28] Jean-Pierre Raison, *Les Hautes Terres de Madagascar* (2 vols, Orstom/Karthala, Paris, 1984), vol. 1, p. 99.
[29] An expression coined by John Wright.
[30] Thomas E. Turner, 'Memory, myth and ethnicity: a review of recent literature and some cases from Zaïre', *History in Africa*, 19 (1992), p. 389.
[31] J. Willis, 'The making of a tribe: Bondei identities and histories', *Journal of African History*, 33 (1992), pp. 191–208.

mythological past. Although the Malagasy term *fihavanana* (sociability based on kinship presented as ideally harmonious and free from conflict) has not been defined as systematically as the *ubunthubotho* of the Zulus[32] according to Inkatha (which has had the advantage of governing the homeland of Kwazulu and which has succeeded in integrating this subject into the state school curriculum). The two are nevertheless similar: they are both expressions of the great power of culture brokers in search of a ground of consensus with those whom they dominate by means of state and administrative structures. *Fihavanana*, like its Zulu equivalent, always leads to the legitimization of the status quo in which current social relations are represented as natural and primordial. In the final analysis, it is the elites who are the beneficiaries of this status quo; their objective was not, and is not, to build a just society. Behind the elite looms the presence of the state which, in most African countries, is essentially a place of accumulation and a means of predation.

*Ethno-nationalism: an instrument in the hands of cultural entrepreneurs and the state*

It is difficult to refute the idea that ethnicity is used by elites, particularly nowadays, in political and social competition. These elites encourage the emergence of an ethno-nationalism in order to mobilize supporters.[33] This type of politicized ethnicity makes its appearance when nationalism extends the field of action of the ethnic community from the purely cultural and social sphere to that of economy and politics.[34] The progressive transformation of Inkatha, which began as a cultural association, into a political organization used by apartheid, is a good example of this.[35]

When it is politicized, ethnicity moves from the mainly private sphere to the public domain. Tangible small units give way to bigger groups. Since 'the principles of predation and redistribution operating in old or modern political formations are ... often at the root of an ethnicization of populations',[36] totalitarian regimes like South Africa under apartheid and the Soviet Union before Gorbachev came to develop identical concepts of ethnicity even though they appeared to be ideologically opposed. Ethnicity became 'a fundamental "scientific" concept applicable to various groups showing "ethnic" traits'.[37] Those who mastermind this transition of ethnicity from the private sphere to the public domain are specialists in 'ethnicity ... myth-makers working for the apparatus of their various states (and parties)'.[38] These are culture brokers or cultural entrepreneurs, intellectuals who make a career in politics.

Historical processes often follow the same course. In the case of the Zulus, for example – but it may equally apply to all of Africa despite its variety – even though the kingdom achieved a high degree of political unification between 1860 and 1870 in the face of external threats, local and regional loyalties remained important. The term Zulu was originally used exclusively for members of the royal family. It was only at the end

---

[32] Praisley Mdluli, 'Ubuntu-Botho, Inkatha's people's education', *Transformation*, 5, (1987), pp. 60–77.

[33] Nicolas Cope, 'The Zulu petit bourgeoisie and Zulu nationalism in the 1920s: Origins of Inkatha', *Journal of Southern African Studies*, 16, (1990), pp. 432–51.

[34] Anthony D. Smith, *The Ethnic Revival in the Modern World* (Cambridge University Press, London, 1981), p. 19.

[35] Heribert M. Adam & K. Moodley, 'Political violence, "tribalism" and Inkatha', *Journal of Modern African Studies*, 30, 3 (1992), pp. 485–510.

[36] Amselle, 'La corruption et le clientélisme au Mali', p. 640.

[37] Pierre Skalnik, 'Union soviétique-Afrique du Sud: les "théories de l'etnos"', *Cahier d'études africaines*, XXVIII (2), 110 (1988), p. 161.

[38] ibid., p. 172.

of the nineteenth century that the *Amakholwa*, Westernized Christians whose social advance was limited by the colonial system, began to develop in the nationalist idiom what we might call the idea of 'Zuluness'. Accepting for their own purposes the fixing of a Zulu territory that had been imposed by the colonizers, they succeeded in propagating the idea that the inhabitants of Natal/Zululand were Zulus by virtue of the fact that their forefathers had been dominated by the Zulu kingdom.[39] Ethno-nationalism thus developed in the very bosom of nationalism.

Nowadays, African universities harbour a number of sorcerer's apprentices whose role behind the scenes is revealed only when dramas take place such as that in Rwanda. Countless theses are dedicated to the dictators who employ them. These cultural intermediaries use their ability to conceive of different cultures objectively in order to represent the ancestral heritage as an autonomous entity, so as to reformulate it in their own interests. In other words, they proclaim themselves as spokesmen of the nation and/or the ethnic group according to the circumstances, while always promoting their own interests in the first instance. They combine knowledge and power in a context where the colonial economy of predation, except in a few rare cases, has left the state as the principal source of wealth and social advancement.

> The [African] intellectual wants to find a place in government, to penetrate those circles where scarce resources, honours and pleasures are accumulated and redistributed. These are the exact places where the national idea and national sentiment are celebrated and where representations of the state are created. The single object of his discourse is the nation, in all its forms.[40]

Once they achieved power, instead of transforming the colonial state in conformity with the democratic aspirations of a relatively large proportion of the nationalist movement, the elites perpetuated it. Those intellectuals who succeeded the colonial ethnographers and administrators promoted concepts such as the single party and the planned economy in order to have control of the accumulative machinery of the state. When disappointment led to opposition, post-colonial states ossified and turned into machineries of repression, as arbitrary, if not more so, as those of the colonial period. This situation had two consequences. Not only did rural societies withdraw into vertical alliances, but the state itself became an object of rivalry between groups defined by vertical solidarities of kinship, clientelism, or, in a broad sense, ethnicity.

Rather than being ethnic in the proper sense of the word, the wars which are prominent in modern Africa are rather conflicts between competing pillars of vertical solidarity in which the populace is more the victim than an active agent. In the case of Rwanda, violence was originally the work of various militias manipulated by factions rather than a clearly ethnic conflict pitting two 'nations' absolutely and systematically against one another. Similarly in South Africa, during the outburst of violence in Natal in August 1985, attacks on Indians, on members of the United Democratic Front and on the Mpondo were the work of vigilantes brought in from rural areas of Natal and generally associated with Chief Gatsha Buthelezi,[41] an ally of the apartheid government but also a member of the local intelligentsia. The renewed outbursts of violence in Natal at the end of the 1980s were motivated by the prospect of political power left vacant by the measures undertaken by F.W. de Klerk. This can be compared with 'warlordism'

---

[39] Carolyn Hamilton & John Wright, 'The beginning of Zulu identity', *Indicator SA*, 10, 3 (1993), p. 45.
[40] Fabien Eboussi Boulaga, 'L'intellectuel exotique', *Politique africaine*, 51 (1993), p. 31.
[41] Shula Marks, 'Patriotism, patriarchy and purity: Natal and the politics of Zulu ethnic consciousness', in Vail, *The Creation of tribalism*, p. 215.

in Somalia[42] or the hiring of young rural illiterates in and around the city of Tamatave to break the democracy movement which was organizing opposition to the socialist state in Madagascar.[43]

However, it would be an illusion to believe that there is no more to ethnicity than the instrumentalist approach, that is, something that has been imposed from above. It is necessary to consider the efficacity of politicized ethnicity or, in other words, the resonances which are created when a population is mobilized by political entrepreneurs and elites more generally.

The relationship between politicized ethnicity and solidarities based on the ties of kinship developed by rural communities is one of the reasons for its effectiveness. The psychological instability caused by a process of Westernization so rapid as to threaten old family structures, for example, can lead to a reflex of 'retribalization' which is particularly noticeable among migrant workers. These workers become particularly receptive to appeals from politicians. Outside Kwazulu, the ethnic mobilization operated by Inkatha during the 1994 election campaign was most effective in the area around Johannesburg where there is a considerable community of migrant workers originally from Natal Kwazulu.

This retribalization takes the form of an extremely conservative return to the grassroots of identity, at the expense of groups like women and youth. A selection from among the symbols of group recognition is used to construct a sense of cohesion which makes it possible to mobilize people. The result is a series of 'reinvented' values which purport to be traditional.[44] In any event, the intention of intellectuals and cynical politicians is to make an appeal to that powerful emotional charge which is one of the by-products of ethnic loyalties. Hence, on the Rand, in the single men's hostels:

> The migrants, at the bottom of the social hierarchy, not surprisingly find solace from their material and symbolic deprivation in their identification with a mythical Zulu pride and fighting spirit . . . Mutilations are reported in many conflicts. People are not just killed, for example, in Yugoslavia or Azerbaijan, but in addition are often grossly disfigured. This horrendous practice points perhaps, to deep-seated feelings of emasculation.[45]

In a rather more prosaic fashion, more material factors such as advantage or the control of violence can explain the effectiveness of ethnic mobilization.

One consequence of the principles of predation and redistribution is that politicized ethnicity transforms an ethnic group into a sort of coalition which is just as capable of predation as it is of redistributing wealth in order to reproduce itself:

> Ethnic groups are in short, a form of minimum winning coalition, large enough to secure benefits in the competition for spoils but also small enough to maximise the per capita value of these benefits.[46]

Clientelist networks or vertical solidarities depart from a central nucleus: the godfather or some other person or group of persons. Next in the scale of the privileged and of

[42] Hussein M. Adam, 'Somalia: Militarism, warlordism or democracy?', Review of African Political Economy, 54 (1992), pp. 11–26.
[43] Anselme Fanomezantsoa, 'Le régicide ambigu ou mouvement de 1991 vu de Tamatave', Politique africaine, 52 (1993), pp. 40–9.
[44] E. Hobsbawn & T.O. Ranger, The Invention of Tradition (Cambridge University Press, Cambridge, 1983).
[45] Adam & Moodley, 'Political Violence', p. 507.
[46] Robert H. Bates, 'Modernization, ethnic competition and the rationality of politics in contemporary Africa', in D. Rothchild & V.A. Olorunsola (eds), State versus Ethnic Claims: African policy dilemmas (Westview Press, Boulder, CO, 1983) pp. 164–5.

the distributors of privileges comes the family, followed by other dependants within the ethnic group. The central nucleus owes these dependants all sorts of services and gifts in exchange for political allegiance. In everyday life small-scale corruption is the most visible sign of clientelist relations and thus it constitutes the reality of ethnic identities as they are actually lived. This small-scale corruption associated with vertical solidarities is undoubtedly a distinctive feature of Africa. Major corruption, at the higher reaches of the state, is as widespread in Africa as it is in the West.

When added one to another, these clientelist relations compete and clash with the formation of other types of solidarity such as class solidarity or reciprocal assimilation.[47] This sort of situation benefits the state and its protégés for whom it is an effective and economic method of managing social conflicts. However, these vertical solidarities also allow inequalities to be made more tolerable. One of the reasons for the durability of the South African homelands, besides control by the police, was the fact that the local authorities, in the form of tribal administrations, were able to distribute resources in the form of pensions, land allocation, and so on.

## Ethnicity from below

An examination of the historical background of ethnicity aids understanding of the fact that an individual has a multitude of ethnic identities at his or her disposal and that not all of these identities imply violence.

Ethnic identities persist, no doubt, also because they are domesticated by the people who have been 'classified' under ethnic labels and who subvert them to their own advantage. Already in the nineteenth century, the persistence of local and regional loyalties in the face of the power of Shaka can be explained by the fact that they supported his power but also resisted his expansionist enterprise. At the same time they competed for power, and in fact it was from one such regional system of loyalties that there arose the power which was to topple Shaka.[48] Similar political practices are still used today at the lower levels of society.

In any event, small groups bound by kinship remain the point of departure and basic building-block of those vertical solidarities with which the rural masses are obliged to define themselves. These extended families, these units of production (the terminology in this subject is as abundant as it is imprecise and inadequate) have survived to the present day, at least in principle. 'The economy of affection'[49] is an attempt to grasp and explain the links between these communities and globalizing groups. This system, which has nothing to do with affection as such, connects disparate economic and social units which would otherwise exist independently.[50] Its function is to provide for essential needs which make survival possible and to ensure the reproduction of society (and ultimately, from Hyden's optimistic point of view, to ensure development).

If the economy of affection makes an effective contribution to the reinforcement and the revitalization of vertical solidarities, two points need to be qualified:

Firstly, on an economic level. It is clear that the market economy has penetrated and

---

[47] Bayart, *The State in Africa*.

[48] Hamilton & Wright, 'The beginning of Zulu identity', p. 45.

[49] Göran Hyden, *Beyond Ujamaa in Tanzania: Underdevelopment and an uncaptured peasantry* (University of California Press, Berkeley, CA, 1980).

[50] Göran Hyden, *No Shortcut to Progress: African development management in perspective* (Heinemann, London, 1983), p. 8.

dominates African rural societies which are not egalitarian groups, independent and isolated from the world. In his description of the 'uncaptured' peasants of Tanzania, (whose study led him to draw conclusions for the whole of Africa), Hyden portrays Tanzanian city-dwellers as sensitive to the needs and interests of networks centred on their village of origin, which precludes any possibility of class solidarity at all levels. In other words, villages are seen as having influence over cities, despite the fact that cities are the seats of power and wealth. There are numerous examples to illustrate this sort of observation, of which Yamoussoukro is among the most spectacular. But for every Yamoussoukro, how many villages and regions are there which are the ancestral villages of ministers, presidents and top businessmen, but which are steeped in poverty? The region where ex-President Ratsiraka – who remained in power for more than fifteen years – is supposed to have his origin is the most backward in Madagascar in terms of communications infrastructure, education and health facilities, to name but a few. Nevertheless, in 1992 the region continued to vote for him, against the trend of what was taking place nationally, which suggests an enduring allegiance.

In consequence of this point, the evolving character of African societies runs the risk of being ignored by the economy of affection. African societies may originally have been relatively little differentiated, but now, on the eve of the twenty-first century, they have come to form sophisticated ensembles which include formidable hierarchies. In every African country, there is a striking contrast between the fortified villas of the most privileged classes and the huts of peasants in the more isolated rural areas, not to mention in the over-populated towns and cities. Through African societies there run veins of solidarity other than vertical ones. And these vertical solidarities, based principally on elements such as seniority and masculinity, are themselves threatened by the growing numbers of young people, by the existence of mass primary education, the beginning of women's emancipation, the emergence of peasant entrepreneurs, migration and immigration, and so on. In South Africa for example, where more than 50 per cent of the population live in the cities,

> The predominant urban black identity has emerged out of a mixture of traditional elements of rural customs, the street wisdom of survival in the townships and places of work, and consumerist aspirations . . . The rural inhabitants and [the] migrants are considered illiterate, unsophisticated country bumpkins . . . The people with rural ties are often looked down upon as ignorant ancestor-worshippers who practise a social life of tribalism and witchcraft.[51]

However, in spite of these nuances, the economy of affection is a reasonable explanation for the vertical solidarities within the basic constituents of the largest groups. Tribes, clans, extended families, segments of lineages, the uncertainty of the generally used terminology is indicative of differences of scale. For a definition of the basic groups, we shall adopt the definition of ethnic groups proposed by Claude Ake, inspired by the studies of Emile Durkheim[52] in regard to mechanical solidarities. For Ake,[53] the ethnic group 'is a descent based group, a segmentary hierarchy with boundaries defined by standards of exclusion and inclusion which are objective and subjective. It is a common social structure of pre-capitalist and pre-industrial societies.' However, for these mechanical solidarities to be functional, the ethnic groups must be of limited size. They are, as we have described, small groups which are conscious of a common existence and interest, unlike large groups such as the Betsimisaraka Antavaratra or the Zulus which resemble

---

[51] Adam & Moodley, 'Political violence', p. 503.
[52] Emile Durkheim, *The Division of Labour in Society* (The Free Press, New York, 1964).
[53] Claude Ake, 'What is the problem of ethnicity in Africa?', *Transformation*, 22 (1993), p. 2.

the model of the imagined communities which are usually artifacts of political entrepreneurs. The Zanamanoro, which are a small group located five kilometres east of Antananarivo, are undoubtedly an extreme case, but nevertheless they are models of these little units described as 'primordial publics'. In 1967 there were 800 Zanamanoro; they doubtless owe their origin to a reaction by peasant societies to historical trials and tribulations. Despite the proximity of the capital city, the group has succeeded in conserving a very clearly defined territory as well as in maintaining a high degree of endogamy.[54]

In this perspective, the ethnic group is considered a means of cultural support rather than with respect to the more or less conflictual links it maintains with its surroundings. In such a setting, it is quite understandable that an individual may have a preference for his or her own community without seeing himself as opposed to other communities. In other words, the ethnic characteristics by which the rural population is obliged to define itself are assimilated and above all domesticated to be used in a strategy of survival. In fact, groups like this represent in Africa the equivalent in many ways of a system of social security, and they are able to make amends for the shortcomings of the state in its regulation of social life, such as, for example, in regard to the management of public security.

Confronted with the appetites of the powerful – like the pillaging barons of the Malagasy monarchy, or the district administrators of the colonial period, or the cynicism of the post-colonial elites which have moved from nationalism via socialism to the rhetoric of democracy – these mechanical solidarities are often the principal counterbalance capable of offering realistic protection to ordinary people who have been subjected to exploitation and repression for generations. (Religious assemblies and opposition parties can also constitute such a counterbalance.) They are part and parcel of civil society, especially in the rural world. To conclude, we shall examine the links between nationalism, ethnicity and democratization in Africa.

## A Perspective: Nationalism, Ethnicity and Democracy

In the aftermath of the elections held in more than half of the 53 African countries between 1990 and 1993, it seems likely that the rural masses have once again been shortchanged in the on-going process of democratization. The view expressed by Jerry Rawlings in 1981 still seems relevant:

> Political parties only profess an interest in the people when it is voting time only to abandon them between elections. Meanwhile, the rich patrons of these parties are desperate to reap the harvest of what they have invested in winning power and constantly use their position for profitable deals.[55]

Politicians' eagerness to jump on the gravy train, to use the expression favoured by South African journalists,[56] is a warning that we should not confuse the recent wave of political liberalization with democratization. The least we can say is that not all such transitions have resulted in the installation of real democracy.[57] The quest for

---

[54] Roland Waast, *Plaine de Tananarive, la parenté* (ORSTOM, Antananarivo, 1967).

[55] *The Believer* (Accra), 5, 10 June 1981, p. 1.

[56] *Weekly Mail & Guardian*, 11, 22, 25 May–1 June 1995.

[57] N.Chazan, 'Africa's democratic challenge: Strengthening civil society and the state', *State Policy Journal* (1992), pp. 279–307; Michael Bratton & Nicolas van de Walle, 'Neopatrimonial regimes and political transitions in Africa', *World Politics*, 46, 4 (1994), pp. 453–89.

democracy is old in Africa even if it has not always been labelled in this way. The real movement in support of democracy is fundamental and takes its place in a country's history only gradually, out of sight. Without entering into a debate on the theoretical possibility of installing democratic regimes in Africa, it is important to emphasize that there exists a popular democratic culture in Africa, formed by struggles against various expansionist states. The movements of 1989–91 constitute only one round in this contest.

### The return of the elites

To a great extent, the motive force in these movements has been urban populations who at present constitute only a minority of the African population, even if urbanization seems set to increase. Nevertheless, the recent movements against dictatorship amount to an irreversible condemnation of nationalism and its variants, which have proved their incapacity to constitute a fair and democratic society. The leaders who came to power during the 1960s and 1970s became prisoners of their nationalist discourse which represented foreign countries as the root of all evil, and were often unable to explain why they turned to foreign donors from the mid-1980s onwards. The model of liberal democracy, not to mention other models, has fallen into disrepute along with nationalism. All of these systems were imported into Africa and superimposed on paternalism and corruption. In spite of this, it has to be acknowledged that debates on the form of democracy which would best suit African conditions remain infrequent and inadequate.

The way in which African elites reproduce themselves, imprisoned as they are in the framework of politicized ethnicity, constitutes an obstacle to democratization. They remain incapable of genuinely sharing power with other groups, particularly poor and ill-educated rural groups and the rapidly growing masses of city-dwellers. Since state resources are diminishing and the bases for recruitment of elites are broadening, the competition for power is becoming more fierce. African elites are obliged to deploy new strategies for the conquest and management of power. This redefinition of elite strategies in Africa currently favours ethno-nationalism. Internal struggles within elites which use, or abuse, ethno-nationalism to achieve their ends, enclose an important part of society in an existing frame of vertical solidarities, but this time in the guise of democracy.

Even in the most hopeful cases, the movement in favour of democratization may be construed as something imposed by a group on others with the aim of reorganizing the protocols governing the distribution of power to its advantage. There is a new generation of elites and they must adjust to a new environment which is now heavily influenced by external aid-donors. The way in which policies of decentralization and privatization are interpreted by elites is an illustration of how they are trying to adapt to the new environment. In Madagascar, the World Bank and the International Monetary Fund's proposal to create development zones around urban centres in an integrated region, has resulted, under the influence of political entrepreneurs such as members of parliament and government ministers, in a new administrative arrangement. This will enable members of parliament to ensure that they are re-elected in the next elections by making use of new patronage networks. Similarly in South Africa, decentralization has been interpreted by a section of the political class as the transfer of prerogatives from the central state to administrative units inherited from the apartheid period, transformed into states in a federalist structure. In both cases, ethno-nationalism turns decentralization to its advantage.

The recourse to ethno-nationalism or politicized ethnicity is a risk to the process of democratization since vertically structured groups can use it in order to acquire political office, which in contemporary Africa is the path to wealth and power. This does not always benefit attempts at macro-economic reform. Such a framework precludes the participation of the masses, imprisoned as they are in vertical solidarities, often in an attempt to defend their interests rather than as active accomplices. It can even encourage the perpetuation of such vertical solidarities through networks of patronage; this is the peace-time equivalent of the warlord system. This is taking place at a time when the internationalization of financial markets, the development of mass communications and unprecedented population shifts are all contributing to the decline of the state which is encouraged by the World Bank and the IMF, leaving the weakest more vulnerable than before. Moreover, African states have entered into a series of crises which mean that they are no longer capable of regulating social life. The state's principal function, since the pre-colonial period, has been that of the extraction and redistribution of wealth. Faced with the gradual diminution of the state, the privileged classes, in search of resources, have turned to ethno-nationalism.

Privatization has been adopted as a policy by elites in much the same way as socialism was two decades earlier. At best, this will lead to an uncontrolled liberalization which ignores the lessons learned from nineteenth-century Europe and more recently from some Asian countries. Since African political elites are often unable to transform themselves into a developmental bourgeoisie, privatization risks becoming a major commercial opportunity for people who were previously advocates of nationalization or for their descendants, with an eye to quick profit. The real beneficiary of privatization should ideally be civil society, consisting both of people from the lower rungs of society and a part of those in the upper strata. It should aim at a revitalization of citizenship within the context of a participatory democracy. The slimming down of the state with a view to improving its economic performance, as recommended by donors and international financial institutions, makes no sense without some stimulus to civil society, that associational life which does not essentially aspire to power, but through which various solidarities are expressed, and which counterbalances the state's aspiration to hegemony.

### The difficult metamorphosis from subject to citizen

In Africa, country-dwellers are obliged to define themselves within ethnic frameworks which have thus become one of the forms of associational life in rural areas. Could these small groups be considered locations in which citizenship could be built or rebuilt? It would undoubtedly be unreasonable to assert that rural societies have succeeded in subverting the system of classification in which expansionist states have installed African peasant farmers throughout history. But it would seem that the durability of ethnic identities is an undeniable sign of cultural pluralism, which is in itself positive. Only when ethnicity is considered as a form of political expression do things become more complicated. In that case, the individual is deemed to exist only within a communal identity even when several competing identities are on offer. In this respect it could be said that:

> The civic public in much of Africa is more potential than reality. What exists is a plurality of publics which may be called primordial publics. These primordial publics are important elements of social pluralism in Africa.[58]

---

[58] Ake, 'What is the problem of ethnicity?', p. 7.

The unanimous or consensual democracy that is said to be active in these 'primordial publics'[59] has been proposed as an African version of democracy, 'democracy seen from the village',[60] which has the potential to mobilize resources to combat poverty.

It is undeniable that democratization in rural Africa must take account of cultural plurality, if we are to consider ethnic groups on the small scale as cultural entities. These small groups are integral parts of civil society. Any project of development which involves the mobilization of rural communities must take into account the cultures in which individuals really live rather than those in which they ought to be living. For groups like this continue to exist and survive despite attempts to dismantle or eradicate them. However, 'the advance of civil society which does not necessarily contain the democratic ideal does not in itself ensure the democratization of the political system'.[61] To idealize all the practices of these small communities would be to lend support to such anachronisms as male chauvinism or gerontocracy, which are incompatible with democratic values. This is illustrated by the development in most African countries of what can be referred to as informal or traditional justice in response to the decay of the state. In southeastern Madagascar, for example, peasants behead suspected thieves in reaction to the inefficiency and corruption of the police and the judiciary, while in certain South African townships the 'necklace', considered as a method of dispensing informal justice, disregards all norms of equity. The development of a democratic culture whose essence is the existence of the rule of the law, is incompatible with such practices.

By the same token, in the field of economics, the emergence of new forces could be hindered by the structures of small communities. Thus in southern Madagascar, following a cotton boom between 1982 and 1986, entrepreneurs who benefited from this prosperity felt themselves obliged to fritter away the fruits of their new fortunes in sumptuary celebrations.[62] The reason for this is that land used for cotton cultivation by these entrepreneurs was considered to belong to local lineages, and the only good locally considered as a capital asset is cattle.

Moreover, whole segments of these communities, such as women and young people, are often excluded from decision-making mechanisms, which means that unanimity becomes an instrument for the oppression of minorities (and other groups, since those under the age of 20 are the majority of the African population) in such communities.

As a rule, the deepening of Africa's economic crisis tends to encourage a sort of cultural fundamentalism, comparable to religious fundamentalism, as an escape for rural populations, constituting an obstacle to genuine democratization.

### *Communitarian democracy or Western democracy?*

The present debates on the nature of democracy in Africa seem to fall into two camps. On the one hand, there are those who propose a specific sort of democracy for Africa, a communitarian democracy which would focus on the community and in which ethnic groups are politically and deliberately rewarded. An extreme expression of this is

---

59 Pierre Ekeh, 'The constitution of civil society in African history and politics', in B. Caron, A. Gboyega and E. Osaghae (eds), *Democratic Transition in Africa* (Institute of African Studies, University of Ibadan/Credu, Ibadan, 1992).
60 Maxwell Owusu, 'Democracy and Africa, a view from the village', *The Journal of Modern African Studies*, 30, 3 (1992), pp. 369–96.
61 J.-F. Bayart, 'Civil society in Africa', in Patrick Chabal (ed.), *Political Domination in Africa: Reflections on the limits of power* (Cambridge University Press, Cambridge, 1986), p. 118.
62 M. Fielloux & J. Lombard (eds), *Elevage et société. Etudes des transformations socio-économiques dans le sud-ouest malgache: l'exemple du couloir d'Antseva* (SME, Antananarivo, 1990).

federalism. On the other hand, there are those who believe it is possible to confine ethnic divisions to the cultural domain, in other words to keep them out of politics in order to promote a democracy in which the individual has priority over the group.

Whatever point of view is adopted, the question of ethnicity is unavoidable in the quest for democracy. Although it is clear that societies benefit from having a multi-ethnic character, the reality is that it is a factor which encourages political instability; or at the very least which considerably reduces a government's room for manoeuvre, especially when ethnic groups receive political rewards.

The multi-ethnicity of most African societies always raises the question of what form the state should assume. In the early 1990s, as at the time of independence, there were debates between supporters of a unitary state and advocates of federalism. In fact, more than the form of the state, the problem posed by multi-ethnicity is how to reconcile the rights of minorities and majority rule, but in a changing context.

The development of a trans-ethnic, indeed trans-national, urban Africa shows that a new logic is emerging. In less than one generation, half of the African population will live in cities which are essentially multi-ethnic. In addition, the population is extremely young. Developments like this suggest that in the long term there will be a reduction in the political expression of ethnicity, in favour of other types of solidarity. In these circles, notions of individuality transcend ethnicity and tend to favour the notion of representative democracy. Foreign observers concede that the electoral processes in the cities, even before 1989–91, are comparable to those in other countries which are considered democratic. Trade unions and national political parties in Africa recruit the majority of their members and militants in these circles. As elsewhere in the world, individual democracy is not easily compatible with the basic economic rights of individuals. Antananarivo, like Johannesburg or Paris, has its share of homeless people, many of whom are children who would in other times be looked after by a family or a clan. In the long term, Africa is generally evolving in this direction.

Any attempt to accelerate this tendency by prohibiting some aspect of ethnicity would immediately lead to the reinforcement of the latter. The phenomenon of group cultural identity, its tendency to acquire a territorial definition and its unavoidable expression in political life are facts of life. But here too the distinction must be maintained between the restricted groups whose reality is tangible, and those large entities where the political entrepreneurs do their work. In the first case, small units, like other elements of civil society, do not compete for political power and often accept the legitimacy of the state inasmuch as legal, judicial and other group rights are respected. The political incentives given to such units by the decentralization of decision-making mechanisms and of revenue allocation are compatible with the spirit of democracy, provided that individual rights are not infringed. The accompanying risk is that of the development of different layers of democracy in the same society. This might be referred to as parochial democracy.

On the other hand, large groups which have been manipulated by political and cultural entrepreneurs, such as Zulus, Afrikaners or Betsimisaraka, for example, pose a real problem, in the short term at least, in the context of the scarcity of resources and the economic crisis of Africa in the 1990s. This context exacerbates conflicts between such entrepreneurs. The problem cannot be resolved simply by appealing to the notion of false consciousness, since these stereotypes are deeply rooted. In the case of Afrikaners, for example, apart from the habitual manipulation of history, one has to take into account their tendency to a racially-based endogamy to protect the colour of their skin, while the 'coloured' population, who speak Afrikaans (language being another symbol of ethnic recognition), are not recognized as belonging to the group. Are we to condemn, on the grounds of anti-racism, what many Afrikaners see as the defence of a cultural minority, especially when a policy of 'affirmative action' is being introduced?

This problem relates more to the construction of a democratic culture than the form to be taken by the state, which, for the time being, is essentially a problem of elites. Democracy requires that the frontiers of an ethnic group should be as porous as possible, enabling free entry and exit.[63] In the opposite case, where there exists a narrow consonance between political and cultural entrepreneurs and the members of an ethnic group, ethno-fascism, a radicalized form of ethno-nationalism, can arise. The more the definition of membership of an ethnic group is centralized, the less this ethnic group is democratic within itself.

Ethnicity pushes institutions and democracy to their limits. It tends to substitute, in place of universal values of human rights and equality among citizens, claims in favour of particular groups. It reduces equal and fair access to resources to rivalries between groups rather than making of it a question of social justice.[64]

The problem facing Africa is not so much having to choose between a collective conception of democracy and a representative conception based on individual choice, but rather how to harness democracy to economic development. In any event, one of the functions of democracy is to instal a framework within which sociability may be negotiated without recourse to violence. Besides other aims, such as greater social justice, it is desirable that such sociability should tend to:

- increase the permeability of ethnic groups.
- confine the cultural identity of a group to the private domain, which means that ethnic identity must not be politically rewarded. However, ethnic identity must be protected in order to guarantee cultural diversity, for ethnic groups are first and foremost vectors of culture. Ethnic groups, just like any other social group, such as homosexuals, should not benefit from a special dispensation but neither should they suffer from discrimination.
- reinforce horizontal solidarities by enriching the components of civil society since ethnic identity is, after all, one of many identities available to an individual. The importance ascribed to ethnicity seems disproportionate to its reality. In South Africa, where 80 per cent of black citizens are members of a Christian church, churches are the second most respected institution after trade unions.[65]

---

[63] Maré, *Brothers Born of Warrior Blood*, p. 4.

[64] Morris Szeftel, 'Ethnicity and democratization in South Africa', *Review of African Political Economy*, 60 (1994), p. 199.

[65] Juan Bosch, 'Christianisme et apartheid', *Travaux et Documents*, CEAN, Bordeaux, 32, (1991), p. 1.

THREE

# *Youth & Violence*

### ALI EL-KENZ

## Common Scenes of Violence

*Dakar, February 1994*

Ibo lives in the little village of Sally, about fifty kilometres from Dakar. He is eighteen years old. His father is a farmer, but for several years the effects of the drought and the collapse in the prices of agricultural produce have meant that he no longer needs Ibo and his brothers to help him with his work. So they have turned to different kinds of employment. His two elder brothers work as cleaners in a tourist hotel. Ibo and his two sisters set out for Dakar every morning, travelling home on the last bus which arrives some time after seven o'clock in the evening. His other stepbrothers and stepsisters have been more fortunate and their more affluent maternal relatives are looking after them.

His youngest sister who is fourteen years old sells cola nuts next to the main mosque. The elder sister wanders around the bus station in the Avenue Lamine Guèye with a few seasonal fruits. Ibo knows that she occasionally works as a prostitute, but what else can she do? As for Ibo himself, every morning he tries to sell clothes given to him by a Lebanese trader to the guests of the hotels in the Plateau district, or to persuade them to visit the shop. Otherwise he cleans and guards cars. He occasionally begs and sometimes, though more rarely because it is more difficult, he even commits petty crimes.

Everything in Dakar is difficult. You have to have a patron, a sponsor, to belong to a network. In order to do any business with the many tourists who visit the country it is essential to belong to a gang. Ibo does in fact belong to a gang, but it is still very new and therefore weak. The other gangs have been around far longer, they have connections with the police and with employees. So Ibo does not even consider approaching the large hotels along the coast, or setting up on the Avenue Pompidou which is the haunt of the more established gangs.

Ibo, like most Senegalese of his age, is generally not given to violence. When he has occasionally had to fight, it has always been in self-defence, with his gang against other rival gangs or against a single opponent. He dreams of one day emigrating to France as many of the young people of the village have done. But he would have to save for years simply for the price of the ticket and the middleman's commission. So they wait together with their families, they persevere, trying not to sink into total destitution, and just get by from day to day. They have adopted what sociologists call a survival strategy. People stick together, they pay more attention to the solidarity of the extended family, the group; often the *marabout*, a holy man of the *mouride* brotherhood, is consulted for his advice. People also pray more frequently, at the mosque, as tradition demands, and Ibo, who has never been particularly devout, never fails to say his *Dhouhr* prayer at one o'clock, even if it means interrupting his work. He occasionally misses an opportunity to earn some money, but he does not mind. In fact, during these services, it is as if he is fortified by the strength of the community which he has discovered to be his own and he feels less isolated as an individual and less miserable.

On Wednesday 16 February 1994, the city bustles with activity as it does every morning. Ibo gets off the bus and heads for the Lebanese shop to pick up any available merchandise. At the crossroads of the Avenue Lamine Guèye and the Avenue Pompidou he spots two cars of the national guard stationed at a right angle in order to survey the two avenues. At the shop the owner tells him there is nothing for him today. Ibo feels rather tense.

Walking back, he meets friends from the village who tell him that a protest demonstration by the unions and opposition parties is planned for that afternoon against the devaluation of the CFA franc, introduced several days earlier.[1] Ibo and his friends are not directly affected by the demonstration. They are neither formal-sector workers nor political militants, but anonymous workers in the informal sector, so, like the thousands of young people who constantly roam the city in search of a source of income, they feel alienated from a society that they are so familiar with but of which they are hardly a part. Besides, being semi-illiterate with very little or no political awareness, they have only a very confused image of modern economic mechanisms and the currency fluctuations which disrupt them.[2]

Walking through the Sondaga market they notice small groups of traders gathered around the shops discussing the devaluation angrily. 'They want to ruin us!'; 'Aren't we poor enough already?'; 'The French are bastards, they're just leaving us!'; 'It is all we deserve after the Gulf War!'. Even at the mosque the discussions are animated, the discontent general. Leaving the mosque after prayers, Ibo follows the crowd heading for Independence Square, where the demonstration is due to set off. Like the others he melts into the angry crowd body and soul and begins to chant the same slogans. He

---

[1] The devaluation of the CFA franc by 50% affected all the countries of the franc zone in a large part of West and Central Africa. Linked to the programmes of structural adjustment applied to the countries of this zone, the devaluation was principally intended to encourage exports and thus to alleviate the growing balance-of-payments deficits of these countries. The measure gave rise to a series of popular demonstrations of which the most significant was the one held in Dakar and its surroundings on 16 February 1994.

[2] It has to be said that they are not the only ones. We are of the opinion that this is partly due to the fact that the major economic decisions are increasingly made by technocrats who do not have to bear the consequences of their actions, except perhaps morally. cf. Hans Jonas, *Le principe responsabilité* (Cerf, Paris, 1992).

experiences an emotion which is profoundly liberating. He can finally give voice to his distress, loudly and forcefully. The crowd is there to justify his shouts.

At the approach to the presidential palace, there are police vehicles blocking the road. The crowd hesitates for a moment and then the clash begins. Again like the others, Ibo finds himself with stones in his hands that he hurls with all his might at the cars parked alongside the pavements – the cars he has so often cleaned and guarded. The first tear gas grenade goes off, creating panic within the seething mass. Then the dry crackle of gunshot disperses the demonstrators. Here and there, cries of *Allah Akbar* can be heard, giving this demonstration – initially politically and socially motivated – a strange and compelling religious overtone.

Ibo is moved. His eyes are burning from the tear gas, but he has never felt so dignified, or so much a man.

After looking for him for three days, Ibo's parents find him at the hospital where he has had one of his legs amputated. Due to a lack of resources, the bullet which hit him was not removed in time and gangrene had set in.

Ibo: a permanent victim of the violence in which he was an actor for one day.

## Algiers, October 1988

The date is Monday, 3 October. The city is filled with rumours of a coup d'état, of revolution, of something about to happen, something important but vague and imprecise. In the popular dialect of Algiers, this is known as *el houl*, like a storm at sea. The workers of the industrial centres of Rouiba in the east of the city have been on strike for several days. They decide to leave their factories in order to demonstrate their discontent. The entire region is surrounded by police and special security forces. Many union officials have been abducted by plain-clothes policemen during the night and carried off to unknown destinations.

The following day the rumours are even stronger. The queues in front of the super-markets grow longer as in times of shortage. Around the primary and secondary schools young people gather together in groups to talk, they roam the districts and gather in the large city squares at the end of the afternoon. In twenty-four hours their attitude has changed considerably. Their voices are now louder and more aggressive. They walk in the middle of the road, their gestures stronger and more animated. The adults, on the other hand, become more discreet, more reserved, almost passive. In the evening there is already talk of several of the large ring-roads being blocked by barricades, tyres being burnt, trees being uprooted. The police are nowhere to be seen.

Boualem is sixteen years old. He lives in Belcourt, a working-class district of the capital, not far from the house in which Albert Camus lived. He does not know this, of course, and probably never will: he left school after the fourth year of primary school and has since forgotten almost everything, including how to read and write. He lives with his five brothers and two sisters in two rooms. He has to leave early in the morning and does not return before the late evening to eat (usually a plate of couscous or pasta or beans) and to sleep, on the floor of the same room as his five brothers. His parents and his two sisters sleep in the other room. His father is a stevedore and spends his days at the docks. Two of his older brothers work at the market as odd-job men. The other two go to school, but nobody pays any particular attention to them. His sisters who are 14 and 17 stay at home and help their mother who is often ill. No one knows exactly what is the matter with her. In any case, in this part of the world, once a girl has passed puberty, she has no business being outside the home except to go to school or college if she is lucky enough to be able to continue her studies, or to work, which is even more unusual.

So Boualem is on the streets from morning till night. And there are many like him. They are known as *hittistes*[3] and they use the name to refer to themselves derisively. With his friends, his gang, consisting of no more than about ten members, he occupies a corner of the pavement of the main road right next to a café.[4] They remain there most of the time, sometimes going to a football match when the Belcourt team is playing, or going to see a film in the local cinema. Like his friends, Boualem does not work, except occasionally when a *trabendiste*[5] of the district gives him jeans or a watch or a radio to sell. The commission he gets – the equivalent of one or two dollars – enables him to get by for a few days. It is enough to pay for a cup of coffee, a packet of cigarettes, a couple of *zatla*.[6]

Boualem is not a thief, except occasionally when a stranger parks his car in the district. Then the radio or the headlights will be stolen. More rarely, when he is really broke, he will venture on to a bus with a few friends in order to steal a woman's jewels, or some middle-class person's wallet. Mostly, however, he can be seen there on the pavement, watching the world go by, especially the girls and the smart cars.

His enemy and the enemy of the whole gang and of all the gangs in the district, and even of all the gangs in the other districts, is the police. The district police force knows them all. It keeps them under surveillance, and the policemen mock them. Sometimes they are taken in to the station for a dressing-down, a few slaps, occasionally a night in a cell. But they remain enemies.

On the morning of 5 October groups of primary and secondary school pupils were told[7] to leave their classes and ransack everything public or belonging to the state. They wrecked supermarkets and ministries, police stations and officials' cars alike. Boualem and his friends joined the movement with enthusiasm, breaking into cars and shops in their turn and especially focusing all their hatred, together with the other gangs of the district, on the police station, which they ransacked. The secondary school pupils who

---

[3] From the Arabic *hit*, which means wall. Since they are often to be seen standing with their backs to the walls of houses, they are literally called: 'those who lean against the walls'.

[4] Each group formed in this way occupies its own small territory and it is difficult for a stranger to gain entrance to such a group. They move around within the district – in Arabic *el houma* – without taking too many risks in the other districts. Certain Algerian sociologists have termed this phenomenon *houmism*. See especially S. Musette, 'Enquête sur les chômeurs dans la région algéroise', (Master's thesis, University of Algiers, 1992).

[5] From the Spanish *trabendo*, which here means 'to trade on the black market'. This phenomenon which was practically unknown in Algeria in the past, or limited to the frontier zones, developed rapidly during the 1980s. With its specializations (women's clothing, jeans, household electrical appliances, car parts), its areas in the large cities, its exponents and opponents, both within the state and within the universities, it has since become an important activity within the economic and social life of the country. See on this subject A. Henni, *Le cheikh et le patron* (Entreprise nationale d'art graphique, Algiers, 1992).

[6] Cannabis cigarettes. Young people generally smoke together in the evenings, listening to a cassette of *chaabi* or *raï* music.

[7] Until now, the analysts of the October 1988 events have not succeeded in solving the mystery of how it all started. Even if all agree on the theory of manipulation by those groups in power who wanted to eliminate their opponents by inciting street riots, the details of the events are still not known with any precision. Whatever the case, the October riots, or, in any event, at least their incitement, were largely manipulated by groups in power. These riots are a classic case of what has been termed 'manipulated violence', which seems to be becoming increasingly widespread throughout the world. Riots in Karachi, Pakistan in December 1994, to which hundreds fell victim, fall into this category. See especially Bertrand Badie, 'Ruptures et innovations dans l'approche sociologique des relations internationales', in 'Etat moderne, nationalismes et islamismes', *Revue du monde musulman et méditérranéen*, 68-9 (1994), pp. 65–74.

had initially led the movement were quickly overtaken by events, and soon the entire unemployed youth of Algiers, together with the unemployed youth of the poorest and toughest suburbs, unleashed their bottled-up violence on the city and its hated symbols.

After the Bab el Oued shootings on Friday the 7th, in which more than fifty people were killed, a state of emergency was declared after prayers. The army entered the city.

Two days later, Boualem fell into the hands of the Republican Guard. Several months later, when he left the rehabilitation camp where he had joined thousands of other young people of his own age, he was unrecognisable, above all in his character. He had become taciturn, sad and silent. It was obvious that he had been tortured, but he said nothing about it and did not wish to put his case before the commission for human rights which was set up for this purpose. Tragically, within the space of a few days he had been robbed of his youth.

Afterwards, like his friends, Boualem left his habitual haunt next to the café. But he did not move far – just a hundred metres away from the road. He began diligently visiting the local mosque. He changed his habits, including the way he dressed.

In March 1992 he disappeared. Some say he was killed by the police, others believe he is now the head of a group of terrorists active in Blida, about fifty kilometres from the capital.

The house where Albert Camus lived is still there, but the small groups of *hittistes* have disappeared from the road outside. Some have gone underground, others are dead, and yet others have joined the police.

It is not good these days to be young in Belcourt.

## Numbers

There are thousands, millions, like Ibo and Boualem. More in the South than in the North, more on the fringes of social systems than at their centre, more and more numerous in the cities, and more and more uncontrollable, aggressive, violent. These are the main characteristics of youth in many countries, lauded by poets in the recent past but today haunting the minds of local, national and international decision-makers like a nightmare. They are destabilizing societies, frightening the middle classes and reinforcing, if not justifying, dictatorships.

What should have been an indubitable sign of scientific, economic and social progress – the drop in the mortality rate – now appears to some to be a catastrophe, and for many at the very least one of the greatest problems of the present era. What has happened in just a few decades? Thomas Malthus[8] and his alarming theories date from an era not comparable to ours in its low productivity and rudimentary technology, and they are not directly applicable.

But it is clear that the facts and the events to which this state of affairs has led have developed far more rapidly than anyone expected. Nowadays, events are proceeding too fast for us to grasp. So reason gives way to emotion and analysis is clouded by fear, a fear amplified by the millenarianism of the end of this century and having the texture of myth.[9]

First, some facts:

Within a few decades, the structure of the world population has undergone a profound

[8] Thomas Robert Malthus, British demographer and economist, 1766–1834.

[9] cf. Dominique Lecourt, *Contre la peur: de la science à l'éthique, une aventure infinie* (Hachette, Paris, 1990).

transformation. Its expansion has been spread unequally over the continents, while the expansion of the world economy has been spread unequally in exactly the opposite direction. This has led to alarming discrepancies between people and resources.

Let us first consider demography. According to the 1993 world report of the United Nations Development Programme (UNDP), between 1960 and 1991 world population increased from 3 billion to 5.4 billion. However, while the population of the industrialized countries expanded by only 280 million at a rate of growth of 0.8 per cent, the population in the developing countries increased from some two billion to more than four billion, at a rate of growth of 2.3 per cent.[10] Within this category as a whole, sub-Saharan Africa is in the lead, with a rate of growth of 2.9 per cent, the highest in the world, which means that its population has increased from 210 million to 520 million. By the early twenty-first century the population of the African continent, including North Africa, will be approaching one and a half billion, twice its present size and close to three times the population of Europe. For the same period the United Nations predicts a world population of close to 8 billion, dominated by three large blocs: Africa, China and India. Experts, and notably those of the United Nations, are of the opinion that this extraordinary demographic thrust, which from the 1950s onwards shifted from the developed countries to the Third World, is beginning to decline, and that it will probably come to an end a century from now. This will signal the end of the demographic transition which began in Europe at the beginning of the nineteenth century. But what is to be done between now and then?

In the 1960s, the fear of impending demographic growth led population experts to come up with a thousand and one formulas for managing the transition and alleviating its effects. This was the era of superficial and narrowly technicist neo-Malthusianism, which sometimes produced an opposite reaction to the one sought as a result of a recognized feed-back effect. This was notably the case in the Islamic countries, where the new technologies were perceived as a fresh tactic by the West aimed at perpetuating its dominance. The world population conference held in Cairo in 1994 clearly revealed the fierce reactions to which a crude technocratic approach to complex and delicate phenomena can give rise. The more clear-sighted analysts and experts have long since passed this preliminary stage. Today it is well known that

> the high levels of fertility which currently exist in Africa, and the sustaining of such high levels of fertility, are related to the pattern of marriage (extremely low incidence of celibacy, early marriages and rapid remarriage following divorce), to the high rate of infant mortality, to social structures which favour the arrival of a child and its early participation in economic activity, and to the fact that the child represents a guarantee for its parents in old age.[11]

Since the key work of Vasant Gowariker on the control of the birth rate in India,[12] it is difficult to isolate demography from the other dimensions of social existence, notably the problems of education and development.

But here we find the core of the problem, which is that this powerful demographic growth has been accompanied in many of the developing countries, and particularly in Africa, by an unprecedented economic crisis. Within a few decades, all the hopes awoken

[10] United Nations Development Programme (UNDP), *Human Development Report* (Oxford University Press, New York & Oxford, 1993), pp. 180–1, table no. 23.

[11] François Gendreau, 'La démographie du développement', in C. Choquet (ed.), *Etat des savoirs sur le développement* (Karthala, Paris, 1993), p. 122.

[12] Vasant Gowariker (ed.), *The Inevitable Billion Plus: Deepening the debate on science, population and development* (Vichar Dhara Publications, Poona, India, 1993). As one of the authors notes: 'a decrease in the rate of demographic expansion is not brought about by sterilization nor methods of contraception, but by economic and social transition.'

by decolonization have gone up in smoke. Africa has not taken off economically and the signs are that the crisis which has struck the region will be both long-term and profound. 'Black Africa's main characteristic at the dawn of the third millennium is the total and over-whelming bankruptcy of its formal economy,' notes J.P.M. Tedga in a sombre tone.[13]

The economic and social results, especially during the last decade, have definitely been worse than the most pessimistic predictions. The annual rate of growth of the gross national product per head of population in Africa fell from 1.5 per cent in the period from 1965 to 1980 to −1.1 per cent for the decade of the 1980s.[14] As Ademola T. Salau reports,

> all the available facts tend to confirm that Africa, more than any other continent, is experiencing increasing poverty and hunger . . . close to 200 million individuals in sub-Saharan Africa are reported to have received less than 90 per cent of the minimum of 2,200 calories a day and are therefore in a condition of chronic malnutrition. In 1988, the average per capita income was $250, which represents only 95 per cent of the real income in 1960, and 29 of the 36 poorest countries in the world are African countries.[15]

According to the Food and Agriculture Organization (FAO) at least a quarter of the population of sub-Saharan Africa is threatened by famine, yet systems of extensive or shifting agricultural production, added to drought, continue their work of deforestation, soil erosion and desertification. So people leave the rural areas for the city (the urban population is currently growing at a rate of 5.3 per cent) or turn to export agriculture, including the export of drugs. This simply further increases the country's food deficit and adds to the social inequalities and political instability.

This serious picture is aggravated by a national debt which grows heavier as the years go by and which can no longer be compensated for by international aid. The donor coun-tries are now reluctant to disburse funds which may be mismanaged or even diverted from their initial objectives. At US$150 billion, Africa's external debt currently represents the equivalent of its total gross national product, and debt service represents 20 per cent of its export receipts as against 4.5 per cent in the 1960s. We are now witnessing the sad paradox of an abortive economic development in an inversion of financial transfers, with a negative balance for the developing world of −$9.2 billion in 1989 in favour of the industrialized countries, as against +$33 billion in 1982.[16]

The main consequence of such a dramatic situation is clearly unemployment and under-employment. In this respect, economic problems affect all countries, including the developed countries where there is increasing talk of growth without employment which requires a rethinking of traditional economic models. But for the developing countries, and especially for Africa, the relative decrease in the supply of jobs comes at a moment when demand is exacerbated by an exceptionally powerful demographic thrust. Every-where, rates of unemployment are rising while solutions to the situation have yet to be found. As far as the experts of the UNDP are concerned, the outlook is bleak. In the developing countries, they observe that,

---

[13] Quoted by R. Buijtenhuijs & E. Rijnierse, *Democratization in Sub-Saharan Africa, 1989–92* (Research Reports No. 51, Afrika-studiecentrum, Leiden, 1993), p. 46.

[14] UNDP, *Human Development Report 1993*, pp. 188–9.

[15] Ademola T. Salau, *Changements écologiques à l'échelle du globe: Programme de recherche pour l'Afrique* (Codesria, Dakar, 1992). There is an abundant literature on this subject, and even if points of view diverge as to the causes and the responsibility for the situation, all observers and experts are in agreement on the diagnosis: the people of Africa are in danger.

[16] Dieudonné Ouedraogo, 'Vers un afflux des réfugiés économiques', in 'Une terre en renaissance' (*Savoirs*, published by *Le monde diplomatique*, Paris, 1993), p. 38.

the total labour force increased by more than 400 million during 1960–1990 . . . [It] will continue to increase by 2.3 per cent a year in the 1990s, requiring an additional 260 million jobs . . . This would imply increasing total employment in developing countries by more than 4 per cent a year in the 1980s[17]

The same report states that such a perspective is illusory. It indicates, moreover, that for Africa a hypothetical increase in employment of 2.4 per cent per year, and thus lower than the rate at which the working population is increasing, at 3.3 per cent per year, anticipates a rate of growth of gross domestic product of 5 per cent. This objective is utterly unrealistic, given the seriousness of the trends outlined above. Therefore, a significant increase in both unemployment and underemployment is to be expected, with the corresponding movements of populations (rural migration towards the cities, emigration to the countries of the northern hemisphere), which could become uncontrollable if they are not already so. One of the greatest fears of the northern hemisphere countries at the end of this century is that they will be submerged by immigrants from the South, and notably from Africa.

The informal sector can certainly continue to absorb considerable surplus labour, but for how long? Moreover, is it not the case that the expansion of this sector is a threat to the stability of the entire social system, because it risks leading to the reconstruction of society on an as yet unforeseeable ethnic, religious and racial basis?[18]

It must be emphasized that the impact of future pressures will be felt primarily by young people. Besides the growth of the population in terms of numbers, we are also witnessing a significant qualitative change in the age structure. In the developed countries the proportion of young people under the age of 15 has decreased, while the same category of the population has noticeably increased in the rest of the world, at rates of 2.02 per cent in southern Asia, 2.92 per cent in the Arab countries, and, above all, 3.25 per cent in sub-Saharan Africa. According to UNESCO,[19] almost seven out of every eight children under 15 years of age currently live in developing countries. In sub-Saharan Africa almost half the population is under 15 years of age, as opposed to just one-fifth of the population in North America, Europe and Japan.

It is for this reason that the economic dependence of young people on the working population as a whole is greater in this region, and perhaps increasingly so, since the ratio has grown from 87 per cent dependency in 1970 to 93 per cent dependency in 1990, measured in terms of the proportion of the population under 15 to the working population aged 16–64. Everywhere else the percentage is falling. It is currently around 53 per cent for the world as a whole and around 32 per cent for the developed countries.[20] This intolerable pressure imposed by young people on Africa's working population often means that they are set to work at a relatively early age. The UNDP estimates that in Africa almost 20 per cent of children are working, more often than not in very poor conditions; it is essential that children help the family to get by.

Children are deprived of their childhood and education, because the dependence of school children on the working population has also become intolerable. The dependency

---

[17] UNDP, *Human Development Report 1993*, p. 37.

[18] The UNDP reports that the informal sector in sub-Saharan Africa developed at an annual rate of 6.7% between 1980 and 1989, thus at a far more rapid rate than that of the modern sector. Between 1980 and 1985 the modern sector created just 500,000 jobs on the urban labour market, while the informal sector created some 6 million jobs. *Human Development Report 1993*, p. 41.

[19] UNESCO, *Rapport mondial sur l'éducation 1991* (Paris, 1991), p. 23.

[20] ibid., p. 40. These figures relate to the ratio of people under the age of 15 to the active population between 16 and 64 years old.

rate is estimated to have been around 47 per cent for Africa in 1970, and it currently runs at 49 per cent, which is significantly higher than that of the rest of the world as a whole (36 per cent and 30 per cent respectively) and than that of the developed countries (26 per cent and 20 per cent respectively). This means that in relation to the hours worked by the working population, the education of school children is far more costly in those countries which are the least developed. In fact there are only two people employed in Africa for each child of school age as opposed to five in the developed countries and therefore – the paradox of poverty! – 'it is in those regions of the world least able to train and pay teachers that the need for teachers in relation to the working population is the most acute'.[21] US$89 were spent annually on each pupil in African countries in 1988, as opposed to $2,888 in the developed countries and $129 in the developing countries as a whole. But related to the GNP of each country, the sum spent is far higher in Africa than anywhere else. 'Sub-Saharan Africa is therefore extremely disadvantaged in its efforts to develop education, since for each additional pupil it is required to spend a higher percentage of GNP than other regions.'[22] So, as in the previous case relating to the dependence of young people, the dependence of school children leads families and governments to redefine their educational objectives. It is anticipated that in the coming decade there will be a significant decrease in all the indices related to education, including the rate of adult literacy which was beginning to gain ground in the 1980s. Throughout Africa the salaries of teachers have fallen considerably during the past decade while working conditions (the number of pupils per class, availability of teaching materials, etc.) have deteriorated.[23] According to UNESCO forecasts for the year 2000, record rates of poor schooling will be held by five African countries, with an average of −50 per cent, the countries in question being Guinea, Liberia, Mali, Niger and Somalia.[24]

In any event, it will be extremely difficult for all countries to sustain the efforts of previous decades to provide education, and to attempt to educate vastly increased populations of young people with fewer financial resources. It would require several hundreds of thousands of additional teachers to educate the hundreds of millions of children, while the priority, according to the designers of structural adjustment programmes, is budget cuts.

This brief outline of the situation in Africa, combined with the economic, social and cultural prospects, clearly indicates that the youth of the continent are entering the next century severely handicapped by the failures of their parents and the unconcern and lack of understanding of the world at large, and especially of the developed world. How should they respond to this situation for which they are not responsible, and of which, it seems, they have no wish to become the willing victims?

[21] ibid., p. 40. [Unofficial translation – ed.]

[22] ibid., p. 41. [Unofficial translation – ed.]

[23] 'There have been no schools or colleges built in Côte d'Ivoire since 1975,' notes Aka Kouassi, 'but given the current rate of growth of the population, registrations for primary school cannot be halted. The result is alarming: more than 70% of children of six years of age are not in school . . . the situation is worse still in the only university, despite the proliferation of inadequate university faculties . . . Most of the facilities for training educators are closed, while the need for training continues to increase at an accelerated rate'. L'évolution de la Côte d'Ivoire; le concentré d'une gestion anti-prospective' (Forum du Tiers Monde, Dakar, 1993), p. 13. This collection of papers is to be published by l'Harmattan, Paris.

[24] UNESCO, Rapport mondial sur l'éducation 1991, p. 77.

## Disorder

'I prefer injustice to disorder,' wrote Goethe on the eve of the great revolutions which were to turn Europe upside down. Goethe was lucky: he still had a choice. For Africa today there is no longer any choice. There is both disorder and injustice, combined in a negative dialectic which draws societies and their environments into an apparently endless process of regression. As J.G. Speth observes, 'We could witness the collapse of vast areas of the world into ethnic violence, poverty, hunger and the disintegration of society and the environment'.[25]

There is still time to act, and voices are being raised both in international organizations and in the countries concerned to alert world opinion and decision-makers to the need and the urgency for action. Some are already acting without waiting, while more and more intellectuals in Africa and elsewhere are a mobilizing force in this respect.

The fact is that the process of regression is already under way, hitting whole countries, regions, social and ethnic groups, disrupting the fragile equilibrium of institutions and traditions, creating new injustices, new social tensions which in turn cause new tragedies. Everywhere, almost, violence is the mode of response to the problems that inadequate political institutions and outdated codes of behaviour have proved incapable of solving.

In all of these countries it is youth which is in the forefront: young people enraged by the injustice and indignity of a situation that they refuse to accept fatalistically. They are using the only means left to them – violence.

If we are to have any hope of dealing with the situation, we have to understand the origins of the wave[26] of violence spreading over the African continent. With this in mind, its origins should be analysed as the result of specific historical circumstances and the response to them, rather than as an isolated fact. The historical situation itself is nothing more than the product of a constellation of diverse economic, demographic, social and cultural factors, which together form an explosive mix that explains the emergence and subsequent expansion of violence as a principal mode of action.

First of all there is the impact produced by the intersection of two curves on a graph, those representing dwindling economic growth and demographic expansion, which are moving in opposite directions, at the precise moment that millions of young people are preparing to become full members of society via the education system, training and work. Their exclusion from the system is both immediate and massive. It is all the more difficult for them to accept since they have grown up in a culture of progress and development,[27] with a fascination for the models of Western consumerism, which were brought to their doorsteps, even in the most remote village, by the globalization of communication and information. For most of these young people, entering adolescence, which is difficult even under normal circumstances, is a descent into hell. The spirit of rebellion which is normal at this age, exacerbated by such deep frustration, is transformed

---

[25] 'Année 2050', in *La situation des enfants dans le monde 1995* (UNICEF, 1995), p. 8. [Unofficial translation – ed.]
[26] The UNICEF report quoted above notes that the conflicts of the last decade have caused more children to be killed and wounded than soldiers. During the course of this period, war has killed some 2 million children, and disabled 4 or 5 million more, while more than 5 million have been sent to refugee camps, and more than 12 million have lost their homes. With Mozambique, Angola, Somalia, Sudan and Rwanda, Africa is at the top of this grisly league table. UNICEF, 'Année 2050'.
[27] The editors of the UNICEF report *La situation des enfants dans le monde 1995* justifiably emphasize the 'synergy between two forces – increasing economic exclusion and social disintegration, which is also on the increase – as the central element in a new wave currently threatening human security'. [Unofficial translation – ed.]

into hatred and into violence. Their nihilism is aggravated by the rapid changes their society is undergoing.

Life has changed dramatically everywhere, both for the main actors and the settings in which they are acting out their parts. We may begin by considering the most significant of these changes, those in regard to central government.

States, authoritarian or otherwise, are ailing or collapsing in the face of repeated battering by a society they have been unable to regulate and an international environment which has changed substantially and which, above all, no longer tolerates the slightest mistake. The tone is set by the unrestrained liberalism imposed on the world economy by the United States during the Reagan period. There are programmes of structural adjustment, but their initiators, the experts of the Bretton Woods institutions, are beginning to look more and more like the merchant of Venice immortalized by Shakespeare four centuries ago. The economic revival they anticipated has still not materialized. Rather, quite the opposite has taken place, while in the meantime the legitimacy of the state has declined, undermined by social movements awakened from their torpor by the ideals of democracy. Michael Bratton has observed that: 'In many African countries, ordinary people are ceasing to regard the state as their own and are refusing to comply with official injunctions. The loss of legitimacy is manifest in numerous ways'.[28]

If, as Max Weber defined it, the modern state is characterized by the power of administration and the monopoly of legitimate violence, it may be that in most cases the state in Africa hardly corresponds to this definition. The state in Africa has lost authority to the international financial institutions and through programmes of structural adjustment, as a result of which it has lost the power to govern and can no longer control the forces of legitimate violence, which split into factional interests and are dissolved in the body of society. At first its collapse was rather welcome to public opinion, opposition movements and intellectuals weary of the authoritarianism of governments, the corruption of leaders and the incompetence of administrations. In many countries the African Spring which began in the 1980s was marked by the ritual of national transition conferences which were supposed to mark the beginning of a new, more just and more humane order.

Youth has often been in the vanguard of democratic revolutions which drive out unpopular dictators in the belief that their departure will be followed by a rapid upturn in the state of affairs. Casablanca in 1984, Algiers in 1988, Bamako in 1991 and, at the time of writing – 23 February 1995 – in Nouakchott: the sequence is identical. Pupils and students emerge on the streets to express their opposition to some unpopular measure: a rise in the price of bread, as in Casablanca or Nouakchott, the death of a political opponent, new regulations for some public service. The demonstrators are rapidly joined by thousands of children and adolescents who roam the city and its suburbs, often out of work, perpetually on the verge of revolt and ready for action. The original groups of demonstrators are swamped, vastly outnumbered by the ragged masses who change the nature of the demonstration but intensify it at the same time. Shop windows are smashed, cars are broken into and widespread looting follows. By the time the police intervene it is already too late, and military reinforcements are necessary. A few days later the numbers of wounded and dead will be published, and they will vary according to the nature of the political change which has taken place. If a dictator has been deposed from power, the dead and wounded will be turned into

---

[28] Quoted by Buijtenhuijs & Rijnierse, *Democratization*, p. 47.

martyrs and heroes;[29] but if, by some misfortune, the movement fails, little will be said, and in referring to the incident people will use words like 'hooligans', 'vandals' and 'criminals'.

Like Ibo in Dakar, many will be handicapped for life. Others, like Boualem in Algiers, will become even more deeply entrenched in the cycle of violence. The remaining majority will gradually return to their miserable daily round.

This sequence of events has now become a common factor in social movements in Africa. It is not the only or even the most important factor, as we shall see, but it does indicate the weakness of the social and political organizations (especially those set up by trade unions and political parties) whose fringes are very often taken over by an informal mass movement. Thus the forms of violence specific to riots, including those used by the police or security forces, often cause movements that are initially pacifist and disciplined to descend into bloodshed and disorder.

If, as in Mali, the movement succeeds in overthrowing the dictatorship, there is euphoria, especially among the elite who were opposed to the old system. But in many cases such euphoria is short-lived.[30] Indeed, national conferences do not often reach the results hoped for, transitions drag on interminably, and the political coalitions charged with the task of administering them are fragile and prone to rapid collapse. The new order is long in arriving while the economic and demographic pressures and their accompanying problems grow.

At this point in time there are not many people who are attentive to 'these social vacuums'[31] which are multiplying and expanding in proportion to the disengagement of the state. Like Michael Bratton,[32] African intellectuals and democrats, disenchanted by the unhappy experience of the African state during these last decades, hope that 'the retreat of the state will create, willy-nilly, an enlarged political space within which associational life can occur'.

Unfortunately, this is rarely the case. A new political space struggles to emerge from a society which is unable to produce an alternative capable of replacing the old order. Coalitions formed with a view to overthrowing those in power turn out to be, in fact, concerned with gaining power themselves. Having achieved this, they split up along lines such as the ethnic or religious identity of a community, the economic interests of a particular stratum, a corporate interest, the autonomy of a certain organization, and so on. And these imperatives can in turn result in the most unnatural alliances and the most surprising combinations, which frequently split and realign.[33] The resulting chronic instability further exacerbates the sense of precariousness felt by people at large and calls into question the values they hold about money, work, violence, and even life. Young

---

[29] This idea is taken from the remarkable work of Jeremy Seekings, *Heroes or Villains? Youth politics in the 1980s* (Ravan Press, Johannesburg, 1993), which concerns young people in South Africa.

[30] After the Malian dictator Moussa Traoré was deposed in 1991, H.M. Magassa and O. Diarrah observed sceptically: 'the intellectual shortcomings of the political class could signal a new trend towards authoritarianism, even dictatorship, if the supporters of the democratic movement currently in power, do not succeed in putting an end to at least some of the problems of Malians, namely: insecurity and increasing disrespect for the law, increasing lack of education, unemployment among young people, old and new endemic diseases, rural migration and the emigration of the working population, urban unrest, etc.' in: *Contribution à la problématique politique et économique de l'alternative démocratique au Mali* (Forum du Tiers Monde, Dakar, 1994 – to be published by l'Harmattan, Paris).

[31] The expression is borrowed from Badié, 'Ruptures et innovations'. It refers to the social spaces which escape the authority of the state.

[32] Quoted in Buijtenhuijs & Rijnierse, *Democratization*, p. 49.

[33] This chaotic (in the mathematical sense of the term) type of structure explains the difficulties encountered by political scientists in their attempts to analyse a situation, and in particular, their incapacity to produce possible alternatives and to propose realistic scenarios when faced with dramatic changes which elude traditional paradigms.

people are of course highly susceptible to this erosion of values, their consciousness divided between two systems of representation corresponding to two equally inaccessible worlds: the old world of their ancestors which is fading into memory, and the other, the world of the West, the image of a distant but pervasive reality. This is the condition of the great majority of African youth, like the young Malians of the new democracy described by Magassa and Diarrah.[34] Easy money, diplomas acquired by bribery or the accepted idea that to be able to pull strings is worth more than years of study, and Western images on the cinema screens which serve to replace African reality, all represent mental schemas which both exclude young Malians and imprison them in an intellectual ghetto, thus bringing them close to a kind of socialized schizophrenia. This leads to phenomena of ostentatious imitation and provokes feelings of envy, frustration and sometimes insanity, all of which have a bearing on aggression. Behind the appearance of a conviviality which is highly prized, Malians conceal a violence which may surface in an open or indirect attack on human life. The fashion for the 'necklace' means of punishment is an outward sign of the hidden reality which the democratic movement must bear like a curse.

What actually happens is that, in the aftermath of the disruption of the state, the fabric of society itself begins to decay. The public space that civil society was supposed to reconstruct around the democratic ideal disappears into social structures which are about as solid as volcanic magma. As Gramsci wrote of Italy in the 1920s, the years which heralded the emergence of fascism: 'The old dies, the new is not yet born, in the semi-shadows monsters emerge.'[35]

The city is the first of these monsters. Everything happens in the African city, whose colonial origins were denounced by Fanon[36] but which has been betrayed by its experience of independence. 'What did independence bring to Fama? Nothing but a national identity document and a ruling party card', just as it has brought nothing to the vast majority of his fellow-citizens, who are victims of the chaos of a city which continues to be marked by the stigma of exclusion and anarchy, observed Ahmadou Kourouma bitterly.[37] Worse, twenty years after this was written, the situation has degenerated.

In the thirty years between 1960 and 1990, Africa's urban population has grown from 15 per cent to 30 per cent of the total population. By the year 2000, it will be close to 40 per cent, perhaps more if the influx of refugees fleeing insecurity and the exodus of farmers leaving arid and difficult areas are not halted. Successive waves of migrants agglomerate around the nucleus of the old colonial city, called in French 'le Plateau', which they eventually surround. They settle in concentric circles and make camps, often in shanty-towns which end up having a permanent existence. The authorities, partly because of corruption and embezzlement, eventually leave them to themselves, if they are not driven out of their homes on the grounds of 'illegal building'.[38] It will not be long before even the police will not dare to venture into the badly-lit and evil-smelling labyrinths which serve as streets.

---

[34] Magassa & Diarrah, *Contribution à la problématique*, p. 20.

[35] Antonio Gramsci, *Quaderni del Carcere* (Einaudi, Turin, 1975), p. 311.

[36] 'The colonial city,' he wrote, 'or at least the African city, the negro village, the medina, the reserve, is a disreputable place populated by disreputable people. People there are born any old how. People die there of no matter what. . .The colonial city is an abject city, a city on its knees, a city defeated.' *Les damnés de la terre* (Maspéro, Paris, 1961), p. 32.

[37] Ahmadou Kourouma, *Les soleils des indépendances* (Le Seuil, Paris, 1970), p. 23.

[38] The extraordinary vitality of African language has succeeded in naming these precarious residents '*les déguerpis*', from the French *déguerpir*, 'to vacate or to evict', and their encampments '*le déguerpissement*'. Those who live there are under constant threat of eviction from plots which they occupy illegally. In Algeria an association of illicit shanty-builders has even been set up, and is entirely legal.

'Here too independence has betrayed its promises. It has not built the sewers it promised and it never will', writes Kourouma.[39] 'The pools of water will continue to stagnate as before and the natives, whether colonized or independent, will continue to have to wade through them until such time as Allah lifts the damnation of the negro.'

Within this urban sprawl, which has little in common with a city as it is usually defined, everything is difficult, uncertain, violent. Vast differences in standards of living and life-styles separate the well-to-do, often nouveaux riches, from the vast majority of residents. The city is cruel. Its anonymity is disconcerting, and it is difficult for people to adapt. Even the old traditions of solidarity and mutual support do not survive when confronted by money, power and force. The elderly are resigned to this state of affairs, but not the younger generation. Quite the contrary.

Among these young people there is anger, a sense of hurt, and revolt. Their needs are greater than those of their parents dut to the ostentation shown by those of their compatriots who have got rich quickly. The frustration of the young is aggravated by imaginations which feed on television, radio and cinema. Young people dream of Paris, New York, London. *Dallas*[40] is a smash hit, as are Bruce Lee, Rambo and an infinite succession of James Bonds, usually made in the USA. Their acculturation to Western standards is selective: what they like best is the speed of the action, but also the images of quick money, violence and weapons. These are the messages which remain imprinted in their memories, accompanied by images of beautiful women, smart cars and alcohol. Can they be blamed if they prefer the shiny image of the Western dream to the sinister reality of daily existence? People in other parts of the world may have the same fantasies but they do not share the same reality, and it is probably this gap between fantasy and reality that constitutes the most specific and original feature of the youth of the Third World, or perhaps we should say the Fourth World.

It is a small step from the culture of violence to its actual practice. This is all the more so because of the social vacuum which has developed as a result of the withdrawal of the state, and in this vacuum, the poorer areas of African cities take on the look of disaster zones and are left to their inhabitants. Youths, organized in gangs with leaders and symbols of group allegiance, perching on the edge of delinquency, grasp their opportunities. Acquiring weapons is easy since the state has lost its monopoly of legitimate violence, and this has resulted in its spread. There are large stocks of arms available in Africa's major capitals as a consequence of the many wars taking place in the continent. These weapons are sold through large international networks, often formed by former officers of state security services who have turned to arms-dealing. Weapons are all the more easy to procure now that state control of the weapons trade has become less vigilant as a consequence of the general weakening of the state.[41]

The dissemination of violence is aided by the state's decline. The major patronage systems which developed around high-ranking government dignitaries have split into as many fiefs as there are centres of power. From this point of view, the weakening of the capacity of the state to administer central government is accompanied by its feudalization in terms of both power and force, including a feudalization of its own armed forces. This is the syndrome of the warlords which emerged in China after the collapse of the

---

[39] Kourouma, *Les soleils des indépendances*, pp. 25–6.

[40] We refer, of course, to the famous US television series of the 1980s.

[41] Six million weapons are currently being privately held in South Africa, while some African states continue to supply weapons to black markets in neighbouring countries. This is not to mention those countries which manufacture arms and continue to sell them to countries unable even to pay for them. Debt forgiveness often starts with military debts.

first republic of Sun Yat Sen. Closer to home, it is also what happened in Lebanon. Sometimes whole sectors of the central bureaucracy organize as a criminal mafia around a leader who may be a former minister, a general, a former security service chief, with the whole network depending on some sort of economic activity and an income based on a specific area of monopoly. This is where an organized group combines with money and violence. It is the young who are called upon to fulfil the last of these functions. The street-gangs of the shanty-towns then turn into militias, sometimes even provided with semi-heavy weapons, as in Somalia.[42] Under the manipulation of their sponsors, it is possible in certain cases for such gangs to gain partial autonomy, becoming new fiefs.

This process of disseminating violence is not simply of a criminal type, as in Colombia. Very often it is closely related to ethnic conflicts (as in Rwanda), religious conflicts (Algeria and Sudan) or political conflicts (Mozambique); sometimes even a complex combination of all three. In any event, this type of violence is in the process of becoming one of the fundamental factors of the political and social life of Africa. The tragedies of Rwanda and Somalia caught the attention of onlookers in the developed countries and led to a wave of international solidarity, but the work of charitable organizations is not complete and is often illusory because it confuses cause with effect, the latter hiding the former.

The myopia of the charitable soul is not specific to African youth and society. The young people living in the less salubrious suburbs of Western cities can in many ways be compared with their African counterparts in terms of frustration and revolt. On occasion curfews have been proposed in major cities in the USA, including the capital, Washington, aimed at young people under 17. This is eloquent testimony.

The fact remains, however, that the extent of the phenomenon in African societies and its proliferation at a time of global unrest, particularly social and political unrest, are cause for concern for the world community, not only on moral grounds, but also strategic ones. It should be emphasized that the quasi-politicized form of violence which is growing in African societies, and in which a large proportion of the youth of these countries can be engaged, could turn quite soon into a third form of violence which will threaten the stability of other parts of the world. All that is required is for these groups to become internationalized for the dissemination of local violence linked to the collapse of the state to extend beyond national frontiers to other regions.

There is no lack of opportunity for this. There are, for example, economic opportunities. This applies particularly to the drug trade, which is beginning to acquire some importance in Africa with cannabis being cultivated in all parts of the continent, and heroin being traded in Nigeria, threatening to link many African economies into the world drugs market. There are also politico-religious opportunities, such as for Islamic fundamentalism, a nebulous phenomenon but a world-wide one, which is capable of turning to advantage the destabilization of districts or regions or of organizing complex terrorist operations. The same, in fact, could apply to any other transcontinental network, such as the arms trade, migrant labour movements, and so on. With globalization picking up speed, the hidden hand which manipulates youth and its violence in the disarray of African institutions, societies and economies is well positioned to connect the local to the universal in its own manner, and to exploit both without concerning itself with international laws and regulations.

The marginalization and exclusion of Africa and African youth have drawn the latter

---

[42] Roland Marchal, 'Les mooryaan de Mogadiscio. Formes de violence dans un espace urbain de guerre', *Cahiers d'études africaines*, 130 (1993), pp. 295–320.

into a cycle and into forms of violence, spontaneous or organized, official or manipulated, which have cowed many of the states of the continent and which can lead to terrible collective tragedies. However, the seriousness of the effects of such forms of violence and their possible extension to other parts of the world, especially the richer regions, confronts the latter with the question, which can no longer be ignored, of the need for collective global security based 'not on weapons but on development'.[43]

[43] Boutros Boutros-Ghali, quoted in UNICEF, *La situation des enfants dans le monde*, p. 5. [Unofficial translation – ed.]

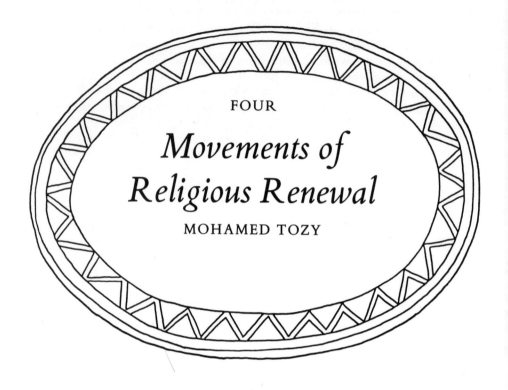

FOUR

# Movements of
# Religious Renewal

MOHAMED TOZY

'The twenty-first century will be either religious or it will not exist at all.' Nowhere
has Malraux's prediction been as accurate as in Africa at the end of this century. The
renewal of the classical religions, the development of numerous centres of prophecy, both
Mahdist and Christian, and the growing importance of forms of so-called fundamentalist
Islamic, Christian and other faiths, pose a challenge to scholars and require them to find
new frameworks of explanation, often differing from the paradigm of modernity/
secularization versus religion/tradition.

Some writers group these complex phenomena under the label 'fundamentalism,' a
word which carries highly negative connotations which impede a proper understanding
of a fluid situation. Others, a minority, prefer to regard them exclusively as a particularist
expression of Muslim civil society. Only a few commentators venture to propose comparisons between different monotheistic systems and to incorporate them in the same
study: making comparisons between the *jama'at attabligh* ('Preaching and propagating the
faith') movement and the Jehovah's Witnesses, for example.[1]

Africa is the continent where the balance both between and within religions may be
described as most unstable. The boundaries between them have hardly been drawn, and
competition between religious entrepreneurs is still lively. For decades a race for conversion has been going on involving the Catholic and Protestant churches and countries
(such as Saudi Arabia, Libya and Morocco) which have taken upon themselves the task of
propagating the faith in Africa. As a result, the statistics concerning religious following

---

[1] G. Kepel, *La revanche de Dieu: chrétiens, juifs et musulmans à la reconquête du monde* (Seuil, Paris, 1991).

58

have become extremely elastic depending on whether the sources are Muslim or Christian.

According to figures published by the Organization of the Islamic Conference during an Islamic Summit in Casablanca,[2] there are sixteen African countries with a Muslim majority; in nine of these, Muslims account for more than 90 per cent of the population. Other sources[3] provide lower figures. According to these estimates, there are only ten countries with a Muslim majority, with Muslims accounting for more than 90 per cent of the population in four of them, for between 80 and 90 per cent in three, and for between 60 and 70 per cent in one; the majority of the other countries have a low level of Islamization. The statistics given by Christian sources are equally imprecise. The two major religions, both of which merge into African traditional beliefs at their margins, provide statistics which often cannot be verified.

One of the characteristics of the religious phenomenon in Africa is its great capacity to adapt to local conditions. The result is a widespread adaptation of imported religions to the realities and needs of specific countries and cultures. This should cause us to reconsider those manifestations of unorthodoxy that are too often interpreted with condescension by outsiders. It is more fruitful to attribute such cultural manifestations to attempts to produce meaning by people interpreting directly sacred texts such as the Bible and the Koran.[4] In this context Achille Mbembe[5] refers to a divine geography with unstable borders, to an informal economy of religion, to families of images, to visions and to metaphors, to representations and beliefs which integrate the miraculous and the marvellous. In the Maghreb, Islamists perform their own exegesis of the canons of their religion and claim a right of direct access to the original text.

The phenomenon which concerns us in the present discussion is the creation of religious movements with new sociological characteristics (for example, consisting of educated young people, only recently urbanized), that can be provisionally classified as 'fundamentalist'. This is expressed through public prophecy or through an equally prophetic reappropriation in the form of a solitary act which rejects the authority of the existing religious establishment.

The religious renewal in Africa often takes the form of male clerics claiming space in the political arena, such as in those Catholic and Protestant churches which were directly involved in the processes of democratization which began in the early 1990s. The clergy played a central role in this process in many places, either by means of pastoral letters sanctioned by the episcopal conferences, or through active participation in the various national conferences. After years of virtually unconditional support for established regimes, the clergy openly sided with opposition forces. In various pastoral letters issued between 1990 and 1993, African bishops denounced corruption in government, one-party systems which dissolved the separation of powers and, above all, the systematic violation of human rights.[6]

At the social level bishops demonstrated their concern about the spread of poverty and the increase of inequality. In this regard, they have condemned structural adjustment

[2] *Le Matin du Sahara*, 8730, 13 December 1994.

[3] Guy Nicolas, 'L'islam au sud du Sahara', *Les cahiers de l'Orient*, 27 (1992), pp. 125–42.

[4] J.-F. Bayart, 'L'énonciation du politique', *Revue française de science politique*, 35, iii (1985), pp. 343–73; Christian Coulon and Denis-Constant Martin (eds), *Les Afriques politiques* (La découverte, Paris, 1991).

[5] A. Mbembe, 'Prolifération du divin en Afrique subsaharienne', in G. Kepel (ed.), *Les politiques de Dieu* (Seuil, Paris, 1993), p. 177.

[6] Episcopal conferences of Chad (18 December 1991), the Central African Republic (July 1991), Benin (1989), Zaire (20 May 1990), Côte d'Ivoire (18 July 1990), Kenya (21 June 1990), and Cameroon (17 May 1990).

policies, while calling for objectivity in the practice of public administration.[7] At the same time, bishops have not hesitated to assume a role as guardians of the public conscience in insisting on the need to adopt policies inspired by the 'light of the Gospel and the social teachings of the church'.[8]

The various national conferences have provided opportunities for the Church to participate more than previously in the political arena. In Benin, the first country to use a national conference as an instrument of political transition, the Church – represented by Bishop De Souza – had the opportunity to influence the process of political change. Benin's example has been followed by some ten other countries which have held national conferences, in more than half of which the Church has played a key role, such as in Gabon, Zaire, Madagascar, Congo.[9]

The national conferences held in the Sahelian countries also presented Islamists with an opportunity both to denounce the corruption of the political classes and to question the principles on which the existing social pact is based. Ten Islamic delegates provoked a long debate on the Islamic or secular nature of the constitution in Bamako in August 1991. In Niger, Islamic associations which participated in the national conference managed to prevent the word 'secular' from appearing in the constitution of the Third Republic, using instead the expression 'non-confessional character of the state'.[10]

North Africa has also been the site of a clerical intervention in the running of public affairs. Paradoxically, it was the governments themselves which appealed to the *ulema*, clerics authorized to interpret holy scripture, to legitimize the status quo.[11] That these governments then went on the defensive in the early 1980s was hardly surprising. The Islamists began by occupying the mosques and using Friday services to denounce the authorities' incompetence, haranguing the masses and transforming themselves into leaders of the process of political change, as happened initially in Egypt and subsequently in Algeria, Morocco and Tunisia.

This irruption of religion into the political arena has generally been treated as a negative development by academic writers, some of whom have seen it as a return of obscurantism and fanaticism. However, the analysis has moved on, and the resurgence of a religious element in public life based on carefully formulated religious expressions can no longer be regarded as something archaic, or as an unthinking reaction to the process of modernization. It is better understood as a phenomenon that accompanies the crisis of states which have failed in their function of allocating resources and managing conflicting interests.

The diffusion of religious movements and modes of expression is in part a consequence of this. It testifies to a widespread call for the redefinition of a new field of politics, capable of managing and directing the activities of new social groups which are often cut off from their communities of origin and driven by demands for social, spatial and economic mobility.

The fact that Africa is underdeveloped does not mean that it is rural and archaic, since underdevelopment has not prevented it from making a spectacular entry into modernity, especially since the general transition from agrarian systems of production in the 1970s.

---

[7] F. Boillot, 'L'Église catholique face aux processus de changement politique du début des années quatre-vingt-dix', *L'année africaine* (A. Pedone, Paris, 1992–93), pp. 115–44.
[8] Episcopal conference of Côte d'Ivoire, *La politique au service du pays. Documentation catholique*, 2012, 2–16 September 1990.
[9] Boillot, 'L'Église catholique', p. 124.
[10] 'Les islamistes à l'assaut de l'Afrique noire', *Jeune Afrique économie*, 185 (November, 1994), p. 103.
[11] M. Tozy, 'Islam et État au Maghreb', *Maghreb-Machrek*, 126 (December, 1989), pp. 25–46.

According to Gellner,[12] agrarian societies are characteristically dominated by a minority which has a monopoly of literacy, underpinned by a distinction between elite tradition and the village tradition, rigid social stratification, and the predominance of a rural way of life. Transition takes place to an industrial society characterized rather by widespread education, a questioning of traditional stratifications, and social and spatial mobility. Defined in this way, modernity cannot be regarded as a world which has lost its sense of the enchanted or the sacred. Modernity is the object of a strategy of appropriation opened up by the prophecies of Islam and the new churches.

It is not our intention in the present essay to sketch a map of religious renewal in Africa, although we firmly believe that the question is one of the development of an already existing phenomenon rather than its creation. Neither do we intend to assess the importance of these movements in determining the political future of each country or region. We have deliberately chosen to lump together religions and regions which are usually opposed (Islam and Christianity; North and sub-Saharan Africa) and which scholars often consider to be marked by different characteristics and approaches. In any event, our analysis is based on the hypothesis that the whole of Africa faces the same problems, despite differences in their rhythms and intensities.

To what extent can religion be considered a cohesive force for the underprivileged strata of society, especially in the cities? What is the relation between this phenomenon and the status of women, especially in North Africa? Are the new religious movements sources for the creation of a new social and political morality?

The reply to these questions will be centred on three points:

1. The religious renewal is usually expressed by so-called 'fundamentalist' movements led by educated young people, who are urbanized and not necessarily marginal in society. Establishment Christianity and Islam are confronted with two types of sensibility: spiritualist (in the form of new churches and Muslim brotherhoods) and rationalist (in the form of new Islamist movements). In West Africa in particular, Muslims are often attached to religious orders called in Arabic *tariqa* (pl. *tûrûq*). This is generally translated as *confrérie* in French or brotherhood in English. The most prominent such brotherhoods are the *tijaniya* and the *mourides*, founded by saints whose memory is revered by devotees of the brotherhoods. They are opposed by devotees of Islamic reform movements, particularly the puritanical *wahabist* movements which regard the brotherhoods as decadent. To what extent do these new Islamist movements correspond to a generational conflict or to a need for social mobility?

2. The withdrawal of the state from the provision of financially expensive services has led to an increase in state intervention in the field of religion, with a view to using religion as an instrument of government. This disengagement of the state leaves the field free for social movements, often expressing themselves in religious terms, to take charge of certain services, especially in the areas of health and education. In Morocco a twin phenomenon is taking place: the setting up of private Islamic schools, starting with those established by followers of the *jama'at attabligh*, the Association for Preaching and Propagating the Faith, and appropriation of the primary school system as well as secondary and tertiary education.

3. The religious renewal mobilizes women as well as men, contrary to what many observers of Islam believe. Within a modernizing perspective and through a moralization of external symbols, Islam offers women the opportunity to move from private to public space without transgressing social norms.

[12] E. Gellner, (trans. B. Pineau), *Nations et nationalismes* (Payot, Paris, 1983).

## Religious Renewal and the Problem of Young People

Any analysis which begins by identifying modernization as a condition in which the sense of enchantment has been lost, and goes on to contrast this with a definition of archaism in which religion is a prominent feature, is confusing two separate issues: it is confusing modernity as an idea with the actual effect it has on specific social structures. Such an approach effectively means that facts collected by social science research are fitted into an inappropriate model. Most analysts of religious revivals have run into this problem; they all note that the instigators, actors and target populations of renewal movements are firmly situated within the framework of modernity, while at the same time designating it as the main enemy. In other words the reformers' struggle is aimed at the signs of modernity rather than its content, and their purpose is to create or reformulate modernity.

In the particular case of the Islamist renewal, which is the most spectacular manifestation of renewal in North Africa, it is not an organized movement, but more a state of mind shared by a population which is often young, recently urbanized, and educated in modern schools. The majority of the leaders of Islamist movements in the Maghreb are in their forties and work within the state education or health services or are prominent within the scientific community.

To explain this phenomenon as the reaction of tradition to modernity would be satisfactory if it did not limit us to an evaluation of the way in which people interpret Islamic texts. The concept of 'traditionalization' is limited to the extent that the political and even ideological work of new reformist groups, such as those mentioned throughout the present essay, shares in a re-creation and interpretation of tradition, within the perspective of the appropriation of modernity and the legitimization of the advance of a younger generation.

The demographic explosion in Africa in the 1960s was associated with a rapid and uncontrolled increase in investment in the training of an elite, even though the structures to accommodate new school graduates did not exist. An overestimation of the mobility conferred by a school education clashed with a system hemmed in by the scarcity of resources, which has in turn exacerbated nepotism and patronage. Educational systems which were established hastily and which lack large-scale resources are now witnessing the adverse effects of their own malfunctioning.

What is the relevance in this context of an explanation based on inter-generational conflict? In any event, the religious renewal is multidimensional. As has often been pointed out, it demonstrates how a revolt against injustice and moral degeneration, as well as an intense desire for self-affirmation in situations of social marginality, can be accompanied by a fear of losing self-esteem or, more generally, a profound crisis of identity. Religious militancy offers the possibility of acquiring a positive, stable and valued self-image.

Membership of lay organizations and other associations gives members access to forms of solidarity which redefine existing social hierarchies by the establishment of criteria which are not necessarily those of society at large. Piety, militant commitment and hard work are in principle valued more highly than age or social background. Allegiances are organized around charismatic personalities outside of any existing hierarchy.

The object of the quest for a new identity is reinforced by the principle of practical efficacy. Once Islamists are liberated from the tutelary power of the older generation which occupies the official positions of authority, they themselves become producers of meaning and leaders of opinion. They do so by patiently undermining the existing structures of mediation and by delegitimizing both the traditional hierarchies and those created since independence.

New strategies are implemented, all aimed at securing a position in the existing system, and only rarely at its destruction. The idea of seizing power from above is only a marginal variant of this youth movement. The promotion of an edifying morality and a work ethic, symbolized by the choice of clothing and even partners in marriage, is another way of challenging dominant values. It creates a parallel society which augments the power of the denunciation and delegitimization of authority with that of exemplary militant behaviour.

The numerous studies that have been published of the rapidly changing Islamic Salvation Front (FIS) in Algeria highlight the predominance of the younger generation, which has been as important as state violence in the choice of zealotry as an option in the struggle for power. Sevrine Labat has written that 'the new generations of radicalized militants are led by an intellectual avant-garde',[13] often drawn from the ranks of the FIS but having broken with the Islamist leaders on account of their alleged politics of prevarication. They include Arabic-speaking primary and secondary school teachers, as well as young ex-army officers, like Said Makhloufi or A. Chbouti.

The technocrats who have been able to make political headway within the FIS are a good example of the model of young leaders of religious renewal movements. The majority of them were born in the 1950s. They are the first generation to be educated after independence. They were trained almost exclusively in the sciences, are French-speaking, and convey the image of modern, upwardly mobile technocratic elites, whose career is often blocked by the predominance of the apparatchiks currently in place.

The conversion of this generation took place through the FIS only late in the day, but this frame of reference was soon replaced by a radical vision marking the transition from mobility through the mosque and piety to mobility through armed resistance and *jihad*.

## Algeria

In fact, the FIS was already starting to rid itself of its founding fathers in July 1991, long before the setting up of armed groups. The emergence of figures like R. Kébir, A. Haddam and A. Hachani foreshadowed a 'total renewal of the leadership'.[14] Even when the military expressions of the Islamist movement – the Armed Islamic Groups and the Islamic Salvation Army (the AIS, close to the FIS) – are analysed closely, it can be seen that the dividing line is not simply between the armed extension of a political movement (the AIS) and that of the unorganized combatants, but rather between generations of militants. The violence of internal conflict within the broad Islamist movement reflects as much the individual careers of combatants faced with humiliation at the hands of the older generation as it does a defined political programme. Descriptions of neighbourhoods like the one presented by Myriam Vergès demonstrate the impasse in which all young people find themselves: 'When you add it all up, you don't remember anything, you realize that you haven't done anything and you don't own anything. It's incredible. Where do I live? What am I doing? What have I done to deserve this? Elsewhere, people of our age are starting out on a career, but for us, there's nothing in our heads. It's

---

[13] Sevrine Labat, 'Islamismes et islamistes en Algérie. Un nouveau militantisme', in G. Kepel (ed.), *Exils et royaumes: les appartenances du monde arabo-musulman d'aujourd'hui* (Presse de la fondation nationale des sciences politiques, Paris, 1994), p. 53.
[14] ibid., p. 57.

better not to think about it, or it drives you crazy' (Morad, 30 years old, hairdresser). 'There [among the Islamists] they have real social justice, everyone receives his due, people say hello to each other and what's more, if they're not *Kuffar* [impious] they go to paradise'.[15] These are not statements of either fascination or resentment, but a simple cry of distress, a demand for a place in the sun which has gradually turned into a commitment to a place in paradise through the quest for the status of martyrdom.

### Nigeria

The case of Nigeria confirms a view of the inter-generational dimension of the religious renewal. It is generally representative of the demographic tension which is a feature of most African countries. As some authors have noted, Nigeria and some other countries in central and southern Africa are poles of geopolitical restructuring. Both the Roman Catholic Church and the Organization of the Islamic Conference designate Nigeria as the 'front line between Christians and Muslims'.[16]

The religious expression of a demand for mobility concerns the renewal of Christianity as much as that of Islam. The renewal of Nigerian Islam, especially among the younger generation, is reflected in the development of groups inspired by the *wahabist* reform movement, such as the *jama'at Izalat al bida' wa iqamat assûnna* ('Movement for the Elimination of Vice'). The sociological characteristics of the *izala* movement[17] are a good example of this quest for mobility. It is claimed that access to the group is dependent on having academic training and the 'need to acquire a formally certified school education'. Fluency in Arabic and some knowledge of literature are highly esteemed, often leading to a stay in Saudi Arabia. Espousal of the reform movement becomes a means of breaking away from the community of origin, and a way of acclimatizing to urban space.

The following statement by a young *izala* follower is interesting in several respects. As well as conveying the exaggeratedly critical attitude of the *tijaniya* Muslim brotherhood against what could be called schismatic tendencies, it also provides us with a clear understanding of where the Islam of the younger generation and that of their parents diverge, the main point being the rejection of parental authority:

> In Garko almost everyone was a supporter of the *tijaniya*, including my parents. We were very attached to the Islam of the *tûrûq* . . . Our teachers told us not to join *izala* because these people are all damned. We were told that they do not respect their elders or their parents, and that they attack people for no reason. It was said that the *izala* followers went to give their parents a sheep, with cola for the father and milk for the mother, and said: 'This is what you gave the day we were born', and changed their names. We were made to hate them with all our strength.[18]

Despite this, the movement's very negative image has hardly scared off the younger generation. A new ethic allows them to match their social status to their position within the ethnic or family group. Affiliation to *izala* entails such things as a commitment to emancipate the younger generation from the power of the elders.

[15] Myriam Vergès, 'La casbah d'Alger. Chronique de survie dans un quartier en sursis', in Kepel, *Exils et royaumes*, p. 75.

[16] Guy Nicolas, 'Le Nigéria: pôle de restructuration géopolitique, ou ligne de front entre chrétiens et musulmans?', *Hérodote*, 56–66 (1992), p. 87.

[17] Ousmane Kane, 'Les mouvements islamiques et le champ politique au Nord du Nigéria: le cas du mouvement Izala à Kano', (Thèse ès sciences politiques, IEP, Paris, May 1993).

[18] ibid., p. 185.

Among the Hausa a tradition of modesty imposes a certain distance between the old and the young. (It is an insult to shake the hand of one's father, father-in-law, uncle, master, husband or employer; one is expected to kneel.) In the mosque the younger members are not supposed to pray beside their elders. The *izala* movement condemns this practice of genuflection: one is only obliged to kneel while praying to God. This transgression of the social code, which was condemned, becomes positive and acquires a legitimate character.[19]

### Senegal

In Senegal, the nascent religious renewal manifesting itself outside the existing Muslim brotherhoods through the *wahabist* connection has been partly neutralized by the activities of the sheikhs of the *mouride* and *tijaniya* brotherhoods, many of whom are wealthy businessmen as well as religious leaders, and their capacity to offer alternative networks.[20] The pressure coming from the younger generation has been absorbed by the brotherhoods through the *da'ira* (i.e. associations affiliated to the brotherhoods). Without creating parallel hierarchies, these allow for a gradual absorption. At a public meeting in 1976, Serigne Ahmad Tidiane Sy, the son of the second caliph of the *tijaniya* brotherhood, castigated the young for not having understood that the 1968–78 decade was manifestly destined for them by Allah the Most High. In his view, if young people continued to show a lack of initiative they would eventually miss the most favourable opportunity for self-fulfilment.

The general strategy adopted by the Senegalese brotherhoods of absorbing pressure from the young through the *da'ira* is accompanied by an intensive programme of conversion among young people. This is conducted through both educational work and religion, the favoured method being the study and prayer groups known as *da'ira*. Both the *mourides* and the *tijaniya* brotherhoods have established their own networks of *da'ira*. A *da'ira* consisting of *tijaniya* students was set up in 1988, drawing in students from the university in Dakar, and has been chaired by Sheikh Ahmed Tidiane Niang since 1988. A tea-drinking circle was created in 1975–6 at the instigation of former pupils from Saint-Louis, associated with Abdoulaye Sarr. This brought together the *mourides* to explain the master's thoughts to them and to teach the writings of Serigne Touba. The circle of friends has been extended to other acquaintances. When students who had completed their secondary education arrived at the University of Dakar in 1975, they established an organizing committee which was later to become the *da'ira* of the *mouride* students. A general meeting in 1983 defined the direction of the movement and enabled the students to re-focus the *da'ira* on the campus, following a period when it was dominated by non-students. The chairman is elected by the members and the committee is chosen by fellow-adherents,[21] students of history and geography.

### Morocco

In Morocco the advance of the younger generation has avoided the anti-brotherhood attitude which was adopted by the Salafiya nationalists, who made it one of the main strands of their approach during the struggle for independence. Since the state strengthened its control over the mosque and religious preaching by institutionalizing

---

[19] ibid., p. 223.
[20] Muriel Gomez-Perez, 'Associations islamiques à Dakar', *Islam et sociétés au sud du Sahara*, 5 (1991), pp. 5–19.
[21] ibid., p. 17.

the clergy, a new category of clergy has emerged, mainly working within the framework of associations or as clandestine 'freelancers'.

The appropriation of the religious renewal by this new elite took place by ignoring older networks and by the use of a new rhetoric. As graduates of modern university faculties, they have opted for the medium of the printed word: periodicals and newspapers instead of preaching in the mosques.

The legitimacy of these often youthful new clergy is based on their ability to grasp the contemporary problems of young people. Conformity to the techniques of traditional textual exegesis is for them of secondary importance. As a result of studying a group of about twenty such clergy holding positions of responsibility, we are able to characterize the theological revolution which has taken place within the framework of what an Islamist periodical calls the *fiqh maqassidi*, meaning objective exegesis which meets the practical needs of life. For these young Muslims,

> it is necessary both to take account of the divine signs and of those inscribed in everyday reality. The first thing that anyone familiar with the *sûnna* [the codified prophetic practice] has to understand is that the *fiqh* [exegesis] is not simply a memorization and exegesis of sacred texts, but a deep assimilation of the profound meanings of the text in order to disclose its rationality; confining oneself to the texts and only taking account of the literal meaning without paying heed to the general objectives of religion always leads to a superficial understanding, and sometimes to error.[22]

The practice of the new Islamic generation challenges the criteria used by the older clergy in the reading of sacred texts. It attempts to undermine the very basis of the function founded on mnemonic techniques and a timeless solidarity with the past.

Each of the four examples discussed above thus reveals a different strategy. Senegal is an exception, since here the sheikhs of the *tijaniya* and *mouride* brotherhoods have been able to control the renewal movement partly as a result of their financial resources and their capacity to control networks which extend to every corner of society and the state. The brotherhoods have been able to offer opportunities for social mobility under their own supervision. The other cases we have examined all show the emergence of strategies aimed at by-passing or discarding old elites.

In Algeria the younger generation has taken control of the Islamist movement in two ways: through the ballot box and by armed insurgency. In Morocco it has been achieved through control of the modern means of textual exegesis and, as a result, by an ethos appropriate to modern university training. In Nigeria, promotion of the new groups has taken the form of the adoption of a new exegesis as well as a break with traditional ethnic and community affiliations, which are characterized by a rigid age hierarchy.

## Agents of Religious Renewal and Civil Society

To demonstrate the importance of ecclesiastical institutions or religious brotherhoods, their strategic role in the structuring of space and their capacity to act in the face of the withdrawal or erosion of the state, let us consider the case of Zaïre.

The Church of Christ, an interdenominational Protestant church, claims to have 12 million members, out of a population of 35 million. These members are divided into sixty-two highly diverse ecclesiastical groups, called 'communities', which are genuine regional or inter-regional Churches, founded by missionary activity. The most important

---

[22] *Revue Al fûrqan*, 14, 1988, p. 2.

groups in numerical terms appear to be the Baptists, Congregationalists, Methodists, and (Reformed) Presbyterians. Various Pentecostalist movements seem to be gaining influence, particularly in the large cities, even among the Catholics. Pentecostalist practices such as ecstatic collective prayer and healing transcend the boundaries of the confessions.[23] Protestantism as a whole, represented by the Church of Christ in Zaire, contains: 11,200 parishes, 3,000 ordained pastors, 2,500 non-ordained pastors, 3,516 primary schools, 1,367 secondary schools, 5 higher institutes of theology, one faculty of theology, 62 hospitals, 348 dispensaries, 137 maternity clinics, 26 sanatoriums and leper colonies, 22 health centres, 13 medical schools, and 200 agricultural, stock-breeding and housing projects.[24]

In 1989 there were 15.7 million Catholics in Zaire, accounting for around 43.5 per cent of the total population. The country is divided into 47 dioceses with 55 bishops, 2,800 priests, and 5,800 other male clerics and nuns. The Church controls a sizeable proportion of the hospitals, dispensaries and schools in the country, as well as the best communications network (all missions have a radio link with Kinshasa). It has also managed to establish a productive, market-integrated agricultural sector.[25]

The case of the Zaïrian churches is not isolated. It is neither a special case of Protestantism largely dominated by an Anglo-Saxon philanthropic sensibility, nor a Catholic phenomenon inherited from the church of the colonial period. The investment in civil society by religious groups can be observed equally among the Islamist groups of North and West Africa and among the Christians.

The clergy, whether they are members of the established congregations or leaders of alternative movements, focus on two activities in the social field: health and education. Certain Islamist groups refer to this approach as a strategic option aimed at changing human personalities as a prerequisite to changing society.

Radical Islamist groups aim to promote a veritable counter-culture based on a rigorous social morality. During the month of Ramadan in 1991, FIS militants in Algeria set up a number of 'Islamic sûq' or markets where goods which are usually scarce during this period were available at wholesale prices. Two years earlier, on 29 October 1989, after the terrible Tipasa earthquake, Islamists had demonstrated remarkable efficiency in organizing help within forty-eight hours. In Morocco the dairy and baking sectors, which require professional standards of conduct which combine integrity and hygiene, are dominated by Islamist entrepreneurs who have managed to project this balance between ideological choice and social and commercial practice.

Every aspect of everyday life is suffused by a dense associative network, which is all the more effective in that it exposes the inadequacies of state policy. Governments often react by restricting civil liberties. At the end of November 1992, for instance, a few weeks after an earthquake, the Egyptian government, after demonstrating its inability to organize assistance, issued a decree prohibiting fund-raising by non-governmental organizations, even for humanitarian purposes. The same thing happened after 17 February 1993, when the minimum participation for valid trade union elections, which traditionally attract a low turnout, was fixed at 55 per cent for the first round and 30 per cent for the second round of ballots; if these levels were not reached, the trade unions were to be placed under judicial control.[26]

---

[23] Ph.B. Kabongo-Mbaya, 'Protestantisme zaïrois et déclin du mobutisme', *Politique africaine*, 41 (1991), pp. 72–89.
[24] ibid. p. 73.
[25] Boillot, 'L'Église catholique', p. 131.
[26] F. Burgat, 'Les mutations d'un Islam pluriel', *Le Monde diplomatique*, June 1993.

Education is the prime strategic objective of religious activists, whether Muslim or Christian.

> We cannot talk about development without linking it to an educational policy. The governments in Islamic countries do not try to develop the creative potential of all social groups. On the contrary, they rely on a philosophy of security based on conservatism and the increase of inequality . . . which leaves plenty of scope for education as a mode of political action.[27]

Islamist groups in Morocco, for example, have pursued this objective in two ways. The first is the establishment of private schools affiliated to various groups, starting at kindergarten level. A case in point is *jama'at attabligh*, which has set up a network of schools since the mid-1970s encouraged by the existence of a private education sector which had been greatly influenced by the nationalist movement ever since the mid-1940s, but which has developed enormously due to the deterioration of state education. A second approach has been to concentrate conversion activities within the educational system. Thus the universities were one of the priority objectives of groups like the *'adl wa al ihssan* ('Justice and Self-commitment') in Morocco, *annahda* ('Renewal') in Tunisia, and *hamas*, an Islamist party in Algeria. At present the student union movement is largely dominated by these groups.

The first manifestation of an organized Islamist presence on the Casablanca university campus appeared in connection with the council of residents on the university site during 1979–80. It was also at this time that the first Islamic cultural week was held after Abdessalam Yacine, the leader of the *'adl al ihssan* organization in Morocco, had included the holding of these events within the activist project of the movement, which still lacked backbone at the time. The city mosque was the nerve centre of the movement, which began to move away from the Islamic Youth movement *Chabiba islamiya*. Towards the middle of the 1980s, the Islamist university movement was organized around three groups: *al islah wa attajdid*, ('Reform and Revival'), *al adl wa al ihssan* ('Justice and Self-commitment') and the militants of *Chabiba islamiya*, divided between the activists and a more political wing inspired by Rachid Ghannouchi, the leader of the Tunisian *nahda*.

Currently, all the leaders of the Casablanca student movement (the object of a survey conducted at the beginning of 1995) are Islamists. These 64 students are from the faculties of law, humanities and sciences at the university. They are relatively young: less than 12 per cent of them were born before 1970, and the average student age is 23. Even though there are no female students among the leadership, women do have a strong presence on the campus and in the lecture halls.

The academic careers of the student leaders appear to be normal. In other words, their average length of study rarely exceeds five years for a four-year course. This is true of 75 per cent of them. Less than 20 per cent have had to repeat a year during their study, even in the sciences. This relatively high rate of success can be explained by the values upheld by the movement, which insists on high performance and tailors student union activity to meet this need: the diffusion of textbooks for examination subjects, photocopies of the best periodicals, group revision, explanatory sessions, etc.

The language of study does not seem to affect the choice for militancy. In the law faculty, the balance between economists and jurists mirrors the characteristics of the membership of the faculty as a whole (55 per cent for the former), which perhaps reflects the existence of an agreed distribution. The only anomaly which could add weight to the language variable is the absence of French-speaking jurists and publicists. In the

---

[27] *Assahwa*, 26, (1993) p. 15.

humanities faculty, Arabic-related courses (Islamic studies and Arabic literature) account for 75 per cent of the students. This is not surprising; what is surprising is that 25 per cent of the student leaders are studying English literature.

Teacher training colleges and secondary schools are the target of intensive cultural activity. Islamist teachers promote extra-curricular activities intended to compensate for the inadequacy of the educational system. Free supplementary courses are provided for pupils who have fallen behind with their studies, free advanced courses and collective revision classes enable Islamists to assert their presence and to recruit among future students and teachers on a large scale. One religious leader, Mohamed Yatim, shows that the cultural activism which was considered by Islamist associations simply as a means of providing opportunities for militants who could not find a place in the existing political structure, has now proved to be an avant-garde activity giving militants a direct relationship with society.[28]

The lowering of standards in the public sector as a result of the increase in class size and the reduction in the number of teachers offers enormous scope for action. In one school in a working-class suburb of Casablanca, an Islamist group infiltrated the administration and part of the teaching staff. With the complicity of the latter, it even created classes for Islamist children, who benefit from special treatment so as to become the best pupils in the school. The comparison with the others is supposed to suggest that their success at school is due to their religious commitment.

In Nigeria, the renewal of Islamic education is a top priority of the *ulema* in the *izala* movement. According to the author of an important book on Islamic political thought, Shehu Umar Abdullahi,[29] education is 'the most effective weapon to combat social and moral decadence and economic stagnation', except that 'the Western-style schools and universities which mould the aspirations and behaviour of the Nigerian elite are based on a secular conception which is bound to result in an amoral materialism'. These criticisms are also directed at the traditional Muslim educational system, which is accused of producing more ignoramuses than educated people. The new clergy, who are often trained in the Saudi universities and only occasionally at Cairo's Al Azhar, have a preference for the Islamya schools and the universities of the North (Kano, Sokoto, Zaria). They also welcome the initiatives of certain reformist Islamic associations such as *jama'at annasr al Islami* ('The Group of Islamic Victory'), *izala* and others.

The *izala* movement claims to have established more than 2,843 schools for married women. This large number is explained by the fact that, apart from the schools founded by the movement, many educated women give lessons at home, which is considered an act of extreme piety. The movement has also set up two secondary schools, which confer a diploma recognized by the committee of the *ulema*. Other centres of Islamic education controlled by the Islamist associations provide continuous programmes offering religious education for adults. The Souleiman Crescent centre is one of the largest centres of religious education for married women.[30]

In the countries of the Sahel, young educated people, having benefited from grants from the Arab countries (Saudi Arabia, Libya, Morocco), favour the *medersa* schools and the modern Islamic university. Lessons are in Arabic. The *medersas* also provide language courses and high quality technical and scientific courses. The aim is to produce an Islamist

[28] *Araya*, 32, November 1992.
[29] Quoted by C. Coulon, 'Les nouveaux ulama et la résurgence islamique au Nord Nigéria', *Islam et société au Sud du Sahara*, 1 (1987), p. 44.
[30] Kane, 'Les mouvements islamiques', p. 226.

counter-elite. In Mali, Niger, Chad and Burkina Faso a veritable parallel system is in the process of construction.[31]

In the field of health, the social activism of the churches influences the nature of the apostolic mission. The content of the religious message tends to conform to the local situation. This leads to the creation of new meanings, referring to indigenous conceptions of illness and healing, piety and sanctity.

A spectacular development of therapeutic centres took place in Brazzaville between 1976 and 1981. The faithful form a healing group through collective prayer led by a pastor. The origin of these therapeutic centres goes back to 1948, when the pastor Daniel Ndoundou cured a paralysed child during a public service. This development is in answer to popular demand, which is itself exacerbated by a chronic lack of health-care facilities.[32]

More than just an attempt on the part of the church to adapt to the conceptions of illness and healing, this represents a major initiative to occupy social space. With 100,000 adult members in 1981, the Congolese Protestant Church, the result of a small Swedish evangelical mission, is the second largest religious group in the Congo today. It has 64 parochial therapeutic centres (11 in Brazzaville) whose operations are based on a 'traditional revealed' approach; they draw on the mobilization of indigenous pharmacological knowledge, collective prayer and mystic gifts, accompanied, recognized or even controlled by the church. 'This therapeutic vocation arises from a mystic movement qualified as "spiritual reawakening"', which marks the beginning of the transformation of the Protestant mission to its local setting.[33] In fact, the mission has merely remained faithful to its ecstatic calling because of its origins as a breakaway from the Swedish Lutheran Church at the end of the nineteenth century, rather than to any specific strategy of acculturation to Africa.

Parochial therapeutic centres owe their success to a double adaptation to urban demand. In contrast to the apathy of the public health services, they present an image of competence, they are local, they are almost free of charge and they offer an incomparable quality of care. In contrast to the various 'traditional healers' (who are often charlatans) and the minor therapeutic sects which are rife in the capital, they guarantee impartiality and unfailing honesty. Finally, as a result of the divine grace appealed to in prayer, they offer a solution to allegedly 'supernatural' afflictions which avoids having to cast doubt on notions of sorcery and also aggravating family conflicts exacerbated by the urban environment and its inequities.

Similar phenomena can be observed practically everywhere in Africa. The religious renewal aims to invade social space by means of the promotion of local services. The new options for development implied in the participatory approach of basic communities, adopted in the face of the incapacity of the bureaucracies of the new states, put the churches in a favourable position. Their experience in social work makes them the leading non-governmental organizations in the field. In the Muslim countries, the phenomenon is less visible because of the absence of clergy. Nevertheless, one can see the same trends in Islamist investments in the health sector and in the renewal of the Islam of the *marabouts*, holy men associated with the brotherhoods. Unlike the traditional clergy, Islamists operate in the field of modern medicine.

[31] 'Les islamistes à l'assaut de l'Afrique noire', *Jeune Afrique économie*, November 1994.

[32] G. Balandier, *Sociologie actuelle de l'Afrique noire* (PUF, Paris, 1982).

[33] Elisabeth Dorier-Apprill, 'Christianisme et thérapeutique à Brazzaville', *Politique africaine*, 55 (October 1994), pp. 133–139.

In Egypt, in the working-class districts of Cairo, Islamic reform groups have opened consulting rooms run by volunteer doctors. The service is almost free of charge and is of good quality, in contrast to the run-down condition of the state hospitals and the exorbitant cost of private medical care.

In Morocco the pietist group, *jama'at attabligh*, whose main function is preaching, has set up a permanent scheme for hospital and prison visits. In a different field, Islamist groups, especially *al islah wa attajdid*, are conducting specific activities in the public hospitals which are abandoned by medical staff who have gone into private practice. It is increasingly these doctors, who are followers of *islah* or *adl wal ihhssan*, who practise with a commitment that draws attention. The term 'Islamist' in this respect is often a synonym for seriousness, competence and moral integrity.

## Women and Religious Renewal

Pictures of Iranian women in long black robes riding brightly coloured toboggans in a Teheran leisure park, or of young girls in white Islamic veils speaking in a lecture hall in front of an audience of students impressed by such self-assurance, riding motorscooters or jogging in the suburbs of Casablanca, call into question clichés which have been dominant for decades. They lead us to question the status of women as victims of 'fundamentalism' and to try and explain why these girls and women take part in the movements of religious renewal on such a massive scale.[34]

It seemed so obvious that women, like minorities, were the victims of rampant obscurantism, that determined efforts have been made to alert them to this fact without considering the opinions of the women themselves, who are after all the people involved. On the face of it, examination of the careers of female militants in the Islamist organizations would imply a certain functionalism in their choice of these options. When one takes the trouble to put it directly,[35] the vital question is: in what respect is the practice of Islam opposed to their access to modernity? Given that the latter is not a universal extension of Western civilization, the reply is not as clear-cut as has sometimes been supposed.

The rift between the situation of women in traditional society and the horizon of expectations opened up through education and urbanization, leads to the emergence of multiple strategies of upward social mobility. The demand for respect for the letter of the religious law is one of them. It enables women to gain access to public space by adopting Islamic dress, and to demand the application of the *shari'a* or Islamic law in order to be able to inherit property, work outside the home, engage in trade, and manage their own inheritance autonomously. Islamic and traditional societies are not necessarily synonymous. The spectrum of Islamic sensibilities is broad enough to accommodate a range of diversities.

There are enormous differences between the policies of the militants of the Armed Islamic Group (GIA) – who have even fired on young school girls – the *hamas* Islamists of Sheikh Nahnah in Algeria, and those of the Reform and Renewal Movement in Morocco. Moreover, within the various movements discussion of doctrine increasingly tends to reveal a certain tolerance, reflecting the liveliness of internal debates. In the last

---

[34] Fariba Abelkhahf, J.-F. Bayart & O. Roy, *Thermidor en Iran* (Ed. Complexe, Brussels, 1992).

[35] Fariba Abelkhahf, 'Femmes islamiques, femmes modernes', *Pouvoir*, 62 (1992), pp. 93–107.

ten years there has been an evolution towards the adoption of certain firm principles that even Islamists can no longer ignore: women's activities, the equality of the sexes, and access to school education. These currents, although sometimes expressed by minority groups, point to a clear distinction between a traditional society which locks women up in a tangle of restrictive rules and makes them figures of the shadows, and their own demands for an Islamist society. They do not speak of a return to the tradition of their mothers.

The emblematic character of the controversy surrounding the wearing of the *hijab* or Islamic veil demonstrates the nuances of the Islamist position. The Islamist view, while based on the texts of the *shari'a*, insists on the objective of dignified access to public space. The example of the young Muslim women who belong to the Islamist Reform and Renewal group in Morocco allows us to make certain distinctions. 'Several explanations', it is said, 'are given for the phenomenon of the adoption of the *hijab* by Muslim women.' It is often taken as a collective rejection of modernity, a response to a situation of poverty and absolute misery. However, it should be pointed out that the *hijab* first emerged among a group of educated young women who are not all poor. The *hijab* is not just a protest against all forms of immorality. Nor do I perceive any relation between the spread of the *hijab* and the demand that women should return to the home and give up their jobs. The *hijab* has been defended by those who work outside the home.[36] According to Rabi'a Sarah, a Muslim graduate in history and geography, the relation of Islamists to the question of women is determined by three factors:

(i) the legacy of traditional society which has dominated for centuries, with all of the static and negative views it upholds on women's participation. This turned women into prisoners who only left their husband's home for the grave. Victims of illiteracy, they were treated like slaves and enjoyed no rights, including those of inheritance;

(ii) the values of modern society which treats women as objects whose only value is that of a commodity;

(iii) the third factor is constituted by the very principles of the *shari'a*, which are interpreted by certain Islamists as favouring an eclectic approach based on a radical and literal reading of the sacred texts. Women are prevented from studying, mixing with men, and appearing in public places, while the spirit of the revelation is based on the fundamental principle of equality.[37]

One cannot judge these positions only by considering them as tactical choices, a sort of historical compromise awaiting the assumption of power. A radical reading of the sacred texts is bound to generate new social practices whose consequences are irreversible, especially when it is performed by militants in a situation of upward mobility who are in positions of power in their own movement.

There is no lack of examples to illustrate this. For instance, the first woman to be elected to the Sudanese parliament in 1986 stood – like her colleague on the executive of the Egyptian medical union in 1992 – on an Islamist list.[38] In 1990–91 the FIS based its campaign on the personal votes of Algerian women, while it was the militants of the governing *Front de libération nationale* (FLN) who resisted the call to ban voting by proxy, and used the ballot cards of their wives, daughters and sisters, to vote in their stead.

On the Kenyan coast, far from being a refuge in tradition, conversion to Islam is a

---

[36] *Revue Al fûrqan*, 11, 1988.
[37] ibid.
[38] Burgat, 'Les mutations d'un islam pluriel'.

necessity for Giriama women who come to the city to look for work and need to avoid the evils of prostitution or at least disrepute and dishonour.[39]

In Nigeria, the *izala* movement excels in the emancipation of women. According to Hausa tradition, women are confined once they are married. A tradition states that 'every woman who crosses the threshold of her home commits an infamy which will bring on a drought or will lead 70,000 of her relatives to hell'. Thousands of girls' schools and adult training centres for women allow for the promotion of women. *Izala* gives this objective top priority in its programme. The number of female pupils is estimated at 1.6 million (although this figure is certainly an exaggeration).[40] The same group promotes a women's section within its own ranks, allows it to take part in the procession on the First of May and opens its newspaper columns to women's literary efforts.

Even outside Islamist circles, in the Islamic brotherhoods, the idea that in Africa, more than elsewhere in the Muslim world, women are the repositories of pre-Islamic religious traditions, is often invalidated by a study of actual religious experience. Women seem able to put into their proper context the often contrived discourses of religious leaders, who are usually men.

The renewal of the Islamic brotherhoods in East Africa has also caused a break with tradition. The brotherhoods emphasize that 'the equality of the faithful and the need for religious education for all, including women and slaves, the interest in magic or ecstatic manifestations and acceptance of a festive dimension in . . . religious ritual (music, *maulidi*) meant that the attitude of the Sheikh towards women differed from conventional attitudes. Not that the Sheikh particularly seeks a female following; simply, the principles of associative activity made them one of the most receptive groups among the under-privileged . . . Admission to the *tariqa* is the result of a free and individual choice for everyone',[41] which is subversive in relation to the clan and tribal order.

> Whatever her social status, a woman's decision to associate with a brotherhood is made personally, independent of the choices made by her husband or family. If she made this choice before marriage, it is not affected at all by marriage. This spiritual choice which creates an allegiance is independent of the vicissitudes of her private life (and therefore of her matrimonial status).[42]

Thus, in a region extending from Somalia to Lake Malawi, the *tariqa* demonstrates that there is room for women's self-determination in an area of life which is neither individually nor socially insignificant: religious affiliation.

In relation to the same point, the case of Sokhna Magat Diop – a female *marabout* from the *mouride* brotherhood in Senegal – may illustrate the mechanisms which enable women to be authentic religious agents and leaders. She has made use of religious culture in the sense of an explicit mystic asceticism (use of the *khalawa* or place of spiritual retreat) in order to remove herself from the public realm (i.e. she may not lead prayers or preside over marriage ceremonies). On the other hand, she is recognized as possessing all the attributes of a *marabout*, notably the exemption from initiation and the granting of the *werd* or special prayer of Ahmadu Bamba, the founder of the *mourides*. Sokhna Magat Diop was admitted to the caliphate of a very powerful *mouride* branch at the age of 26.[43]

---

[39] R. Peake, 'Comment on devient swahili. Stratégies des femmes giriama en ville', in F. Le Guennec-Coppens & P. Caplan (eds), *Les swahili entre Afrique et Arabie* (Karthala, Paris, 1991), pp. 95–107.
[40] Kane, 'Les mouvements islamiques', p. 226.
[41] F. Constantin, 'Condition féminine et dynamique confrérique en Afrique orientale', *Islam et société au sud du Sahara*, 1 (1987), p. 63–4.
[42] ibid., p. 64.
[43] C. Coulon & Odile Reveyrand, 'L'Islam au féminin: Sokhna Magat Diop, Cheikh de la confrérie mouride (Sénégal)', Centre d'Étude d'Afrique Noire, University of Bordeaux I, *Travaux et documents* 25 (1990), p. 4.

These examples are not intended to absolve religion from its historical responsibility, but simply to avoid over-simplifications and to suggest different ways of viewing the changes that are currently taking place. Strategies of modernization may take the path of religion just as easily as that of political authoritarianism. Movements of religious renewal tend to serve, among other things, as the framework for a renegotiation of social pacts. The promotion of morality as a mode of operation also entails the establishment of the biological category of femininity as a fundamental social category capable of creating a process of individuation which develops in spite of the actors themselves. They often invent modernity while believing that they are engaged in a scrupulous respect for tradition.

## Conclusion

Religious renewal movements do not necessarily take on the same form in every country and in every religion, despite the fact that resemblances can be found everywhere. In a religion like Catholicism, which is centred on a single church, new movements are mainly to be observed in the institutional field, while in Islam it is the ideological vector which tends to be the most important. Nevertheless, this essay allows us to underline certain constants. Religions confront the question of political choices directly.

They adapt to their environment through a redefinition of orthodoxy and a great capacity for syncretism. The demand for political participation by a new generation is asserted violently whenever states restrict opportunities for expression. The object of the renewal is still, at this stage, the organization of society. But the question of power is not far from this call for a better appreciation of the primordial human factors which create the wealth of nations, and nor is the redefinition of morality.

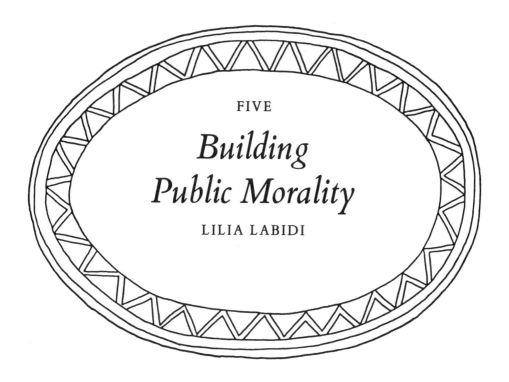

FIVE

# Building Public Morality

LILIA LABIDI

With the arrival of independence in Africa, the popular imagination came to be dominated by two models. New nation-states promised a remedy for the continent's underdevelopment; at the same time, the young in particular were offered a Western model of progress and consumption. Two decades later, the failure of theories of development and the limits of what welfare states were able to achieve were already becoming obvious, and contradictions increasingly evident. A feeling of bitterness set in. The improvement in some social welfare indicators led among other things to a demographic explosion.[1] This has caused an immediate deterioration of the prospects for the younger generation whose basic expectations could not be fulfilled and whose rights could no longer be guaranteed. It is the tensions resulting from this state of affairs which have led to the social crises which are to be found throughout North Africa; in Algeria and Egypt the most acute expressions of this are problems of unemployment and housing. Some sections of the population feel they have been cynically abandoned by their

---

[1] World Bank, *World Development Report 1992: Development and the environment* (Oxford University Press, New York 1992). In the case of North Africa, for example, Algeria has a fertility rate of 3.7 and a total foreign debt of $26,806 million, Egypt has a fertility rate of 3.1 and a debt of $39,885 million, while Tunisia's fertility rate is 2.7 and its debt amounts to $7,534 million. These figures show how the demographic situation of Africa, which has the highest population growth rate in the world, is a threat to its economic take-off. Within one generation, the continent's population will increase from 682 million to 1.6 billion. The average fertility rate is six children per woman, but in certain instances reaches seven or more.

leaders, a sentiment which the Algerian writer Rachid Mimouni describes in his novel *Tombéza*.[2]

Among the leading victims of this situation are women. Eking out skimpy budgets, they literally pay with their lives. Since 1991, hundreds of women have been singled out for murder in Algeria. The victims include secondary school students, young girls, mothers, employees, doctors, artists and militants. These modern-day equivalents of Scheherazade[3] become the ornaments of their executioners' distress. Each of these murders typically appears to be the act of people obsessed[4] with notions of defilement, sin, transgression of a religious code. These women are no longer even seen as objects, but as figures of utter abjection. Their murders are a reflection of their murderers' social frustration and moral confusion.

These are the symptoms of societies which have lost their senses, and have come to trade in human lives. This takes a number of forms, including the trade in domestic servants for purposes of every sort, juvenile prostitution, marriages of pubescent girls to rich men of advanced age, and the trade in human organs as the ultimate solution for people in economic adversity. Such violence may be located within a history of the human body in Africa, marked by the slave trade and the trade in eunuchs that have obscured the experience of happiness. A search for understanding of the lengths to which human beings will go in response to extreme economic difficulties leads us to consider the nature of the relationships between citizens today and the independent states of Africa. This requires an appreciation of the evolution of popular thinking about personal and family morality in relation to the rights and duties of the welfare state.

## Economic Crisis or Crisis of the Individual?

The data for the present essay are drawn from a number of extreme cases from Egypt and Tunisia. The purpose of studying these is to arrive at an understanding of the issues raised by such behaviour as the sale of human organs and the maltreatment of children as responses to economic difficulties, and to discover what this might reveal about the relationships developed by citizens born in the generations since independence.[5] Common to these situations is an aggressiveness towards human life and a series of assaults on the human body. What sort of political culture is connected with such actions, and what are the psychological imperatives which produce such behaviour as the following?:

- people who make use of the possibilities of modern technology in order to sell their own internal organs in order to survive;
- children who are suffering from extreme malnutrition but are not taken to hospitals or clinics, where preventive care is free, until they are at the point of death.

### The language of symptoms

Hayet has been divorced by her husband because he can no longer pay for her medical treatment. She begins selling her possessions one by one until she eventually decides to

---

[2] R. Mimouni, *Tombéza* (Editions Laffont, Paris, 1984).

[3] Scheherazade is a character in *A Thousand and One Nights*. Every night she had to tell a story to keep the sultan awake until dawn; this was the only way she could avoid being another victim.

[4] J. Kristeva, 'L'expérience imaginaire', *Le Monde*, 5 November 1993.

[5] This material is drawn from a comparative study I have been directing since 1994 on 'Death, popular cultures and modern medicine in the contemporary Arab world' both in hospitals and among the population in general.

sell one of her organs. In a local newspaper she reads an advertisement placed by someone wanting to purchase a kidney. When she arrives at the place mentioned in the advertisement, she finds that other people have already responded to the same advertisement. Some time later, a citizen of an Arab country offers her £E20,000 for her corneas, one to be transferred immediately and the other after her death. The doctor refuses to carry out the operation. Finally, she reaches the point of placing an advertisement in a newspaper offering to sell her corneas in order to be able to gain an honest living.[6]

Naoufal wants to sell a kidney but, out of shame, prefers to exchange it for a house. He enters into a negotiation about the location of the house: one house costs £E50,000, another £E22,000. Finally, vendor and buyer agree on a house priced at £E25,000; the house is to be resold as soon as the organ is handed over.[7]

Kamel, aged 27, has been selling his blood for fifteen years. For a litre of blood he gets £E20.[8]

Omrani, a young student, offers his kidney for £E12,000, but the middleman disappears with the money.[9]

Moustapha, aged 35, married with seven children, in order to raise the money for school fees goes to a laboratory and offers to sell a kidney for £E10,000.[10]

People whose kidneys are no longer able to function efficiently generally require repeated dialysis treatment.[11] A longer-lasting solution for a person suffering from a kidney malfunction of this sort is to receive a kidney transplant, which allows patients to return to full health and to resume their family and professional life. In Egypt, the demand for kidney transplants is estimated to be between 2,000 and 3,000 cases a year, although other sources put the figure at 5,000,[12] only a tenth of which is currently met.[13] The shortfall between those who receive a kidney transplant and those on a hospital waiting-list opens up the possibility for a range of malpractices and creates a market in low-income societies. These figures do not take account of foreigners who pass through Egypt specifically for medical care, most of whom are treated within the private sector and whose numbers are not recorded.

Women participate in the trade in human organs less than men. However, there are both men and women who sell or attempt to sell their organs, often because of their inability to cope with their daily problems or because of the lure of quick money.

The ages and the amounts involved vary. Sellers of organs can be young or old. Some are Egyptian and others are from sub-Saharan Africa. The buyers can be either local people or from neighbouring regions.[14] The price of organs varies. Thus, placentas sell for £E2 each. The price of bones is somewhere between that of a placenta and blood, which costs £E20 per litre. Kidneys vary greatly in price, from £E10,000 to £E30,000. Corneas can fetch £E20,000. The liver, as the most valuable product on the market, can sell for £E1 million per kilogram. Naturally, all those involved are aware that an organ sold

[6] *Saout El Arab*, 4 January 1987.

[7] *Akhar Saa*, 5 March 1989.

[8] *Echaab*, 8 November 1988.

[9] *Akhar Saa*, 20 September 1991.

[10] *El Lioua El Islami*, 13 October 1991.

[11] J.P. Wauters, 'Système de santé et mortalité: un exemple néphrologique?', *Médecine et hygiène*, 23 February 1994. The author shows how terminal chronic kidney incapacity provides a good example of the interaction between health-care systems, mortality, morbidity and quality of life on the basis of an example drawn from the United States.

[12] *El Akhbar*, 6 June 1990.

[13] *Akhar Saa* and *El Akhbar*, 27 March 1987.

[14] *El Ahali*, 11 April 1990; *El Akhbar*, 2 April 1989.

for £E10,000 can be sold in the West for 15 times as much, or about £30,000 sterling.[15]

The last few years have seen efforts by Arab countries to define a legal framework for organ transplants from corpses. Paradoxically, Egypt, the first country in the region to establish a modern medical school in 1830, has yet to legislate on this subject. The authorities leave it to the patient to find a donor within his or her family. It is this which leads to situations in which the poor are prepared to allow themselves to be mutilated in return for the money they need to live. In October 1994, a 36-year-old unemployed Sudanese national was arrested in Egypt for selling organs taken from Sudanese and resold for between £E10,000 and £E20,000 to Arab customers, on the basis of false medical documents.[16]

We have not encountered such cases in Tunisia, where problems of this sort are not as acute as in Egypt and where legislation authorizing the transplant of organs from corpses was enacted in 1991. However, a rumour which circulated during the 1980s is eloquent with regard to the tensions that have begun to emerge: it was rumoured that a young girl had been found in the street of a working-class suburban neighbourhood with a kidney removed.

A continuation of this line of inquiry is based on an investigation of mothers of malnourished children affected by kwashiorkor during the 1980s.[17] Kwashiorkor is a disease which affects some children in the months following their weaning, essentially as a result of protein malnutrition. They lose weight, suffer from diarrhoea, oedema, changes in their skin, nails and hair, which becomes dry, thin, faded and brittle. The children's behaviour is apathetic. They are generally fearful and listless, and either become introverted or hostile and irritable, while their malnutrition makes them more vulnerable to other infections. The disease leads inevitably to the child's death unless an appropriate programme of remedial nutrition is adopted in time. The condition is found only in developing countries, where it is known as the 'disease of poverty'.

Interviews conducted by psychologists with a group of sixty-two mothers reveal a distinctive characteristic of these cases. In this group, the children affected by the disease were the only ones among their siblings to be affected by it; the other children in the family were healthy. Why do mothers wait so long before seeking treatment? Their answer is generally that they did not notice that anything was wrong, that they are single mothers, that they have no money and have no confidence in doctors. What do these children represent? What information can we glean from these cases? We shall try to put into words a situation which is the product of a culture of silence, and to draw conclusions from the experience of mothers of malnourished children, in the belief that this might provide further material for reflection on aspects of social reality.

Two-thirds of the children surveyed in our sample were weaned before their third month. Almost half (45 per cent) of the mothers recognized that their children had responded badly to weaning. 81 per cent of the mothers came from rural areas and were alone when they gave birth. 42 per cent of them did not want their pregnancy, and their families had an average of three children. 42 per cent of them lived in a single room, 47 per cent did not have running water in their homes and 72 per cent used only a brazier for heating. 40 per cent of the couples were consanguineous, 52 per cent of

[15] *El Ahram*, 22 January 1990; *Akhbar El Yaoum*, 20 August 1991.

[16] *Jamhouria*, 30 October 1994.

[17] S. Khadraoui, L. Labidi & B. Hamza, 'Mères d'enfants malnutris', *Revue tunisienne de pédiatrie*, 7, 1 (1986). Regarding marital expectations, see H. Moore, *Is There a Crisis in the Family?* (UNRISD, Geneva, 1994).

the women did not plan their pregnancies and 20 per cent admitted to having conflicts with their partners.

Such cases of the sale of body organs and of the maltreatment[18] of young children have in common an element of violence, in the first case directed at the self and, in the second, against another. Further, both types of case are relevant to a broader discussion of the economic crisis that has overtaken North Africa since the late 1970s. We refer to these cases as a means of better understanding the experience of these marginalized people, of identifying the precise context in which such events happen, and of examining whether they might reveal something about the wider political and cultural system. The cases mentioned here are data for the analysis of those societies in Africa where women are held in low esteem, where corruption is rampant and drains countries of their resources – thus destroying any meagre savings the poor might make – , where the expansion of the market has had a negative effect on local economies, and where the system of education inherited from the colonial state makes traditional values obsolete. Finally, these cases occur in societies in which the young move from the countryside to the cities where many lead an existence on the margins of society.

The cases we have described provide material for four distinct debates which are taking place within the region: first, on the precariousness of mechanisms for the protection of women's rights; second, on corruption; third, on the existence of economic and educational models of development which mark a break with local and regional traditions; and fourth, on the exodus of the young to the large urban centres. The examples we have given are admittedly extreme ones, but they do nonetheless illustrate the real oppression which exists in these societies as they undergo profound transformation. They may lead us to consider the reasons why people in situations of hopelessness and who are unable to overcome their economic problems turn their anger on themselves or their children, or both. What ideology underlies such behaviour? What type of culture produces it?

## Self-hatred

To establish a connection between these things and the ideology and culture within which they are embedded, it is first necessary to recall some of the dominant elements of the culture of the region in order better to grasp the significance of such transgressions of moral behaviour. Popular culture in North Africa maintains that the human body belongs to God. Man is only the guardian and is not responsible for the body's existence, whether in life or in death. It is this conception of the body which prevents the passing of legislation in Egypt to authorize the transplant of organs from corpses. The argument is clearly based on Islamic culture, but its antecedents go right back to the heritage of the pharaohs which continues to exercise a powerful influence on Egyptians today. In Egypt, there is a fundamental conception that the living owe a debt of honour to the dead, which is fulfilled by burying a corpse immediately after death so as to protect it from decomposition and to preserve its dignity. Some medical practitioners go so far as to reject the medical definition of brain death and subscribe to a theologically-based definition of death.

---

[18] cf. S. Siala, 'Incidence de la malnutrition protéino-calorique' (Doctoral thesis in medicine, Tunis University, 1977). Of the 845 children who attended a mother and child care centre in a semi-rural district on the edge of Tunis, 33.85% were malnourished (of whom 54.20% were girls). K. Limam, "Enquête sur la malnutrition protéino-calorique dans la région de Moknine. Étude comparative entre le milieu urbain et le milieu rural' (Doctoral thesis in medicine, Tunis University, 1981), demonstrates that girls are more exposed than boys to malnutrition.

The attacks against human life that have occurred in these societies since the 1980s have been aimed at the body. Such self-destructive practices, generated by aggression against the self, are reminiscent of the compulsion to self-punishment found in clinical studies of melancholia. In Western societies, manifestations of this sort can even lead to suicide, which is strictly forbidden in Islamic societies. Attempts to live in situations of such acute distress or humiliation as to drive people to the sale of their own organs are extreme examples whose study can help us discover the motives for behaviour of this general type. Naoufal, for example, whose case is cited above, is ashamed of selling his own kidney, but does so by disguising the trade as a real-estate transaction; this is suggestive of self-punishment as a motive, although his action is superficially the unwanted consequence of certain immoral and violent actions.

The aggressiveness involved in the sale of organs, a crime against life, is a reflection of the pernicious silence which surrounds the corruption and violence of a justice system which excludes those who do not have friends in the right places, and of the unbearable pressures which lead towards conflict which surfaces in the form of sporadic outbursts of popular violence. When popular violence does occur, it is testimony to the lack of effectiveness of those organizations which are supposed to oversee the interests of the poor and the excluded and, similarly, of the ineffectiveness of those social movements which represent the marginalized, other than religion in which people can locate their identity and express their ideal ego. The work of H. Nunberg[19] shows how the ideal ego of subjects, whose structure is similar to the cases in our study, is defined as a strongly narcissistic ideal, based on the same model as infantile narcissism to which, in cases of psychosis, the adult strives to return. Lagache[20] suggests that the ideal ego involves an identification with the mother, invested with absolute power, which he describes as a heroic identification with prestigious personalities. For Lacan,[21] the ideal ego is essentially a narcissistic phenomenon, which originates in the mirror stage and is a product of the imagination. The ideal ego has sado-masochistic implications, notably in the negation of the other, correlative to the affirmation of the self, and is characterized by its dual character.

An identification suggested by the prevailing religious code transforms the mother into *aoura*,[22] because of her identification with her sexual organ, thus obliging her to veil herself. This leaves the subject with only two alternatives in reaching the oedipal phase: either an identification with the aggressor, with all the implications of obedience, submission, subordination to the leader and the social consensus, or an escape to the margins of the situation.[23] This reading throws some light on the reasons for violence directed at the self and absolves the locus of power from any fundamental challenge, thus confirming the group consensus which surrounds the established order, rendering the excluded subject guilty and responsible for his or her condition.

What, then, is the relationship between the voluntary sale of organs and the murder

[19] H. Nunberg, *Principes de psychanalyse* (PUF, Paris, 1957).

[20] D. Lagache, 'La psychanalyse et la structure de la personnalité', *La psychanalyse*, VI (1957), pp. 41–43.

[21] J. Lacan, 'Remarques sur le rapport de Daniel Lagache', *La psychanalyse*, VII (1958), pp. 133–46.

[22] See note 25 below.

[23] L. Labidi, 'Le passé ou le pouvoir de l'abject', in *Psychologie différentielle des sexes* (Centre d'Études et de Recherches Économiques et Sociales, Tunis, 1984). A.B. Bozeman establishes similarities with what we have pointed out. Physical violence might be used in human relations 'on a prodigious scale without offending social values and norms'. However, we regret that he attributes this characteristic to African societies in general. Quoted by Rob Buijtenhuijs and Elly Rijnierse, *Democratization in sub-Saharan Africa* (Research Reports No. 51, Afrika-studiecentrum, Leiden, 1993), p. 5.

of children through malnutrition? Before answering this question, we propose to return to what such acts might signify in order to grasp what the children suffering from kwashiorkor represent and what message they convey. During the course of research with mothers and children, we encountered 'diminished'[24] women, that is, women brought up in the culture of silence, who are moving hesitantly towards modernity, a condition into which they are often thrust with very limited resources. They reorganize their relationship to sexuality after ceasing to perceive themselves as a vessel of male desire and after becoming able to form a critical opinion of the male Other.[25] This path is often full of pitfalls, that is if women do not end up in madness or taking refuge in the *hijab*, the Islamic veil.

The mothers of children with kwashiorkor in our survey have crossed the dividing line between wanting the death of their children and the passage to acts of infanticide, and this appears to be a message which we may read into these cases. The women are no longer able to gratify their own narcissism. Following their uprooting from rural areas, these isolated and disoriented women are no longer entirely part of the world of tradition, nor are they entirely situated in the realm of modernity. They are unable either to reactivate the traditional mechanisms of mutual help or to overcome their economic difficulties by access to the social assistance provided by the state and the legal system. Their mistreatment of their own children is an index of their own failure. They wean their children early because they are no longer able to control their own unconscious aggression, identified by H. Deutsch[26] in her analysis of breast-feeding mothers. They oscillate between their own fear of being devoured and their impulse to destroy the child, which recalls the primitive fear of death in childbirth. This experience is strongest amongst those women who were alone when they gave birth. Women feel a strong need for a maternal substitute at these times, even if they have in fact rejected their own mothers. Among the women in our group, 81 per cent were alone when they gave birth and 32 per cent had acute problems during their pregnancy. Their anxiety and aggressive feelings affected their ability to produce breast-milk.

Fear and aggressiveness combine with their daily worries, sapping their strength and distracting them from their maternal duties which require them to limit their own narcissism, leading them to feel devalued. Two-thirds of the mothers weaned their children abruptly, disturbing the normal pattern of feeding. In refusing the child the appropriate nourishment, they inflict on it an oral frustration while also damaging their own maternal feeling of tenderness. The child's basic needs are no longer closely related to the mother's capacity to identify with the ego of her child nor to her need to satisfy the child's own requirements. Having become the victims of their own children, prematurely aged by the strains of life, the mothers project an indifference which they use to protect themselves against depression. The home, the place where love is properly expressed, is transformed into an arena of struggle for survival, not a place of life.

Other cases of criminal acts endangering life have been reported in Tunisia.[27] Criminal cases brought before the law-courts between 1970/71 and 1986/87 increased

[24] L. Labidi, *The Origins of Tunisian Feminist Movements* (in Arabic, 2nd edition, Tunis-Carthage, 1989).

[25] L. Labidi, *Cabra Hachma, Séxualité et tradition* (Dar Ennawras, Tunis, 1989). The author here deals with the redefinition of the status of sexuality and the passage from the status of the *aoura* woman, a sexual object who cannot make any part of her body visible to men, to that of an 'individual', who attempts to negotiate her relationships on new bases.

[26] H. Deutsch, *La psychologie des femmes* (PUF, Paris, 1973).

[27] A. Belloumi, 'La criminalité en Tunisie de 1970–1989: essai d'explication', in *Les déterminismes socio-culturels de la pauvreté en Tunisie* (CERES, Tunis, 1994).

from 13.8 per thousand to 27 per thousand. Acts involving a threat to life represented approximately 50 per cent of the total, with a large proportion of the cases resulting in convictions occurring in the major cities of Tunis, Sousse and Sfax. The rate of change in the crime statistics increases in line with rises in the cost of living, and diminishes when the standard of living improves. This supports the hypothesis of a disintegration of the moral frame of reference for those who move from a rural environment, accompanied by a breakdown in cultural mechanisms when rural and urban values are in conflict with one another. This happens all the more easily in the anonymity of the big cities.

The behaviour of citizens born since the time of national independence in response to economic difficulties reveals the psychological conflicts experienced by subjects of study who mutilate themselves in response to their inability to deal with new economic circumstances. The sale of bodily organs is a form of response to this situation in the absence of the development of a new ethics, whereas other victims express their solitude, dysfunction and loss of any sense of direction by ceasing to breast-feed their children. These are symptoms of economic difficulties which drive people to self-destruction. In the absence of a discourse that might reorganize and give expression to these feelings, such experiences can lead to violence perpetrated in conformity with the conventions of a culture which offers to men the prospect of submission to the political order and, to women, submission to the sexual order. This is a victory of tragedy over dialogue. In such circumstances, what ideas of personal and family morality in regard to the state might be developed?

## The Passage from Social Practice to Law

To understand relations between the citizen and the welfare state, we shall focus on the medical field because of its relevance to the cases examined above. It should be remembered that this field has undergone at least two profound changes over the last 30 or so years: first, in response to rapid technological and demographic change and, second, in the form of organizational changes consequent to the implementation of structural adjustment plans. Since the 1980s, reforms throughout North Africa designed in consultation with the IMF have aimed at encouraging households and insurance funds to pay a greater share of the expense of health care, in tandem with a progressive decrease in the role of the state, which is to limit itself to the provision of assistance to the poorer strata of society.[28] This is in contrast to the previous situation where, in the aftermath of independence during the 1950s, health-care policies generally enjoyed the full support of international organizations and attracted high levels of investment.

With the participation of international organizations such as the World Health Organization (WHO) and other United Nations agencies (UNICEF, UNDP, UNFPA, etc.), health care was extended to the poorer sections of society by means of mass prevention campaigns.[29] In our view, the economic limitations of the states which emerged at independence reveal the nature of the morality that governs each individual's view of personal and family responsibility. We may wonder if it is possible for this to pose a threat to the existence of the modern state in which the passage from social practice

---

[28] M. Ben Hamida et al., 'Analyse de quelques aspects du système de soins en Tunisie', Cahiers de sociologie et de démographie médicale, 32, ii–iii (1992).
[29] B. Tekçe, L. Oldham & F.C. Shorter, A Place to Live: Families and child health in a Cairo neighborhood (American University in Cairo Press, Cairo, 1994).

is translated into law. States which govern North African societies regard themselves as immune to a widespread revival of the traditional model of social morality known as *acabya*, in which the members of a tribe join together to oppose the central power, and from the intellectual crisis of its elite. We shall base our investigation of this possibility on the following:

• the cases of doctors who, due to lack of resources, send terminal patients home, thus saving the face of the welfare system by offering patients the opportunity to die in their own home, a practice approved by traditional morality. This occurs after the patients have been given a sense of being cared for and a prospect of a better quality of life.

• the cases of sick people who have to pay for their own treatment, thus exposing themselves as prey to criminals and professional middlemen who profit from the misery of others.

### The institutional limits

It is appropriate to consider the experience of health-care professionals in hospitals when they are confronted with patients for whom they can no longer provide the proper care. These doctors and nurses, like their patients, have to face a situation in which patients cannot be guaranteed care of the requisite quality because of poor hospital conditions. A patient diagnosed as being in the terminal phase of a disease is generally discharged to die at home. Powerless to prevent cases of preventable deaths, hospital staff attribute their failure to poor working conditions, the absence of proper equipment and insufficient human resources.[30] In situations where a doctor's priority is to save a patient's life, these limitations produce a strong sense of failure and frustration. Medical personnel generally are well aware of their status as the agents of a welfare state whose responsibility is to implement the ideals expounded during the struggle against colonialism. One of them told us the following:

> Unfortunately, there are patients that we could save and whose death we are unable to prevent. Although such cases are rare, that does not make them any less difficult for us to live with. . . . They are real nightmares. Many patients who die reach us when their diseases are already very advanced or after something has gone wrong during an operation. . . . it's very distressing.

An analysis of the medical discourse of the 1990s demonstrates how the practice of discharging terminal patients takes place within a situation of general crisis in the countries of the South, and which is broadly related to the post-colonial context, the failure of development policies and theories and the dependence of countries of the periphery on a centre whose achievements in technology and research are constantly improving. The shortage of resources means that hospital staff have to make decisions which, in effect, amount to passive euthanasia. Patients can be left feeling abandoned when they see the limits of the welfare state, after they have been led to expect a very different experience as a result of their exposure to images of modern medicine through the media or sometimes through travel.

In Côte d'Ivoire, for example, the devaluation of the CFA franc in January 1994 has led to a marked revival of traditional medical practices. The price of clinical medicines rapidly increased by 30 to 70 per cent, beyond the reach of many, and this has led to a five-fold increase in the price of a piece of tree-bark traditionally used as a treatment

---

[30] L. Labidi & T. Nacef, *Deuil impossible* (Sahar, Tunis, 1993).

for malaria. Sick people are making increased use of traditional healers, whose professional association has witnessed a membership increase of some 50 per cent in a few years, while attendance at university teaching hospitals dropped by about half in one year. According to nurses, patients without money for medicines are left untreated.[31]

These examples are an indication of the sense of unease of some of those working within public health-care institutions. The way in which sick people experience these same problems also has to be taken into account. Below, we describe two cases, one of a person suffering from chronic kidney problems, who hopes to benefit from a donated organ but who risks being exploited by unscrupulous middlemen. The second case relates to patients who are treated within state hospitals and have had organs stolen from them while they are still under the care of these institutions. The complicity of the medical profession in these practices demonstrates the gulf which separates the law from what actually takes place.

> Ali, having undergone one transplant, returns to dialysis after his body rejects the new organ. At the same time he places an advertisement in the newspapers in a search for a kidney donor. Four people respond. He has to pay all the expenses involved in checking the compatibility of donor and recipient. One of the donors meets the requirements, but the price he asks is very high. The deal falls through. The patient returns to square one and places another advertisement.[32]

> Hamza, on the advice of friends, travels from the interior of the country to a big city for treatment. In view of the high costs of dialysis and other problems, friends advise him to seek a transplant. No member of his family is prepared to donate an organ. He decides to buy a kidney on the open market. After several attempts, he finds a person to whom he gives, in part-payment, an advance of £E3,000. Although the preliminary analyses are inconclusive, the donor refuses to return his deposit. Another donor is found at a price of £E10,000 but he refuses to donate his kidney. Hamza is forced to sell his land to pay for treatment and to meet the costs he has incurred.[33]

There are cases of people who have entered hospital for treatment and have left, dead or alive, after having had one or more of their organs removed without their consent:[34]

> A family which discovers that their twelve-year-old deceased son has had his corneas removed and replaced by cotton wool, lodges a complaint against the hospital where he had been treated.[35]

> Hassen discovers that one of his kidneys has been removed without his consent. The response of the doctors at the hospital where he had been admitted is clear: they say that it is impossible that anyone could have stolen one of his kidneys. He continues: 'What would have happened if I had gone to a private hospital? They have stolen my youth, they have stolen my life, I have been handicapped at a time when I am still able-bodied . . . it happened so many years ago, I can't even lodge a complaint against the doctors. My story is simple, even if it sounds fantastic. It could happen to anybody and may have happened to others, but there was nobody to make their stories public. . . . One day I felt a pain in my abdomen and I went straight to the hospital . . . a large hospital offering free treatment. I was told that I had cancer. . . . After some X-rays they asked me to undergo surgery. . . . I entered the hospital in November 1979 and was discharged only on 14 June 1981. . . . There were further complications. I was hospitalized a number of times. . . . Once, when I was ill. . . . I was sent to another hospital closer to home. . . . A doctor asked me: 'When did you have your left kidney removed?' I couldn't believe what he was asking me and I said to myself: 'Has he just left medical school?' During another stay in hospital, the doctors confirmed his diagnosis. . . . Some of the staff advised me to keep quiet and to watch out for myself. . . . The real anguish is that I don't know who did it nor do I know who my kidney went to.'[36]

---

[31] 'Dévaluation et médecine traditionnelle', in La Presse (Tunisia), 15 March 1995.
[32] El Ahram, 13 July 1991.
[33] Akhar Saa, 10 December 1991.
[34] El Ouaf, 2 and 5 April 1989.
[35] El Ahram, 15 July 1991.
[36] Akhar Saa, 27 May 1990.

Cases in which organs are removed without the consent of the donors themselves or of their families are considered immoral and have been the subject of indignation on the part of the public, doctors and clerics.[37] The fact that such things have occurred within state hospitals makes them no better than middlemen. A doctor disclosed in an interview published in a Cairo newspaper that 50 per cent of the corneas removed from corpses are re-sold to private clinics and to Arab countries for hard currency.[38] This has provoked outrage from those who have to tolerate sub-standard medical treatment. Fear and distrust cloud the relations between patients and medical staff, and hospitals become objects of a suspicion which is hardly conducive to efficiency.

The introduction of an open market economy without the accompanying construction of an appropriate ethos is taking place at a time of crisis, including in the medical field which, thanks to the democratization of education, has experienced a significant growth in demand and jobs. Salaries, however, have tended to fall. Those doctors who do not have the means to go into private practice often choose to work abroad, in the Gulf states, Saudi Arabia or the West, or to join the public health system. This is also true of women in nursing and para-medical occupations. For example, figures from Kuwait in 1975 showed that 37 per cent of the country's doctors and 25 per cent of its nurses were Jordanian.[39] The complexity of the situation which arises from a general crisis of confidence in the medical profession has led to all sorts of distortions throughout the medical sector. After having worked for five years in Saudi Arabia, a young Egyptian paediatrician returned to his country following the Gulf War with savings of £E100,000. However, financial speculation had put his dreams out of reach. He finds that an apartment of approximately 200 square metres costs between £E130,000 and £E200,000 in either the public or the private sector, and he therefore decides that he has no other option than to emigrate once again and work and save for another ten years to fulfil his ambition.[40]

How many doctors want to leave their country and are waiting only for an opportunity? The disengagement of the state has had a profound effect on people who have invested so much hope in the education offered by the welfare state as a means of social advancement, but who now find themselves obliged to do a second job to survive. Faced with the difficulty of meeting their daily needs in a manner which they consider morally acceptable, both patients and doctors end up having to come to terms with practices involving violence perpetrated on the human body. The integrity of the body which is called into question by affairs of this sort has both psychological and ethical consequences. The need to introduce a new morality into the health sector has been the occasion for clerics in Egypt to intervene publicly on moral grounds and to question the authority of a state which can no longer fulfil its functions since it can no longer uphold public morality.

The same dissatisfaction exists, though in less extreme form, within the Tunisian medical world. In response to a journalist's question as to 'whether he would make the same choices if given a chance to do it all again', a doctor working within the public sector replied: 'Without hesitation – and for personal reasons – yes. But I would make

---

[37] *El Siassi*, 14 July and 11 December 1988.

[38] *El Ahram*, 8 June 1992.

[39] Abdullah Nazem, 'The return of Jordanian/Palestinian nationals from Kuwait: economic and social implications for Jordan, Amman', September 1991. Quoted in Brigitte Curmi, 'Jordanie: les médecins militaires, précurseurs de la modernité scientifique', *Monde Arabe Maghreb: Machrek*, 146, (1994), p. 50.

[40] *El Ahram*, 29 March 1995.

sure that I did not end up in such a difficult material situation.'[41] Following the massive exodus of the best teachers to the private sector in the 1980s, the state, concerned by its loss of prestige, increased the attention it gave to those who remained in the state sector and, simultaneously, to such nebulous areas as the tradition of *acabya*, which is potentially subversive of state action. The government is working to improve the image of the public sector, to make hospitals more attractive and to win the support of the medical elite whose good opinion it holds dear. Health-care professionals at all levels who agree to work in rural or remote areas are given social benefits, and extra funds are being directed for training and retraining, while staff at the university hospital are given opportunities to travel to conferences abroad. At the same time, mobile health-care services have been organized to bring treatment closer to the people.

### Reformism in question

The troubles of health-care professionals and of their patients are symptomatic of a moral crisis, caused by economic difficulties,[42] which threatens the role of the law in social life, a central objective of state technocratic reforms which has led, in the case of Tunisia, to the promulgation of the Personal Status Code (*Code de statut personnel*).

Independence had a profound effect on both public and private life, constituting a clear epistemological break with previous models of interpreting personal responsibility. Commitment to the rights and duties of the individual citizen was inscribed in the Constitution and became a central element in the vision of a better future. The reforms introduced by a state committed to the individual welfare of its citizens and by the effort of national development were aimed at emancipating society. Among the changes resulting from the radical departure represented by this technocratic view of the future, three at least were to become some of the most important symbols of the nation-state: the ideal of the new family (based on the couple, on love and on family planning), education and health care for all, and social security. These different areas became parameters for the reorganization of the human personality.

In Tunisia, these changes consolidated the legal rights of women from 1956 on. The judicial rights acquired by women include the equality of the sexes, the abolition of polygamy with penal sanctions for offenders, and the prohibition of divorce by repudiation. Divorce instead became a judicial act. The consent of a woman to marriage is mandatory and the age of marriage was raised to seventeen. Other amendments introduced since 1992 provide for the further emancipation of women, by allowing them to obtain and transfer their nationality on the same basis as men. They have full judicial recognition of their civic rights upon reaching the age of twenty and their husbands have no administrative power over them. Women can be summoned before the judicial courts under their own names. The education of girls has improved, after experiencing

---

[41] Interview given to *L'Observateur* (Tunis), 88, 28 September 1994. The increase in the size of the health-care sector has had the positive effect of bringing care to the population in general. For example, in 1965 Egypt had one doctor per 2,300 inhabitants, and in 1984 the ratio was one per 770. There is assistance at only 24% of births and the child mortality rate per 1,000 births is 66. Of the women of child-bearing age, 38% are protected by some form of contraception. In 1965, Tunisia had one doctor per 8,000 inhabitants, and in 1980 the ratio was one per 2,150. 60% of births take place in controlled surroundings and the child mortality rate is 44 per 1,000. 50% of Tunisian women of child-bearing age use a form of contraception. The rapid increase in the number of doctors has led to a weakening of the power of the professional body, which is dominated by state employees.

[42] Sick people in Egypt and Morocco launch public appeals for charity to help them cover the costs of their medical treatment. See *Jamhouriya*, 30 October 1994; *L'Opinion*, 25 December 1994.

a decline during the 1970s, and this has led to an improvement both in the fertility rate and in the standard of living of families. Nonetheless, women's participation in the formal political arena remains very limited, and the Islamic inheritance laws (where a sister's share is equal to one-half of a brother's share) have not been changed.

In order to reinforce the separation of state and religion, post-independence governments introduced a new method of managing mutual aid. Social security opened up new horizons and Tunisians were aware of the advantages it offered. The idea that personal security could be offered by the state exercised a profound influence on the popular imagination, reflected in demand for public-sector employment. The attraction of state employment is less a result of the salaries offered than of job security and other social benefits. Another change was the reform of the curriculum at the Zeitouna theological university in Tunis with a view to producing new generations of clerics and judges. The university itself was reformed. Its graduates are paid, as teachers of civics and religion, on the same salary level as other public servants. The allocations of the state budget are testimony to the state's concern to establish new forms of management in conformity with its objectives of rational reform. In 1990, for example, 6.1 per cent of the budget was allocated to health care, 16.3 per cent to education and only 6 per cent to defence.[43]

The deep-seated break with the past represented by independence in Tunisia has provided the conditions necessary for social equilibrium, for the redistribution of wealth and the equality of all before the law, encouraging the growth of a middle class which is the bedrock of the state and its objectives. In public discourse, this cultural revolution nurtured a structure in which relations are negotiated rather than ascribed.

Since January 1995, the Egyptian government has been preparing to change the marriage laws to protect women from polygamy and to introduce the right of divorce in the marriage contract (a right to be based on the mutual consent of both parties), as well as the right for women to travel abroad if required to do so for professional reasons or for study. This reform of the law was introduced in 1979, but pressure from Islamic fundamentalists led to the law's amendment in 1984, assigning to magistrates the responsibility of judging whether the taking of a second wife would be detrimental to the first wife. The family and relations between family members remain subject to theological ethics.

The Egyptian film industry during the 1950s and 1960s adopted the notion of social welfare and contributed to its dissemination throughout the Third World, giving people the hope of maintaining their dignity even in the face of life's major risks, such as accident, illness or death. These rights have eroded very rapidly, as the state budget shows: 2.8 per cent allocated for health care, 13.4 per cent for education and 12.7 per cent for defence. Al Azhar, the Cairo theological university, has maintained its influence over cultural life and social matters.

There is a clear divergence in the different models of the relations between the citizen and the type of state created at independence. This is manifested in the extremes of behaviour of some individuals, the sense of insecurity of others, and the sense of unease among people working in the medical field. In the absence of a new ethics and a new social mythology, poverty has become a terrible handicap: we now see emerging what Clifford Geertz calls, in relation to Morocco, a hyper-individualism in public actions,

---

[43] World Bank, *World Development Report*. In 1965, the number of girls per 100 boys in primary school was 64 in Egypt and 52 in Tunisia. These levels had increased by 1989 to 81 and 83 respectively. The same trend is evident in secondary schools, where female attendance increased from 41 per 100 boys in Egypt and 37 in Tunisia in 1965, to 77 and 75 respectively in 1989.

and today this has reached the bosom of the family.[44] The sale of organs and the death of children from kwashiorkor point to new developments in the field of popular ideas concerning personal and family morality in regard to the responsibilities of the state. Can the state based on modern law, the subject of criticism from the elite, come under threat from a longing for a political model which reformers want to consign to the past?

Instead of reassessing the difficulties and elaborating a new ground for legitimation,[45] intellectuals, when they break their silence at all, often denounce the measures introduced by the welfare state. In the late 1970s, the Tunisian sociologist A. Bouhdiba severely criticized the new apparatus evolved by the state to deal with social insecurity by means of social security budgets, mutual aid funds, mutual benefit societies, and national and international humanitarian organizations, for having introduced a juridical and bureaucratic quality into a social solidarity 'whose secret can only be expressed in a spontaneous, internalized manner, and because it is practised with loving kindness'.[46] He notes that in a context of profound crisis and failure, older concepts of solidarity have lost their value, and he attributes this change to the 'extraordinary and unprecedented changes' undergone by society since 1956. His thinking is based on the theological reasoning which is at the root of the traditional family model – a model he sees as absorbing the psychic energy of social groups, in which individual feelings are subsumed in those of the group, just as in the model of the *acabya* described by Ibn Khaldoun in the fourteenth century, where solidarity is based on consensus.

The fundamentalist movements base themselves precisely on what some intellectuals call the 'divergence from theological ethics', which is said to have caused crises within the family, religion, morality, and, ultimately economic, social and political structures. Other intellectuals point out the difficult work done by Islamic militants for the poor, which clashes with an official, technocratic vision in which the existence of flagrant inequality and of social injustice is denied, and in which poverty is perceived as essentially a question of the rehabilitation of individuals and their families.[47] The Tunisian elections of 1989/90 had among other merits that of shedding some light on the social tensions throughout the country.[48] Public debate concentrated on the poor, unemployment, health care, the legal system, transport, water, sanitation, roads, etc. The fact that these questions were taken up by political candidates tends to vindicate the reformist view of the technocrats. Politicians made televised tours to explain the round of price rises and privatization supported by the IMF in a campaign steeped in sentiment. Television viewers 'suffer at long distance'[49] and feel gratitude for the intervention of the state, perceiving a certain rationality in the politicians' show of concern and advice.

[44] C. Geertz, *Observer l'Islam* (La découverte, Paris, 1992).

[45] A. Abdel Moat, *La répartition de la pauvreté dans le village égyptien* (in Arabic, La Nouvelle Maison de la Culture, Cairo, 1979).

[46] A. Bouhdiba, 'La solidarité aujourd'hui', in A. Bouhdiba (ed.) *Raisons d'être* (CERES, Tunis, 1980).

[47] M. Nasraoui, 'Les réactions des Tunisiens non pauvres à la vue des pauvres', in *Les déterminismes socioculturels de la pauvreté en Tunisie* (CERES, Tunis, 1994).

[48] L. Labidi, *Choisir, Voter, Élire* (forthcoming).

[49] L. Boltanski, *La souffrance à distance* (Ed. A.M. Métailié, Paris, 1993). The author deals with the politics of pity created by audio-visual media.

# Conclusion

A study of the sale of organs and the mistreatment of children enables us to recognize in 'isolation', as Freud suggests,[50] 'the exaggeration of conditions which would otherwise have remained hidden in normality'. Such responses to economic difficulties are an indication of what, for the individuals concerned, are life and death issues. Economic crisis and individual crises both share the same origin. Some intellectuals lament the erosion of an ethics based on religion which represents the figure of the mother as despicable, repulsive, thus favouring an identification with heroic figures, as the basis of their ideal ego. Others believe that society has not yet moved far enough from the older religious-based concepts to put an end to the oral libido and to represent women as objects rather than as figures of abjection. They attempt to refute the view of the religious intellectuals which bears a similarity to perversion since it is founded on notions of defilement, transgression and images of women as a source of danger.[51]

This dialectic, based on various readings of unconscious motivations and of cultural phenomena, lays bare the foundations of the debates conducted by rationalist intellectual reformers since the end of the nineteenth century in Egypt and during the twentieth century in Tunisia, in their discussion of those traditional values which delay the process of assimilating modernity. The lack of any further elaboration of critical discourse, since the time of independence, on the causes of the violence at the roots of political culture, today hinders discussion of modernity, in which the individual has to see himself as both subject and object of continuous change, rather than as an abject figure.[52] The symptoms that have been developed in the form of crimes against life – self-mutilation and abuse – demonstrate the unconscious motivations and the perverse thoughts which are common to these two societies, which differ in terms of the expression which they give to the complex of politico-religious concepts and the welfare state, the state which takes the place of providence.

We have seen how a social dynamic unable to rid itself of the servility generated by a political culture founded on the durability of traditional values and a consensual morality, can be stopped in its tracks, in spite of the epistemological break which is the foundation for new identifications. A policy based on reason and the responsibility of each person to others in society should be founded on a renegotiation of the social contract around a constantly renewed consensus. It is indeed the case that daily life in countries burdened by debt and witnessing the withdrawal of the state is intolerable to those who are excluded from the system, who have not managed to participate in modernity. For the states themselves, weighed down by debt, it is equally difficult to manage social policies without undermining fundamental human rights under conditions of structural adjustment. In the absence of a vision which incorporates a new, multi-faceted social contract, these societies will not be able to control, on the basis of consensus, the development of internal violence which they generate, as long as they remain prisoners of a political culture based on an ethic generated by the centre, and founded on consensus and shame.

[50] S. Freud, *Nouvelles conférences d'introduction à la psychanalyse* (Gallimard, Paris, 1984).

[51] L. Labidi, 'Circulation des femmes dans l'espace public-cimetière, carrefour du politique et du religieux dans le monde arabo-musulman'. Paper delivered to Fourth Conference on Women. French Ministry of Health and City of Paris, 1995.

[52] A. Laroui, *Esquisses historiques* (Centre Culturel Arabe, Casablanca, 1993).

# II

*Institutions & Policies*

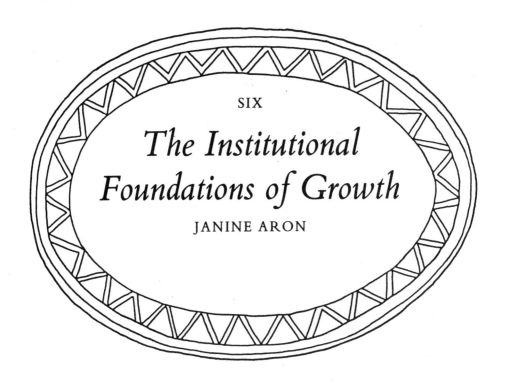

SIX

# The Institutional
# Foundations of Growth

JANINE ARON

Africa faces a significantly altered international environment in the mid-1990s, and new global trends have enormous implications for its future economic path.[2] One important feature of the 1990s is the growing internationalization of the global economy. Revolutions in information and communications technology have facilitated international transactions in trade and finance, and the mobility of capital and industry amongst countries has consequently risen strongly. Science and technological changes are more easily transferable, creating pressures for exporters to innovate, diversify and adapt. Furthermore, there has been significant progress recently in freeing non-tariff barrier restrictions, and the newly formed World Trade Organization has an ambitious agenda which includes reducing trade barriers in agriculture and the services sector. The prospect is one of larger volumes of trade and foreign investment being competed for internationally by developing (or 'emerging') countries. Thus, the policies of individual governments will be more constrained by considerations of international competitiveness, and the trend is to similar policies across countries.

These policy constraints will assume increasing importance in Africa. It is widely accepted that growth rates, after 15 years of structural adjustment programmes in a wide

[1] I am grateful for comments from Will Cavendish, Stephan Dercon, Carolyn Jenkins, Pramila Krishnan, Sanjaya Lall, John Muellbauer and Megan Vaughan.
[2] The present chapter is limited to discussion of Africa south of the Sahara, and also excludes South Africa from some sets of statistics. This is in conformity with the practices governing the gathering of macro-economic data for much of the period under discussion. Major monitoring organizations, such as the Bretton Woods institutions, regarded North Africa and sub-Saharan African as separate categories.

sub-section of African economies, lie far below the rates needed to erode large and growing levels of poverty. According to the World Bank, even the fastest growers will need to double current growth rates of 5 per cent per annum. For many small, open economies in Africa, with low domestic savings rates and stagnating private investment, and heavily indebted public sectors, the impetus for economic growth in the 1990s would seem to fall mainly on export growth and increases in foreign investment. Unfortunately, African countries have seriously diminished their international links, after decades of domestic macro-policies hostile to outwardly oriented trade, and inimical to foreign investment. The region's growth in the volume of exports fell from 2.8 to 2.4 per cent per annum between 1970–80 and 1980–92, as compared with a growth from 3.6 to 6.8 per cent for South Asia over the same periods,[3] while Africa's share of the flow of foreign direct investment to developing countries in 1993 amounted to nearly 3 per cent of the estimated total of around $87 billion per annum (compared with 30 per cent for East Asia and over 50 per cent for Latin America).[4]

Successful outward trade orientation requires diversified exports. Yet most African countries continue to export primary goods and raw materials, while importing their capital and industrial goods mostly from OECD countries. Indices of the degree of outward orientation of economies place the sub-Saharan African countries lowest in the ranking of developing regions;[5] and the region's share of primary commodities in total exports (including oil), which was around 93 per cent on average in 1971, continues to be very high at over 80 per cent in the 1990s. Apart from the highly undesirable vulnerability to commodity price shocks from such a narrow export base, the gains from this type of trade are limited. Competing internationally for foreign investment requires a favourable policy environment, whereas most African governments continue to impose, either by action or inaction, tremendous constraints on investment. Africa could also increase its aid dependence from the region's current high levels of nearly 10 per cent of GNP; and indeed in many countries aid remains the sole international link. Taking a longer-term view, it is hard to see how African countries can escape forging new links with the competitive world environment described above, and delays could prove costly.

A second profound change in the world environment with far-reaching consequences for Africa has been the ending of the Cold War, and the collapse of most highly centralized economies after 1989. The sharp ideological polarization of foreign funding in African countries has mutated in recent years, arguably becoming more development-oriented and less strategic in motivation. The flow of funds has increased not decreased, with sub-Saharan Africa receiving about 30 per cent of global net aid transfers in 1991. This change has brought with it a peace dividend, particularly in the southern African region. Reinforcing the peace prospects has been a dramatic ripple effect from the political revolutions in Eastern Europe: in early 1989, only four countries in sub-Saharan Africa permitted a multi-party system, but over 30 national elections have taken place in Africa in the last five years, accompanied by greater freedom of the press and associational life. In the economic sphere, and again catalyzed by events in Eastern Europe, there is an apparently growing consensus in the developing world that more decentralized, market-driven or market-oriented economies with strong international linkages may be better

---

[3] Paul Collier, 'The Marginalization of Africa' (Mimeo, Centre for the Study of African Economies, University of Oxford, September, 1994).

[4] Jack Glen & Mariusz Sumlinski, *Trends in Private Investment in Developing Countries 1995: Statistics for 1980–93* (Discussion Paper 25, International Finance Corporation, Washington DC, 1995).

[5] David Dollar, 'Outward oriented developing countries really do grow more rapidly: Evidence from 95 LDCs 1976–85', *Economic Development and Cultural Change*, 40, (1995), pp. 523–44.

and more flexible performers in the achievement of growth. During the last five years, over 30 African economies have enacted liberalizing reforms, but with mixed results, including policy reversals. The juxtaposition of these tendencies to greater economic and political liberalization in African countries is thus potentially of great significance. In principle, political liberalization should allow a wider debate on appropriate economic policies, and these may be more deep-seated, credible and persistent as a result. The increasing acceptability of democratic ideas could facilitate fundamental constitutional reform, and with it a more effective application of the rule of law governing state institutions and private contracts. This would rid Africa of a principal constraint to investment. A broader political voice may also prevent some of the negative income and wealth distributional consequences of market reforms (that have so disgraced the privatization of state enterprises in Russia, for instance). However, in the absence of significant constitutional reform, it would be naïve not to recognize the continued dominance of a small elite in the political process, with the majority, especially in rural areas, *de facto* disenfranchised.

A third global event is the recent reassessment, fifty years after the foundation of the Bretton Woods organizations, of the role these global institutions should play in the new international environment.[6] Over the last five years, the multilateral agencies have been extended by an enormous research and operational input in the transition from socialism of Eastern European and ex-Soviet Union countries. Transition in many of these countries has involved the attempt to construct, from scratch markets and market institutions, representative government and the capacity to manage and regulate, and the rule of law in enforcing contracts of various kinds. By contrast, in African countries many of these markets and the various institutions have long existed in differing degrees of dysfunction (in some cases on paper only), and arguably reform requires the deepening of markets and the long-term renovation of existing institutions.

During the preceding decade, Bretton Woods policy conditionality has unquestionably placed far greater emphasis on short-term, deflationary demand management and price liberalization in many African economies than on such structural measures. Taking the longer-term and gradualist approach obviously poses increased risk for creditors, given uncertain outcomes and the greater resources required. It has been mooted that the World Bank – whose formal role is intended be the encouragement of longer-term, structural change – has been intellectually subservient to the IMF and its short-term goals.[7] Indeed, efforts were focused on ridding economies of the controls that distorted and weakened them, not reforming the institutions that administered the controls. One might argue that the 'short-term' policy goals applied over 15 years have been myopic, and a wasted opportunity for African countries. After all, on an Africa-wide measure, the gains in macro-policy and performance as assessed by the World Bank itself are fragile in the realm of fiscal policy, incipient though promising in monetary policy, and disappointing in trade.[8] The main achievement has been in liberalizing prices and deregulating markets, and there have been sectoral improvements as a consequence. Yet price liberalizations are easily reversed, and there have been a number of such reversals in recent years (e.g. in Nigeria and Gambia).

---

6 Peter Kenen (ed.), *Managing the World Economy* (Institute for International Economics, Washington DC, 1994); and idem, 'Bretton Woods: Looking to the future', Background Papers for the Committee on the Future of the Bretton Woods Institutions, Washington DC.
7 Mahbub Ul Haq, 'The Bretton Woods institutions and global governance', in Kenen, *Managing the World Economy*, p. 409.
8 World Bank, *Adjustment in Africa: Reforms, results and the road ahead* (Oxford University Press, New York, 1994). This broad measure obviously conceals a wide spectrum of performance.

Furthermore, rapidly liberalizing prices such as the exchange rate, in thin markets with rudimentary institutions and little regulation, may create less of an efficient market price and allocation than is commonly supposed.

While accepting that demand management constitutes an essential precondition for successful supply expansion, and that price liberalization provides appropriate incentives to producers, the clear trend today is that economists are trying to understand the surprising (to many people) failure of supply response in Africa after 'getting the prices right', on the basis of cumulative institutional impoverishment. This has been reinforced by foreign donors' experiences in the transitional economies in the 1990s, which have refocused attention on the importance of institutional issues, and by the increasing acceptability of democratic ideas post-Cold War which makes such reform feasible.

This chapter draws on a range of recent literature to trace the argument that future prospects for growth in Africa are strongly circumscribed by its political, economic and legal institutional foundations, including the oversight or monitoring structure for these institutions. An implicit theme of the chapter is the importance of path dependence or hysteresis in African economic reform. Hysteresis is a term borrowed from materials science and refers to the plasticity of a material after stress. Hysteresis in an economic sense refers to the long-term persistence of initial conditions, or of changes to capacity, incentives or reputation after episodes of reform or adjustment to shocks. In other words, the finding that there is hysteresis, or 'path dependence', in the evolution of a variable, basically means that history matters for the outcome. The chapter explores hysteresis in the changing capability and reputation of the state in Africa, from independence to the present day. Given the imperative of growth through international linkages, it examines the likely determinants of growth in Africa, drawing on endogenous growth theory empirical models, which emphasize the path dependence of growth and stress the role of institutions and the cultural environment in which they operate. Finally, it examines the way in which history matters for the evolution of institutions, which has important implications for the process of institutional reform in Africa. The last section draws together the argument and concludes with a realistic assessment of the role of the state in Africa from the 1990s.

## Macro-economic History: The Evolving Role of the State

The state in Africa in the past has presented an odd dichotomy between a strong state and a weak one: at once authoritarian with enormous power often concentrated in the person of the president, and yet weak in institutional and administrative capacity, with limited material means, indebted, and with little control over peripheral regions in some cases.[9] In recent years, the state in Africa has frequently been redefined, under the influence of exogenous shocks of various kinds, and when applying (or reversing) policy conditionality. In general, this process has involved a progressive move towards a smaller state, with a far more limited interventionist role in the economy, given the economic damage wrought by excessive controls; its smaller scope is also the result of budget constraints. The austerity measures followed and the contraction of the state have unfortunately also further exacerbated its areas of weakness. The state has become completely inadequate as a provider of social services and its economic and legal institutional

---

[9] See Rob Buijtenhuijs & Elly Rijnierse, *Democratization in Sub-Saharan Africa 1989–1992*, (Research Report 51, Afrika-studiecentrum, Leiden, 1993), p. 19.

capability has worsened. For instance, this is manifest through a loss of control over economic decision-making given the drain of skilled personnel, which has induced the substitution of foreign technical assistance to implement policy conditionality. Poor commitment associated with lack of ownership of programmes, and limited accountability to the populace, has seen the consequent decline of governments' reputations domestically and internationally. In recent years these changes have been coupled with an apparent greater accountability to the population, though such 'democracy' could be construed as an attempt merely to legitimate authoritarian states.[10]

In this section we examine the economic evolution of the African state, in distinct phases from independence to the present day. This somewhat stylized approach does lend insights into the usefulness of particular state constructs in the context of Africa's predominant structural characteristics: thin markets, primary commodity dependence and vulnerability to shocks, rudimentary institutions in many cases, skill shortages, capital shortages and high population growth. Moreover, the historical perspective highlights the importance of hysteresis in these economies, and the consequences will be linked to the constraints on growth.

*A small but interventionist state: the economic legacy at independence*[11]

The colonial legacy to the newly independent African states was small government. The national accounts figures for the post-World War II period estimate governments' contribution to national income as typically less than 10 per cent. Social sector expenditure for Africans was segregated from that for Europeans, and left mostly to the missionary societies. These were dualistic economies, comprising a wealthy export-oriented sector, largely foreign-owned, and a subsistence agricultural sector lying largely outside the money economy. In mineral economies the share of mining plus manufacturing was about 30–50 per cent of national income, with agriculture contributing about 25 per cent. In agricultural economies the structure was very different, with over 70 per cent of national income due to agriculture. The economies were undiversified, and potentially vulnerable to commodity price fluctuations; but the potential for growth and diversification was large in the climate of world growth in the 1950s and 1960s.

Before 1945, colonial governments tended not to be developmentalist, and indeed in mineral economies did not even benefit from royalties. Subsequent to World War II, there was major intervention to develop the agricultural sector on the part of French and British governments, but peasant farmers were taxed by state monopoly marketing boards largely for the benefit of the colonial powers. The exchange rates were pegged to colonial rates, themselves fixed to the gold standard; and weak forms of capital controls were in force. Price and wage controls were administered.

The years preceding independence saw substantial export-led growth from private mineral extraction and plantation or smallholder agriculture. There was a small secondary growth in private manufacturing and services, largely allied to the export sectors; similarly, an often extensive private infrastructure of transport and utility services for exports was established. African entrepreneurship, while substantial in some parts of Africa, was overshadowed by expatriate and immigrant ownership of firms elsewhere

---

[10] See Chapter 2 in the present volume by Solofo Randrianja.

[11] See also Paul Collier, 'The economic history of Africa: 1990–94' (Mimeo, Centre for the Study of African Economies, Oxford University, 1994); and Gavin Williams, 'Africa: Retrospect and Prospect', in *Africa South of the Sahara 1995* (Europa, London, 1995).

in the continent, and sometimes actively prevented, as in the case of constraints on Northern Rhodesian African farmers.

At independence, well-functioning administrative, regulatory and judicial structures were left intact, and new parliamentary systems following the Gaullist and Westminster models were established. However, it should be noted that the longer colonial government tradition was one of autocracy and centralization.

### The rise of the state: African socialism in the 1950s to mid-1970s

The type of African economy that evolved in the early decades after independence was influenced by socialist theories of various hues, by liberal interpretations of Keynesian economics, and by infant-industry protection and terms-of-trade arguments for growth. This was a fairly general pattern amongst developing countries, reflecting the development ideology of the day, and for the most part supported by donor countries. Given the lack of capital, and a distrust of foreign capital stemming from the colonial era, most countries chose the path of state-led industrialization. Agriculture was relegated to the status of the provider of resources for this transformation; and this contrasted with the colonial impetus for enhanced agricultural growth.

Building on the colonial heritage, virtually every aspect of the economy was subject to varying levels of state intervention in the subsequent two decades. Governments administered price controls and increasingly regulated and intervened in labour markets, mining, agriculture, manufacturing and financial markets. Partly through appropriation of existing enterprises and financial institutions, the share of the public sector in the economy as producer and employer grew hugely. In many mineral economies, the mining sector was nationalized, and public monopolies were created for the marketing of agricultural exports.

Foreign exchange was administratively allocated, and the parastatals were major beneficiaries. The exchange rates were originally constrained in regional currency boards, but these were disbanded after independence, with the exception of the francophone region; exchange rates were then pegged to European currencies or the US dollar, and exchange controls from colonial days persisted. Credit market intervention occurred through interest controls and high reserve requirements, and credit was directed to selective sectors, especially public enterprises.

A restrictive trade policy and an inward-looking import-substitution growth strategy were followed. Import licensing was pervasive and certain categories of imports were banned, but there was liberal licensing of capital and intermediate goods imports. These quotas were reinforced by a complicated tariffs system. This trade strategy served to promote import dependence in capital-intensive industries, and this dependence quickly rose with industrialization. Although exports grew strongly in this period, the export base remained narrow. In fact there was a strong anti-export bias, with heavier taxation of agricultural and mineral exports than in the pre-independence period. Agricultural producers were largely forced to sell crops through marketing boards and received real prices that were half those of producers of similar crops in other regions.

In combination, these policies created a strong bias against the private sector, including rural farmers. This was reflected in expropriation of private property; the favoured allocations of credit, foreign exchange and trade licences to parastatals and rent-seekers; and the very high taxation of exports. The inevitable result was the contraction of exports and a decline in private investment and confidence.

These interventionist governments rapidly became over-extended. For the most part they did not possess the administrative capacity to play so large a role in the economy. The judicial and regulatory functions deteriorated, not least because of political interference. Governments tried to meet their electoral promises of massive social sector expenditure, but the public provision of services became progressively more inefficient. Large discrepancies between rural and urban wages induced migration of unskilled workers to urban centres, while, simultaneously, expanding education poured skilled workers on to the market. Governments then resorted to deficit financing for employment generation, regardless of capacity utilization levels. Even before commodity prices faltered in the mid-1970s, most countries' public finances were in deficit (with the exception of the CFA countries). Since the tax base was heavily dependent on the traditional export sector, the subsequent commodity price falls significantly worsened the budget deficit. The incipient balance-of-payments crises were not alleviated by contractions in spending in most cases, nor by devaluation. Instead the exchange controls and trade controls were tightened, and the result was overvalued currencies defended by the rationing of foreign exchange.

### The unsustainable state: external shocks in the 1970s

The region's GDP per capita growth for the period 1965–73 was about 2.4 per cent, but this stagnated or declined during 1974–80. The two oil shocks of the 1970s turned the terms of trade against agricultural exporting countries, and these were only partially offset by temporary agricultural commodity price booms. Mineral-exporting countries also experienced export contraction and sharply declining terms of trade. Foreign-exchange earnings and fiscal revenue were both contracted by the shocks, and growth declines in import-dependent sectors followed the cycles of import compression. Mineral discovery countries, on the other hand, experienced Dutch Disease effects, such as Nigeria, where the huge inflows of foreign exchange financed wasteful investment and capital flight.[12] (Botswana is a notable exception.) While foreign aid and financing was extended to ailing countries from the mid-1970s, this only partially compensated for the terms-of-trade losses.

Those countries which had experienced commodity booms in the pre-1973 period generally behaved as if the price rises were permanent. Public investment was expanded (thereby incurring large future recurrent costs), while recurrent expenditure in the budget was sharply raised. Faced with commodity price shocks in the mid-1970s, governments found it difficult to reverse the high levels of expenditure. Public investment was generally curtailed, but recurrent expenditure on defence, public debt service and pensions grew strongly, while politically sensitive expenditure on civil servants' salaries and consumer subsidies fell somewhat in real terms, and there were serious reductions in government services. A further budgetary drain was due to extensive loans, subsidies and increased equity holdings in the ailing parastatal sector. By the late 1970s, the region's government consumption expenditure as a percentage of GDP reached over 16 per cent, as compared with 10 per cent for most other developing regions. Moreover, given the earlier fiscal profligacy, limited international reserves were available to bolster the economies against external shocks.

Far from adjusting exchange rates to accommodate balance-of-payments crises, ever

---

[12] David Bevan, Paul Collier & Jan Willem Gunning, *Controlled Open Economies* (Clarendon Press, Oxford, 1990).

more stringent exchange and trade controls were applied. Importers and urban consumers benefited from the fixed overvalued exchange rates; but overvaluation acts like an implicit tax on exports. The reduced profitability due to both explicit and implicit taxation exacerbated the effects of falling commodity prices in contracting exports, further squeezing the revenue base. Furthermore, thriving parallel markets for foreign exchange (and informal markets for goods) began to emerge. Relative to other developing regions, the parallel premia[13] and the size of these markets have tended to be far larger in African economies.[14] This induced considerable diversion of trade into illegal channels – smuggling – further narrowing the tax base. Flight from domestic currency also reduced the savings base for domestic investment, undermining the long-term growth potential.

## Diminishing the state: structural adjustment in Africa in the 1980s

By the early 1980s, with few exceptions, declines in GDP per capita had spread throughout the region: the World Bank estimates that real GDP per capita for roughly two-thirds of Africans was lower than in the mid-1970s (i.e. around $500). Africa was already receiving higher net transfers than any other region in the 1970s, at about 3.8 per cent of GDP, but incurred further debt to pay for the bloated recurrent public expenditures, existing debt service, and continued imports, partly based on the expectation that commodity prices would recover. With petrodollar recycling between 1974 and the eventual collapse of private bank lending in 1982, a large expansion occurred in short-term financial transfers at flexible rates from private banks to developing countries (which was many times the long-term lending from donors and development agencies). Africa was not structurally able to assimilate these large flows: they were not used to adjust economies from the crisis of the late 1970s, nor to invest wisely in improved infrastructure. Monetary and fiscal policies continued to be loose, and trade and exchange controls were maintained to prevent the politically sensitive adjustment of the exchange rate. Balance-of-payments problems and fiscal deficits were aggravated by huge capital flight as confidence deteriorated in domestic economic management.

Also by the early 1980s, high debt stocks and high interest rates, in consequence of the OECD countries' deflationary stance, simultaneous with the onset of adverse terms of trade, made debt service unmanageable. Many African countries accumulated large arrears on their huge debts. With slowing export growth, Africa lost market share abroad (except in oil). Agriculture stagnated; but mineral economies were hardest hit, with losses of around 20 per cent of GDP (a terms-of-trade fall of 50 per cent) over the period 1970–86. The income loss from declining terms of trade in sub-Saharan Africa, but excluding Nigeria, was about 5.4 per cent of GDP between 1970–73 and 1981–6. Taking account of external transfers, this income loss was 3 per cent of GDP or about 0.2 per cent per annum.

Faced with the problems of negative transfers from African countries, and the virtual cessation of private sector finance in the 1980s, the Bretton Woods organizations altered the nature of existing agreements and devised new lending mechanisms. Previously most IMF lending was by very short-term stand-by agreements incorporating stabilization

---

[13] The black market or parallel premium is a measure of the percentage difference between the official exchange rate operating in the official or legal market, and the exchange rate determined in the illegal or black market, or sometimes a quasi-legalized bureaux de change market.

[14] Miguel Kiguel, J. Saul Lizondo & Stephen O'Connell (eds), *Parallel Market Exchange Rates in Developing Countries* (Macmillan, London, and St. Martin's, New York, forthcoming).

policies, and by project loans, where conditionality focused on project preparation and evaluation, institution-building, procurement, technical pricing and marketing issues, with disbursements following specific stages in implementation. Given the huge balance-of-payment problems, more medium-term programme and adjustment lending mechanisms were tailored, with specific macro- and sectoral policies directed at stabilization and structural adjustment. Typically, this conditional lending has included reducing budget deficits by cutting subsidies to urban consumers and protected, inefficient parastatals; civil service retrenchment; state asset privatization; promoting all exports; maintaining tight control over monetary policy to reduce high levels of inflation; ridding the economy of the vast range of controls on economic activity (and institutions administering the controls), thereby deregulating markets such as the foreign-exchange and credit markets; and more recently there has been attention to restructuring the financial sector and to civil service reform.

In other words, the transformation required was a radical redefinition of the economic role of African governments to small government, with an overriding responsibility for prudent fiscal and monetary management, limited intervention in markets, and the provision of essential social services. However, a by-product of fiscal austerity has been diminished social services and infrastructure provision, as well as a further decline in the institutional capability of the state. Transition on the scale required by most developing countries had no precedent. There have been frequent policy reversals. Influential domestic interest groups, privileged under the controlled regimes, were opposed to the reforms, and in conditions of economic crisis, and popular uprisings in some cases, wielded considerable political power. Furthermore, governments did not possess comparable capacity with the development institutions to devise and debate programme conditionality, and in this sense policies were often not home-grown, and governments were not wholly commited to them. Reversals damaged the reform credibility of governments both domestically and abroad, decreased the countries' creditworthiness abroad, gave rise to huge capital flight, and promoted the tendency to short-term hoarding and speculative behaviour by the private sector rather than productive activity. Governments thus required even more effort in subsequent reforms to sustain them. This we may regard as a symptom of hysteresis.

### The fragile state of Africa in the 1990s

Recent World Bank analyses of about 30 adjusting countries in sub-Saharan Africa compare reforms enacted since 1988 and their impact, with the situation in the early part of the 1980s.[15] The intention of these reforms was threefold: to strengthen the state's management of monetary and fiscal policy; to decrease the state's interventionist role in private markets by promoting liberalization, particularly of the exchange rate and agricultural producer prices; and to reduce the size of the state by promoting privatization of state enterprises. The first two points also reflect an increased emphasis on promoting agricultural and mineral exports and diversifying the export base.

The overall conclusion by the World Bank is that no country has achieved a good macro-economic framework, although macro-policies have definitely improved since 1985

---

[15] World Bank, *Adjustment in Africa*; and an updated summary: Lawrence Bouton, Christine Jones and Miguel Kiguel, *Macroeconomic Growth and Reform in Africa: Adjustment revisited* (Policy Research Working Paper No. 1394, World Bank, Washington DC, 1994). For a critique, see Nguyura Lipumba, *Africa Beyond Adjustment* (Policy Essay No. 15, Overseas Development Council, Washington DC, 1994).

in over half the adjusting countries.[16] The fiscal stance remains fragile overall, but monetary policies have strengthened. Countries such as Ghana and Uganda have made considerable progress, and twelve other countries were classified as having a fair framework.[17] Since the report was published there have been policy reversals in Nigeria and the Gambia. Most other countries were considered to have very poor macro-policies.[18] Even the best performers lag far behind the policy stance of the best developing countries outside the region such as Thailand, Chile and Malaysia. Furthermore, while there has been progress in liberalizing and deregulating markets, particularly the foreign-exchange market, the majority of stable countries, including Ghana, have maintained medium to heavy government intervention in markets. Public enterprise reform, clearly a long-term objective, has not been satisfactorily achieved.

On the fiscal balance, while there has been some improvement in some countries in recent years, the regional achievement has been rather moderate, and budgets display an unduly high dependence on foreign aid. We consider the average fiscal deficit excluding grants, which measure emphasizes the fragility of the public finances vis-à-vis changes in foreign aid.[19] For the sample of 30 adjusting countries, the average fiscal deficit (excluding grants) as a percentage of GDP rose from 8.7 to 9.8 per cent between 1981–87 and 1988–93. In fact this measure has not altered much since the early 1980s, showing that African countries depend heavily on external support to balance their budgets. Evaluating countries by this measure classifies most of them as having a poor fiscal stance (exceeding 7 per cent of GDP). Very few showed a fair to good fiscal stance in 1991–2, with the best performers such as the Gambia and Tanzania still relying heavily on foreign grants.

Most countries possess a poor revenue base, which is a function of low tax collection and pervasive tax evasion. Government revenue for the region averages 18 per cent of GDP, which masks wide variation among countries. At least one-third of the countries in the sample had revenues less than 12 per cent in 1988–93, covering only interest payments and the wage bill; another third were greater than 20 per cent, with the others falling in between these two groups. On average, revenues have fallen over the last decade, but have improved for countries that have devalued with flexible exchange-rate regimes. Partly this reflects the move back to legal channels of trade with the elimination of parallel market premia. At the same time there has been an effort to broaden the tax base and improve collection procedures.

Total expenditure, capital plus current, averaged 28 per cent of GDP for the sample of 30 adjusting countries in 1988–93. Government expenditure has seen falls in the last decade, focused on capital expenditure, with recurrent expenditures unchanged on average. In a number of cases, including Senegal, Sierra Leone and Côte d'Ivoire, capital spending has fallen to under 4 per cent of GDP, well below replacement rates. Current non-interest expenditure (including social sector expenditure) has been cut back in all but middle-income and oil-exporting countries (where wage bills rose). However, this

---

[16] A number of countries were omitted from the analysis, including small countries such as Equatorial Guinea, non-adjusting countries with civil unrest such as Angola and Ethiopia and other non-adjusting countries such as Botswana and Mauritius.

[17] Burundi, Kenya, Mali, Malawi, Mauritania, Senegal, Togo, Gabon, Madagascar, Burkina Faso, the Gambia and Nigeria.

[18] Mozambique, Sierra Leone, Benin, Cameroon, Côte d'Ivoire, Niger, Rwanda, Tanzania, Zimbabwe, Congo, Zambia and the Central African Republic. The following reforming countries offered too few statistics to be classified: Chad, Guinea and Guinea-Bissau.

[19] This draws on the World Bank, *Adjustment in Africa*; and Karim Nashashibi and Stefania Bazzoni, 'Alternative exchange rate strategies and fiscal performance in sub-Saharan Africa', *IMF Staff Papers*, 41, 1 (1994), pp. 76–122.

decrease in current expenditure has been cancelled by a rise in interest payments (from 2.5 to 4 per cent of GDP between 1981–6 and 1988–91), with the worst affected being Nigeria and Côte d'Ivoire, and the least affected, Malawi and Mauritius. A major item of current expenditure is the bloated and inefficient civil service. Reform here faces political resistance, particularly given the lack of viable private-sector alternatives to absorb retrenched state employees.

Basic social services have been the victim of budget cuts or freezes, and the erosion of the health and the skills of the population represents a loss of capacity that African economies can ill afford.[20] By contrast, countries which have rapidly eroded poverty – Indonesia, Malaysia, Thailand, and more recently China – invested heavily in basic social services at an early stage.[21] Aggregate public sector data are reported for health and education expenditures as a percentage of GDP for a range of 15 African countries, contrasting the two periods 1981–6 and 1987–90.[22] The mean averages for all countries (and those with complete annual data) are a fall in health expenditure from 1.34 (1.20) to 1.20 (1.10) per cent, and in education from 3.60 (3.12) to 3.31 (2.95) per cent, across the two periods. Only Niger, Ghana and Zimbabwe saw a growth in both types of social spending, while Kenya and Cameroon expanded educational expenditure. Given that GDP growth was negative for a number of these countries, while overall population growth averaged 3 per cent for the region, these average figures understate the deterioration, and even some better performers saw real spending per capita stagnating or declining. Poor data complicate investigation of the composition of spending on education, but the averages appear to be about 50 per cent on primary education, 30 per cent on secondary education and 20 per cent on higher education.[23] Higher education spending is high even by South Asian levels, and there is a similar bias towards secondary and tertiary health care.

The outlook is similarly negative for infrastructure provision. One-third of capital investment in roads has been eroded through poor maintenance, and this adds an estimated 17 per cent to freight costs. Rail traffic has declined in recent years and many national airlines are seriously in deficit. Rail freight costs are twice as high as in Asia, and port and air freights are markedly higher. The state of the rural infrastructure is worse, with 50 per cent of the road network requiring rehabilitation. Water supply and sanitation coverage is low in rural areas, and worsening in urban areas, despite gains in the 1980s. There is a slow improvement in the efficiency of power sector provision, but telecommunications coverage is the lowest in the world. The overwhelming trend, already in progress, is to transfer many of these services to the private sector.

On the monetary situation, the structure of financial markets in African economies, where securities markets are usually absent or very thin, makes indirect methods of monetary control, such as open-market operations, largely out of the question. Typically, governments have intervened directly in financial markets with such measures as

---

[20] Education seems to have been regarded as a luxury rather than a necessity, and one might speculate on what African institutional weakness allowed such indiscriminate budget cuts during adjustment, in contrast to adjusting Asian countries. Was military expenditure in Africa subject to similar pressures for cutbacks? Data are scarce, and cover only recorded, not illegal arms transfers: the statistics show a decline from 1.9 to 1.1% of the region's GDP between 1984–87 and 1988–91 (World Bank estimates). These figures, however, exclude the enormous domestic expenditure on the military, for which data are generally not available.

[21] The importance of basic health and nutrition in economic development has been much emphasized in recent literature, e.g. Partha Dasgupta, *An Enquiry into Well-being and Destitution* (Oxford University Press, Oxford, 1993).

[22] Nashashibi & Bazzoni, 'Alternative exchange rate strategies'.

[23] David Sahn, 'Public expenditures in sub-Saharan Africa during a period of economic reforms', *World Development*, 20, 5, (May 1992), pp. 673–93.

administered interest rates, reserve ratios and intervention in credit allocation. In recent years the emphasis has been on tight monetary and credit policies to restrain aggregate demand and bring down inflation, or in the case of the CFA countries, to support the fixed exchange rate. There is a clear distinction in the performance of the CFA and the non-CFA zone countries in terms of monetary policy. The former group enjoyed very low inflation (averaging under 1 per cent of GDP in 1991–2), and low seigniorage rates[24] (averaging 1 per cent of GDP in 1981–6, and declining further in 1987–92), under the discipline of the fixed exchange rate. Those non-CFA countries with a poor fiscal stance saw rising inflation (a median of 20 per cent, and about 8 countries considerably higher) and rising seigniorage (a median of 1.8) from the early 1980s to the 1990s. However, most of the adjusting countries in the early 1990s had low or moderate seigniorage (less than 1.5 per cent of GDP), and most had moderate inflation (under 10 per cent). Only a few countries (Tanzania, Zambia and Sierra Leone) demonstrated both high inflation and high seigniorage rates in the past five years.

Real interest rates have been high and positive in the 1990s for most CFA countries (a mean of 7.5 per cent), and while some non-CFA countries still have high negative rates in the face of high inflation and government controls (Sierra Leone), most countries have positive real interest rates. This indicator may be of limited value, given the thinness of the financial markets and limited institutional development. The recent linkage of interest determination to the Treasury Bill auctions, which were instituted to roll over short-term government debt, has seen very high interest rates emerge in some countries, damaging productive activity (e.g Zambia and Ghana in 1993/4). This has been described as an unforeseen circumstance of interest-rate reform.

In the realm of price and trade reform, considerable progress has unquestionably been made in liberalizing the exchange-rate regimes in several countries (but there have been reversals, such as in Nigeria in 1994). This reform is crucial, given the small, open nature of most African economies, where overvalued exchange rates have caused long-term damage. But it is difficult with thin markets to find an 'equilibrium' rate, and especially given the starting point of distorted rates in many countries. Black-market premia in 1993, for a range of 17 African countries, are lower, and in some cases substantially lower, than in 1981–6, before gradual market-based liberalization. The most dramatic changes have occurred for Zimbabwe, Uganda, Tanzania, Mozambique, Ghana and Guinea, with falls from over 200 per cent (and over 400 per cent in some cases) to levels below 25 per cent (probably compatible with the maintenance of some capital controls). Countries with large falls in the premium also effected large real depreciations: the non-CFA countries achieved on average 100 per cent real official depreciation between 1981–6 and 1987–92; the CFA countries, on the other hand, lost competitiveness until the franc was devalued in January 1994. While the terms of trade for CFA countries fell from an index of 100 in 1985 to about 60 in 1993, and rose slightly to just under 70 in 1994, the real effective exchange rate rose from 100 in 1985 to 135 in 1993, a real appreciation of one-third. The devaluation of the CFA franc in 1994 was to an index of just under 90, a real depreciation of one-third from 1993.

The donors have pushed for a rapid move to interbank markets, where the exchange rate is determined by transactions between banks and customers, and between banks themselves, and where the central bank is not a major seller or buyer but intervenes

---

[24] Seigniorage measures the resources gained from printing money (the higher the seigniorage the greater the money expansion), and is defined as the difference between this and the previous period's M1 over GDP, minus the ratio of M1 to GDP, times real GDP growth.

periodically to accumulate international reserves and for smoothing operations. Where price liberalization has been sustained, it has been accomplished through a gradual process (e.g. Ghana, Uganda), broadening the market by institution-building and progressive liberalization, with a supportive framework of compatible macro-economic policies, and where the reform has been at least to some extent home-grown. These facts need recognition. The interbank markets are of recent duration and there has been little assessment to date of the outcomes. Liberalization of exchange rates into thin markets which depend on temporary aid flows, private transfers and a narrow base of export earnings raises the possibility of considerable exchange-rate volatility, a deterrent to investment and damaging to manufacturing. Given the undeveloped nature of money markets, active intervention on the part of the central bank to smooth fluctuations is limited by its inability to sterilize the monetary consequences of intervention. Furthermore, weaknesses in the financial institutions have prevented the smooth functioning of interbank foreign-exchange markets. Finally, the state may not be a small player given the preponderance of foreign aid in the foreign-exchange market, or it may own major export industries.

Trade liberalization has usually occurred in the context of aggressive exchange-rate liberalization (e.g. Uganda, Ghana and Zambia in the 1990s). The distortionary trade practice of controlling official imports by the manual allocation of licences, has largely been replaced by automatic licensing in adjusting countries, and the substantial reduction of imports liable for licences (except Cameroon, Côte d'Ivoire and Tanzania). Although there has been significant progress in rationalizing tariff structures, reducing the spread of tariffs and the number of tariff categories, nominal average tariffs have not declined much, and at 40 per cent in the 1990s are much as they were in the 1980s. This contrasts with a figure of 30 per cent for South Asia. Given the conclusions on the poor revenue base above, this fact is not surprising: trade taxes are a high component of public revenue. In some countries the pressure in adjustment programmes for the rapid liberalization of tariffs has led to widespread bankruptcies of manufacturing firms, and has induced resistance to trade reform (e.g. Zambia). Replacing quotas by gradually reduced tariffs is precisely the South Asian policy.[25] While African states probably do not have the capacity to administer the system of selective and temporary tariffs for different export sectors used with such success in South Asia, gradual, across-the-board tariff reduction is surely better than widespread destruction of manufacturing firms, which may have formed the basis of a more diversified export sector.

Exports have been favoured by the removal of direct disincentives, given the strong emphasis in recent years on export expansion for growth. In addition to real depreciation, most reforming countries have lowered explicit taxes on exports, and limited the scope of export licensing. Again there is conflict with the traditional fiscal dependence on such taxes, but devaluation has partially compensated. Agricultural exports have benefited from the raising of producer prices in a number of countries (e.g. coffee producers); but in real terms, given the primary commodity price falls of the past decade, the change in the real producer price for agricultural exports was positive between 1981–3 and 1989–91 for only 10 of the 27 countries examined. State monopoly export crop marketing boards have been eliminated in some cases. Non-traditional export promotion has been an important recent focus, and for many adjusting countries for much longer, but alarmingly these exports still occupy a tiny share of exports. The poor supply response has to do with implementational problems or the limited scope of existing direct incentive

---

[25] See for example, Sanjaya Lall, 'Structural adjustment and industrial development in Africa', in *The African Development Report 1995* (African Development Bank, Abidjan, 1995).

105

schemes (e.g. duty drawback or tax rebate schemes, export credit, marketing information, promotion zones), but depends crucially on deeper structural problems such as deteriorated infrastructure and institutions.[26]

## The Determinants of Growth

The radical redefinition of the state in Africa in the past three decades has left us with a disturbing picture of a fragile state in the 1990s. Even for countries with good performance, the fiscal position remains highly vulnerable to changes in foreign aid; there has been a drastic decline in the quality and scope of social services and infrastructure provision; and significantly, the administrative capacities of many institutions of the state, including the legal system, have become seriously impaired. It seems inevitable that private-sector provision of many services traditionally in the government's domain will accelerate, assuming a capable private sector exists.

Thus, the full circle has been completed to the small state of pre-independence days. However, quite apart from the deterioration of the state-provided legal system, infrastructure and skills, there remain tremendous policy impediments which raise the cost of trade, business and investment in Africa. Moreover, the short-term political imperatives towards damaging policy reversals often hold greater sway than the economic necessity of sustained and consistent macro-economic policy.

### African growth prospects

The overall growth performance of the 47 sub-Saharan African countries during 1988–93 averaged −0.9 per cent GDP per capita per annum. This figure masks the very different performance of different groups of countries. Some 25 countries experienced negative per capita growth rates, including populous war-torn countries and those with internal unrest such as Zaïre, Rwanda, Liberia and Somalia. Some 21 countries saw positive per capita growth, and of these, about 12 achieved at least a 4–5 per cent growth rate in real GDP.[27] The growth for some of the good performers was export-led. Exports in 1988–93 increased in real terms by 4.4 per cent per annum, reversing the trends of 1981-7, when earnings fell annually by 0.3 per cent, according to World Bank data. Since the recession in 1988–93 in OECD countries (which import about 80 per cent of Africa's exports) resulted in lower commodity prices, export growth has been largely devaluation-driven and due to a catch-up effect in volumes in the traditional export sector. Non-traditional export growth has for the most part been disappointing, reflecting a long-term continued reliance on primary commodities.

With typical population growth rates of around 3 per cent per annum, the World Bank estimates that even the fastest growing African countries need to double their current annual per capita growth rates of 5 per cent, if they are to make any impact on poverty in the medium run. This would imply a doubling of the level of investment, assuming a constant efficiency of investment. The average rate of investment across sub-

---

[26] Sanjaya Lall, 'Structural problems of African industry', in F. Stewart, S Lall & S. Wangwe (eds), *Alternative Development Strategies in Sub-Saharan Africa* (Macmillan, London, 1992); S. Lall, G. Navaretti, S. Teitel & G. Wignaraja, *Technology and Enterprise Development: Ghana under structural adjustment* (Macmillan, London, 1994).
[27] In order of decreasing per capita GDP growth rates, these countries are: Botswana, Lesotho, Mauritius, Seychelles, Nigeria, Equatorial Guinea, Cape Verde, Chad, Uganda, Guinea-Bissau, Ghana and Tanzania.

Saharan Africa is quoted by the World Bank as around 16 per cent of GDP in 1988–93, little changed from 1981–7. Where investment has grown this has been due to public investment: yet the fragility of the fiscal balance, and the necessity for more social sector and infrastructural spending, makes any large and sustained contributions from the public sector improbable. Most investment in African countries is due to private investment, comprising about 60 per cent of total investment, but this has universally stagnated across Africa.[28] The source for private investment lies in private saving; and while data are not generally available, what there are suggest little recorded growth of private domestic savings over the past decade. While the oil economies have increased savings substantially, for most countries recorded aggregate savings rates lie below 10 per cent, and others are dissaving (e.g. Tanzania, Uganda, Lesotho, Guinea-Bissau). Yet, based on empirical research into the financial systems of five African countries, Nissanke[29] concludes that the emphasis on domestic capital shortages is exaggerated. Potential savings are substantially understated, since domestic resource mobilization is highly fragmented, and there is inefficient intermediation between savings and investment. Segmentation has occurred into formal and informal sectors, and there is little interaction amongst the formal institutions. However, the transmission of savings into investment is not just a matter of financial intermediation. Inconsistent and incredible macro-economic policies reverberate down to the household level and together with biased or short-lived micro-policy interventions, create an uncertain environment for households. This emphasizes the precautionary motive for household savings and induces high levels of liquidity.[30] Thus, in addition to the deepening of the financial structure, fairly long-term macro-measures to create a favourable investment climate, and effective micro-measures to enhance household security, will be required to translate savings into investment.

Given the small contribution likely to arise from private and public investment in the short to medium run, foreign investment will have to be a major source of investment in many African economies if they are not to incur further indebtedness. Foreign direct investment has proved negligible in the last decade, largely due to the unattractive macro-policy and regulatory environments in African economies. Rates of return on investment in Africa are comparatively lower than in other regions, and African government debt in international secondary markets is priced the lowest for developing regions. Another possible source of funds for investment is the return of flight capital, which has indeed comprised a large flow recently in such countries as Zambia and Uganda. This fact underlines the importance of strong macro-policies in encouraging such flows.

It remains an important question whether African economies should increase their debt levels further. Sub-Saharan Africa has become increasingly aid-dependent, with aid flows rising at 6 per cent per annum in real terms in the past five years. Evidence above showed the sensitivity of public finances to reduced aid flows, even in countries with the best growth performance. Imports too are highly vulnerable to alterations in balance-of-payments support. One estimate is that sub-Saharan Africa receives about five times more net official transfers per capita than South Asia does, and that aid constitutes 9.3 per cent of African GNP, compared with 2.1 per cent in South Asia.[31] Many commentators believe that aid flows have allowed politicians to postpone the essential adjustments, and

---

[28] Glen and Sumlinski, *Trends in Private Investment in Developing Countries 1995*.

[29] Machiko Nissanke, 'Financial sector reform and intermediation performance', in Willem van der Geest (ed.), *Negotiating Structural Adjustment in Africa* (James Currey, London, 1994), p. 171.

[30] Timothy Besley, 'Saving, credit and insurance', in Jere Behrman & T.N. Srinivasan (eds), *Handbook of Development Economics* (vol. III, North Holland, Amsterdam, forthcoming).

[31] Collier, 'The marginalization of Africa'.

indeed have made damaging policy reversals easier for some governments.[32] Many countries already cannot sustain their debt burdens. Total debt in sub-Saharan Africa (excluding South Africa) was $179 billion at the end of 1992, representing a 25 per cent increase on 1988, and two-thirds of the increase was due to the accumulation of debt-service arrears and interest capitalization on outstanding debt. Most of this is official debt, and the majority of it is bilateral not multilateral debt. In an analysis of 45 African countries the World Bank concludes that 19 countries have manageable debt burdens, meaning that the net present value of debt service to exports is 200 per cent or less. The remaining countries need more than export growth to cope with their debts. However, the options are few for limiting Africa's aid dependence in the light of administratively and financially impaired governments, with poor delivery of social services and infrastructure.

### Endogenous growth theory models

Africa needs high rates of economic growth. Yet, as we have seen, save for remarkable growth in a few countries, performance in general has proved disappointing. What are the likely determinants of growth in African countries, given their often common structural characteristics? There is a large and growing empirical literature in the spirit of the 'new growth theory' models,[33] and some interesting results have been achieved using African data. The theory stresses the path dependence (or hysteresis) of growth: that is, initial advantages or disadvantages, and interim shocks, can have long-lasting effects on growth, and these effects can be compounded. Thus, initial economies of scale in production, transport and technology can achieve a virtuous circle of falling costs and further investment. The empirical endogenous growth models include variables for initial conditions (e.g. human capital; physical capital, including infrastructure; income and income distribution; political stability); exogenous events (e.g. terms of trade or climate shocks, and war); economic spill-over effects from growth and development in neighbouring regions; and a range of country characteristics including policy variables (e.g. indicators of fiscal, monetary, trade, financial, tax and exchange-rate policies, and policies affecting research and development), and cultural considerations (e.g. political configurations and the legal culture).

An important feature of these models is the attention accorded to the powerful influence of legal, financial and other institutions as factors in growth, and the social considerations which may impinge on the character of these institutions. This accords with the results of a spectrum of earlier research, which has for instance found that governments' administrative competence was the single most important factor explaining the differences in growth among many developed countries,[34] and that safeguarding civil liberties and political stability also increase growth.[35] This attention might be symbolic at best, given the limits of the data and the complexities of institutions: one

---

[32] ibid.

[33] Robert Barro, 'Economic growth in a cross-section of countries', *Quarterly Journal of Economics*, 106 (1991), pp. 407–43; and the papers and references from 'How Do National Policies Affect Long-run Growth?', World Bank Conference, 8–9 February 1993 (organizers W. Easterly, R. King, R. Levine and S. Rebelo).

[34] G. Reynolds, *Economic Growth in the Third World: 1850–1980* (Yale University Press, New Haven, CT, 1985).

[35] R. Kormendi & P. McGuire, 'Macroeconomic determinants of growth: Cross-country evidence', *Journal of Monetary Economics*, 16 (1985), pp. 141–63; and G. Scully, 'The institutional framework and economic development', *Journal of Political Economy*, 96, 3 (1988), pp. 652–62.

empirical challenge for these models is to devise innovative measures of institutional competence.[36]

Typically in the African context, cross-country regressions of endogenous growth based on fundamental variables, such as government policies and initial conditions, find a persistent effect due to an Africa dummy variable, suggesting that the traditional fundamentals cannot fully explain the African growth experience.[37] A recent paper, examining a wider array of factors influencing long-run growth than any previous study on Africa, improves on past analyses of African growth and renders the Africa dummy insignificant.[38] The study finds that slow growth is associated with low educational performance, political instability (proxied by the number of assassinations per million population), poorly developed financial systems, large black-market premia (indicating macro-economic distortions), large government deficits and inadequate infrastructure. Furthermore, ethnic diversity both slows growth and reduces the possibility of adopting correct policies. Societies with sharp ethnic divisions, particularly where the sizes of groups are large and similar, may face competitive rent-seeking inimical to smooth decision-making within state and private-sector institutions. Finally, there are large spill-over effects of growth from neighbouring regions; so that regional cooperation, or at least the absence of damaging wars and economic deterioration in neighbouring regions, will serve to enhance trade, and facilitate transport routes to the sea for the many land-locked countries.

These sorts of conclusions are reinforced by investment survey results, included in the World Bank's private-sector assessments carried out in a number of African countries.[39] These surveys find in general that the major deterrent to investment is political and economic policy uncertainty; and other important factors are the lack of currency convertibility, poor infrastructure and regulation, rudimentary financial and business services, breaches of contract and high taxation. Accordingly, economists are now paying increasing attention to the role of well-functioning state institutions in policy-making, regulation and administration, as well as to private-sector financial and business institutions.[40]

The weaknesses of the state look very serious in the light of the results of the above models. Cutbacks in social services have seriously damaged the delivery of education and vocational training, health services, and infrastructural development and maintenance. Inconsistent macro-policies reflected in high deficits and black-market premia are the consequence of past failures in policy as well as current policy reversals by state economic institutions, in addition to limited risk diversification against external shocks. Poorly functioning financial institutions can also be attributed to an environment of high and

---

[36] Stephen Knack & Philip Keefer, 'Institutions and economic performance: cross-country tests using alternative institutional measures', *Economics and Politics* (forthcoming, 1995) and Paolo Mauro, 'Corruption, country risk and growth', (Mimeo, Department of Economics, Harvard University, Cambridge MA, 1993), use data from country risk services for international investors, capturing corruption in business dealings with government, contract enforcement, nationalization risks, bureaucratic delays and the integrity of the legal system.

[37] See Ibrahim Elbadawi & Benno Ndulu, 'Long-term development and sustainable growth in sub-Saharan Africa', SAREC International Colloquium on New Directions in Development Economics, Stockholm, March, 1994.

[38] William Easterly & Ross Levine, 'Africa's growth tragedy' (Mimeo, World Bank, Washington DC, November 1994). Pooled cross-country regressions are used for all countries with data (excluding the Gulf oil states): the dependent variable is the average annual growth rate of GDP per capita in the 1960s, 1970s and 1980s; explanatory variables are decade averages, except for those controlling for initial income (at the start of each decade). Note that the use of decade averages for explanatory variables may introduce endogeneity problems.

[39] 'Private sector development in IDA countries' (Private Sector Development Department, World Bank, Washington DC, 1994).

[40] Paul Collier, 'The role of the African state in building agencies of restraint' (Mimeo, Centre for the Study of African Economies, University of Oxford, February, 1995).

correlated risks and the inability to manage these risks.[41] Improved design and conduct of macro-economic and financial policies by state economic institutions matter, as well as the availability of institutions to manage commodity price stabilization.[42] International relations are weak amongst African states, with limited successes for formal or informal regional integration. While political instability has many probable causes, the lack of a constitution-based politics sensitive to pressures from civil society, and an inequitable income distribution, must be emphasized. The impact of ethnicity in many cases has been to rationalize a one-party state on grounds of national unity, with the damaging effects of limited economic accountability. The question remains highly debatable whether multi-party democracy engenders ethnic strife, but recent analysis discusses how legislation in Botswana and Mauritius, for example, may help to prevent ethnic conflicts from interfering with the multi-party system.

## The Role of Institutions and Constitutional Reform

Cross-country empirical tests of 'new growth theory' models, in which African countries are a significant part of the sample, lend support to the notion of the path-dependency of growth, and the substantial influence of institutions and the environment in which they operate. Typically this hysteresis is thought to originate in initial conditions of income and capital, and transitory shocks, which have long-lasting effects. However, a recent critique by Paul David of the 'new institutional economics' argues that the evolution of institutions themselves is path-dependent, and this suggests that initial conditions for these models should include institutional capacities.[43]

### The path-dependence of institutional change

The fact that institutions evolve is self-evident. What is in contention is the mechanism of this evolution. In David's view, three fundamental micro-institutional features can help to explain path-dependence. First, in order to function effectively, institutions need to evolve mutually consistent expectations amongst individuals within the organization, or social conventions, which can coordinate the actions of individuals, without the need for centralized direction. For instance, a firm engaging in commercial transactions will require particular behaviour to be adopted associated with well-defined roles. Reliable control of behaviour will typically depend on shared historical social experience, such as prior investment in socialization and ethical education. Second, for even a minimum viable level of efficiency, an organization needs to establish communication channels and particular ways of processing information. Once specialized information systems are adopted by an institution from a range of possible choices, learning the 'code' for an individual represents an irreversible investment. In fact, these systems are more likely to be refined and ingrained over time. In this respect, the early choice of codes resembles sunk capital. Third, complex institutional arrangements may fit together, forming complementary 'institutional clusters', which are self-reinforcing. Thus, historical prece-

[41] Nissanke, 'Financial sector reform and intermediation performance'.

[42] Ronald Duncan & Christopher Gilbert, 'Two statements on commodity price risk management', UNCTAD Ad Hoc Group of Experts on Risk Management in Commodity Trade, Geneva, 26–28 October 1994.

[43] Paul David, 'Why are institutions the "Carriers of History"? Path dependence and the evolution of conventions, organizations and institutions', *Structural Change and Economic Dynamics*, 5, 2 (1994), pp. 205–20. See also Kenneth Arrow, *The Limits of Organization* (W.W. Norton, New York, 1974).

dent can shape the whole institutional cluster: rules chosen early on, for which the rationale is now obsolete, are perpetuated because removing them may disturb other operations, and with significant adjustment costs. According to David, where these features are pronounced, organizational structures can become locked into narrow subsets of routines and goals. In this case, change will occur incrementally, and possibly imperceptibly, with new functions adapted to interlock with the pre-existing structure.

This approach contrasts with a more conventional view that current characteristics of economic institutions have evolved as efficient solutions to resource allocation problems, and internal organization and modes of functioning represent the consequences of rational optimizing decisions. This analysis suggests a ready adaptation or plasticity of institutions, and consequently, '. . . the implicit presumption that institutional arrangements are perfectly malleable seems to be a persistent predilection on the part of many mainstream economists'.[44] While the 'new institutional economics' is essentially prescriptive, with suggestions for improved incentive structures and better organization that are expected to result in greater institutional efficiency, it does not consider the actual implementation difficulties. David's is a functional analysis, the important contribution of which is to focus attention on the process of transition, and the reasons for resistance to reform, via the sunk capital of conventions and codes necessary for the functioning of an institution, as well as its historical links to other institutions. A further implication is that, where cross-institutional links are well-developed, there will be economies of scale in institutional reform, such that piecemeal reform may be less effective than reforms applied in concert to a range of interconnected institutions.

This perspective raises policy questions about institutional reform and growth in Africa. With path-dependent institutions, empirical growth models without comprehensive proxies for initial institutional conditions, and shocks to institutions, may seriously underestimate the adjustment costs to new higher growth equilibria. We have argued above that reform and development of state economic, political and legal institutions are of paramount importance for growth, but one cannot necessarily hold a sanguine view of the outcome. Institutions are the products of their environments and the negative impact of past distortions will persist. The capacity to reform through the transfer of technical knowledge may in practice be very limited. Further, many institutions in Africa are dominated by networks of the elite,[45] who may resist adaptation to prevent the obsolescence of their organizational capital. Two practical instances of these points are the often poor transfer of technical economic capacity to African institutions, and the resistance experienced in the privatization process.

On the other hand, given the low capacity and skills-scarce environment in which most African institutions operate, the act of completely destroying institutions, with a view to beginning anew, may simply bring about a permanent loss of capacity, and massive postponed adjustment costs. For instance, in the important area of commodity price risk management, some commentators have somewhat controversially criticized the Bretton Woods organizations ' . . . who in their enthusiasm for liberalizing structural adjustment have allowed much of the stabilizing and risk-reducing experience of state marketing boards to be washed away with the monopolistic bath water'.[46] An instance of destruction of private-sector institutions (that is, firms), with their particular

[44] David, 'Why are institutions the "Carriers of History"?', pp. 206–7.
[45] See for instance Nicolas van de Walle, 'Political liberation and economic policy reform in Africa', *World Development*, 22, 4 (1994), pp. 483–500.
[46] Duncan & Gilbert, 'Two statements on commodity price risk management'.

experience of doing business under African conditions, is the recent rapid trade and interest-rate liberalization, which has damaged existing capacity in the manufacturing sector in such countries as Zambia and Zimbabwe.

These considerations point to the necessity of fairly far-reaching reforms within existing institutions, thus allowing accumulated skills and experience to be harnessed and rechannelled. Such changes could eventually be sustainable without aid, despite the increased call on government recurrent expenditures, in view of the smaller number of motivated civil servants reaping efficiency gains from a low base. An instance of a successful transformation along these lines is the creation of a quasi-autonomous revenue board in Uganda, where salaries were raised, staffing curtailed, processes streamlined and computerized, and on-the-job technical training was given.

### The oversight structure for institutions

It was emphasized above that where cross-institutional links are important, the major pitfalls to a credible reform of institutions will lie not only in such internal problems, but crucially in the broader context in which institutions operate. These links are particularly important amongst state institutions. A number of questions concerning the institutional environment get to the heart of the matter. By whom, and by which criteria, are managers, and others, in the institution appointed? Who controls the funding available to institutions? Does the institution have clear and non-conflicting objectives, and how are these objectives arrived at? How easy is it to change the appointments system, the funding and the objectives of organizations, and is the process of change transparent? Are there effective oversight agencies or watchdog bodies to monitor the institution? To whom do institutions and agencies report, and how accountable publicly is their performance?[47]

Typical answers to these questions for the many institutions influencing African economies, and the myriad oversight structures (some dating from the colonial era), help to explain much of the failure of these bodies. Senior figures in these institutions are frequently political appointments, often made by the president or by his appointees with his approval (e.g. governors of central banks, permanent secretaries of ministries, state auditors, judges, chief executive officers of parastatals). Subject to the skills-specificity of posts, there may be a rapid turnover of such appointments, or at least the threat of easy removal. This discourages taking responsibility or stepping out of line, and indeed the incentive to master the job. People may be appointed for the wrong reasons: political favours rather than merit, or passivity.

Many oversight agencies have been weakened by very low levels of funding, often politically controlled. With limited resources and ineffective management, these agencies cannot be effective. Low and uncertain salaries in African public institutions have created poor incentives, by lowering morale, attracting poor quality applicants, raising staff turnover, and limiting the time incumbents can devote to the job (since they may have to hold other jobs too).

The objectives of institutions may be multiple, unclear and conflicting. Using the channel of political appointments, they may easily and without transparency be altered from what should be core objectives to overtly political and short-term objectives. The ability

---

[47] These types of questions fall in the tradition of a huge literature on principal-agent analysis: e.g. see J. Laffont & J. Tirole, 'The politics of government decision-making: a theory of regulatory capture', *Quarterly Journal of Economics*, CVI (1991), pp. 1089–127.

to divert institutions from core objectives can be seriously detrimental to economic growth: the obvious example is policy reversals enacted by state institutions. Thus, political or interest-group interference with appointments, funding and objectives introduces hysteresis into institutions by permanently degrading their efficiency or their reputation.

Oversight agencies may report to parliament, and there may even be some debate and criticism from parliamentary committees. But typically these committees are under-resourced and have no formal mandate to act. The problems are worsened in areas of technical complexity. With limited democracy, accountability is minimal. Often state institutions report directly to the president.[48]

Thus, it is clear that a series of interlocking institutions, a cluster, will achieve and collectively reinforce a sub-optimal *modus operandi* in such an environment. Even where an act of parliament governs an institution's operation and oversight, one has to turn to the fine print.[49]

Collier[50] has recently drawn attention to the lack of effective agencies of restraint in African countries, by which he means oversight agencies for state and private economic institutions, or professional bodies which set standards for private-sector institutions. He critically examines a range of current policies for strengthening restraint, which could impact on three important deterrents to African private investment. The deterrents he considers are endemic corruption; the uncertain economic reputation of governments, due to a finite probability of policy reversal (which through hysteresis worsens if there have been past reversals); and the illiquidity of firms' fixed assets, attributed both to the breakdown of the private audit profession in verifying firms' accounts, and of the civil legal system in establishing and enforcing legal title.[51]

In fact, the domestic policies Collier considers for strengthening restraint are not strictly concerned with improving oversight. Rather they focus on narrowing the set of specific objectives to be followed by the institution in question, and thus seem to embody an element of commitment by government. Examples of commitment to a narrower set of objectives are legally enshrining central bank independence; the adoption of procedural cash budget rules by the ministry of finance (e.g. in Zambia); and granting quasi-autonomy to revenue boards (e.g. Uganda). However, in the absence of a working constitution, there is no effective sanction to government itself, should it break the rules:[52] and there is no binding of successive governments to the rules. In other words, these commitments are reversible. Yet, it is widely accepted for a range of economic phenomena that if policies are to be perceived as credible, they should be tied to an irreversible pre-commitment or investment.[53] To create a perception of credible reform,

---

[48] A study exploring these points to explain the dismal performance of Zambia's most important parastatal, is Janine Aron, 'Political capture of a mining parastatal: the case of Zambia Consolidated Copper Mines Limited 1981–91', (Working Paper, Center for International Development Research, Duke University, Durham, NC, 1992).

[49] A case in point is the Anti-Corruption Commission, set up under President Kaunda's government in Zambia, which even recently has been held up as an effective preventative of corruption simply by the fact of its existence. Scrutiny of the Act shows that the President controls the funding, the appointments, the objectives, the oversight, what is published, and whether reports are acted upon; and he may covertly change any of these at any time (The Corrupt Practices Act, 1980).

[50] Collier, 'The role of the African state in building agencies of restraint'.

[51] See T. Besley, 'Investment and liquidity in Ghanaian agriculture', *Journal of Political Economy*, (forthcoming).

[52] Indeed as Collier points out, the observed absence of correlation of central bank autonomy and low inflation for developing countries is probably due to the weakness of the judiciary in enforcing autonomy (see A. Cukierman, S. Webb & B. Negapti, 'Measuring the independence of central banks and its effect on policy outcomes', *World Bank Economic Review*, 6 (1992), pp. 353–98.

[53] D. Rodrik, 'Promises, promises: Credibility policy reform via signalling', *Economic Journal*, 99 (1989), pp. 756–72.

governments may build in a fiscal sanction by enacting liberalizing reforms, such as interest-rate and capital-account liberalization, that are attractive to investors, but which would prove costly in terms of domestic and foreign debt for fiscally irresponsible governments. However, the increased policy risks of this 'poison pill' (Collier's phrase) are more likely to outweigh the initial effects of improved credibility.

There are foreign agencies which can and do provide limited oversight for public and private sector institutions. In some cases, oversight works because of the cost of voluntarily reneging on the agreement. Thus, donor conditionality carries the threat of the withdrawal of aid and debt relief; and cooperative behaviour in a currency union, currency board or trade grouping (e.g. CFA franc; the North American Free Trade Area), or membership of a cartel (e.g. De Beers diamond marketing organization), carries the threat of lost benefits of membership. A poor credit rating from international accreditation agencies (e.g. Standard and Poor) penalizes risky financial and macro-policies. Private and public international sanction influences respect for human rights. International trade bodies influence trade policy. There are many other examples. In other cases, there may be a firm binding by governments to the oversight of contracted organizations (e.g. the Swiss Société Générale de Surveillance monitors the prices of exports and imports in many African countries to check for misinvoicing). Further, in many subsidiaries of international financial and accounting firms in African countries, limits on firm behaviour are set by the parent company. Yet once again, while international standards of economic and legal behaviour are influential and more or less welcome, these agencies still do not bind public and private institutions in a way that is subject to challenge by the populace.

### Constitutional reform

There is probably no viable long-term alternative to the oversight problem other than deep-seated constitutional change. Institutionalization of the rule of law gives more emphasis to the basic rights of individuals, and improves the balance between state and society. Constitutional reform is distinct from the rather loose notion of 'democracy' that the mere fact of multi-party elections is sometimes considered to guarantee. Rather, constitutional change can carry democracy to the level of citizens, de facto enfranchizing them. However, an effective constitution assumes the existence of a strong civil society which can challenge the state through a variety of means, which may be developed to differing degrees in various countries. Constitutional reform would have to be accompanied by other institutional reforms such as land reform and decentralization of political power to give the masses the power to make states responsible. Further, it is crucial that a constitution creates a fully independent judiciary, specifying the mode of appointment and funding of judges. For without well-paid and competent judges, free of political influence, a constitution cannot be defended. We have argued above that such institutional reforms may be costly and slow to achieve, particularly in such a skills-specific area as the judiciary. While constitutional reform is undoubtedly the root to the oversight problem, its effectiveness, even if well-designed, is likely to be only slowly cumulative. However, constitutional change need not be a lengthy procedure. South Africa's interim constitution bears this out.

Constitutional change potentially embodies a range of economic benefits. A constitution can bind in the sorts of economic rules discussed above, and act as a genuine oversight agency for government. It can thus clarify objectives in a range of economic and other institutions (e.g. South Africa provides for an independent Reserve Bank, which has stated exchange-rate and balance-of-payments objectives). Current governments will have to make the firm commitment that their institutions will operate with account-ability and transparency, and be operationally free of *ad hoc* political interference; and they will *de jure* tie future governments into this commitment.[54] Such an act would prove very attractive to foreign and domestic private business sectors, as a substantial pre-commitment. A constitution can also guarantee freedom of the commercial press and freedom of information. This transparency is itself a powerful check on governments. A constitution can provide a social safety net or basic needs for sectors of society, com-mensurate with its current ability to fund such obligations. In South Africa's interim constitution, childrens' basic needs only are guaranteed. Respect for property and human rights and freedom from racial and gender discrimination obviously have a spectrum of benefits. This removes, for instance, the fear of expropriation of property (a significant deterrent to investment), while the important role of women in the development process is increasingly recognized.

Overturning constitutional obligations should be a matter for referendum (as it is in Malawi), or for an independent constitutional court appointed by independent selectors (as in South Africa). On some specified economic policy matters, rules could conceivably be altered by a majority in parliament. In South Africa and Malawi, wide debate has preceded the adoption of constitutional rules. Furthermore, in South Africa it has been decided to allow ordinary courts to try constitutional cases, to encourage a broad familiarity with the constitution and to entrench it with the whole judiciary. Recently, the interim constitution was seen to bring even a popular President to book.[55] It is to be hoped that this constitution rides out the recent threats to limit its provisions, for example on central bank independence.

Ideally, constitutional reform should be undertaken voluntarily by committed govern-ments. African countries could turn to the shining local examples for expertise and advice. However, there is no loss of sovereignty entailed in donors trying to force the issue, because the long-term welfare and rights of the population are at stake, and that is the proper focus of sovereignty, rather than avoiding offending current governments. Donors could offer substantial debt relief in exchange for comprehensive and effective constitu-tional change, and there is now a window of opportunity with the increasing accep-tability of democratic ideas, post-Cold War.

## Conclusions

This chapter has drawn on a range of recent literature to develop the argument that Africa's future growth prospects are overwhelmingly circumscribed by its institutional foundations. These encompass a broad range of state legal, political and economic institu-tions, and private-sector financial and business institutions, as well as an effective over-sight or monitoring structure for these institutions. At root, sustainable institutional development will depend on deep-seated constitutional reform.

---

[54] This is a more permanent and prospective structure for government commitment than the World Bank's (never-theless useful) current suggestion that commitment be evaluated on evidence of retrospective extensive consultation on policies, nationally and with the private sector; that past fiscal management be a key indicator, showing respect for the budget constraint, and allocation of spending towards social sectors and away from military expenditures (see also Tony Killick, 'Conditionality and the adjustment-development connection', Paper presented to the Con-ference on Fifty Years after Bretton Woods, Madrid, 1994).
[55] 'Winnie Mandela sacked again', *Financial Times*, 15/16 April, 1995, p. 2.

Africa's growth performance is inadequate if it is going to address its large and growing levels of poverty. According to the World Bank, even the best economic performers need to double their current economic growth rates of 5 per cent, if they are to make any inroads into poverty. Moreover, poverty reduction requires growth with redistribution. However, there are limited sources of capital to provide the investment towards any significant acceleration of growth in the short to medium run. Severe constraints on government expenditures rule out any large and sustained contributions from the public sector. Most investment in African countries is due to private investment, which has stagnated across Africa in the last decade. The source for private investment lies in private savings. While low (recorded) savings rates have much to do with the highly fragmented nature of domestic resource mobilization in Africa, improving savings and translating them into investment will depend on consistent macro-policy and improved household security, as well as long-term financial restructuring measures. Another possible source of funds for investment is the return of flight capital, which is difficult to quantify, though there have been large inflows recently in such countries as Zambia and Uganda. This fact underlines the importance of strong macro-policies in encouraging such flows. In addition, the small size of domestic markets implies a limited absorptive capacity for home-produced goods. It seems inevitable that an early impetus for growth will require many African countries to increase their now limited international (including regional) linkages in the form of a deeper and more diversified export base and larger flows of foreign direct investment. The costs of delay now are continued stagnation and greater aid dependency, and a yet more fluid and competitive international environment to grapple with in the future.

What are the determinants of growth in the African context? In recent years, economists have increasingly turned for inspiration to the practical example of successful growth through international linkages in South-East Asian countries. The tendency, however, has been to overemphasize the role of export orientation in achieving high growth, and to downplay the importance and effectiveness of government intervention in these countries.[56] In Africa, consequently, structural adjustment policies have typically concentrated on liberalizing prices and marketing arrangements, and providing export incentives, with scant attention to the institutional environment, human capital investment and the importance of equitable growth. The surprising lack of a supply response in reforming African countries in the 1990s, especially in diversifying to non-traditional exports, has refocused attention on these issues. Global events after the Cold War have probably reinforced this trend. This includes the experiences of foreign donors in East European economies, with little in the way of market and democratic institutions, but also the new feasibility of improving executive, legislative, regulatory and other institutions given the increasing acceptability of democratic ideas in Africa.

One recent and influential strand of research on the determinants of growth is the estimation of empirical models in the spirit of the new endogenous growth theory. The theory stresses the path dependence, or hysteresis, of growth: that is, initial conditions and interim shocks can have long-lasting effects on growth. The empirical growth models, in which African countries form a significant part of the sample, lend strong support to the role of state institutions in developing human capital, providing and maintaining infrastructure, facilitating research and development, promoting political stability

---

[56] World Bank, *The East Asian Miracle: Economic growth and public policy* (Oxford University Press, New York, 1993). For a critique see Dani Rodrik, 'King Kong meets Godzilla: The World Bank and the East Asian miracle', (CEPR Discussion Paper No. 944, April, 1994).

and regional links, and, importantly, in making consistent macro-economic policy and sticking to it. Private institutions matter too, including the depth and efficiency of the financial system, as does the social environment of institutions, such as bureaucratic delays and corruption, the integrity of the legal system, and sharp ethnic or religious divisions. Surveys of investors in Africa broadly support the conclusions of these growth models. Yet, empirical analysis of this type is still in its infancy in Africa. It is particularly important to test for the positive effects of growth found elsewhere, using measures such as income and wealth distribution and land reform.[57] There are limited data, particularly in the institutional sphere, which may underestimate the importance of institutional capacity. Moreover, as one prominent commentator has suggested, these models are highly stylized, with accumulated decades of institutional field experience 'simplified to the point of distortion . . .'[58]

What is the capacity of the African state to deliver the above growth-promoting conditions? If African states were in the position to follow East Asian governments' strategies, interventionist policies would be highly advantageous, given the increased growth and the increasingly competitive international environment. Contrary to popular opinion, there is no unique East Asian model, but rather variants of industrial policies which employ differential strategies to address market failures. Clearly the type of state that can successfully implement these often highly targeted policies needs strong administrative capacity, plus the institutional strength to discriminate between winners and losers. However, a significant theme of this chapter has been to trace the macro-economic history and radical redefinition of the state's economic role in Africa, culminating in a disturbing picture of a fragile state in the 1990s. The state in Africa has come full circle to the small government of pre-colonial days; but with the additional hysteresis effect from past shocks of a seriously depleted current institutional capability, deterioration in the current quality and scope of social services and infrastructure provision, coupled with a fiscal position highly vulnerable to changes in foreign aid. The drastic impairment of the state looks serious in the light of the results of endogenous growth theory models. Its very weaknesses are important determinants of growth, while its past and current weaknesses are being compounded over time.

It is clear that long-term and sustainable growth needs the reform and development of state and other institutions. The private sector can substitute for the state in the provision of services traditionally in the government's domain, only up to a point. A path-dependent view of the evolution of institutions has been presented in this chapter, which has significant practical implications for institutional reform in Africa. It suggests that empirical growth models without comprehensive proxies for initial institutional conditions, and shocks to institutions, may seriously underestimate the adjustment costs to new higher growth equilibria. First, the path-dependent perspective focuses attention on the process of transition, and the reasons for resistance to reform, via the sunk capital of conventions and codes necessary for the functioning of an institution, as well as its historical links to other institutions. Institutions are not very plastic: they are the products of their environments and the negative impact of past distortions will persist. The inherited capacity to reform through the transfer of technical knowledge may in practice

---

[57] Torsten Persson & Guido Tabellini, 'Is inequality harmful for growth? Theory and evidence' (CEPR Discussion Paper No. 581, September, 1991).
[58] Paul David, 'Rethinking technology transfers: institutions and knowledge-based industrial development', Paper presented at the British Academy/Chinese Academy of Social Sciences Joint Seminar on Technology Transfer, April, 1995.

be limited. Further, many institutions in Africa are dominated by networks of the elite, who may resist adaptation to prevent the obsolescence of their organizational capital. However, given the low capacity and skills-scarce environment in which most African institutions operate, scrapping institutions may needlessly destroy capacity, and introduce large adjustment costs. This argues for far-reaching reform within existing organizations and there are recent success stories in Africa.

Second, where cross-institutional links are well developed, there will be economies of scale in institutional reform, and piecemeal reform will be less sustainable than reforms applied in concert or at least sequentially to interconnected institutions. These links are particularly important for state institutions, and thus the broader question of the oversight structure for institutions needs to be addressed. One conclusion is that the micro-institutional design matters. The myriad institutions, including oversight agencies, in African countries have been weakened through acts of parliament allowing political appointments, politically controlled funding, and multiple and conflicting objectives, with appointments, funding and objectives all subject to alteration in a non-transparent fashion. Further, with limited democracy, accountability of oversight agencies and other institutions has been minimal. Clearly, a series of interlocking institutions will achieve and collectively reinforce a sub-optimal *modus operandi* in such an environment.

Improving oversight for state and private-sector institutions could significantly reduce many important deterrents to African private investment. However, simply narrowing the set of specific objectives of institutions (e.g. budget rules, or legalizing central bank independence), without providing a binding sanction to government itself (and future governments), should it break the rules, is little more than a reversible commitment by government to such policies. Relying instead on foreign agencies to enforce some international benchmark of economic and legal behaviour achieves a limited oversight, and may work quite well, but still does not ineradicably bind governments to their obligations to the populace.

There is probably no viable long-term alternative to the oversight problem other than deep-seated constitutional change. Constitutional change potentially embodies a range of economic benefits. Institutionalization of the rule of law gives more emphasis to the rights of individuals, and improves the balance between state and society, but does depend on the existence of a strong civil society which can challenge the state. Constitutional reform would have to be accompanied by other institutional reforms such as land reform and decentralization of political power, to give the masses the power to make states responsible. Further, it is crucial that a constitution creates a fully independent judiciary, specifying the mode of appointment and funding of judges. Yet we have concluded that such institutional reforms may be costly and slow to achieve, particularly in such a skills-specific area as the judiciary. For these reasons, while constitutional reform is undoubtedly the root of the oversight problem, its effectiveness, even if well-designed, is likely to be only slowly cumulative. Hence it should not be delayed.

What, then, is the reality for the role of the state in Africa from the mid-1990s? Probably very small government with highly circumscribed options. The constraint is to act now to increase international linkages for growth, but this involves a set of policies of which only a small sub-set can actually be carried out by weakened African governments. Feasible elements of the policy set towards improving the initial conditions for growth could still be adopted, with some reaping important future benefits.[59]

---

[59] Amartya Sen, 'Beyond liberalization: social opportunity and human capability', *DEP*, 58 (Development Economics Research Programme, London School of Economics, November 1994).

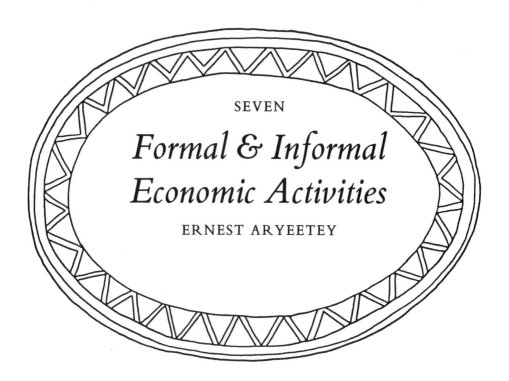

SEVEN

# Formal & Informal Economic Activities

## ERNEST ARYEETEY

It was generally expected that in African countries that have undergone economic reform in the last decade, the relative sizes of their informal sectors would diminish as more formal private-sector activities were encouraged by the reform measures. It is in this regard that some concern has been expressed about poor investment responses in Africa,[1] at the same time as various studies have shown more positive responses by small and micro-enterprises to structural adjustment.[2] Formal sectors were expected to take over market share from both the public sector and the informal sector. There does not appear currently to be any empirical evidence to support such a position in Africa, however.[3]

The reference to informal sectors in this chapter covers both informal real-sector activity and informal financial activity, making a distinction between the two when necessary. The 'informal real sector' here is a subsector of what is more fashionably referred to as the micro-enterprise sector in much of the recent literature on enterprise development,[4] characterized by a labour force of under four persons. Most informal real activities are characterized by self-employment and hardly any record-keeping. They are

[1] World Bank, *Adjustment in Africa: Reforms, results and the road ahead* (Policy Research Report, Oxford University Press, New York, 1994).
[2] W.F. Steel & L.Webster, 'How small enterprises in Ghana have responded to adjustment', *World Bank Economic Review*, 6, 3 (1992), pp. 423–38.
[3] E. Aryeetey, *Informal Finance in Africa* (African Economic Research Consortium, Nairobi, forthcoming).
[4] e.g. N. Molenaar, M.S.S. El-Namaki & M.P. van Dijk (eds), *Small-Scale Industry Promotion in Developing Countries* (Research Institute for Management Science, Delft, 1983), pp. 120–31.

almost always not registered by any national authorities. 'Informal finance' in Africa is defined here to embrace all financial transactions that take place outside the functional scope of various countries' banking and other financial sector regulations. This definition permits the inclusion of a wide range of financial activities whose operational scope may differ across countries. Various studies suggest a wide variety of such informal savings and lending units in the region.[5]

The relative dynamism of the informal-sector response to reform is also exemplified in a number of studies which suggest that informal finance has responded much more positively to various growth stimuli than have formal financial-sector operations.[6] But informal finance is a direct function of informal real-sector activities. Informal finance grew faster only because the growth rate of the informal real sector outstripped that of the formal sector. Our view is that market reforms under structural adjustment policies do not necessarily remove those structural features of developing economies that give rise to informal activities designed to meet the demands from distinct market niches. We shall explain this phenomenon in this chapter.

The expectation of a diminishing informal sector as the result of the reforms is derived from the general perception of what constitutes the informal sector. Notwithstanding our definition of informal economic activity, many descriptions of economic activities as informal have been confusing and have tended to suggest that informal-sector activities are mainly those economic activities that thrive when public policies do not favour or support the formal sector. For example, theories on financial repression suggest that curb markets abound in developing countries as a result of repressive financial policies, ironically designed to strengthen formal finance.[7] Structuralist economists have tended to view informal economic activities as residual activities or second-best choices after all manner of economic agents have failed to find optimal conditions in formal economic structures.[8] The inability of those economic agents to find optimal conditions is generally attributed to market failure, with the assumption that, under ideal conditions, all economic agents would operate from formal structures. As a consequence, when attempts have been made to distinguish between formal and informal sectors, these have varied between definitions derived on the basis of ease of entry, scale of operations, regulated versus competitive markets, the use of indigenous resources, the prevalence of family ownership, self-employment as opposed to wage employment, technological choice and the low productivity of labour. When such distinctions have been employed, it is to be presumed that any modifications to market conditions that sought to improve the functioning of those indices would automatically result in reductions in the relative size of informal economic activities.

This chapter discusses how reforms under structural adjustment and their outcomes have influenced the activities and size of the informal sector in sub-Saharan countries.

[5] D. Aredo, 'The informal and semi-formal financial sectors in Ethiopia: a study of the Iqqub, Iddir and savings and credit co-operatives' (AERC Research Paper No. 21, Nairobi, 1993); E. Aryeetey, *Financial Integration and Development in sub-Saharan Africa: a study of informal finance in Ghana* (Overseas Development Institute Working Paper 78, London, 1994).

[6] M.S.D. Bagachwa, *Financial Integration and Development in sub-Saharan Africa: a study of informal finance in Tanzania* (ODI Working Paper 79, London, 1994); A. Soyibo, *Financial Integration and Development in sub-Saharan Africa: a study of informal finance in Nigeria*, (ODI Working Paper 89, London, 1995); C. Chipeta & M.L.C. Mkandawire, *Financial Integration and Development in sub-Saharan Africa: case study of the informal financial sector in Malawi*, (ODI Working Paper 87, London, 1995).

[7] M.J. Fry, 'Models of financially repressed developing economies', *World Development*, 10, 9, (1982), pp. 731–50.

[8] S. van Wijnbergen, 'Macroeconomic effects of changes in bank interest rates: Simulation results for South Korea', *Journal of Development Economics*, 18 (1985), pp. 541–54.

Our argument is basically that informal activities will continue to thrive so long as structural impediments to the transmission of macro-economic incentives prevail. But the rapid expansion of informal-sector activities would not necessarily lead to rapid and sustainable growth of the wider domestic economy in the long term. This is mainly because of the fragmented nature of much informal activity which imposes a constraint and some cost on the flow of resources among economic agents. For the initial expansion of the informal sector in economies undergoing reform to be conducive to wider growth, the various fragments must have strong links to the rest of the economy.

To study the changing dimensions of informal activity in relation to formal activity, we first review the changes in the role of the state in sub-Saharan Africa expected as a consequence of economic reforms and how these have impinged on formal and informal activities. A consideration of the generally poor response of the private sector to macro-economic reform is briefly introduced in the section which follows. Thereafter, we attempt to explain the difficulties the formal private sector encountered in its attempts to take advantage of the macro-economic incentives provided under adjustment policies. The strong re-emergence of informal activities after the reforms, both in the real and the financial sectors, is then discussed, looking at the factors that have propelled the sector forward much faster than the formal sector. The chapter ends with a review of the impact of the prevalence of informal economic activities on the macro-economic performance of African countries in the past decade, looking at such indicators as fiscal performance and the savings-investment nexus.

## Structural Adjustment and the Role of the State

As the state attempts to give up its role in various areas, has the formal private sector been able to take over some of the new functions being handed to it? We look first at how the role of the state was intended to change and the responses as well as factors that influenced the actual or current outcomes.

The practice of government in a number of sub-Saharan countries after independence relied on a heavy involvement of the state in direct production and service activities.[9] It was therefore not surprising that, with the trend of declining agricultural and industrial productivity in the 1960s and 1970s, some pressure was exerted on governments to transfer the ownership or responsibilities of state-owned enterprises to the private sector. Towards the end of the 1970s and in the early 1980s, the major criterion for allocating roles between the central government and the rest of the economy was whether activities led to direct production or only facilitated productive activity. The role of central government was often defined as only to create an acceptable macro-economic environment for the private sector to undertake production, and to facilitate this process by creating the necessary infrastructure.

In fact, however, central governments had difficulty with such approaches for determining roles. The public sector's involvement in production grew substantially. In Ghana, for example, employment in public enterprises grew from 11,000 in 1960 to 241,600 in 1984, representing 27.6 per cent of formal-sector employment. There were 329 public enterprises in 1984, the number having doubled in the preceding 10 years. Many other countries, including Kenya, Tanzania and Mozambique, also had more

[9] See Chapter 6 in the present volume, by Janine Aron.

than 200 public enterprises by 1992,[10] the number having grown substantially since 1970.

It is not surprising that, since the 1980s, donor-sponsored reform programmes have exerted increasing pressure on governments to reduce state involvement in a number of activities. While the privatization of public enterprises has become a major issue, the role of the state in reforming economies is being more narrowly defined in reaction to what has generally been perceived to be the failure of government in many countries. It is sometimes suggested that some state functions that were previously generally regarded as administrative should be delegated to non-governmental organizations.[11] This includes the contracting out of the construction of infrastructure and the provision of some public services.

Most commercial services are now slated for privatization, and there is increasing pressure to use traditional authorities, religious bodies, non-governmental organizations and the private sector for various activities. The rationale behind public-sector reform is generally: 'let others do it, if they can be more cost-effective'. The roles which the state gives up do not have to be only in direct production, as was the dogma of the 1970s and early 1980s. As a consequence, public-sector reforms that have accompanied structural adjustment programmes have adopted the approach of reducing the size of the public services through the retrenchment of public servants involved in administration and attempts at privatizing public enterprises or parastatals. The pressure to delegate some administrative roles of the state to other bodies has certainly intensified in the 1990s.

Even though we shall discuss the response of the private sector to structural adjustment in the next section, the point has to be made here that the expected change in the role of the state as a result of the reform has not fully materialized in many countries; and this has contributed to the inability of the formal private sector to take over from the state in many areas. The state continues to be a major player in many countries. While privatization has been difficult in most countries, the retrenchment of public servants has often taken place, and has thus become the most conspicuous outcome of attempts to reform the public sector. But this has seldom led to any significant changes in the composition of the government's recurrent budget, the implications of which we shall discuss later. 'Only a handful of countries have divested more than 40 per cent of their enterprises. And half the countries have been extremely slow to privatize any enterprises. In Kenya there have been almost no sales [of public enterprises] in ten years. A few countries have even expanded their public enterprise sector.'[12]

Reasons for the slowness of privatization have varied from the most common (too much political interference in the process) to the absence of willing buyers. In many instances, governments have not been able to reach acceptable arrangements with potential buyers, while in other cases they have had to confront the problem of how to compensate the labour that is shed by the privatization exercise.

Interestingly, while the state remains a major player in the productive sectors of economies, it has liberalized entry into most areas within those economies in the hope that this will foster competition and make public enterprises more efficient and less dependent on economic rents. The liberalization of exchange-rate regimes in many countries and the removal of import licences and other international trade restrictions facilitated closer links with foreign economies in the process. The irony of all these efforts is that

---

[10] World Bank, *Adjustment in Africa*.
[11] ibid.
[12] ibid., p. 104.

many governments have been unable directly to initiate a new role in production for the formal private sector because they have omitted to put in place adequate supportive regulatory frameworks and facilities to encourage that sector either to take over state-owned enterprises or to set up competing industries.

This has often led to the situation where a large number of potential investors, unable to acquire state enterprises and finding it difficult to compete with these subsidized entities, have found their way into activities which are not so heavily dominated by the state. Such activities include import trade and other services, which are more dependent on international partners than on the state. But most trade and services linked to it in African cities are informally organized: hence a boom period for the informal sector. Whatever productive activities resulted were dominated by the informal sector. In Tanzania, for example, where the state dominated all economic activities under a socialist regime for a long time, recent liberalization has produced a considerable expansion in the number of informal production and trading activities along the streets of Dar es Salaam. We discuss some economic factors leading to this trend below.

In addition to the inability of the formal private sector to take over state enterprises, the retrenchment of public servants in such countries as Uganda and Ghana released a large portion of the labour force onto a malfunctioning labour market, resulting in significant unemployment. When governments later tried to remedy the situation with assistance packages for promoting self-employment, as under the donor-sponsored Programme of Actions to Mitigate the Social Costs of Adjustment (PAMSCAD) in Ghana, the resulting economic activities were almost always informal in nature, even if some effort was made to register them.

## Private Sector Response to Structural Adjustment

One of the most remarkable outcomes of structural adjustment in sub-Saharan Africa has been the slow response of investment to stimuli provided by macro-economic reforms.[13] The average investment rate for the region rose from 15.9 per cent of GDP in 1965–73 to 22.2 per cent in 1974-80. Between 1981 and 1987, however, alongside declining saving rates, the investment rate fell to an average of 16.7 per cent, and has not recovered since.[14] In general, the slow growth in investment as a ratio of GDP is attributed to the expectation that growth in public spending in the capital budget might have been restrained as governments sought to reduce the fiscal deficit.[15] The private sector was expected to make up for reductions in public capital investments. The evidence from sub-Saharan Africa suggests, however, that in the few countries where governments actually cut back on capital spending this has not been replaced by private investment. If the private sector was unable to carry out the required investments, then the public sector was expected to step up its capital spending.

Indeed, in most reforming countries, public spending patterns have continued as before, with no change in capital expenditure growth rates. Hence the slow growth of total investments. Whatever improvements were made in the fiscal balance can be traced

---

[13]P. Mosley, J. Harrigan & J. Toye, *Aid and Power: the World Bank and policy-based lending* (2 vols., Routledge, London, 1991).
[14] In a number of countries, lending as part of a structural adjustment programme may have enabled public investment to recover.
[15] World Bank, *Adjustment in Africa*.

to revenue improvements in the early stages of the reform, as in Ghana. There is hence little empirical evidence to support the notion that current private investment is dependent on public spending. Both public and private investment were low in relation to GDP before the reforms and have continued to be low. Only in a handful of countries has private investment actually seen any growth, a development that the World Bank attributes to macro-economic reforms.[16]

In Ghana, for example, where one of the most comprehensive sets of reforms has been pursued, private investment recovered only marginally after the reforms began. In the decade of structural adjustment, the target for private investment of 15 per cent of GDP per annum was never attained. Private investment increased only from 2.9 per cent in 1983 to 5.4 per cent in 1985 before falling to 2.4 per cent in 1986. Between 1987 and 1990, it increased from 5.5 per cent to 8.7 per cent.[17] But most of the later growth in fact came from a sizeable increase in foreign direct investment in the gold mining sector, an activity that has been heavily supported with multilateral assistance and significant guarantees.

The performance of the rest of the formal Ghanaian private sector, particularly manufacturing, has not been encouraging. In the reform years, new private investment fell well below planned targets and the capacity utilization of existing firms remained low. A survey of 30 manufacturers[18] showed that less than 10 per cent of respondents undertook any major new fixed investments after 1982, thus recording a sharp drop in the value of total fixed investments as a proportion of annual turnover. Also, a study of 133 small and medium-sized firms in Accra, Kumasi and Takoradi by Aryeetey and others[19] showed that the average number of staff employed by firms dropped from 22 in 1980 to 16 in the absence of technological improvements. This was directly attributed to lower fixed investments during the period, even though many firms purchased equipment after the reforms.

While formal private-sector institutions were unable to take advantage of the macro-economic incentives offered under the reform package for a number of reasons that we discuss below, growth, which had largely been stimulated by donor funds and also remittances, encouraged more positive responses from the rest of the economy. The poor response of private-sector investments in manufacturing occurred at the same time as the considerable expansion of the service sector in general, and distributive trade in particular. But these were activities with much lower sunk costs and shorter turnover periods and were organized largely informally. It is apparent that positive responses occurred mainly where investors made only short-term commitments at any specific time.

By 1993, the service sector contributed 35 per cent of GDP, more than half of which originated from the distributive trade sub-sector, largely organized informally. The sub-sector's output was only marginally below its 1970 level, but its share of sectoral output had been very consistent, and growth since 1985 had been steady. As in many other parts of Africa, the booming distributive trade sub-sector, trading mainly imported consumer items, is quite conspicuous. It is usual to hear the remark in Accra that 'Ghana

[16] The World Bank has observed that 'Nine countries increased (private) investment, and in seven of them the increase coincided with an improvement in macroeconomic policies. . . . The investment response thus is moving in the right direction.' ibid., p. 155.

[17] Y. Asante, *Investment Determinants in Ghana: final report* (African Economic Research Consortium, Nairobi, 1994).

[18] Aryeetey, *Financial Integration and Development*.

[19] E. Aryeetey, A. Baah-Nuakoh, *et al.*, *The Supply and Demand for Finance among SMEs in Ghana* (World Bank Discussion Paper, Washington, DC, 1994).

has become a nation of traders'. Alongside this, informal processing activity has been shown in a number of surveys[20] to have revived considerably since 1986.

With this development, the important question remains why the formal private sector is unable to respond in similar fashion. One conclusion we draw from the above trend is that the reforms pursued in many countries mainly addressed issues arising out of inappropriate policies affecting pricing in markets. When transaction costs rose as a result of constraints in formal institutional structures, it was only those enterprises that could operate outside these structures that benefited from the markets that had been opened up. Hence, the booming informal sector.

## Constraints to Formal Private-Sector Growth

Most studies of supply response after reform have focused on the constraints derived from fiscal policies, infrastructure, market conditions and institutional support. A number of studies of enterprise performance in sub-Saharan Africa after the reforms, and notably the World Bank's Regional Program on Enterprise Development in Africa (RPED),[21] have reported a number of structural constraints in the process. RPED results indicate that small and medium-sized enterprises in sub-Saharan Africa face a large number of problems that may not necessarily be unique to enterprises in the region. These include poor access to credit for both working capital and fixed investments as well as poor demand in the face of rising competition from cheaper imports from East Asian countries. Other major problems found in the countries studied centred on the over-regulation of labour markets in relation to large formal enterprises and the inadequacy of currently applied technologies. In Cameroon the study noted a low level of business confidence as well as 'uncertainty in the government's industrial policy', similar to what the RPED study and also Asante[22] reported for Ghana.

Indeed the issue of uncertainty as a constraint is receiving considerable attention in the recent literature on investment in developing economies. Rodrik[23] suggests that poor response from the formal private sector has been largely due to a perception of uncertainty in the environments under reform, which may be traced to the low credibility and sustainability of the reform processes themselves. In many countries, businesses have viewed the reforms as being unsustainable as a consequence of the government's poor track record with policy reversals, the heavy involvement of donors in the process of managing adjustment and the conditionalities attached to structural adjustment credits. Unsustainable reform policies create instability by creating uncertainty about their own life span and by aggravating instability with macro-economic imbalances.

An illustration of such trends of instability arising from a background of uncertainty is presented by the Ghanaian experience where the persistently high level of inflation

[20] J. Riedel, E. Aryeetey et al., Small-scale Manufacturing and Repair Activities in the Urban Area of Techiman, Ghana (Department of Development Studies, IFO-Institute for Economic Research, Munich, 1988).
[21] A. Baah-Nuakoh & F. Teal, Economic Reforms and the Manufacturing Sector in Ghana. (Report for Africa Regional Program on Enterprise Development (RPED), Private Sector Development and Economics Division, Africa Technical Department, World Bank, Washington DC, 1994); IIEC Montreal, Manufacturing Enterprises under Adjustment in Cameroon: a survey perspective (Report for Africa Regional Program on Enterprise Development (RPED), Private Sector Development and Economics Division, Africa Technical Department, World Bank, Washington DC., 1994).
[22] Asante, Investment Determinants in Ghana.
[23] D. Rodrik, 'How should structural adjustment programs be designed?', World Development, 18, 7 (1990), pp. 933–47.

on the heels of dramatic exchange-rate adjustments led to a series of temporary palliative measures, including more frequent introductions of new Bank of Ghana rediscount rates and constant revisions of banks' reserve requirements.[24] The resulting variability of credit flow to the private sector has, among other things, further undermined its confidence in the banking system and reinforced the tendency to view the investment climate with uncertainty. In general, businessmen expect governments under pressure to reverse macro-economic reform policies, as happened in Nigeria, for example. The consequence is often a tendency for businesses to shorten the time horizons of their own commitments. But 'such shortening of time horizons is the chief obstacle to eliciting the desired private sector response to economic policies'.[25] When private investors perceive a high probability of change in policy in the short to medium term they cannot be expected to make mainly irreversible decisions by committing investment capital to long-term projects.

In situations where formal-sector firms are uncertain about the future, their responses to reforms are often informal. A good illustration of this in many countries is in the hiring of labour. In Cameroon, after changes to bring in a new labour code in 1992 in support of structural adjustment, firms found the new code still too rigid. In the hiring of labour, therefore, while a few formal-sector establishments tried to abide by the new regulations with great difficulty, a large number of firms completely disregarded the code and used their own guidelines. A third category of employers tried the approach of engaging labour only indirectly. This was done through the use of informal-sector agents and was characterized by the absence of enforceable contracts between the firms and their employees. 'These newly unregulated formal firms are presently sitting on the fence separating the informal sector from the formal sector.'[26]

This Cameroonian example is by no means unique to that country. The construction industry in a number of African countries abounds with similar arrangements. In Ghana the use of so-called casual or temporary labourers on a more or less permanent basis has recently given the government cause for concern. The important point to note about firms simply straddling the formal and informal sectors is that their activities may not necessarily be illegal. They simply take advantage of loopholes in regulatory frameworks when operating from the formal sector proves too costly.

## The Growth of Informal Activities After Economic Reforms

The liberalization of various markets following structural adjustment has certainly reduced the requirements for entry into a number of economic sectors in many sub-Saharan countries. While it is generally true that the numbers of entities operating in specific sectors in growing African economies have expanded significantly, informal operators have invariably responded much more actively to new macro-economic policy stimuli. As indicated earlier, this is because of their ability to deal more spontaneously with problems of a structural origin that are reflected in rising transaction costs in the early phases of adjustment and changing informational needs that might otherwise lead to adverse selection and moral hazard in contractual relationships. In this section we illustrate the situation with

[24] Institute of Statistical, Social and Economic Research, *State of the Ghanaian Economy Report 1993* (University of Ghana, Legon, 1994).
[25] Rodrik, 'How should structural adjustment programs be designed?'
[26] IIEC Montreal, *Manufacturing Enterprises under Adjustment in Cameroon*, p. 263.

a look at the performance of selected activities of the informal sector as they cut across the real and financial sectors of a number of sub-Saharan countries.

### The costs of transacting business in the real economic sector after reform

Apart from removing policy bottlenecks that restricted the scope of economic activities in repressed economic regimes, reforms often sought to provide regulatory frameworks more conducive to the conduct of such activities. The essence of these arrangements was to make it profitable for economic agents to utilize more fully market-based arrangements for the production and distribution of all goods and services. Thus, transactions between producers and consumers were expected to take place at minimum cost to the parties.

In practice, however, relaxation of the regulatory frameworks and the removal of other structural impediments usually lagged far behind the macro-economic reforms introduced in the liberal environment. A frequent result was that formal-sector economic agents could not take full advantage of the liberal macro-economic environment established. As depicted earlier, while straddling the two sectors may be a way out of the dilemma for many formal operators, a faster growth of purely informal operators could be observed.

In Ghana, for example, the realignment of the exchange-rate regime with major external currencies took place far in advance of the removal of restrictions on labour engagement as well as the re-writing of the investment code to deal with such issues as firm ownership and source of investment capital. The World Bank RPED study in Ghana suggests that an adverse regulatory framework affected the transactions of larger (formal) enterprises trying to export more than it did smaller (often informal) enterprises. When relatively large firms wanting to export found it difficult to raise the necessary capital for investment in new technologies because foreign ownership of enterprises was limited under the pre-reform investment code, small informal exporters of near-similar products responded much more readily in the non-traditional export sector (fruits, crafts, etc.).

Whereas larger firms complained about the regulatory framework surrounding such arrangements as the retention of foreign exchange from export earnings, access to bank credit, the use of foreign equities, business registration, etc. and were sometimes unwilling to bribe their way through the difficulties, small informal operations took place involving the export of one or two cartons of fresh fruit as luggage for a number of travellers and destined for specific niche markets among immigrant communities in Europe. While the marginal financial costs of transacting business remained high for both informal and formal operations, informal arrangements ensured that such exports went unhindered by regulation for many years. The informal sector's greatest gain in this area of activity was therefore with respect to the non-financial transaction costs, exemplified by time-saving. As the regulatory framework improved, many informal operations in the export sector have actually been 'formalized' through registration but continue to operate informally in the financing of their businesses.

### Inadequate information in the real economic sector after reform

All transactions between producers of goods and services and their customers entail a contractual arrangement that may be fulfilled either immediately a purchase is made or over an agreed period of time. In many African economies, because of low incomes in many households, contractual arrangements that extend payments over a period of time tend to be quite common. For such arrangements, the suppliers of goods and services require ample

127

information about their customers in order to make decisions, but this information is not always easy to obtain as they face many dispersed low-income customers. It is certainly much easier for a supplier who lives in the same community as a customer to obtain information than for a large formal entity located outside that community.

For this reason formal-sector operators prefer to link up with informal operators in agency relationships. This is particularly conspicuous in the textile and food and beverage industries in many countries south of the Sahara. Informal operators are used by formal industries for the distribution of their produce across the length and breadth of countries, and even for exports. The role of traders across West African borders is a clear example of this link between the formal and informal sectors in an attempt to minimize the risks associated with inadequate information on the part of formal producers. Textile producers are generally known to promote these arrangements by providing goods on credit to informal distributors for channelling to final consumers. The present arrangements also explain the rapid growth of informal trading activities in many African cities following the initial growth arising from economic reforms.

Such agency relationships do not extend to production by informal operators. There are few agency links in production where the informal supplier, acting as the principal in this case, and using the formal buyer as an agent, may gain access to sophisticated larger (export) markets. In all the RPED studies there was little evidence of vertical integration in production between formal and informal operators in the countries studied. Formal buyers may lack information on the quality, capability for on-time delivery, etc. of the informal supplier. But they can often find the same items elsewhere or can organize the production themselves, and therefore do not need the informal supplier.

### The costs of transacting business in the financial sector after reform

In dealing with transaction costs in the financial sector, households often have some asset choices to make, with a view to minimizing the relevant costs. We look here at factors affecting the selection of real assets and informal financial assets, as well as some trends in these choices.

Households have two basic choices in saving: either to acquire financial assets or to settle for real assets. The choice depends mainly on the nature of the risk-adjusted returns on the asset. There are certain risks that a potential saver can do little or nothing about, such as inflation or government policies and attitudes towards wealth. There are other risks that can be more easily dealt with, such as theft of the asset, bankruptcy or insolvency of the banking institution, etc. This can be done through insurance schemes, for example. In a relatively stable economic environment, depositors often take the first set of risks for granted and make decisions based primarily on the second, placing their assets where they will be reasonably secure while yielding the highest possible returns. There is not much variation in risk and the risks are relatively low. Depositors therefore switch from instrument to instrument or from institution to institution (given that the institutions are present and functioning), looking for high yields and security.

On the other hand, when the macro-economic environment is not stable, or when institutions for holding the assets are not functioning well, the first set of risks becomes very important. In this case, the question faced by the potential saver is not 'which asset?' but whether to hold financial assets at all. Many holders of real or non-monetized assets do so for a combination of the two reasons. They perceive the economic situation to be not quite as stable as they would wish and the financial market does not function well.

It is generally believed that non-monetized savings far outweigh monetized or financial savings in many African economies.[27] Non-monetized savings in Ghana, up to the 1980s, were predominantly a rural phenomenon. One study[28] estimated that in rural Ghana over 80 per cent of total household savings were in real assets. In northern Ghana a larger proportion of these savings are held in the generally liquid forms of stored produce and live animals. This may be attributed to seasonality in production, as it allows them to smoothe consumption. In southern Ghana where incomes are generally less seasonal and cyclical, larger portions of rural savings are held in less liquid forms such as building materials, partially completed construction projects and cleared land.

As a structural feature of the economy, the holding of real assets is attributable to the relatively low degree of monetization of the rural economy. There are simply not enough facilities for channelling unconsumed income into worthy financial assets. The occasional explosion of such savings, particularly in urban centres, is derived from such factors as inflation and other sources of uncertainty, as for example, took place in the period prior to 1988, when confidence in the financial system was at its lowest.[29] Non-monetized savings are often difficult to convert into productive investments while yielding no immediate utility to their owners. Nevertheless, there are indications that this form of saving in Ghana grew considerably in the period 1980–1990.[30] In other countries, such as Tanzania and Nigeria, there are indications from studies conducted by Bagachwa[31] and Soyibo[32] respectively that savings in real assets also grew in the same period.

In a number of African countries experiencing growth after reform, informal financial-sector activities have grown considerably since the reforms began, and not only in absolute terms but also in relation to the formal financial sector.[33] In Tanzania, the total volume of deposits mobilized by savings and credit associations increased by 57 per cent in real terms in the period 1990–92, with significant growth in the numbers of depositors.[34] In Ghana, over the three-year period 1990–92, we observed relative stability in the mean real deposits collected monthly by *susu* groups as monthly contributions by members averaged US$10,[35] an amount equivalent to 10 per cent of the monthly salaries of junior civil servants. The numbers of depositors also grew significantly. Other deposit mobilizers in Nigeria and Malawi have also shown considerable growth.[36]

The formal financial sectors of many countries south of the Sahara are having a difficult time recovering deposits after the reforms. The banks have not achieved any significant financial depth since the reforms began in many countries, as measured by $M_2/GDP$

---

[27] C. Udry, 'Credit markets in Northern Nigeria: credit as insurance in rural economy', *World Bank Economic Review*, 4, 3 (1990), pp. 251–69.

[28] Interdisziplinaere Projekt Consult GmbH (IPC), *Rural Finance in Ghana. A research study on behalf of the Bank of Ghana* (Frankfurt, 1988).

[29] E. Aryeetey, Y. Asante *et al.*, 'Mobilizing domestic savings for African development and diversification: a Ghanaian case study', (Mimeo, International Development Centre, Queen Elizabeth House, Oxford University, 1991).

[30] IPC, *Rural Finance in Ghana*; Aryeetey, *Financial Integration and Development*.

[31] Bagachwa, *Financial Integration and Development: Tanzania*.

[32] Soyibo, *Financial Integration and Development: Nigeria*.

[33] Aryeetey, *Informal Finance in Africa*.

[34] Bagachwa, *Financial Integration and Development: Tanzania*.

[35] Aryeetey, *Financial Integration and Development*.

[36] Soyibo, *Financial Integration and Development: Nigeria*; Chipeta & Mkandawire, *Financial Integration and Development: Malawi*.

ratios.[37] The fact that deposits with informal deposit mobilizers appear to have recovered faster than bank deposits since the financial sector reforms may be related to the fact that informal deposits are targeted at the purchase of some specific item. At the same time as informal deposit mobilization grew, so also did informal lending by the various lending units.

The above-mentioned studies on informal finance in Africa suggest that the activity thrives under both repressive and liberal financial-sector policies. Its performance in many countries indicates that informal finance will do well so long as the level of activity within the economy calls for increasing financial services from groups that cannot be reached by the existing financial institutions. Whenever a demand arises for short-term credit, particularly among traders, farmers and consumers, an informal unit is also likely to emerge to meet that demand. Thus, contrary to the expectation that informal finance will diminish after financial sector reforms in many countries, this has not happened because the growth in the real sectors of those economies has created a suitable environment for informal finance.

Formal finance is unable to step into the niches created by the new growth because it is ill-equipped to deal with the problems of transacting business with the small borrowers described earlier. Financial-sector reforms, focusing mainly on liberalization, have in many places not helped to reduce banks' transaction costs in lending to small borrowers.[38] So long as the most important responses to adjustment stimuli remain those of small informal real-sector operators, informal finance will continue to grow faster than formal finance.

Informal finance can deal with small borrowers in distinct market niches. The process of matching informal units with distinct market niches is explained by Hoff and Stiglitz as the ability of the lender to screen particular borrowers and enforce particular kinds of contracts. 'Only an individual who markets his surplus through a trader can be matched with that trader-lender.'[39] Informal lenders select those borrowers that lead to minimal transaction costs. These include the cost of administering the loan and the default risk cost, which is partly to do with the information that lenders possess about borrowers, which we discuss below.

### Inadequate information in the financial sector after reform

A distinguishing feature of informal finance in Africa is that, in minimizing loan administration costs, many informal lenders tend to attach more importance to proper loan screening than to loan monitoring and contract enforcement,[40] suggesting greater interest in the problems of adverse selection than of moral hazard. While we recognize from a number of studies[41] that many African commercial banks also tend to do the same, placing emphasis on loan screening in the administration of loans, the types of information sought and available are different and less reliable for banks, thus forcing them to devote relatively greater resources per loan to monitoring and contract enforcement than informal financiers would.

---

[37] P. Popiel, *Financial Systems in sub-Saharan Africa: a comparative study* (World Bank Discussion Paper 260, Africa Technical Department Series, Washington, DC, 1994); M. Nissanke, 'Financial linkage development in sub-Saharan Africa', in African Economic Research Consortium, *Economic Policy in Africa: What have we learned?* (AERC, Nairobi, 1994).

[38] Nissanke, 'Financial linkage development'.

[39] K. Hoff & J. Stiglitz, 'A theory of imperfect competition', in *Rural Credit Markets in Developing Countries* (Institute for Policy Reform, Working Paper Series IPR 49, Washington DC, 1993), p. 6.

[40] Aryeetey, *Financial Integration and Development*.

[41] See note 6 above.

The more effective loan screening of informal finance derives from the fact that informal units believe they can rely on their relatively solid communalized information base for proper loan screening. This is an advantage which is completely missing in formal finance. A brief look at some screening practices will help explain the practice better. In community- or group-based arrangements (such as savings and credit associations), standard screening practices are based on the group's observations of individuals' habits and the group's obligations towards applicants. The groups are aware that their members have joined principally because of the possibility of borrowing, which obliges them to meet that need. In 'screening' applicants, therefore, the emphasis is not necessarily on whether members can repay loans they have taken out, but on the commitment of members to the group's goals. The group must also decide whether it has effective disciplinary measures that could be exercised if problems arise. Most of its screening, therefore, has to be done before members join. The major criterion in screening loan applications is the character and reliability of the applicant. Moneylenders, on the other hand, usually lend to people who have been recommended by old clients or other acquaintances. The most important criteria for many moneylenders are the character of the applicants and their position. Only a third of the moneylenders we studied in Ghana indicated any clear creditworthiness criteria.[42] They often arranged interviews with applicants during which they tried to establish their backgrounds and the intended use of the loans. Their trust in the person introducing the borrower and their knowledge of the borrowers are major factors in the process.

Banks are not usually in a position to obtain the kind of information that informal lenders get through these screening practices. This difficulty forces them to limit the scope of their lending to relatively well-established formal activities. As such firms have had difficulty expanding significantly after structural adjustment, the banks have been compelled to reduce their lending to the private sector as a whole in many countries. Uninterested in lending to the private sector, banks labouring under excess liquidity tend in many countries to lend to the public sector.[43] In contrast, individual informal lenders have a limited capacity to lend, thus effectively reducing loan sizes to small amounts for short periods. As a consequence, while formal loans are often difficult to come by, the informal loans that are available are usually not attractive to a number of small firms that want to expand. The financing needs of growing small firms cannot be met by the informal sector, thereby leaving a huge credit gap to be filled in many countries.

## The Impact of Growing Informal Activity on Macro-Economic Performance

A broader feature of macro-economic performance in most sub-Saharan African economies in the reform years has been the persistence of macro-economic instability.[44] We conclude this chapter with a discussion of how the growing domination of the informal sector contributes to such instability. We first discuss some aspects of the instability before associating it with rising informal economic activities.

Macro-economic instability in sub-Saharan Africa is not unique to any one country. Indeed, the fact that macro-economic instability among African countries has been greater

---

[42] Aryeetey, *Financial Integration and Development*.
[43] Nissanke, 'Financial linkage development'.
[44] W. Easterly & R. Levine, 'Africa's growth tragedy' (Mimeo, World Bank, Washington, DC, November 1994).

than in other regions of the world has not escaped attention.[45] Policy reversals in a number of countries, following difficulty in maintaining macro-economic stability, are quite commonplace. Nigeria, for example, has had to renege on financial-sector reforms, as it has on monetary and fiscal policies. In many countries instability is reflected in growing fiscal deficits, rising inflation, negative real interest rates, and rapidly depreciating exchange rates. Notable exceptions may be found in the CFA zone.

In many countries, there are indications that instability is often induced through uncontrolled rises in the fiscal deficit. The rises come in two forms: one, steady yearly growth in public expenditures alongside stagnant or decreasing revenues, and secondly over-spending (i.e. beyond budgetary limits) when governments are subjected to internal pressures. A major difficulty has been to achieve sustained growth in public revenues over the reform period. While governments have had considerable difficulty keeping expenditures down, little expansion in the tax base in the reform years has led to the re-emergence of substantial recurring budget deficits. The World Bank[46] has indicated that public revenues are about 18 per cent of GDP for Africa, whereas public expenditures take as much as 28 per cent of GDP on average. Indeed in more than half the sub-Saharan countries carrying out structural adjustment, public revenue (as a percentage of GDP) did not increase. For the region, the median tax revenue as a share of GDP fell by 0.5 per cent in the period 1986–91.

Outside the CFA zone, countries have recorded significant increases in seigniorage to finance the deficit, leading to significant inflation. The continued rises in money supply in the process have resulted in difficulties in maintaining stable exchange rates, which have in turn been fed back into further inflationary pressures. It does not appear that much can be done about macro-economic instability until budgetary pressures come down or are contained by rising revenues. In the short run rising revenues can come mainly from improved revenue collection. In the long run, this is tied to growth, which requires that there should be significant improvements in the productivity of labour and capital. This calls for increased investments in areas that will have a greater impact on production. As social and political pressures mount on governments transforming their politics to more liberal and democratic regimes, such long-term solutions appear unattainable.

While some of the decline in tax revenue is attributable to declines in trade taxes in some countries,[47] in many others it was a consequence of severe falls in domestic tax revenue following administrative bottlenecks in the collection of taxes. For Ghana, the World Bank[48] recommended among other things 'vigorous tax collection efforts across the board' to improve the revenue base for accelerated growth. It was obvious that difficulty in reaching some sectors of the economy (particularly small informal operations) confined tax collection mainly to formal-sector activity. In essence, the growth and domination of scattered informal activity made tax administration cumbersome and relatively costly, which would explain why, after an early rapid growth in tax revenues after the reforms, their growth rate has slowed down in relation to economic growth. It is thus obvious that while growing informal activity holds some hope for many reforming economies, realistic approaches at making such informal activity accessible to the

---

[45] ibid.

[46] World Bank, *Adjustment in Africa*.

[47] Particularly in the oil-exporting countries that saw falls in oil prices and appreciation of the exchange rate.

[48] World Bank, *Ghana 2000 and Beyond: setting the stage for accelerated growth and poverty reduction* (Africa Regional Office, Western Africa Department, World Bank, Washington, DC, 1993), p. 55.

public-sector administrative machinery cannot be ignored if there is to be sustainable growth and development.

In the light of the persistent macro-economic instability in reforming countries, most economies have been characterized by low and declining saving and investment rates, as indicated earlier. Average savings for sub-Saharan Africa rose from 13.9 per cent of GDP in 1965–73 to 19.5 per cent in 1974–80 and then fell to 12.9 per cent in 1981–7. By 1992, they had fallen to 12.4 per cent after a small increase in 1991. The decline in aggregate saving rates in many countries occurred at the same time as the composition of private savings between financial and real assets tended to favour the latter, as noted earlier. Similarly, financial savings in informal instruments have grown at the expense of formal instruments.

Various studies of savings trends in a number of sub-Saharan countries have attributed the decline in aggregate domestic savings to a number of factors, which themselves are not unique to the region, but probably occur much more intensely there than in other developing regions. These are 'low income and sluggish growth, public sector dissaving, macrofinancial instability and financial repression, institutional weaknesses and lack of financial markets and instruments, and financial distress'.[49] The combined effect of these factors is to reduce confidence in the operations of the formal financial system and economic transactions, resulting in an increase in non-monetized and informal-sector savings.

The presence of informal financial agents in the market is by itself not harmful to the effective development of the financial markets. The worrying thing is the persistent fragmentation of the market. Since the segments of the informal financial sector are collectively poor intermediators of funds but hold a substantial portion of total financial savings,[50] the actual intermediation occurring is substantially less than the potential, thereby weakening the link between savers and investors in the economy generally.[51] The low intermediation effectively reduces the availability of term finance to investors in general, and in particular financial flows to small (informal) operations that want to expand. The consequences are further fragmentation of the goods and services markets, limiting further the volume of production and growth within the economy. Private investments tend in most cases to be very small and often inefficient.

The consequence at the micro level has been inadequate supply response in many countries, which has been manifested in many sub-Saharan countries in the limited recovery of export volumes and difficulties in improving the quality of so-called non-traditional exports. While exports grew by an average 3.6 per cent per annum in 1987–91, having risen from 1.2 per cent in 1970–86, this was far below the average 9.2 per cent achieved in other developing regions. The performance was clearly uneven over the period as many countries recorded declines in export growth. Biggs and his colleagues[52] suggest that a major contributory factor to the limited growth of non-agricultural exports is the domination of such exports by the informal sector. In their paper, *Africa Can Compete*, they highlight drawbacks related to African business strategies that impose a constraint on their entry and remaining in US markets for garments and home products. They attribute the inability of African exporters to survive in the US garments market to the

---

[49] Popiel, *Financial Systems in sub-Saharan Africa*.
[50] A number of studies have estimated that the informal sector controls more than half of total financial savings in some African countries. Aryeetey, *Financial Integration and Development*.
[51] Aryeetey, *Informal Finance in Africa*.
[52] T. Biggs, G. Moody & J.-M. van Leeuwen, *Africa Can Compete! Export opportunities and challenges for garments and home products in the U.S. market*, (World Bank Discussion Paper 242, Washington, DC, 1994).

following factors: (a) mismatch in scale and technical competence of the African exporter and the US buyer; (b) inability of the African exporter to negotiate a realistic price; (c) lack of familiarity on the part of the African exporter with financial institutions and instruments in international trade; (d) differences in business culture. They suggest further that 'the largest impediments to Afrocentric home products are the difficulty in organizing the production of many remote small producers, the need to provide working capital, and unfamiliarity of small African producers with market standards. The production constraints emanate from a void in the African supply chain.'[53]

## Conclusion

We have shown that informal activities have continued to do well in spite of the general expectation that informal activity would diminish following the removal of distortions that lead to market failure. There is ample evidence that informal economic activities will thrive so long as structural impediments to the transmission of macro-economic incentives persist.

The problem for many African countries with strong informal sectors, however, is that their rapid expansion will not necessarily lead to rapid and sustainable growth of the wider domestic economy in the long term. This is a consequence of the fragmented nature of most informal economic activity, which imposes a constraint and some cost on the free flow of resources among economic agents. If the growing informal sectors in various African economies undergoing reform are to have any impact on economy-wide growth, there must be a firmer integration of informal activity with the rest of the economy.

The absence of integration among formal and informal units is manifested in many countries in difficulties in sustaining growth at the macro level. In the financial sector, for example, the observation that each lender type (formal/informal) satisfies the demands of a distinct niche in the market with none meeting the needs of certain categories of borrowers, such as micro-enterprises attempting to expand, illustrates clearly the nature of the financing gap that many African entrepreneurs face and hence some of their difficulties in obtaining needed investment. These gaps embrace all those potential borrowers who cannot enter the circles of informal lenders because they do not find the financial products of these lenders attractive for their business purposes, and yet cannot gain access to formal circles as they are considered unsuitable candidates for bank credit. Obviously the scope of specialization of all types of lenders has been too narrowly defined to be meaningful for effective financial intermediation and investment. But poor private-sector investment response lies at the bottom of the macro-economic instability observable in many countries.

In the real economic sectors, the small and fragmented nature of various activities is reflected in the inability to meet the new product demands of growing African economies anxious to enter and exploit expanding export markets overseas. The informal sectors of African economies simply cannot compete with well-organized overseas competitors without restructuring.

We consider it unlikely that either the formal or the informal sectors of sub-Saharan Africa can, on their own, make the necessary structural adjustments to accommodate an expansion of the niches they control in order to embrace new areas or produce goods

---

[53] ibid., p. 3.

and services at the levels expected to lead to significant growth. In view of the historical development of these niches and their line of progression outlined above, we tend to be sceptical about the capability of either the formal or the informal sector broadening the scope of their specializations in order to embrace the demand for their services that is excluded. Our studies suggest that the most dynamic ways forward have been provided by those institutions that have responded to market stimuli by making their operations semi-formal; keeping to informal principles in their operations, but being flexible enough to accommodate some formal operational structures, including modern record-keeping methods. An issue that needs to be considered in discussions of market integration is whether the development of such semi-formal institutions that link informal and formal segments may help significantly in the process of market integration.

EIGHT

# The Diversity of
# Adjustment in Agriculture

JEAN-PAUL AZAM

From the 1980s onwards the era of structural adjustment has brought a growing awareness of the need to liberalize agriculture in order for it to contribute fully to economic development. Healthy and progressive agriculture is the starting point for a dynamic development of the rest of the economy, which in due course should supplant it within the structure of national production. The interventions imposed by African governments over the past years have resulted in a wide variety of experiments in adjustment, in which both the instruments of economic policy and the results achieved often vary considerably from one country to another.

The aim of this chapter is to illustrate the diversity of experiments in adjustment introduced in the agricultural sector of various African countries, whilst at the same time emphasizing the fundamental unity of the policies adopted. In effect, these policies always aim to reduce the direct or indirect margins which exist between actual net prices paid to producers after the various levies have been deducted, and the final prices paid by the consumer or foreign buyers. In many cases these margins represent a distortion in relation to the efficient functioning of the markets, leading to the creation of profits in the form of 'rents'. It is sometimes difficult to identify clearly where these margins originate, as the interventions which create them are themselves well hidden.

This interpretation differs from the general view according to which the liberalization of agricultural markets within the context of structural adjustment programmes tends to systematically favour export crops at the expense of crops produced for the domestic market. In reality, the objective pursued is an improved functioning of the markets in order to achieve an efficient use of resources. In order to illustrate this distinction clearly,

136

the following section presents a brief review of the various measures implemented by different governments before the era of adjustment, in an attempt to extract large revenues from the agricultural sector. This is followed by an account of the diversity of experiments in adjustment, starting with the extremely unorthodox case of Morocco, where the labour market has contributed significantly to the rehabilitation of the agricultural system. The subsequent section demonstrates how the impact of adjustment policies can be decisively affected by the reactions of intermediaries, even if the quantities produced do not show a clear response. The final section highlights the role of certain macro-economic policies in agricultural recovery.

## The Variety of Levies Imposed on Agriculture

The difference between the price paid to the producer and the price paid by the end consumer or foreign buyer comprises various components which can be grouped into three categories: fixed transport and transformation costs; direct or indirect taxes; and profits or rents. Within these categories a number of hidden factors such as the artificial inflation of certain costs of commercialization and transport, and a plethora of administrative interventions, need to be taken into account. We intend to focus specifically on taxation and profits, which are generally the target of reforms.

### Direct or indirect taxation

The most obvious way to impose levies on agriculture is via taxation. Export crops in particular are primarily subject to taxation in developing countries because it is extremely easy to control their passage at the border, and thus through customs, as well as at various stages during their transformation.[1] On the other hand, it requires a fairly sophisticated fiscal administration in order to levy taxes on the products sold on the domestic market, especially in rural areas. The case of the export crops of Côte d'Ivoire, particularly coffee and cocoa, has been studied in depth.[2] In this particular country, the levies on export crops were imposed directly by means of an export tax known as DUS (Droit unique de sortie), or indirectly via the agency of the Stabilization Fund (CSSPPA), intended to protect the peasants from fluctuations on the world market. The former accounted for up to 25 per cent of Côte d'Ivoire's operational budget, whereas most of the CSSPPA deductions were channelled into the Special Budget for Investment and Equipment, directly supervised by the presidency.[3] These sums were used, for example, to fund a redistribution of wealth from the southern forested area which is relatively affluent to the Sahelian zone in the north which is much poorer.[4] This redistribution probably helped significantly to cement the national unity of the country, whose population is

---

[1] V. Tanzi, 'Structural factors and tax revenue in developing countries: a decade of evidence' in I. Goldin and L.A. Winters (eds), *Open Economies: Structural adjustment and agriculture* (CEPR/OECD, Cambridge University Press, Cambridge, 1992).

[2] E.g. J.-P. Azam & C. Morrisson, *La faisabilité politique de l'ajustement en Côte d'Ivoire et au Maroc* (Etudes du Centre de développement, OECD, Paris, 1994); D. Benjamin & A. Deaton, 'Household welfare and the pricing of cocoa and coffee in Côte d'Ivoire: Lessons from the living standards survey', *World Bank Economic Review* 7 (1993), pp. 293–318; P.K. Trivedi and T. Akiyama, 'A framework for evaluating the impact of pricing policies for cocoa and coffee in Côte d'Ivoire', *World Bank Economic Review*, 6 (1992), pp. 307–30.

[3] B. Laporte, *Les réformes des systèmes de commercialisation et de stabilisation des filières café et cacao au Cameroun et en Côte d'Ivoire* (Ministry of Cooperation and Development, Paris, 1992).

[4] Azam & Morrisson, *La faisabilité politique de l'ajustement en Côte d'Ivoire et au Maroc.*

divided among four distinct ethnic groups.[5] Until the collapse of the world price in 1987, the levies exacted were generally around 50 per cent of the export price. Trivedi and Akiyama[6] have shown that, ideally, the levies on coffee should have been lower – the production of coffee was actually discouraged somewhat – than on cocoa, in which the country had something of a monopoly. Despite this taxation, however, Côte d'Ivoire may be held partly responsible for the collapse of the world price in 1987; it more than doubled its cocoa production within a decade, while it was already the leading world producer during this period. We may therefore maintain, along with Trivedi and Akiyama, that the government would have done better to impose a relatively lighter tax on coffee than on cocoa in order to encourage more diversified agricultural growth. This point illustrates the fact that optimal organization of the agricultural sector does not necessarily imply that the state should not intervene. What it does mean is that this intervention has to be guided by principles which are based on proper economic analysis. In the present case, the theory of optimal customs dues should serve as the reference framework.[7]

Many other countries have also imposed direct or indirect taxation on export crops, using a stabilization fund system. Cameroon is just one example of this.[8] In other countries, however, especially English-speaking countries, the state has often intervened more directly, assuming a monopoly of the commercialization of export crops. Thus in Ghana, for example, the Cocoa Marketing Board (Cocobod) was for a long time the only authorized operator on the cocoa market. This resulted in a drastic cut in the real price paid to the producer, especially during the 1970s, a time of considerable wastage mainly due to Cocobod's[9] oversized work force. In fact, unlike the system of stabilization funds in which the state is content to control and tax the commercialization of export products and where most of the revenue ends up in the state budget, the system of public monopoly encourages an element of rent-seeking which does not particularly benefit the state. Probably one of the most striking examples is that of ONCAD in Senegal. This public body was given the task of organizing the production and export of groundnuts, which for a long time was Senegal's primary export crop. However, it was diverted from its original objective and became a means of distributing unearned favours to various privileged members of the regime. A great deal of extravagance, especially the employment of numerous unnecessary and expensive officials, led to the collapse of the organization, leaving behind an enormous debt.[10] Thus groundnut producers were indirectly taxed in order to fund the government's patronage network. Not only that, these public bodies generally obtained loans to finance their defective functioning, with inflationary effects. So in this case, the burden of inflation is added to the drop in prices paid to producers in order to finance the distribution of undeserved privileges to the protégés of the regime.

However, state intervention may take on other, more devious forms, in which the dimension of indirect taxation is less apparent. For example, fiscal theory has taught that

[5] J-P. Azam, 'How to pay for the peace? A theoretical framework with reference to African countries', *Public Choice*, 83 (1995), pp. 173–84.
[6] Trivedi and Akiyama, 'A framework for evaluating the impact of pricing policies'.
[7] E.g. J.N. Bhagwati & T.N. Srinivasan, *Lectures on International Trade* (MIT Press, Cambridge, MA., 1983).
[8] Laporte, *Les réformes des systèmes de commercialisation et de stabilisation*.
[9] J.-P. Azam & T. Besley, 'The case of Ghana', in J.-P. Azam, T. Besley, J. Maton, D. Bevan, P. Collier & P. Horsnell, *The Supply of Manufactured Goods and Agricultural Development (Ghana, Rwanda, Tanzania)* (Development Centre Papers, OECD, Paris, 1989), pp. 13–65.
[10] J.-P. Azam and G. Chambas, 'The groundnuts and phosphates boom in Senegal (1974–1977)' in P. Collier & J.W. Gunning (eds), *Trade Shocks in Developing Countries* (Vol. 1, Oxford University Press, Oxford, in press).

it is necessary to make a distinction between the effective payment of the tax and the monetary collection of the tax. Since the work of David Ricardo in 1817, we know from the theory of tax incidence that a tax burden can be transferred up or down by the agents who collect it by means of the relative prices of products. For example, in applying these principles it has been possible to demonstrate that Moroccan agriculture actually pays certain indirect taxes, which are borne by the producers via the intermediary of the prices of the inputs used. However, following several years of drought, this sector was exempted from taxation by the king of Morocco in 1984.[11] This type of repercussion is fairly simple to analyse, provided reliable data on the relations between agriculture and the other sectors of the economy are available. Other fiscal interventions, however, while relatively frequent in Africa around 1980, are far less visible.

### Shortages and parallel markets

Many Marxist-Leninist governments put pressure on agriculture by provoking a shortage of consumer goods, particularly manufactured goods, in rural areas. This kind of approach has been studied in particular in Madagascar,[12] Mozambique,[13] and Tanzania.[14] However, a distinction needs to be made between the development of a more or less effective network of parallel markets, and shortages due to the suppression of private trade. This is what happened in Mozambique in the late 1970s and early 1980s, when the army executed *candongeiros*, traders on the parallel market. Under these circumstances shortages were extreme, and cash crops collapsed. For example, exports of cashew nuts, the main export crop of Mozambique at the time, fell to one-tenth of what they had been during periods of shortage.[15] In this case the government pays for the agricultural products with money which has no real purchasing power, and the peasants soon realize this.[16] In such cases they fall back on subsistence crops and virtually abandon cash crops. If the real price paid to the producer is calculated not by deflating the nominal price by means of the ordinary price index – which includes the prices of products unavailable on local markets – but with a virtual price which genuinely reflects the scarcity of consumer goods, then clearly this policy of shortage will result in the farmer being paid a price well below the real price paid at the border. Azam and Besley[17] provide a theoretical analysis of agricultural supply during a shortage, while Azam, Berthélémy and Morrisson[18] also present various econometric analyses. In these situations

[11] J.-P. Azam, *Tax Incidence on Agriculture in Morocco (1985–1989)* (Middle East and North Africa Discussion Paper No. 11, World Bank, Washington DC, 1994).

[12] J.-C. Berthélémy, 'Le cas de Madagascar', in J.-C. Berthélémy, J.-P. Azam & J.-J. Faucher, *Offre de biens manufacturés et développement agricole (Madagascar, Mozambique)* (Textes du Centre de développement, OECD, Paris, 1988), pp. 11–81.

[13] J.-P. Azam & J.-J. Faucher, 'Le cas du Mozambique', in Berthélémy, Azam and Faucher, *Offre de biens manufacturés et développement agricole*, pp. 82–172; J.-P. Azam, 'L'effondrement des cultures de rente en économie de pénurie: le cas du Mozambique (1981–1985)', in M. Benoît-Cattin, M. Griffon & P. Guillaumont (eds), *Economie des politiques agricoles* (Vol. 2, Editions de la Revue Française d'Economie, Paris, 1994), pp. 123–48.

[14] D. Bevan, P. Collier & P. Horsnell, 'The Case of Tanzania', in Azam, Besley *et al.*, *The Supply of Manufactured Goods and Agricultural Development*, pp. 141–203.

[15] Azam & Faucher, 'Le cas du Mozambique'.

[16] J.-P. Azam, P. Collier & A. Cravinho, 'Crop sales, shortages and peasant portfolio behaviour', *Journal of Development Studies*, 30 (1994), pp. 361–79.

[17] J.-P. Azam & T. Besley, 'Peasant supply response under rationing: the role of the food sector', *European Journal of Political Economy*, 7 (1991), pp. 331–43.

[18] J.-P. Azam, J.-C. Berthélémy & C. Morrisson, 'L'offre de cultures commerciales en économie de pénurie', *Revue Economique*, 42 (1991), pp. 553–73.

of shortage, structural adjustment policy must be based on an increase in the supply of consumer goods in the countryside and on a steep rise in the price of these commodities, in order to absorb the monetary funds accumulated by the farmers, with a view to encouraging them to produce instead of buying consumer goods solely on the strength of their accumulated funds. Generally, this type of case necessitates a devaluation.[19]

Fortunately for the populations concerned, the state is not always able to suppress the intervention of private traders, and parallel markets may develop which alleviate the shortage somewhat. This was particularly the case in Ghana[20] and Nigeria.[21] In these countries the activities of traders on the parallel markets made it possible partly to avoid the total collapse of the rural sector and of the economy, as had happened in Mozambique. In Tanzania prior to liberalization, on the other hand, it seems that the parallel markets were never able to develop sufficiently to relieve shortages to any appreciable extent.[22]

It is possible, therefore, to extrapolate that the diversity of measures employed by governments or other social groups with a view to exacting more or less visible levies from agriculture, corresponds to the many different ways adjustment has been experienced. Morocco is a striking illustration of the case in point.

## Morocco: A Case Of Heterodox Adjustment

Morocco is generally considered a good pupil as far as structural adjustment is concerned, especially in view of its exchange-rate policy.[23] Its adjustment programme dates back to 1983, with loans from the IMF and the World Bank.[24] Initially it comprised a graded series of devaluations, reaching a rate of 16.4 per cent between 1983 and 1986, followed by a devaluation of 9.25 per cent in May 1990.[25] Edwards[26] has shown that the Moroccan dirham has never been overvalued in recent years; it has, in fact, at times tended towards undervaluation. The devaluation policy has not led to any significant rate of inflation, thanks to a rigorous policy of macro – economic stabilization and the effect of rapid growth in agricultural production, which serves to contain the increasing price of foodstuffs.[27] Fiscal reform was introduced in the 1980s,[28] including the introduction of VAT and general income tax. Furthermore, as noted above, several years

[19] Azam & Faucher, 'Le cas du Mozambique'.

[20] E. May, *Exchange Controls and Parallel Market Economies in sub-Saharan Africa* (World Bank Staff Working Paper No. 711, World Bank, Washington DC, 1985); J.-P. Azam and T. Besley: 'The case of Ghana', in Azam, Besley, et al., *The Supply of Manufactured Goods*.

[21] J.-P. Azam, 'Cross-border trade between Niger and Nigeria, 1980–87: the parallel market for the naira', in M. Roemer & C. Jones (eds), *Markets in Developing Countries: Parallel, fragmented and black* (ICS Press, San Francisco, CA, 1991), pp. 47–61.

[22] D. Bevan, P. Collier & J.W. Gunning, 'The persistence of shortages in rural black markets', in Roemer & Jones, *Markets in Developing Countries*, pp. 63–74.

[23] S. Edwards, 'Structural adjustment, stabilization and real exchange rates: Morocco in the 1990s' (unpublished, World Bank, Washington DC, 1991).

[24] Ch. Morrisson, *Ajustement et équité au Maroc* (Etudes du Centre de développement, OECD, Paris, 1991); idem, 'Adjustment, incomes and poverty in Morocco', *World Development*, 19 (1991), pp. 1633–51.

[25] D. Ben Ali, 'La politique économique marocaine de l'indépendance à nos jours' in D. Ben Ali & A. Maertens (eds), *Analyses de politique économique appliquées au Maroc* (Collection GREI, Mohammed V University, Rabat, 1993), pp. 5–46.

[26] Edwards, 'Structural adjustment, stabilization and real exchange rates'.

[27] E. Cardoso, 'Food supply and inflation', *Journal of Development Economics*, 8 (1981), pp. 269–84.

[28] M. El Ktiri & N. Akesbi, *La réforme de la fiscalité marocaine à l'heure de l'ajustement structurel* (Editions Toubkal, Casablanca, 1987).

of drought led the king to exempt the agricultural sector from all taxation.[29] Other institutional reforms were also applied, including privatization and the revision of the investment code.[30]

In addition, at the end of the 1980s Morocco liberalized the commercialization of agricultural products on domestic and foreign markets by significantly reducing the role of the public marketing organizations. Customs duties on imports were cut drastically: the maximum rate fell from 200 per cent in 1983 to 45 per cent at the beginning of 1986. Through licences or even prohibitions, quantitative restrictions still affected all imports in 1983, but restrictions applied to only 37 per cent of imports in February 1986, at which point all quantitative restrictions were lifted.[31] This package of measures helped re-launch Morocco's performance in terms of growth, inflation, and external and internal deficits. This performance is analysed below for the period 1983–90. The early 1990s – a period characterized by the consequences of the sharp devaluation of May 1990 and in particular the difficult agricultural-climatic conditions – have not been taken into account.

Table 8.1: Performance Indicators (1983–90)

| | Rate of growth (annual %) | Rate of Inflation (annual%) | Balance of Payments (% GDP) | Budget Deficit (% GDP) |
|------|------|------|------|------|
| 1983 | −0.56 | 6.2 | −6.3 | −10.6 |
| 1984 | 4.34 | 12.5 | −7.8 | −6.4 |
| 1985 | 6.33 | 7.8 | −6.7 | −7.7 |
| 1986 | 8.30 | 8.7 | −1.3 | −4.8 |
| 1987 | −2.55 | 2.8 | +0.9 | −5.0 |
| 1988 | 10.39 | 2.3 | +2.1 | −4.7 |
| 1989 | 1.49 | 3.1 | −3.6 | −4.4 |
| 1990 | 2.64 | 6.7 | −0.8 | −3.4 |

Source: Direction de la Statistique

## A recovery led by agriculture

Table 8.1 lists the most important performance indicators for an evaluation of the adjustment implemented in Morocco at the beginning of the 1980s. The first column shows the rate of growth of real GDP. Generally speaking, it is fairly high, averaging 3.8 per cent for the period 1983–90. There are, however, significant conjunctural variations. As the average demographic rate of growth for the same period was 2.9 per cent, the period shows positive growth in per capita GDP. There are therefore no signs of the deceleration of growth often associated with structural adjustment.

The second column lists the figures for inflation rates, calculated on the basis of the rate of growth of the consumer price index. It exceeds 10 per cent only in 1984, the devaluation year, subsequently dropping to very low levels in 1987–9. This is all the more impressive given the fact that this period began with a devaluation which could have unleashed high inflation.

[29] Azam, Tax Incidence on Agriculture in Morocco.
[30] Ben Ali, 'La politique économique marocaine'.
[31] F. Bourguignon, Ch. Morrisson & A. Suwa, 'Adjustment and the rural sector: a counterfactual analysis of Morocco' in Goldin & Winters, Open Economies, pp. 93–116.

The third column represents the current account of the balance of payments. It shows a continuous improvement of the current account deficit, even becoming a surplus in 1987 and 1988. The slight relapse in 1989 was brought about by a legal dispute with Morocco's main buyer of phosphoric acid, without any great significance. This drop in the need for external funding is accompanied by a striking improvement in the financial situation. In the mid-1980s, the World Bank included Morocco among the 17 most indebted countries in the world. It was dropped from the list in the early 1990s, notably after Saudi Arabia had written off its debts in 1991. These amounted to approximately 25 per cent of the Paris Club debt.

The fourth column shows that the improvement of the central government budget deficit (as defined by the IMF) has been slower. This has been calculated after debt cancellation. It shows a regular reduction in the budget deficit which fell by around two-thirds as a percentage of GDP during this period. All the same, the 1990 figure of 3.4 per cent of GDP is by no means negligible.

Table 8.2 shows the developments of total GDP and agricultural GDP together with their deflators. It reveals much more rapid growth in the agricultural sector than in the economy as a whole. On average, the agricultural growth rate for the period 1983–90 is almost double that of the total economy. If one compares this performance with the relative developments of the deflators of total GDP and agricultural GDP, an unexpected result emerges. By comparison with the relative development of the deflator of the economy taken as a whole, that of the agricultural sector indicates a deterioration in the terms of internal exchange between agriculture and the rest of the economy. Thus the dynamism of agriculture during this period cannot simply be explained in terms of a conventional neo-classical model. On the contrary, such a model would predict a deceleration in the relative growth of agriculture, whose relative prices dropped during this period.

**Table 8.2: Sectoral performance**

|  | GDP (constant prices) | | GDP deflator | |
|  | Total | Agriculture | Total | Agriculture |
|---|---|---|---|---|
| 1983 | 100 | 100 | 100 | 100 |
| 1984 | 104 | 104 | 109 | 108 |
| 1985 | 111 | 123 | 118 | 116 |
| 1986 | 120 | 168 | 130 | 117 |
| 1987 | 117 | 128 | 135 | 125 |
| 1988 | 129 | 169 | 142 | 124 |
| 1989 | 131 | 173 | 147 | 125 |
| 1990 | 135 | 161 | 156 | 135 |

*Source:* ibid

Table 8.3 shows the figures for external trade in goods, presenting the figures for total exports and agricultural exports on the one hand, and for total imports and agricultural imports on the other. It shows that the agricultural sector has not been a major performer as far as exports are concerned. While its growth in this area was not negligible in absolute terms, it fell behind the growth of the economy as a whole. In other words, the composition of Moroccan exports over the course of this period of adjustment altered in favour of non-agricultural products. Similarly, the table reveals that, in relation to total imports, agricultural imports also dropped significantly.

Thus Moroccan agriculture not only participated in the economic recovery by leading

**Table 8.3: External trade in goods**
**(constant prices)**

|      | Exports | | Imports | |
|------|---------|-------------|---------|-------------|
|      | Total   | Agriculture | Total   | Agriculture |
| 1983 | 100 | 100 | 100 | 100 |
| 1984 | 104 | 100 | 108 | 128 |
| 1985 | 104 | 103 | 108 | 106 |
| 1986 | 108 | 109 | 111 | 101 |
| 1987 | 120 | 106 | 123 | 118 |
| 1988 | 142 | 122 | 135 | 99 |
| 1989 | 124 | 122 | 145 | 94 |
| 1990 | 151 | 119 | 164 | 102 |

*Source:* ibid.

the growth of the economy as a whole, as seen above, but it also contributed directly to improving the balance of trade by substituting some local production for imports of agricultural goods. This example is a striking illustration of the fact that agricultural adjustment is not to be confused with the recovery of agricultural exports; on the contrary, it may be characterized by an effective substitution of imports, obtained by reducing initial imbalances.

Moreover, this improvement in performance was accompanied by a striking rise in the standard of living of the poorest sectors of the population. All indicators point to the fact that Morocco has achieved remarkable success in the struggle against poverty.[32] Thus a report by the World Bank[33] shows that poverty had almost halved in the years between the Household Consumption survey (1984/85) and the Household Standard of Living Survey (1990/91). During this period the percentage of those living below the poverty line dropped from 32.6 per cent to 18 per cent in rural areas, and from 17.3 per cent to 7.6 per cent in urban areas. In the countryside, the poorest people usually come from agricultural labourers' families.

The fundamental determinants of this recovery in production have been highlighted by Azam.[34] The structural adjustment in Morocco has been the subject of a number of studies.[35] However, none of them has correctly assessed the importance of the particular functioning of the labour market in Morocco. More precisely, various studies suggest that the minimum agricultural wage (Guaranteed Minimum Agricultural Wage, or SMAG) contributes significantly to employment opportunities and production in this sector. Azam[36] presents econometric results which both corroborate this idea and provide the theoretical base for this relation. Pascon and Ennaji also provide many observations

[32] Ministère du Plan, *Niveaux de vie des ménages, premiers résultats – Vol. 1: Rapport de synthèse* (Direction de la statistique, Rabat, 1992).

[33] World Bank, 'Kingdom of Morocco: adjustment, growth and poverty', (Report No. 11918-MOR, unpublished, 1993).

[34] J.-P. Azam, 'Salaire minimum et ajustement structurel au Maroc', in G. Benhayoun & S. Bazen (eds), *Salaire minimum et bas salaires* (L'Harmattan, Paris, 1995), pp. 281–300.

[35] E.g. World Bank, 'Kingdom of Morocco'; Bourguignon, Morrisson and Suwa, 'Adjustment and the rural sector'; Morrisson, *Ajustement et équité au Maroc*.

[36] J.-P. Azam, 'The agricultural minimum wage and wheat production in Morocco', *Journal of African Economies*, 1 (1992), pp. 171–91; idem, 'Employeurs dominants et salaire minimum dans l'agriculture marocaine', *Revue Economique*, 44 (1993), pp. 1151–68; idem, 'Salaire minimum et production agricole au Maroc', in Benoît-Cattin *et al.*, *Economie des politiques agricoles*, Vol. 3, pp. 331–44.

which corroborate this analysis in their sociological work.[37] On the other hand, it would appear that, while it is not negligible, the role of the minimum wage in the other professions is far less important.[38] Moroccan legislation on the minimum wage dates back to 1936. Benhayoun and Bazen[39] give a brief account of the legal and administrative context of minimum wages in Morocco. However, their study concentrates on the modern urban sector, while Azam's theoretical models[40] show that this legislation makes it possible to counter the inefficiency of the market wage analysed in these models. This is yet another case where the responsibility of the state is not the cause of the imbalance; the latter is the result of the autonomous functioning of the labour market. But the state is nevertheless involved to the extent that it has the power to rectify such an imbalance by imposing a minimum wage.

## The role of the minimum wage

Azam[41] has presented a model of a buyer's monopoly directly inspired by Stigler's pioneering article.[42] The market strength of large-scale agricultural employers entails an equilibrium on the agricultural labour market where the marginal productivity of labour is superior to the wage paid. It is not in the employers' interest to offer to raise the level of the minimum wage, since this would provoke a general wage rise and an increase in the total wage bill which would exceed the value of the extra production resulting from it. As they are also unable to cause a drop in wages if they respect the minimum wage, the result is an equilibrium on the labour market similar to the system of surplus demand for work analysed by Malinvaud[43] and Benassy.[44] The employers are bound by the labour supply; increasing the minimum wage, and thus the labour supply, allows them to increase production, partly bridging the gap between the marginal productivity of labour and the wage paid. This entails an increase in efficiency by dissipating a part of the buyer's monopoly profits, provided that the prices of products adequately reflect optimal prices.

Two independent econometric tests are provided in this article for the wheat market. First, a supply equation is calculated and rigorously tested. The positive effect of the minimum wage on the level of production is significantly higher than zero. Secondly, this result is confirmed by an equation explaining price formation on the wheat market. Besides various control variables which largely concern state interventions, the minimum wage appears significantly in the equation with a minus sign. This is exactly what one would expect assuming a positive effect on supply.

Besides these econometric results, this model provides explanations for the stylized facts found in the sociological work of Pascon and Ennaji.[45] For example, these authors report that certain agricultural producers arrange to take on female labour from the towns during the seasonal peak. Moreover, they note that the agriculturalists complain openly

---

[37] P. Pascon & M. Ennaji, *Les paysans sans terre au Maroc* (Editions Toubkal, Casablanca, 1986).

[38] World Bank, 'Kingdom of Morocco'.

[39] G. Benhayoun & S. Bazen, 'Salaire minimum et structure des salaires au Maroc', in O. Bahraoui & G. Benhayoun (eds), *Restructuration économique et développement régional et urbain au Maroc* (Kingdom of Morocco, Ministère du Plan, Rabat, 1991).

[40] See note 36.

[41] Azam, 'The agricultural minimum wage and wheat production in Morocco'.

[42] G. Stigler, 'The economics of minimum wage legislation', *American Economic Review*, 36 (1946), pp. 358–65.

[43] E. Malinvaud, *The Theory of Unemployment Reconsidered* (Basil Blackwell, Oxford, 1977).

[44] J.-P. Benassy, *The Economics of Market Disequilibrium* (Academic Press, New York, 1982).

[45] Pascon & Ennaji, *Les paysans sans terre*.

in field surveys about the shortage of labour. These observations thus indirectly confirm the econometric analysis presented above.

Azam[46] proposes a more general version of this result with a theory more firmly anchored in Moroccan rural sociology. This dominant-employer model uses arguments similar to Scherer's dominant-firm theory.[47] The model described in the preceding paragraphs is a particular case. Now, we shall suppose that there is a competitive sector where the marginal productivity of labour is equivalent to the wage, alongside a sector of dominant employers. In the competitive sector, there is a full continuum of situations, ranging from the smallest farmer with a micro-holding earning most of his income from wage labour, to the well-to-do farmer able to take on extra hands at peak seasons. This corresponds pretty well to the Moroccan situation, where the supply of agricultural labour is the work of small-scale proprietors much more than of landless farmers.[48] In this country, almost 80 per cent of landholdings are smaller than 5 hectares, and taken together they account for only 25 per cent of the workable agricultural surface area. The fragmentation of plots is inherent in the Moroccan system of landholding, for the Islamic law of inheritance lays down that land is to be shared among all the children of the deceased proprietor, with female descendants receiving half as much as male descendants.[49]

The demand for wage labour essentially originates from the modern large-scale enterprises with irrigation. They are situated on the edge of the main irrigated areas and in pluvial agricultural zones, in the favourable zones where it has proved possible to develop a little private irrigation in recent years. It is self-evident that the marginal productivity of labour in these modern enterprises is superior to that on the more traditional types of property. The theory of dominant employers referred to above provides the microeconomic basis of this result, which would be difficult to explain in terms of a conventional model of a competitive agricultural labour market. The dominant employers make their decisions to take on labourers taking into account the residual supply of labour in the competitive sector, which determines a Stackelberg-type equilibrium. The disparity between the marginal productivity of labour in the dominant sector and the wage paid also yields a profit, as in the preceding model. Thus an increase in the minimum wage involves a reallocation of labour between the competitive sector – with its low level of marginal productivity of labour – and the sector of the dominant employers, where marginal productivity is higher. As in the preceding model efficiency improves – provided that product prices are optimal – through a reduction in the profit deriving from scarcity which is appropriated by the dominant employers.

This model has been tested in the same way as the one described in the article cited above. The positive effect of the minimum wage is tested on eight agricultural supply functions, referring to the crops which on average account for almost 75 per cent of the cultivated land in this country. These are the main types of cereal, the main types of pulse, and the main industrial crops. There is therefore no reason to doubt the representative nature of the result. These equations corroborate the hypothesis proposed.

Azam[50] first presents an econometric result corroborating and generalizing these partial results on the basis of national statistics. He then proceeds to propose a different

[46] Azam, 'Employeurs dominants et salaire minimum dans l'agriculture marocaine'.
[47] F.M. Scherer, *Industrial Market Structure and Economic Performance* (Rand McNally, New York, 1980).
[48] Pascon & Ennaji, *Les paysans sans terre*.
[49] H. de Waël, *Le droit musulman* (C.H.E.A.M., Paris, 1989).
[50] Azam, 'Salaire minimum et production agricole au Maroc', in Benoît-Cattin *et al.*

explanation of this phenomenon, based on the theory of the effective wage, combining it with a simple analysis of the family, conceived in Beckerian terms[51] as an institution in which income is shared to pay for consumption. Conceived in this way, the family is an important limit to the achievement of the effective wage by the play of market forces. Take the case in which the worker's productivity depends on his level of consumption.[52] If each employer is aware that part of the wage that he pays his employee is in fact used to pay for the consumption of a relative of that employee who is employed elsewhere, he will not be encouraged to raise the wage paid to maintain the level of consumption and productivity of his own employee. He will even be encouraged to adopt a 'free rider' attitude, resulting in a reduction of the wage paid to his employee if the family income is supplemented from elsewhere. This is an external effect which renders Nash's equilibrium inadequate. The employers do not take into account the symmetry of the problem when they decide on the wage to be paid, and are therefore led to pay a wage below the effective wage.

The minimum wage makes it possible to correct this lack of coordination, since it involves a simultaneous increase in the wages of all the members of a household, so that the increased wage paid by the employer benefits his employee fully. He therefore benefits from all of its consequences for his production. According to this theory, then, the state is able to correct the inefficiency of the market by enabling employers to pay the effective wage. A major difference from the two works previously cited is that in one case the imposition of the minimum wage has an effect which is favourable for the employers and ambiguous for the employees, while in the other cases the effect is favourable to the employees and unfavourable to the employers.

These results therefore reveal the important role of a 'heterodox' component in Moroccan structural adjustment, namely the rapid growth of the minimum wage in terms of the agricultural product, which has a positive effect on agricultural production in this country. Now, the economic reorganization of Morocco during the 1983–90 period can be largely attributed to a strong growth 'pulled along' by agriculture. Agricultural GDP increased in real terms by 61 per cent between 1983 and 1990, while total GDP only increased by 35 per cent. Moreover, this increase also played an important part in reducing poverty in the rural areas.

All the same, it is doubtful whether this positive effect of the minimum wage can still be exploited in the future in Moroccan economic policy. In fact, it rose from the very low level in real terms of 1978, increasing at an annual rate of 7.85 per cent between 1978 and 1983.[53] It is therefore not certain that the minimum wage will be able to function as a growth factor in the future as it has probably done in recent years, since it has now reached a level in real terms that is much higher than the 1978 level. In fact, if it were to rise too much, it could reduce employment and create unemployment in the rural areas instead of strengthening agricultural growth. The various theoretical models used to explain this positive relation, which have been briefly described above, clearly indicate this risk.[54]

Thus the heart of a structural adjustment in the agricultural sector can be in the rural

---

[51] G.S. Becker, *A Treatise on the Family* (Harvard University Press, Cambridge, MA., 1981).

[52] C. Bliss & N.H. Stern, 'Productivity, wages, and nutrition', *Journal of Development Economics* 5 (1978), pp. 363–98; P. Dasgupta & D. Ray, 'Inequality as a determinant of malnutrition and unemployment: theory', *Economic Journal*, 96 (1986), pp. 1011–34.

[53] Azam, 'The agricultural minimum wage and wheat production in Morocco'.

[54] See note 36.

labour market, as the example of Morocco has shown. In general, however, it is more likely to be found in the market for agricultural products itself, where the reactions of the intermediaries play a major role. We shall now proceed to illustrate this point.

## Some Examples of the Reactions of Intermediaries to Adjustment

When the state exercises close control of the commercialization of agricultural products, reforms of the institutions of agricultural markets are in theory important, and they make it possible to bring the prices of the various market sectors in line with one another. However, their effects depend to a large extent on the behaviour of the intermediaries who are at the heart of market operations. Depending on the initial situation, reforms may have a very strong impact if the traders react as expected. In certain other cases, the traders may have anticipated the institutional changes, so that the latter have only a reduced impact.

### Anticipation of reforms in Côte d'Ivoire

This is illustrated by the case of Côte d'Ivoire in the second half of the 1980s. World prices for Ivorian exports (coffee, cocoa, etc.) had then collapsed, severely testing the system of price stabilization for producers. At first, President Houphouët-Boigny refused to consider the fall in world prices as a lasting phenomenon, and he refused to sell the 1988 harvest, speculating on a resurgence of the world price and somewhat overestimating the market strength of his country. Moreover, he realized that France would not leave him without aid, and this gave him a certain confidence in his action. Consequently, he refused initially to pass on the low world prices to his producers. After all, significant levies had been exacted on coffee and cocoa exports for many years in the name of price stabilization, and the president was aware that it was only fair for the state to repay some of this money when the need arose. However, the government had actually invested this revenue in fixed assets, such as the sugar refineries in the north of the country, and he could not easily convert them to meet his obligations.[55] He was thus soon forced to lower the prices paid to producers in 1989. The president felt this decision to be a personal defeat, and the events of 1990 proved him to be right on this score.

However, there are good reasons to suppose that the traders had begun to lower the price paid to producers long before this date. After the drop in the world price in 1987, it seems that the Lebanese traders had already followed the drop in prices, and that they were paying the producers prices which were below the official ones. Numerous subsequent declarations, including the threats issued by the president against traders who bought products below the legal price, bear witness to this problem. To go beyond this anecdotal level, Azam and Bonjean[56] have econometrically tested the relative influence of the official and international prices on the quantities of cocoa traded in Côte d'Ivoire. The idea of this test is the following: if the traders actually pay the

[55] Azam & Morrisson, *La faisabilité politique de l'ajustement*.

[56] J.-P. Azam & C. Bonjean, 'Le rôle des intermédiaires dans la détermination du prix effectif au producteur: analyse par la théorie des jeux et applications à la Côte d'Ivoire et à Madagascar', in G. Etienne, M. Griffon & P. Guillaumont (eds), *Afrique-Asie: Performances agricoles comparées* (Éditions de la Revue française d'économie, Paris, 1993), pp. 191–207.

official prices to the producers, it is likely that the supply will be affected by these prices rather than by international prices; on the other hand, if the traders fix a price that is directly linked to the prices on the international market, as the anecdote recounted above suggests, one would expect the function of the supply of cocoa to be affected by the international price rather than by the official price. This is exactly what the econometric calculations show: the international price is without doubt more significant than the official one, which seems in fact not to play any part in this supply function. Thus these results lead one to suppose that the prices effectively paid to the cocoa producers by the traders are linked more directly to international than to official prices. Under these conditions, the reforms of the system of commercialization and stabilization of the prices of export products in Côte d'Ivoire should be considered less a problem of stimulating production than a problem of the distribution between the state and the producers of the margin between the price paid at the border and the price paid to producers.

Elsewhere, state control of traders has been stricter, and reforms have achieved notable successes. This is the case in Ethiopia, where the Mengistu government (the *Derg*) liberalized grain sales in 1990, about a year before its fall. It is an extremely interesting case, which shows how the private sector is capable of reacting very rapidly to a favourable reform, even in a situation complicated by war.[57]

### The reaction of traders in Ethiopia

The Mengistu regime had imposed severe controls on the grain market in Ethiopia, which were removed in March 1990.[58] They had particularly dramatic consequences at the time of the famine in 1984. A system of quotas had been set up in 1979, under which farmers were obliged to sell a determined quantity of grain to a parastatal, the Agricultural Marketing Corporation (AMC), at a price fixed below the market price, and were only allowed to sell the rest on the free market. The intention of this measure was to make more grain available on the urban markets. The declared objective of the system was to keep grain prices at a reasonably low level in the urban centres, despite the negative effect on farmers' incomes. Furthermore, the *Derg* had set up traffic barriers to prevent the free transport of grain from one region to another and to appropriate the profits which private traders could have made through arbitrage on the markets. This system was made even more restrictive by forcing them to sell a part of their purchases – between 50 and 100 per cent – to the AMC at a price fixed at 4 or 5 birrs above the official price for purchases from the farmers. Only what was left after these transactions could be supplied directly to the open urban markets. This imposed an additional business expense on the traders, since the AMC price was lower than the free market price. Thus this system taxed the farmers *de facto*, by forcing them to sell a fixed part of their harvest below the market price, and the traders, by forcing them to sell a portion of their purchases at a low price to the AMC.

This system of market control was abandoned in March 1990, roughly a year before the fall of the Mengistu regime. The reaction of the markets to this change of policy

[57] J.-P. Azam, 'La levée des contrôles des marchés de grains en Ethiopie (mars 1990)', *Revue d'économie du développement*, 94/3 (1993), pp. 79–104; S. Dercon, 'Food markets, liberalization and peace in Ethiopia: an econometric analysis', in J.-P. Azam, D. Bevan, P. Collier, S. Dercon, J. Gunning & S. Pradhan, *Some Economic Consequences of the Transition from Civil War to Peace* (World Bank, Washington DC, 1994), pp. 47–86.
[58] ibid.

provides good information on the capacity of private traders to take immediate advantage of the opening up of new commercial possibilities. The absence of a reaction, on the other hand, would have proved that other constraints prevented the markets from functioning properly, apart from those which had been lifted. Moreover, the proper functioning of the markets was not only disturbed by the regulatory policy, but was also rendered difficult by the war. It is therefore no easy task to provide a clear analysis of the effect of the removal of grain market controls in Ethiopia in 1990, but the available studies point in the same direction.[59] The difficulties connected with the war make the results obtained even more interesting, showing the capacity of private traders to overcome many difficulties, in particular those arising from a lack of security.

The costs resulting from the control of the grain markets under this system can be broken down into two points, which are summarized in the works by Azam and Dercon already cited. Firstly, there is an effect on the average level of grain prices, since the system of quotas affects the determination of prices on the rural and urban markets. Secondly, there is an effect on the spatial dispersion of prices, since the business costs are opposed to the effective arbitrage of the traders. The benefits of the liberalization can be evaluated in terms of these two points: price levels and dispersion.

Azam proposes a theoretical framework for the study of these questions, applied to the Ethiopian case. He first uses a theoretical model to analyse the probable effects of the system of quotas and its suspension on consumption and production prices. This effect may be positive or negative, depending on whether the system primarily affects the farmers or the traders. The observed reaction of prices to the policy of liberalization suggests that the traders were affected the most by the quota system. The drop in business costs resulting from the removal of the controls was passed on to the consumers, indicating that the commercial sector is both competitive and capable of reacting to the emergence of new possibilities. Dercon extends this analysis to come up with similar results, showing that the *Derg* government, which claimed to be following an official pro-urban policy, used the pretext of keeping urban food prices down to implement a system which actually maintained them at a level which was too high. We do not know what effect this had on the prices paid to the farmers, but it is likely that they increased.

The second effect expected from the reform concerns the spatial dispersion of prices and its effect on the standard of living. The theoretical analysis of the effect on the standard of living of the dispersion of prices and of their unification somewhat generalizes the conventional analysis of the gains from international exchange. It shows that the unification of the markets through arbitrage has a positive effect on the standard of living of households, by reducing the spatial dispersion of prices. Applying these ideas to the development of the prices of certain grains in various urban centres in Ethiopia in 1989–90, Azam finds that arbitrage on the markets was probably improved as a result of the implementation of the liberalization policy. Dercon's results, based on more complete figures, corroborate these findings.

However, private traders do not only contribute to the well-being of the population by reducing the spatial dispersion of prices, for they can also contribute to reducing the temporal dispersion of cereal prices. This is shown by the study of the effects of liberalization on seasonal variations in the price of rice in Madagascar.[60]

---

[59] ibid.
[60] J.-P. Azam & C. Bonjean, 'La formation du prix du riz: théorie et application à Antananarivo (Madagascar)', *Revue Economique*, 46 (in press).

## The stabilization of the price of rice as a result of liberalization in Madagascar

The free operation of the rice market in Madagascar has long been affected by numerous obstacles. Various public bodies were involved in the production and commercialization of paddy and rice, and they enjoyed a certain buyer's monopoly, at least locally. A liberalization programme was implemented in stages during the 1980s, culminating in 1987. From then on, private traders were allowed to intervene on this market unhindered, and numerous husking plants have been set up in the countryside.

The first commentators on these measures, in particular in regard to the events which took place between 1985 and 1987, thought that the main effect of the liberalization would be a significant increase in the price paid to producers.[61] In fact, the increase in the price of rice in terms of non-agricultural goods at this time should be perceived as a speculative movement based on anticipation of devaluation.[62] For many of the people of Madagascar, paddy is the main asset against inflation that one can have in one's portfolio. Sensing the approach of devaluation, many of them stockpiled paddy, driving the real price of rice up very high in 1985 and 1986. Once the devaluation had taken place in 1987, however, the real price of rice tumbled to a level below the pre-liberalization one, while the international exchange rate had increased considerably.[63] What is more, imports were drastically curtailed in that year, and production did not increase appreciably. This is confirmation that the soaring price of rice in 1985–6 was primarily a speculative phenomenon, given the fact that there is no marginal exchange for rice in Madagascar. In fact, as an island, Madagascar is not in direct contact with the world rice market. Imports are shipped in by the 10,000 tons, which requires funding to the tune of $2.5 million. As a result, this indivisibility, combined with the country's balance-of-payments problem (its currency is not convertible), means that the price of rice in Madagascar is determined mainly by domestic supply and demand. It follows that the policy of austerity which accompanied the adjustment policy, and the restoration of confidence in the national currency which resulted from it, had a depressing effect on this price.

Does this mean that the policy of liberalization failed? Not at all, if one considers that the objective was to improve the efficiency of the market by reducing the previous imbalances. The spatial dispersion of prices has been reduced,[64] and we saw above that this has a positive effect on the standard of living. Excessive margins were previously found in the trade between the areas of production and the areas of consumption, which the competition introduced by liberalization has reduced. More important still, the opening up of the market to private traders has favoured a certain seasonal linking of prices. Under the previous system, admission to the rice trade was restricted, and only a few public companies engaged in storage. Their dominant position enabled them to pay low prices at harvest time, and to sell at high prices at the end of the cycle when demand was at its peak. Moreover, their bureaucratic inflexibility prevented these bodies from close management of their stocks, which normally determines seasonal price fluctuations. The econometric analysis carried out by Azam and Bonjean[65] shows that liberalization

[61] E. Berg, 'The liberalization of rice marketing in Madagascar', World Development, 17 (1989), pp. 719–28; P.A. Dorosh, R.E. Bernier & A.H. Sarris, Macroeconomic Adjustment and the Poor. The case of Madagascar (Monograph 9, Cornell Food and Nutrition Policy Program, Cornell University, Ithaca, NY, 1990).

[62] Azam & Bonjean, 'La formation du prix du riz: théorie et application à Antananarivo (Madagascar)'.

[63] C. Araujo-Bonjean & J.-P. Azam, 'La libéralisation du riz à Madagascar ou l'ajustement sans croissance'. (Paper delivered to the second academic meeting of the Economic Analysis and Development network, AUPELF-UREF, Rabat, 1995).

[64] ibid.

[65] Azam & Bonjean, 'La formation du prix du riz'.

brought about a reduction in the fluctuations of the price of rice in the capital Antananarivo at the time of peak demand. Thus the success of this policy of liberalization of the rice market should not be evaluated in terms of its effect on the average price of rice, but of its ability to reduce the temporal and spatial dispersion of that price.

These various examples indicate that the intermediaries are generally capable of reacting favourably to reforms, or even of anticipating them, as the case of Côte d'Ivoire demonstrated. In many countries traders had considerably reduced the imbalances by trading on the parallel markets. The latter generally arise in response to significant and artificial price disparities between different sectors of the market, provided that the state does not repress them too violently. This is particularly the case when the price paid to the domestic producers is too low in relation to the price that private agents can obtain across the border. In these cases, liberalization can have extremely beneficial effects by bringing products back on to the official markets, even if the effects on production are less spectacular.

## Macroeconomic Adjustment and Parallel Markets: Ghana, Ethiopia, Angola

When the government makes every effort to pay producers a price which differs too sharply from what they can obtain across the border, an active parallel trade develops unless the government has the means of imposing this price difference by force. Azam and Besley[66] have provided a theoretical framework for the study of these phenomena by means of a small-scale model of general equilibrium. Their econometric application shows that, despite the attempts of the government of Ghana before the 1984 economic reorganization plan, the markets of this country were to a certain extent tied to those of neighbouring Côte d'Ivoire. In particular, the prices of consumer goods in the two countries were significantly intercorrelated. May[67] and Azam and Besley[68] show that at this time the favourable exchange rate on the parallel market and the difference between the Côte d'Ivoire and Ghana in the price paid to the producer had a significant negative effect on the sales of cocoa to Cocobod. Thus, as in the case of Côte d'Ivoire considered above, the situation in Ghana before adjustment was one in which the state did not really have complete control of the marginal price paid to the producer. Under these conditions, one may wonder what the contribution is of a reform of the institutions of the agricultural markets. Roemer[69] deals with this question and shows that there is a danger that the effects of such measures will be different from those intended if the existence of these parallel markets is not taken into account.

### Return to the official circuit

In particular, one should clearly distinguish between the effects of the reforms on the reorientation of commercial flows between the official and parallel segments, on the one hand, and their effects on farmers' production and income, on the other. In general,

[66] J.-P. Azam & T. Besley, 'General equilibrium with parallel markets for goods and foreign exchange: theory and application to Ghana', *World Development*, 17 (1989), pp. 1921–30.
[67] May, *Exchange Controls and Parallel Market Economies*.
[68] Azam & Besley, 'The case of Ghana'.
[69] M. Roemer, 'Simple analytics of segmented markets: what case for liberalization?', *World Development*, 14 (1986), pp. 429–39.

in the economies characterized by active parallel markets, the former are much greater than the latter. Thus there can be no doubt that the rapid recovery of cocoa sales to the Cocobod from 1984 on is due less to a recovery of production than to a reduction in clandestine exports to Côte d'Ivoire.[70] It takes a long time to replant cocoa plants or to obtain a clear recovery of production. This return of exports to the official circuits is generally a good thing for the economy. It makes it possible to improve the efficiency of trade, because smuggling implies costs in terms of resources and rent-seeking activities which may have negative effects. Moreover, it means that payments in currency return to the official exchange market, which allows a more efficient allocation of resources if the market institutions are also reformed.

Kidane[71] has studied the effects of the economic policy reforms in Ethiopia after the fall of the Mengistu government in 1991 from this perspective, and in particular the effects of the devaluation of October 1993. In this country, where coffee was discovered in the eighteenth century, a large proportion of the production was for a long time secretly exported to Kenya because of the low prices paid to the producers by the marketing board and because of the rate of exchange on the parallel market. Kidane shows that the response of the supply to devaluation was much stronger than what one could predict on the basis of a normal elasticity of supply. We may therefore concur with him in stating that one of the benefits of the devaluation for Ethiopia has been to divert part of its coffee exports from the clandestine sphere and to recapture it within the official circuits.

### Remonetization in Angola

In a similar way, one can observe a very strong response by coffee sales to the improvement in the economic situation in Angola in 1988 during a brief cease-fire in the civil war.[72] Here, the real collapse of prices paid to coffee producers manifested itself as a shortage of consumer goods, as in the case of Mozambique described above. Because of the presence of the army and insecurity, the parallel market was only developed on a very small scale outside the capital Luanda. Even there, the severity of the shortage had driven the prices of consumer goods up to record levels, especially in 1986. At the same time, the farmers did not sell their coffee to the marketing board. According to the authorities, the farmers had actually retained up to eight years of stocks, despite the physical losses this implies in terms of rotting and deterioration of quality. In this situation of absolute scarcity, the currency had lost all liquidity, and coffee was the only reserve available to the farmers.

In an attempt to recover this coffee, the authorities tried to barter consumer goods against farmer stocks, recognizing the *de facto* demonetization of the kwanza in the countryside. Then the Ministry of Agriculture launched the Emergency Programme for Rural Commercialization (PECC) in 1984, reinforcing it in 1986. In a similar way, at the beginning of the 1980s the government of Mozambique had tried to relaunch the production of commercial crops by organizing a supply of consumer goods to the countryside with French aid.[73] However, such actions, whose rates of return appear interesting, are

---

[70] Azam & Besley, 'The case of Ghana'.

[71] A. Kidane, *Exchange Rate Policy and Economic Reform in Ethiopia* (Interim Report, African Economic Research Consortium, Nairobi, 1993).

[72] Azam, Collier & Cravinho, 'Crop sales, shortages and farmer portfolio behaviour'.

[73] Azam & Faucher, 'Le cas du Mozambique'.

bound to have only a marginal effect unless they are accompanied by an improvement in the macro-economic situation. In Angola, around 1986, it was the relaxation on the inflation front, not the effect of the PECC, which was responsible for reviving coffee sales.

Coffee sales tripled between 1986 and 1988, while sales of consumer goods by the PECC only increased by 52 per cent, and the real price paid to the producer, in terms of official prices, fell by 26 per cent. Thus this recovery of the supply cannot be explained by the conventional theory of agricultural supply, which only takes the real price paid to the producer into account, nor by the theory of supply in a situation of scarcity, which takes rationing on the consumer goods market into account.[74] The explanation advanced by Azam, Collier and Cravinho[75] is based on farmer portfolio behaviour. Between 1986 and 1990 the general level of prices on the parallel market dropped by an annual rate of 10 per cent because of a greater toleration of contraband on the part of the authorities and an improvement in the monetary situation. Under these conditions, the relative rates of return of coffee and currency changed completely. While coffee deteriorates to some extent when it is stored under farm conditions, resulting in a negative rate of return if its price remains constant, the purchasing power of money increased during this period at an annual rate of 10 per cent. In this situation, the farmers obviously preferred to sell their coffee stocks to make monetary savings. This creates a vicious circle, because the improvement in coffee exports increases the size of the foreign-exchange reserves, and hence encourages higher imports. There is thus an increase in the availability of goods.

## Conclusion

In this chapter we have illustrated the diversity of experiments in adjustment in the agricultural sector in Africa. This corresponds to a certain extent to the diversity of initial situations encountered, partly due to the variety of measures employed by governments to exact levies from farmers. However, despite this apparent diversity, we have underlined the profound unity in adjustment policies in the agricultural sector, which are aimed at restoring the efficiency of the markets by reducing the differences existing between the real prices of products in the various segments of the market, and especially between the real prices paid to producers and those paid by consumers.

This is in opposition to a widely held view which regards adjustment within the agricultural sector as a policy aimed at relaunching the production of export crops. The best possible example to the contrary is that of Morocco, one of the better pupils as far as structural adjustment is concerned. In Morocco the policy of adjustment was based on a strong recovery in agricultural production as a substitute for imports. Among the imbalances present on the agricultural markets in this country, the most important was found to be that concerning the agricultural labour market. Because of the sociological structure of the agricultural sector in Morocco, there is a disparity between the marginal productivity of labour and the wage paid in the modern, irrigated sector. This imbalance operates as a profit exacted by the landowners in this sector. The increase in the minimum wage has made it possible to reduce this profit significantly, with a significant positive effect on production.

---

[74] D. Bevan, A. Bigsten, P. Collier & J.W. Gunning, 'Peasant supply response in rationed economies', *World Development* 15 (1987), pp. 431–9.
[75] Azam, Collier & Cravinho, 'Crop sales, shortages and peasant portfolio behaviour'.

We then proceeded to illustrate the effectiveness of private intermediaries in the agricultural markets. In the case of the commercialization of export crops in Côte d'Ivoire, we suggested that the prices paid to the producers are actually linked much more directly to international prices than is recognized by the literature on the effects of the Stabilization Fund. The underlying significance of the reform is therefore altered, and emphasis needs to be laid on the distribution of the commercialization margin between the state and the traders, rather than on incentives for production. In Ethiopia, we saw how the intermediaries reacted to the liberalization of the grain markets in 1990, despite particularly difficult circumstances. This reform benefited consumers by allowing a fall in prices on the urban free markets, and above all by facilitating a reduction in the spatial dispersion of prices. Similarly, the liberalization of the rice market in Madagascar resulted in a slight drop in urban prices, improved market unification, and linkage to seasonal price fluctuations. These three effects had a positive influence on the standard of living.

Finally, we discussed the reforms in those economies where parallel markets are highly active. In Ghana, for example, a large part of cocoa production escaped across the border into Côte d'Ivoire before adjustment. Modifying incentives by raising the official price paid to the producer and reducing the exchange rate on the parallel markets led farmers to sell more through the official channels, with positive consequences for the country. Similarly, in Ethiopia, devaluation in 1993 brought a percentage of coffee exports back into the official circuits, with favourable macro-economic effects for the country. Finally, we illustrated, by means of the example in Angola, the analytical difficulties posed by economic situations which have got out of hand. No conventional scheme of analysis can be applied to explain the development of coffee sales in this country, where the shortage of consumer goods and the timid emergence of a parallel market had led farmers to use coffee as a value reserve to counter inflation and demonetization. Only a sustained policy of deflation in the late 1980s enabled the country to remonetize its transactions and encouraged the farmers to sell their stocks of coffee. These three examples show how export crops can correspond to a wide variety of more or less deliberate recovery policies depending on the specific initial situation.

Thus if structural adjustment is generally considered to work in the various African agricultural sectors, this is due to a pragmatic approach to problems, taking the specifics of each country seriously into account. No miraculous and universal cure has been found, and the solutions adopted must be rooted in the historical and political specifics of the various countries. Nevertheless, when correctly adapted to specific local circumstances, economic theory is still the privileged guide to reform in its ability to delineate clearly the objective to be attained: the restoration of market efficiency.

# NINE

# Constraints to
# Manufacturing Production

### LINDANI NDLOVU

Successful manufacturing requires factors of production that are readily usable, such as skilled labour and capital. Reasonable and growing investment and appropriate technology are major requirements. Investment creates the capacity to process and produce. Before commitments on investment can be made, it is essential that the market for products exists or at least can be developed. With production units established, both the raw material inputs and the working capital that will keep production at the required levels and enable it to proceed smoothly and uninterruptedly must be ensured.

Production is also enhanced by a supportive macro-economic environment, a set of incentives and an efficient structure and organization of production on the shop floor, a high level of infrastructure and affordable finance. A lack of these will without doubt hamper the progress of production. Production is targeted for a market, and it is natural to expect competition from domestic and foreign suppliers. Therefore competitiveness is an important dimension of production targeting and of marketing. Constraints to manufacturing production in Africa can be attributed to some or all of these aspects. They range from the narrow and more direct factors that impact on production – technical factors such as the availability of equipment, labour costs and raw materials – to the wider and more indirect factors such as the legacy of political instability in several regions of the African continent, inadequate infrastructure, an uncertain investment climate and the unwillingness of countries to sign investment agreements, a lack of convincing legal structures in some countries and issues of corruption, institutional weakness or the absence of appropriate institutions, and loss of skilled personnel.

The story of Africa's declining manufacturing production has been cause for concern now for more than a decade. In Pickett's classification,[1] two-thirds of sub-Saharan countries were classified in the lowest-income category. In spite of the efforts of various development organizations there seems to be no solution to the continued decline. There is evidence that at independence in the 1960s the state of development and the level of production in Africa were ahead of those of the less developed Asian countries.[2] Since then Asia has experienced improved production. Africa over the same period has experienced a progressive continuous decline despite the many efforts to reverse it. Obviously, this development continues to worry many sections of the international community. The biggest question to be answered before any meaningful attempt can be made to resolve the situation and reverse the trends is: why this continuing decline? The range of arguments, explanations and recommendations often indicates a significant misunderstanding of Africa's problems.

This chapter outlines the perceived major constraints on productive activities in African industry, which explain the low levels of manufactured production and trade in the 1990s. The chapter is divided into five sections. Section two considers the nature and scope of the problem. In section three, various constraints are discussed, and in section four some of the internationally competitive products are outlined. Conclusions are drawn in section five.

## The Nature and Scope of Production and Marketing Constraints

The general decline in African economic activity and production and the crisis that the continent faces are readily visible from the tables below. In the manufacturing sector, evidence of decline is provided by the figure for manufacturing value added (MVA). The share of manufacturing in gross domestic product over time and the growth of output in this sector indicate what has happened. An evaluation of Africa's trade performance is also essential to show the share of traded manufactures in total world trade.

The decline in Africa's participation in world trade is shown in Table 9.1, where African performance is compared with that of other regions. Both African exports and imports fell: exports by 3.7 per cent and imports by 1.9 per cent per annum in the 1980s. In the 1990s these trends have largely continued and in some cases worsened. The magnitude of these declines becomes much clearer when compared with performances over the previous decade, 1970–80, when both exports and imports grew by more than 20 per cent per annum. Between 1980 and 1992 some eight African countries showed an export growth of more than 5 per cent per annum.[3] Manufactured exports from Africa constituted 0.42 per cent of the world total in 1989, marking a reduction of the 1970 share but an improvement on the 1980s' performance. These exports grew at the rate of 16.34 per cent between 1970 and 1980 and fell to 9:82 per cent between 1980 and 1989. Although the fall was substantial, it was comparable with, and in fact better than, performance in the developed economies of Europe, North America and Japan. It was, however, well below the performance of developing economies where South and

---

[1] J. Pickett, 'The low-income economies of sub-Saharan Africa: problems and prospects', in J. Pickett and H. Singer (eds), *Towards Economic Recovery in sub-Saharan Africa: Essays in honour of Robert Gardiner* (Routledge, London and New York, 1990), p. 217.

[2] F. Cheru, *The Silent Revolution in Africa: Debt, development and democracy* (Anvil Press, Harare, 1989), p. 3; World Bank, *Sub-Saharan Africa: From crisis to sustainable growth* (World Bank, Washington DC, 1989), p. 17.

[3] Exports grew by more than 5% in Benin, Burkina Faso, Burundi, Cameroon, Ghana, Malawi, Mauritius and Tunisia. P. Braunerhjelm & G. Fors, *The Zimbabwean Manufacturing Sector: Current status and future development potentials* (The Industrial Institute for Economic and Social Research, Stockholm, 1994), p. 11.

**Table 9.1: Annual average growth rates of exports and imports, 1960–90 (Current prices)**

| Region | Exports (f.o.b.) | | | Imports (c.i.f) | | |
|---|---|---|---|---|---|---|
| | 1960–70 | 1970–80 | 1980–90 | 1960–70 | 1970–80 | 1980–90 |
| World | 9.2 | 20.3 | 6.0 | 9.1 | 20.2 | 6.0 |
| Developed market economies | 10.0 | 18.8 | 7.7 | 10.2 | 19.5 | 7.2 |
| – North America | 8.7 | 17.0 | 5.9 | 10.9 | 19.1 | 8.0 |
| – Europe | 10.1 | 19.3 | 8.2 | 9.7 | 19.5 | 7.4 |
| – Japan | 17.5 | 20.8 | 8.9 | 14.4 | 22.0 | 5.1 |
| Eastern Europe including former USSR | 8.7 | 18.0 | 2.3 | 8.1 | 18.3 | 3.0 |
| Developing market economies | 7.2 | 25.9 | 2.2 | 6.5 | 23.8 | 3.1 |
| – Africa | 9.2 | 21.7 | – 3.7 | 4.7 | 22.2 | – 1.9 |
| – North Africa | 11.5 | 23.9 | – 4.5 | 2.9 | 25.6 | – 1.9 |
| – Sub-Saharan Africa | 7.8 | 20.0 | – 3.0 | 6.2 | 20.1 | – 3.0 |
| Asia | 7.7 | 30.1 | 3.6 | 7.0 | 26.9 | 5.7 |
| – Western Asia | 9.3 | 34.3 | -6.8 | 7.4 | 33.6 | – 2.7 |
| – South and South-East Asia | 6.7 | 25.8 | 10.8 | 6.9 | 23.5 | 9.6 |
| – China | 1.3 | 20.0 | 12.8 | 1.9 | 23.5 | 13.5 |
| Latin America | 5.0 | 20.8 | 0.8 | 5.6 | 20.6 | – 1.3 |

Source: United Nations Industrial Development Organization, *Industry and Development Global Report 1993/94* (Unido, Vienna, 1993).

**Table 9.2: World share and annual growth rates of manufactured exports in current prices by region, 1970, 1980 and 1989 (%)**

| Region | World share | | | Annual growth rate | |
|---|---|---|---|---|---|
| | 1970 | 1980 | 1989 | 1970–80 | 1980–89 |
| World | 100 | 100 | 100 | 19.04 | 7.65 |
| Developed market economies | 84.43 | 82.26 | 77.87 | 18.73 | 6.99 |
| – Europe | 54.6 | 54.08 | 49.61 | 18.93 | 6.62 |
| – North America | 19.27 | 15.59 | 14.7 | 16.54 | 6.95 |
| – Japan | 9.41 | 11.31 | 12.56 | 21.25 | 8.91 |
| Eastern Europe including former USSR | 9.49 | 7.18 | 4.35 | 15.76 | 1.81 |
| Developing market economies | 5.51 | 9.68 | 16.34 | 25.95 | 14.1 |
| – Africa | 0.44 | 0.35 | 0.42 | 16.34 | 9.82 |
| Asia | | | | | |
| – Western Asia | 0.24 | 0.59 | 0.78 | 30.05 | 10.93 |
| – South and South-East Asia | 3.27 | 6.65 | 12.73 | 27.8 | 15.71 |
| Latin America | 0.98 | 1.46 | 1.89 | 23.92 | 10.76 |

Source: ibid.

South-East Asia excelled (15.71 per cent). With reference to Table 9.2, Africa's world share of manufactured exports at less than half a per cent (0.42 per cent), indicates a very low participation in the international trade in manufactures by the continent. This low trade performance may simply be symptomatic of low manufacturing performance in the continent's economies.

Constraints to industrial production can be divided into two groups: technical and non-technical. We shall look at these groups separately.

## Constraints to Production and Marketing

### *Technical constraints to manufacturing production*

Technical constraints are those related to the organization of production, such as the type of equipment, technology, labour and inputs required during the processes. These are discussed here under eight sub-headings.

#### LACK OF INVESTMENT AND DECLINING PRODUCTION CAPACITY

Investment creates capacity that can lead to growth and increased production. African countries are increasingly faced with declining investment in their manufacturing sectors. Much of Africa's inability to attract significant levels of investment has been attributed to conditions on the continent: the security of investments is largely threatened by the state and the absence of the rule of law or by political instability. Much of the decline occurred in the 1990s, when economic environments had been altered significantly by the impact of structural adjustment. Bennell found that between 1989 and 1994 over half of British manufacturing firms based in anglophone Africa disinvested on account of shortage of foreign exchange, massive currency devaluations and low profitability.[4] Underlying reasons given for disinvestment were 'stalled industrialization in Africa' and 'interestingly, the SAPs [structural adjustment programmes].' The countries most affected are Kenya, Nigeria and Zimbabwe where 65 per cent of equity investment was located. In all, the 14 countries affected account for 54.6 per cent of sub-Saharan Africa's population and have been the origin of 58.6 per cent of the region's manufacturing value added. These massive withdrawals may represent a universal disinvestment by investors from other major investing countries.

The consequence of a lack of investment growth is that there is no creation of new production capacity and sometimes a failure to maintain production equipment which has either become obsolete or has fallen into disrepair. Either way, production cannot be maintained. Old machinery and outdated equipment operate less efficiently. Frequent breakdowns interrupt production.

Investment in African economies was controlled and needed government approval up to the late 1980s. Investors had to obtain permission to invest. Often the requirements investors had to meet were stringent and the bureaucratic procedures formidable. The cost of gaining approval was very high before a company could channel resources into production. Much of the bureaucratic maze has been reduced by economic reform programmes implemented by countries all over the continent, but more still needs to be done to improve the chances of attracting more outside investment. Other factors such as the cost of finance and lack of capital equipment discourage domestic investment.

[4] P. Bennell, *British Manufacturing Investment in Sub-Saharan Africa: Corporate responses during structural adjustment* (Institute of Development Studies, Brighton, UK, 1994).

COSTS OF PRODUCTION

Competitiveness is a key factor in Africa's failure to produce and market its products, especially manufactures. As already indicated, capacity utilization levels impact on costs. Explaining the importance of capacity utilization Gunning *et al.* state that 'increased usage of installed plant capacity means that existing fixed capital assets yield greater output without incurring any additional investment costs'.[5] Reduced levels of capacity use and low production volumes implying increased unit costs are thus one reason for uncompetitive prices. High rates of capacity underutilization provide no incentives for firms to introduce new technical innovations requiring investment, implying further underutilization. This capacity underutilization was found to be a main cause of the decline of output, technical regress and falling productivity growth rates in Tanzanian manufacturing.[6] In Nigeria, the average rate of capacity utilization in the entire manufacturing sector in 1992 was 34.5 per cent.[7] This shows considerable waste of installed capacity which would make it very difficult to achieve efficient production and underlines a disturbing propensity towards decline in production.

Costs of production are also increased by poor infrastructural provision and regulatory constraints. The infrastructural constraints include a poor telecommunications service, and poor road and rail networks, and electricity and water services. Telecommunication systems have been state-run and lack of investment has made it difficult for business to conduct transactions with distant clients. Braunerhjelm and Fors show that sub-Saharan countries had some of the lowest numbers of telephone mainlines per 1,000 people and recorded high faults per 100 mainlines.[8] This under-provision created problems of congestion and therefore increased faults. Poor investment in, and maintenance of, roads has affected communication and transportation systems in Africa. Power cuts, long regarded as the scourge of African manufacturing and investment, have hit many countries. This may be as a result of drought or simply be due to inadequate expansion to meet increasing demand or poor repairs and maintenance. Load-shedding and forced rationing or blackouts affect the operation of manufacturing equipment and, hence, production. Power shortages cause excessive wastage, and some machines may take as long as four hours to return to full production levels after the power is restored. There is also inadequate investment in water resources, a much needed resource in African manufacturing given the continent's frequent droughts. Water is a vital part of many manufacturing processes.

In Ghana, demand for telephone services is estimated at 300,000 lines against current supply levels of 50,000 lines. This situation represents a general trend in African economies. Most of the time lines are out of service, making it difficult to cope with the traffic. Many countries have dilapidated rail networks facing financial difficulties; Mozambican port facilities have been unable to cope with traffic from neighbouring countries. In the 1990s Zambia, Zimbabwe and, at present, Kenya are some of the countries

[5] J.W. Gunning, T. Mumvuma & M. Pomp, 'Capacity utilisation and investment', in J.W. Gunning (ed.), 'The manufacturing sector in Zimbabwe: dynamics and constraints'. (Mimeo, University of Zimbabwe, Harare, and Free University, Amsterdam, 1994), p. 79.

[6] K. Kulindwa, 'Input substitution, technical change, productivity and capacity utilisation in the Tanzanian manufacturing sector: a disequilibium factor demand model', Memorandum No. 189, Department of Economics, University of Goteborg, Sweden, 1993, quoted in Gunning *et al.*, 'Capacity utilisation', pp. 79–80.

[7] United Nations Industrial Development Organization, *Industry and Development Global Report 1993/94* (Unido, Vienna, 1993), p. 57.

[8] Braunerhjelm & Fors, *The Zimbabwean Manufacturing Sector*. The countries concerned are Botswana, Burundi, Ethiopia, Morocco, Rwanda, Togo, Tunisia, Zambia and Zimbabwe.

to be affected.[9] The drought in Southern Africa in 1991/92 caused some firms to relocate from areas with water shortages and in some cases these moves have been permanent.

The state in Africa has had a larger than normal involvement which has made production costly and unprofitable. The nature of the controls was such that in general they impeded development. Operating costs in Nigeria are as much as 33 per cent higher than elsewhere, while investment costs in the same country are estimated to be some 50 per cent above international standards. This should indicate that profitability and competitiveness are difficult to achieve or maintain.

The implementation of structural adjustment across the continent further increases the costs of production by raising the cost of finance for investment and working capital. This is a result of the price-raising effects of devaluation which in turn lead to higher interest rates. The contractionary monetary and fiscal policies accompanying devaluation lead to increased rates of inflation and hence increase the cost of borrowing. Interest rates that in the 1980s were low and negative because of government controls have increased significantly. Liberalization brought about increases in interest rates in several countries including Kenya, Tanzania, Zimbabwe and Zambia. The high cost of money makes it difficult for those companies which depend on borrowing to finance production; it therefore becomes a constraint. In Zimbabwe, Canadian investors seeking partners for joint ventures have been scared by the high interest rates, diminishing the partners' chances of raising capital locally.[10]

## LACK OF RAW MATERIAL INPUTS

As indicated above, one of the major requirements for successful constraint-free production is unimpeded availability of materials. Production in many African countries suffered from a shortage or non-availability of the necessary imported raw materials. One of the major reasons for this is a serious shortage of foreign currency to purchase materials. This aspect is dealt with elsewhere.[11] Lack of materials has led to lower capacity utilization and declining productivity of investment, even with ideal production equipment. In some cases production has come to a complete halt. These trends continued in the 1990s as the problems of the 1980s have not been resolved, in particular balance-of-payments problems and the associated shortage of imported inputs.

## LOW AND DECLINING PRODUCTIVITY

Productivity is the relationship between the output of an economic unit and the inputs employed to produce it. There are many possible indices of productivity for one production unit but partial productivity indices of labour and capital are commonly used.[12] Labour productivity improves with investment in equipment and technology. A useful approach to measuring productivity is to express inputs and outputs in value terms, giving the return per unit invested. The cost of labour in Africa is still rather low by international standards and could be a main attraction for investors, should other aspects be

[9] *Business Herald* (Harare), 6 April 1995.
[10] ibid.
[11] See Chapter 6 by Janine Aron in the present volume.
[12] There are conceptual problems in defining and measuring capital, given the various forms of fixed assets required during production. For this reason, labour productivity calculations are common. However, incremental capital output ratios are also used as a productivity indicator.

put right. However, the control and determination of minimum wages by most governments has increased costs and thus reduced labour productivity. Old equipment and obsolete technologies in African economies lead to declining efficiency and productivity of labour and other investment. Low capacity utilization levels also add to the inefficiency of production and indicate falling productivity. Reasons for the decline are a lack of raw materials, foreign exchange shortages, low demand, and shrinking markets. Falling productivity implies increased costs of production and reduced competitiveness of products.

### FOREIGN-EXCHANGE SHORTAGES AND CONTROLS

The main use of foreign exchange in production is to purchase imported inputs for investment, for replacement (repairs and maintenance) and generally for raw material inputs. The other main use is to service debts, in other words for the payment of interest or the repayment of capital on external loans.

The increased importance of these factors in the 1980s and into the 1990s has made shortage of foreign exchange a major constraint on production. It implies a reduction in the value and volume of imports, which imposes choices about where cuts can be made and results in an inevitable impact on the economy as a whole. Decline in the 1980s created the need to borrow, thus increasing obligations which require the use of foreign exchange. Past policies which attempted to replace imports through local production (i.e. import substitution) left lasting effects with no base established to generate foreign exchange. Fluctuations in availability were difficult to predict while growth of earnings remained limited, thus making import-based production hazardous. Essential imports – mainly of capital equipment and raw materials – could at times not be further reduced without affecting production. Such reduction eventually leads to lower production and lower use of installed capacity.

All countries in sub-Saharan Africa have faced foreign-exchange shortages and controlled its use at some point in response to balance-of-payments problems.[13] Foreign exchange continues to be generally in short supply, causing supply-side constraints. Ghana, Kenya, Nigeria, Tanzania, Uganda, Zambia and Zimbabwe, among others, all suffered from foreign currency shortages and have not generated sufficient growth in export earnings to solve the problem. However, import compression because of the increasing costs of imports as a result of devaluation and higher costs of money has reduced demand.

### LACK OF COMPETITION AND QUALITY OF PRODUCTION

The lack of competition and the existence of an assured market provided no incentive for manufacturers to strive to improve product quality and reduce costs, both of which are key to competitiveness, in both domestic and export markets. Inward orientation constrains production and there would have been benefit from a parallel programme to encourage exports for foreign-exchange generation. Such a structure (emphasizing import replacement and export production) would be a natural way to progress in the process of industrialization and is the path that the major industrialized countries followed. While African economies recognize the problems of this approach as a result of the

---

[13] Botswana, which did very well in the 1980s but is now said to face some problems, was an exception in regard to shortages but, like the rest, had foreign-exchange controls. The oil-exporting countries of North Africa were an exception as regards shortages.

pressures which stem from opening up, attempts to improve quality and to be competitive will take some time and need sustained support in the difficult period of adjustment. Much of the support provided by government is no longer available and the investments required for competitiveness cannot be made in the present circumstances because of uncertainty and the costs of borrowing.

Investments previously approved by governments did not emphasize quality. Protection of the domestic market through licensing of imports provided domestic producers with a sellers' market. It was a very lucrative place for these firms to do business, offering assured higher rates of return. Foreign markets were uncertain, difficult to penetrate and required considerable investment to develop. There was no pressure or incentive to reduce costs as a result. There was no prioritization of industrial imports.

### TECHNOLOGY AND TECHNOLOGICAL CAPABILITY

The technologies used in African production are supplied by the developed world. They are not suited to African conditions and are generally very high-cost and capital-intensive, and do not recognize Africa's endowment with labour which could be a major source of cost reduction. African economies have not invested in technology development for use in the continent to boost production volumes and quality of output. African economies are today littered with technologies from several generations back which are old and obsolete. Outdated production equipment is a hindrance to efficient manufacturing production in the 1990s. The acquisition of old equipment was necessitated by cost and other factors constraining investment.

The types of technologies in use and the state of knowledge, including the necessary operating skills, all influence the competitiveness of the finished product. Structural theories on competitiveness suggest that industries in the early stages of formation and setting up have problems competing with more established operations. For this reason they need time to grow and be nurtured before they can compete. This was used in the past to justify protection against outside competition and to allow new industries to improve their performance and reduce their costs of production and become efficient, initially under protected conditions. In the African context, the infant-industry argument for protection was used to justify protective structures but was not used to compel producers towards maturity and competitiveness. These are the producers who, with liberalization, have been unable to withstand competition. This is clearly apparent in the case of those economies currently undergoing structural adjustment.

The problems identified have been compounded by the use of outdated production equipment and old technology. Constraints on technology acquisition lie in its cost and the unavailability of adequate funds for the purpose. Policies according low priority to technology have also been responsible for the deterioration.

### IMPORT-SUBSTITUTION ORIENTATION

In the past, stringent foreign-exchange allocation conditions made the domestic market an attractive place in which to manufacture and sell since it was possible to determine what was in short supply. In this way, economies re-oriented to focus on import-substitution production.

There can be a danger in focusing on replacing imports of manufactures. Often there is a tendency to forget that import substitution continues to require large amounts of foreign exchange to service and maintain production equipment and, more importantly, to supply raw materials. A number of countries in Africa found themselves in a situation where they were working to replace imports and in the process found that foreign exchange continued to be required. The ensuing continued or increasing foreign-exchange requirements put pressure on systems which were not geared towards generating foreign exchange, or in other words, were not geared for export production. This internal orientation in production created a shelter for domestic producers against competition.

### Non-technical constraints

In addition to those constraints relating to the organization of production there are others that affect the environment within which production takes place. In the African context, these have played as important a role as those relating to technical arrangements. Among them are factors such as the political environment, economic uncertainty, macro-economic instability and a lack of observance of legal contracts and inadequate protection of patents.

The question of unfavourable environments continues to this day. Political and economic instability do not encourage investment by foreign or domestic firms. Africa competes for the attention of investors who are quite selective and who are sensitive to the conditions on offer in the host countries, including policies and incentives. In addition, the environment in which they invest should offer security, stability and assured returns. This has not always been guaranteed in Africa and as a result investment has not occurred in sufficient volume to stimulate economic growth, especially in the key sectors of industrial production.

#### POLITICAL STABILITY, IDEOLOGY AND POLITICS

Africa has a legacy of political violence and instability dating from struggles for majority rule and rooted in despotic one-party state systems and dictatorships. Coups d'état have been common. In 1993 there was another military takeover in Nigeria. The political system and the style of governance that developed created a system of economic management which paid little attention to development issues. Van der Kraaij notes that until recently only four countries were democratic exceptions to authoritarian rule in sub-Saharan Africa.[14] Elections have been held in more than 25 countries since 1989 leading to changes of government in many countries. Disagreements over non-acceptance of election results in Angola (1991) ended in renewed civil war. The 1992 annulment of the general election in Algeria led to violence. There are ethnic conflicts in Rwanda and Burundi and fighting in Sudan, Sierra Leone, Liberia and Somalia. According to Van der Kraaij, political stability is as important a precondition as, for example, a good macro-economic policy for social and economic development. Most of the countries affected by coups have not recovered from instability and have experienced a continuous decline in their economic performance.

Poor economic performance persists in many countries. Because successful economies are difficult to come by, countries like Côte d'Ivore, Egypt, Ghana, Kenya, Malawi,

---

[14] F. van der Kraaij, 'Background notes to sub-Saharan Africa' in R. van der Hoeven & F. van der Kraaij (eds), *Structural Adjustment and Beyond in Sub-Saharan Africa: Research and policy issues* (Netherlands Ministry of Foreign Affairs, James Currey and Heinemann, The Hague, London and Portsmouth, NH, 1994), pp. 240–57.

Swaziland and Zimbabwe can all be regarded as reasonable performers. And yet some of them face serious problems.

The production constraints in such cases derive from the unstable economic environment which has undermined the manufacturing sector in particular. Fosu has concluded that political instability played a major role in the relatively stagnant economies of sub-Saharan Africa and reduced the region's GDP growth over the period 1960–86.[15]

Instability discourages investment, a requirement for increased production. This applies to foreign as well as domestic investors. If investment has already occurred and production is under way, instability disrupts systems; it cuts routes for exports and imports (as happened to southern African economies in the 1980s); it deprives production units of valuable imports; it breaks up domestic markets as it reduces disposable income; and it increases the costs of production. Unstable African economies have experienced increased inflation leading to investor losses and serious disruption of production. The disinvestment by British manufacturing firms identified by Bennell was a result of instability that led to reduced profitability.[16]

MACRO-ECONOMIC POLICIES AND STRUCTURAL FACTORS

The macro-economic policies adopted by a country have a significant and lasting impact on its development, particularly on production. In Africa, imbalances in the macro-economic variables – balance-of-payments and large budget deficits leading to high inflation rates and high interest rates – combined to bring about declining investment performance. As a result, there has been a serious lack of investment. This may be explained by other factors as well. For example, in Zambia, falling rates of manufacturing and overall growth originated from before the 1980s. A large foreign debt and a poor balance-of-payments position had adverse effects which largely explain the low investment.

The structure of African economies inherited from the colonial era was deformed and has constrained their development. First, the gearing of production in favour of small minorities affected operations. Independence and the desire for equity between inhabitants saw a failure of systems to cope. The inability to respond to changed circumstances, such as increased demand, underlined the deformities. Ownership was largely concentrated in the hands of a few, mainly with strong external connections.

Even in the 1990s, many African countries have been unable to change these inherited structures. Much of the failure to transform the structural characteristics has been attributed to policies pursued by governments and variable conditions in the external economic environment such as the oil price shocks and, for Africa, frequent droughts. These are cited as evidence of the failure of African economic policies to adapt to changing conditions over very long periods. Structural deformities explain the inability to increase production and exports and its consequences, including negative and widening balance-of-payments deficits, rising inflation and declining foreign-exchange earnings. It is these constraints that structural adjustment programmes (SAPs) implemented with World Bank and IMF assistance are trying to cure. SAPs are intended to bring about structural reform, enabling economies to respond to and to make greater use of market mechanisms. They are also designed to re-orient production away from the domestic market to the production of tradeables.

---

[15] A.K. Fosu, 'Political instability and economic growth: Evidence from sub-Saharan Africa', *Economic Development and Cultural Change*, 40, 4, (July 1992), pp. 829–41.
[16] Bennell, *British Manufacturing Investment*.

Most African countries have experienced macro-economic instability in the form of balance-of-payments problems, high inflation rates, and large public-sector deficits in the 1980s. In the 1990s, different macro-economic policies have been generated by the economic reforms. However, the legacies of past policies are entrenched in the system, and their effects will take some time to reverse. As a result, a number of countries, including Ghana and Kenya among others, have undergone a series of structural adjustment programmes which have not completely reversed the effects of previous policies.

### EXCHANGE-RATE MANAGEMENT

Related to foreign-exchange constraints, in the past, was the issue of the price at which foreign exchange was available. Exchange rates affect the demand for imports for manufacturing and other purposes. Exchange rates were managed and controlled by central banks. It has been argued that the price of foreign exchange encouraged the demand for imports for use in manufacturing production and for consumption and did not encourage diversification into using local raw materials. In Zimbabwe, manufacturing sub-sectors such as chemicals had an import content of their production as high as 85 per cent.[17] The level of imports required in manufacturing production in Nigeria in the 1990s was 55 per cent. This level of import dependence seriously affected production as foreign-exchange availability varied, leading to falls in manufacturing output.

Exports of manufactures have largely been, and continue to be, uncompetitive in international markets. This is sometimes affected by the price of foreign exchange, which tends to favour imports and discourages the drive to increase exports, causing very low or declining earnings in foreign exchange. Production changes intended to increase the supply of exports take some time to set up and run at full capacity. This is combined with what has consistently looked like an unwillingness by developed country markets to import. These factors affect earnings of foreign exchange and its price.

### EXTERNAL FACTORS, GOVERNMENT INTERVENTION AND MISMANAGEMENT

Some of the constraints to production have been largely viewed as external, over which African economies have little influence.[18] Such a view places this factor outside the domain of rational government activity, implying that no one can do anything about it and therefore no one should be blamed. To an extent, it is true that external factors impinge on the design and implementation of policy. Commonly discussed external factors impinging on Africa are drought, fluctuating commodity prices and the external economic environment. However, other factors can be attributed to irrational or unclear policy and inappropriate responses to situations, such as over-expenditure and outright mismanagement by government. Many African governments have spent huge amounts on arms and support a large military apparatus and the obligations they took on to finance this have continued to impact on their national budgets. The effect is to divert limited resources to non-productive activities at a time when large amounts are required to facilitate investment.

Further constraints to manufacturing production and development in Africa result from the extent of government intervention in economic activities. In the past, a typical

---

[17] Government of Zimbabwe, *The Socio-Economic Review of Zimbabwe 1980–85* (Government Printers, Harare, 1986).
[18] F. Cheru, *The Silent Revolution in Africa*.

African economy was very heavily regulated. According to Marsden and Belot, the range of regulations that have had a negative impact on the performance and, hence, the growth of manufacturing industry in Africa included barriers to entry and obstacles to foreign investment, high levels of taxation, labour regulations and price controls.[19] Most of these operated in the 1980s but have, in many cases, continued into the 1990s. The biggest problem is how to deregulate them without an adverse impact on various sections of the population.

African governments have a record of over-expenditure and limited resources with which to finance it. A consequence of this is the use of excessive rates of taxation as a source of government revenue. Governments have had difficulty in balancing fiscal policies with the need to raise revenue, or in creating adequate incentives to work, invest and save.[20] The authorities have also been unable to recognize the need to avoid distortions in the returns to various economic activities after tax. Very high rates of corporate income tax were experienced in, for example, Ghana, Sudan and Zaïre, where it was at times levied at 60 per cent. Such rates of taxation took away incentives and worked to kill investment in manufacturing industry by the corporate sector. Multinationals with a choice of where to invest were not presented with difficult choices when it came to Africa. Top marginal rates of income tax as high as 80 per cent were charged in Rwanda and Zambia, while the top rate was 70 per cent in Sudan and 60 per cent in Ghana and Zaïre. These high levels of personal income tax discourage workers who seem to work for the state and benefit little from their effort.

Excessively high rates of taxation generated further negative effects. For example, they undermined manufacturing's capacity to save and to finance expansion, to re-equip or to maintain its productive assets and investment in other opportunities. This resulted in a worsening performance leading to decline of production. High levels of taxation also discouraged small enterprises from making the transition to formal-sector activities, while some small formal enterprises may have been forced underground in order to avoid paying very high tax. Associated with taxation are issues of dividend remittability and repatriation of profits in the case of foreign investors who have been constantly under threat from governments at times of balance-of-payments crisis, which were common in the majority of African countries, particularly in the 1980s. Affected by drought and under severe foreign-exchange constraints, with large deficits on the current and invisibles account in the early 1980s, the Zimbabwean government suspended remittances and outflows on the invisibles account in March 1984.[21] The historical influence of the ever-present possibility of the suspension of factor payments outside these economies continues to constrain activity.

Excessive controls and regulations were exercised in labour markets. Over-regulation reduced efficiency, leading to lower productivity and, hence, lower profitability. Keen to expand and maintain employment, governments forced employers to expand or not to lay off their workers. Security of employment became entrenched without taking account of specific production circumstances, thus removing any motivation for workers to perform. Zimbabwe in the 1980s had regulations requiring employers to seek government permission to retrench their work force, which could be denied even in the face

---

[19] K. Marsden & T. Belot, 'Private enterprise in Africa: Creating a better environment', in G.M. Meier & W.F. Steel (eds), *Industrial Adjustment in Sub-Saharan Africa* (Oxford University Press for the World Bank, Oxford/London/New York, 1989), pp. 163–8.

[20] ibid., p. 165.

[21] Government of Zimbabwe, *Socio-Economic Review 1980–85*.

of falling profitability. The government also determined minimum wages, but this was abolished in 1993. Employers wanting to cut back on staff in countries like Burkina Faso faced similar difficulties and required government approval.[22] Botswana labour legislation stipulates the rights of employers and their employees, including, for example, job protection, the length of annual and maternity leave and the procedures employers have to follow when hiring and terminating employment. Details of how to deal with misconduct are also a feature of the elaborate over-regulation common in Africa. Besides the loss of worker motivation, entrenched employment made employers reluctant to take on staff and scared outside investors who were not willing to commit their investment funds in these instances.

Overall, African bureaucracies imposed legal and procedural requirements which were clearly painful and discouraging to would-be investors. In the 1990s, African economies have not succeeded in transforming the myriad of regulations and controls that guided and discouraged industrial activity. They still labour under constraints created in the past. For example, many governments controlled prices for a number of manufactured and other products and services and some still do so today.

Other mechanisms of control and intervention which reduce the pace of industrial production and growth are import-licensing measures and investment regulations. Government intervention in the past created numerous problems that make production and marketing of African industrial products difficult. Structural adjustment programmes, widely implemented by African governments, represent an acceptance of past errors. SAPs have led to a sudden and unplanned opening-up which gives little opportunity for real adjustment and creates serious possibilities of undermining whatever industry had developed. As Bennell found,[23] British manufacturing firms' disinvestment in English-speaking African countries was made imperative by lower profitability due to devaluation and structural adjustment.

### INDEBTEDNESS AND RISING DEBT SERVICE

In most discussions of the African crisis, the question of the extent of the indebtedness of African economies to the developed countries and international financial institutions has featured prominently. It is argued that economic growth has ceased in many countries, with debt the single most important cause of Africa's present inability to develop.[24] The logic of the argument is that debt service, more than repayment, absorbs whatever little foreign exchange these economies generate without leaving much for use locally to develop and increase the capacity to generate more. As a result, most economies produce and export to service their debts rather than to manage the industrial development process. Vast amounts of resources are transferred from Africa to the developed countries. The World Bank has highlighted the enormous growth in indebtedness over the 1970s and 1980s with little sign of improvement.[25] According to Bush and Szeftel, Africa's debt in 1993 was estimated at US$199 billion, constituting roughly 90 per cent of the continent's gross national product.[26] In the same year, sub-Saharan Africa paid out US$11.3 billion in debt service, with an increase in the level of arrears equal to

---

[22] Marsden & Belot, 'Private enterprise', p. 167.

[23] Bennell, *British Manufacturing Investment.*

[24] R. Bush & M. Szeftel, 'States, markets and Africa's crisis', *Review of African Political Economy*, 21, 60, (June 1994), pp. 147–56.

[25] World Bank, *World Development Report 1992* (Oxford University Press, New York, 1992).

[26] Bush & Szeftel, 'States, markets and Africa's crisis'.

US$16.3 billion. These levels of indebtedness and consequent transfers show how little remains for Africa's own use, including for deepening industrial production and development.

## Marketing constraints

The successful international marketing of industrial production requires substantial investment in investigating and developing markets. The quality of the products being marketed, the punctuality of deliveries, the assured consistency of supply by producers and price competitiveness are key considerations upon which success is built. It has been demonstrated that African economies have focused on production for the domestic market. They have not invested adequately in developing export markets and invariably lack the experience required to break into them in the 1990s. It was shown earlier that price competitiveness has not been achieved and therefore remains one of the areas of weakness. So too are issues of quality and sustained supply delivered on time.

### DEPENDENCE ON PRIMARY PRODUCTS AND DECLINING TERMS OF TRADE

In addition to these general problems, there are others that characterize African marketing problems. For example, Africa relies to a great extent on trade, and its exports and imports account for nearly half of the countries' gross domestic product.[27] The danger it faces from this reliance on trade is that of being an insignificant player in world markets: its share of world trade is slightly over 1 per cent. This reliance on trade is clearly a problem when cast against the background of Africa's dependence on trade in primary commodities such as cotton, coffee (in Uganda), cocoa (in Ghana) and minerals such as copper (in Zambia). Coote found that primary commodity exports constituted more than 60 per cent of export earnings in the period 1982–1986 in 23 countries in Africa.[28] Oxfam further notes that overall, some 85 per cent of all the region's exports derive from primary commodities and in the majority of cases this comes from one or two commodities.[29]

Commodity prices are highly variable and unstable. Export revenue fluctuations mean instability of income for exporters. Where export income comprises a significant portion of an economy's GNP, a fall in export income may lead to a foreign-exchange crisis, reducing the economy's capacity to import. Continued falls lead to serious balance-of-payments problems with constraints on production which have already been discussed. Africa was much affected by the relationship between foreign exchange and import availability in the 1980s. In this period, the prices of most commodities tended to fall. This was made worse by Africa's tendency to import manufactures and the fact that the prices of imports were generally on the increase. The result was a sharp fall in Africa's terms of trade. The purchasing power of export proceeds from commodities eroded rapidly. The reduction in purchasing power has been of the order of 50 per cent since the early 1980s.[30]

---

[27] Oxfam, *Africa Make or Break: Action for recovery* (Oxfam, Oxford, 1993).

[28] Of these countries, 10 derived more than 90% of earnings from primary commodities, 5 more than 80%, 4 more than 70%, and the rest more than 60%. Countries like Mauritania (fish and iron ore), Zambia (copper), Rwanda (coffee), Niger (uranium), Burundi (coffee), Uganda (coffee) and Namibia (uranium and diamonds) were at the top with upwards of 95% of earnings from these primary commodities. B. Coote, *The Trade Trap: Poverty and the global commodity markets* (Oxfam, Oxford, 1992).

[29] Oxfam, *Africa Make or Break*, p. 7.

[30] ibid.

## PRICE CONTROLS

Price controls were imposed on services such as transport, electricity, and telecommunications to minimize input cost variations in order that manufacturers might ensure competitiveness; to safeguard the position of low-income groups and their access to basic necessities; and to control inflation. Price controls increased the need for staff and as a result the costs of the bureaucracy. Producers and traders invested both time and resources in beating the system, distracting them from productive activities. A number of African countries have at one time or another succumbed to the temptation and pressure to control prices.

Zimbabwe's fairly complex price-control system only fell away with the introduction of the economic reform programme in the 1990s. It had established a comprehensive system of price controls in 1982 that was administered by the then Ministry of Trade and Commerce.[31] The system included a Price Control Committee and the Prices Board which advised the Minister on issues of the price control system, and checked on profiteering elements as well as ensuring that essential basic commodities reached the general public at reasonable prices.[32] The new system controlled prices by fixing a national maximum selling price, requiring ministerial approval for price increases or a change in pricing formulae, and setting price limits by allowing for specific mark-ups on landed costs where price increases would be by permitted percentages.

In Kenya, ceiling prices on a wide range of goods were set by the Price Controller in the Treasury.[33] Companies were in practice permitted to meet cost increases, especially arising from higher costs of imports, by increasing prices. There was no incentive for firms to reduce costs, especially if the sources and reasons for increases could be documented. Quantitative restrictions on imports ensured that there were no competing imports to push prices down, which meant that firms using domestic resources did not consider buying cheaper and better quality inputs from international markets, thus further pushing up their cost structure. A firm that succeeded in reducing, or had the potential to reduce, unit costs by exporting (at a price above marginal but below average cost), was likely to be forced to reduce the domestic market price by the Price Controller.[34] This practice reduced firms' incentives to move into producing for export as gains from exporting were then lost due to domestic price decreases. Industrial production did not benefit from such conditions and could only be negatively affected.

Ghana, Ethiopia, Malawi, and Zambia are other examples of African countries where price controls and regulations were widespread and popular. Once introduced, they become politically sensitive and difficult to abolish.[35] Price controls distort opportunity values and prices cease to be indicators of international comparison since they are artificially determined. By and large, they have been one of the main reasons why economies turn from the production of tradeables to non-tradeable production for the

---

[31] This was caused by price increases which followed the legislation of minimum wages. It was thought that the price increases were without sufficient basis and tended to be *ad hoc*, designed to defeat the government policy on minimum wages. R. Riddell (ed.), *Manufacturing Africa: Performances and prospects of seven countries in sub-Saharan Africa* (James Currey, London, 1990), p. 355.

[32] Government of Zimbabwe, *Socio-Economic Review 1980–85*; Government of Zimbabwe, *Report of the Commission of Inquiry into Taxation under the Chairmanship of Dr. R.J. Cheliah* (Government Printers, Harare, April 1986), p. 195; L.B. Ndlovu, *The System of Protection and Industrial Development in Zimbabwe* (Avebury, Aldershot, UK, 1994).

[33] J. Sharpley & S. Lewis, 'Kenya: the manufacturing sector to the mid-1980s', in Riddell, *Manufacturing Africa*, pp. 206–41.

[34] ibid., p. 222.

[35] In Zambia the increase in the price of maize meal following deregulation in 1987 and the subsequent riots and reversal of price increases by the Kaunda government are an illustration of this sensitivity.

domestic market. The internal orientation of production, as already indicated, does not foster international competitiveness since producers become isolated and cannot compare their performance with those of external and overseas competitors. Once a gap is allowed to develop, there is a problem in rectifying it. Many African economies are to this day struggling to reform or abolish the system and eliminate the effects of their past management practices.

## PROTECTION OF DEVELOPED COUNTRY MARKETS

The marketing of African products faces a hostile international market bent on protecting local producers. As a result African products have not had it easy entering developed country markets. Protection is effected through a variety of controls such as quotas, or the use of quality and hygienic requirements where standards are difficult to establish, leaving room for the use of discretion by those in charge, and international trade agreements. The establishment of regional trade groups has strengthened protection. The European Union, the United States and Japan have strict requirements that make it difficult for African products to enter their markets. This means that African producers must produce goods to acceptable quality standards as specified by developed market consumers in order to break the cycle.

Much of the protection is non-tariff, for example in the form of stringent hygiene standards. A Global Coalition for Africa report found that the tariff and ad valorem equivalents for non-tariff protection against sub-Saharan exports were highest in the European Union.[36] Tobacco (46 per cent), clothing (42.2 per cent), furniture (21.8 per cent), fruit and vegetables (13.5 per cent) and fish and fish products (9.2 per cent) were considerably protected. All these are major exports of African countries. In the same study, tariff equivalents of non-tariff barriers in Japan were highest for fruit and vegetables (86.6 per cent), fish and fish products (28.9 per cent), clothing (19.4 per cent) and textiles (13.5 per cent). The US tariff equivalents for non-tariff barriers hit clothing (52.1 per cent), textiles (11.7 per cent) and tobacco (10.3 per cent) hard among sub-Saharan Africa's exports. The non-tariff barriers show the impediments African exports face in developed country markets.

The product markets in developing countries are small. Thus, the volumes they produce are small and do not allow expansion except by those who have successfully penetrated export markets. Levels of disposable income and purchasing power have also fallen over the years. SAPs have contributed to significant reductions. As a consequence of the small size of markets, the costs at which these economies produce are high and thus undermine competitiveness. A UNIDO study of Zimbabwean manufacturing found that lack of domestic and external demand posed serious constraints.[37]

### Institutional constraints

In addition to technical and non-technical and marketing constraints, institutional arrangements or their absence can impose constraints. In this case, a lack of institutional support has created difficulties for manufacturers.

---

[36] Global Coalition for Africa, *African Social and Economic Trends* (Global Coalition for Africa, Washington DC, 1992).
[37] UNIDO, *The Manufacturing Sector in Zimbabwe* (Unido, Vienna, 1986).

## LACK OF APPROPRIATE INSTITUTIONS

The question of ownership of the means of production is still largely unresolved. At stake is the position of indigenous people in the economics of production in their countries. Their continued marginalization and the apparent syphoning off of resources and attendant profits by large multinationals are a worrying feature in the development struggle. Mechanisms need to be put in place for people to identify with economic activity. There is need for the establishment of, and support for, institutions encouraging improved production and marketing, such as export/import banks and production centres to develop and test new technologies and production methods.

## LACK OF SKILLED PERSONNEL AND ASSOCIATED COSTS OF LABOUR AND OTHER TECHNICAL FACTORS

There are indications of serious shortages of skilled manpower for employment in the industrial sector and this affects the sector's performance overall. Economic development and industrialization depend critically on the quality of human capital.[38] African economies facing a lack of appropriately skilled personnel have resorted to the use of expatriates who are not effectively replaced when they leave and remove their skills. The skill categories affected are engineering, science, management and technical skills, which require local skilled personnel. There is a shortage of professionals and technicians in plant supervision and quality control, in management, marketing, finance and accounting, repairs and maintenance.

Two main reasons explain this shortage of skilled and professional personnel. The first is the level of investment in human resource development; the second is the level of remuneration, the frustration and the unconducive work environment which has caused many Africans to seek greener pastures elsewhere, mainly outside the continent. African investment in human capital has been disappointingly low. There is a wide gap in terms of 'various indicators of human capital accumulation' between Africa and other regions.[39] For example, the average number of years of schooling in Africa in 1993–4 was 1.6 compared with 3.7 years for all developing countries, and 10 years in the developed countries. Literacy levels were also low and varied, the arithmetic mean for the continent being 51 per cent. In addition to these low indicators of investment, other indicators show that Africa had only 2.8 students undertaking training of a vocational nature per 1,000 inhabitants. These levels of performance are highlighted by the reductions in expenditure on education in the 1980s of nearly 50 per cent. These reductions continued into the 1990s mainly due to the heavy fiscal constraints imposed by the economic reform programmes being widely pursued in Africa.

Secondly, a major 'brain drain' has attracted professionals and skilled personnel – engineers, doctors, research scientists, accountants and economists – away from Africa to the developed countries, thus imposing constraints on Africa's production. It is largely the highest qualified and most experienced, with the most to offer in the formulation and design of policy, who leave. The extensive use of expatriates by African governments and the marginalization of local expertise have bred frustrations which push professionals out to countries where their skills are both appreciated and recognized. Frustrations also arise from these professionals being given positions which do not carry commensurate

[38] UNIDO, *Industry and Development Global Report 1993/94*, p. 113.
[39] ibid.

responsibilities. Researchers and policy-makers have misgivings about the ability of African governments to commit adequate resources for them to pursue their careers. This has resulted in the impoverishment of African countries as they are unable to retain a significant number of their highly qualified professionals. On the other hand, the continent is faced with a growing army of job-seekers without vocational training. Unemployment of young school leavers has increased significantly over the last two decades and has reached 100 million.[40] This demands that a carefully planned and well articulated human resource development policy be urgently put in place in most countries. Such a policy would aim to provide adequate training and to develop a programme to retain a certain number of professionals with the requisite skills that would ensure development went on uninterrupted in all countries. To produce benefits, the areas of skill shortage have to be identified and policies devised to attract people into these areas as part of the overall plan.

## SCIENCE AND TECHNOLOGY, RESEARCH AND DEVELOPMENT

Industrial development experience, especially in South-East Asia, underlines the important role played by technological progress in generating export growth and as a source of economic growth generally.[41] A comparison with African industrialization quickly indicates the absence of any meaningful development of local technologies and pinpoints one reason why Africa has failed to catch up. Concern in most developing countries has been restricted to the choice of technology at firm level and the possibilities for substitution among factors, a concern arising from the need to provide employment for growing populations.

Africa's industrialization experience has promoted large-scale, capital-intensive technology which is largely inappropriate. Tanzania's industrialization programme provides an example of this approach.[42] This leads to a set-up which is both economically and technically inefficient. Most of the equipment required for production and most spare parts are imported, thus requiring the commitment of large foreign-exchange outlays at the project implementation stage. Manufacturing plants used in Africa are designed abroad, underlining a technological dependence that threatens self-sustained industrial development. There is a general lack of research and design skills and capability. Some local research and development capability needs to be nurtured with both an understanding of, and interest in, the development of minimum local technology. Hobday describes how the four South-East Asian dragons developed on the basis of export-led technology.[43]

The development of export-led technology in Africa requires that education curricula be geared towards science and technology. It is necessary to establish scientific and research institutes that cater for the development of skills needed in technology development. Greater emphasis on the development of research education is required, with a focus on vocational, polytechnic and university education in technical and scientific subjects. To develop technological capability at the various national levels, the countries involved have to increase the number of personnel with technical and scientific skills.

[40] Bush & Szeftel, 'States, markets and Africa's crisis', p. 149.
[41] M. Hobday, 'Export-led technology in the Four Dragons: the case of electronics', *Development and Change*, 25, 2, (April 1994), pp. 333–61; F.T. Moore, 'Technological change', in Meier & Steel, *Industrial Adjustment*, pp. 212–15.
[42] F.C. Perkins, 'Inappropriate technology choice', in Meier & Steel, *Industrial Adjustment*, pp. 215–18.
[43] Hobday, 'Export-led technology'.

In this endeavour, industrial training centres and facilities need to be expanded. These are essential for long-term development which would enable sustained production in the future.

## Internationally Competitive African Manufactures

Africa still successfully exports unprocessed commodity-type products. There is scope for the growth of resource-based industry involved in further processing. For many countries in Africa, mineral and agricultural commodity processing could easily form the basis for growth. Some countries have moved towards trade in manufactures, among the most successful of which are textile products. With a 14.9 per cent manufactures share in total exports in 1990, Zimbabwe was one of the countries with a high export ratio. Others with significant levels of manufactured exports are Côte d'Ivoire (17.8 per cent) in 1989, Mauritius (21.2) in 1989, Cameroon (7.4) in 1988, Gabon (3.8) in 1988, Kenya (3.7) in 1987, Senegal (5.5) Zaïre (4.4) and Zambia (4.9) all in 1989.

There are the prospects and potential for further industrialization and increased exports of manufactures from Africa if a conducive environment and stable domestic and international economic environments are maintained. Further agro- and mineral processing as part of the value adding process is possible only if exporting remains a major objective. The domestic markets of African countries remain small and economic production volumes can only be supported by a deliberate drive to produce for export. Further processing not only adds value to products but tends to deepen inter-industry linkages which are a pre-condition for significant industrial growth.

Resource-based industries such as textiles and clothing offer the most potential. Cotton is grown in Mali, Côte d'Ivoire, Burkina Faso, Sudan and Zimbabwe, among others, which are major exporters of unprocessed cotton. Also leather goods-processing industries based on tanning and processing, including footwear, have great potential, given that cattle do well under natural conditions in Ethiopia, Botswana, Kenya, Zimbabwe and Zambia. Currently, Ethiopia, Kenya, Mali and Niger are known exporters of raw hides and skins. Footwear exports could increase with design improvements and reduced costs of production, and with an appropriate selling price. The potential of leather goods industries can extend to meat processing for export. Other resource-based industries with potential in world markets and which provide scope for African industrialization are food, beverages and tobacco and metal products.[44]

Countries such as Uganda with important forest resources have hardly exploited these for the export of timber and wood products. Processing of timber to produce plywood, blockboard, flush doors and furniture with tropical hardwood finishes competitive in international markets for wood and furniture products offers great potential. With the development of other sub-sector industries, there would definitely be further scope for the growth and expansion of paper products, especially packing and packaging, although this would be basically for domestic markets. The forest resources, and hence the products potential, also exist in Liberia and Cameroon.

Mineral-related industries displaying potential include the processing of iron ore, copper, tin, manganese and phosphate rock. However, the choice of which potential industries to develop should be guided by resource endowments but should not depend

---

[44] G.B. Assaf & P. Hesp, 'Profiles of key branches of agro-industries in sub-Saharan Africa', *Industry and Development*, 30 (1991), pp. 1–41; UNIDO, *Industry and Development Global Report 1993/94*.

on them alone. Rather, decisions should also be based on wider considerations concerning technological and operational constraints. Some important considerations include the scale and size of operations, the complexity of the technology involved, the size of the domestic market and the scope and prospects for exporting, skill requirements, infrastructural demands, and many others. These are important in determining the minimum conditions that will make manufacturing and possible export attractive. High-technology and capital-intensive processes are still beyond the scope of a large part of the African economic environment. The development of identified sectors improves the chances for others to become economically viable. Chemicals are used in several production processes and an expansion of others is likely to make the manufacture of chemical products possible at viable levels.

## Conclusion

This chapter has outlined perceived constraints to industrial production and marketing in Africa. The major constraints are lack of investment and technology, foreign-exchange shortages and others that affect production processes directly and indirectly. It has been shown that it is not possible to discuss this subject without reference to the systems operative in the past. Many of the constraints to production being experienced in Africa are linked to past policies, experiences and problems. According to Viner (1953),[45]

> Economic development is not merely a matter of more capital, or more acres, or more [minerals] in the ground, but also of the growth and effectiveness of management and of manual effort through better education, better health, better motivation, and better political and social organization.

This makes the point that the requirements for successful and growing production are many. Production also depends on the complex relationship between factors. This is also true for Africa, but in terms of trade the relationship with the developed world and international organizations is especially important. African economies need to address and change those aspects which are controllable and obtain assistance in those areas where external players have influence in order to reduce the constraints affecting production and marketing of products in the past.

Numerous constraints that impeded and constrained production of goods and services have been discussed. It is clear that these have had varying effects on African production. However, the overall effect has been a decline in production over two decades that has led to crisis on the African continent. An attempt at solutions must recognize the mistakes of the past as a basis for planning future recovery. The structural adjustment programmes being implemented may reverse some of the constraints but will also create other problems. The changes African economies may implement will make little impact as long as there is no change in the current world order. On the other hand, Africa must start to assert its position in the world production and trading system.

---

[45] J. Viner, *International Trade and Economic Development* (Clarendon Press, Oxford, 1953), quoted in Perkins, 'Inappropriate technology choice', p. 216.

TEN

# An Agrarian Continent in Transition

DEBORAH FAHY BRYCESON
& JOHN HOWE

From the 1960s, when most African nations achieved independence, until the 1980s at least, Western donor countries' development policy recommendations revolved on two central axes: the promotion of export crop production in rural areas and the nurturing of an industrialization process. Although there was much debate as to the relative priority of these strategies, for much of this time there was substantial agreement between African governments and donor agencies regarding the two strategies' potential to deliver an improved standard of living.

However, they have yielded disappointing results. The lack of material improvement experienced by most people in sub-Saharan Africa is evident. Economic decline beginning in the 1970s entrenched itself in the 1980s with a marked decrease in per capita income, deteriorating rural living standards and stagnant, if not declining, agricultural production in many places.

Over the past three decades, sectoral change has occurred but not in the form intended. It is estimated that the percentage of the sub-Saharan African population engaged in industrial labour was stationary at 8 per cent between 1965 and 1990–92. Meanwhile, there has been a pronounced shrinkage in the size of the agricultural sector from 79 per cent of the total labour force in 1965 to 67 per cent in 1990–92 (Table 10.1). This relative decrease in agricultural employment has been mirrored by a similar decline in the proportion of the population resident in rural areas, estimated at 85 per cent in 1960 and 69

[1] We would like to thank Eddy Akinyemi, Tjalling Dijkstra, Jan Herman Koster, Laurens van der Laan, Marius de Langen and Henk Meilink for their comments and criticisms although we alone are responsible for the views expressed in this paper.

175

**Table 10.1**
**Statistical indices of African de-agrarianization 1960–92**

| Country | Population million 1992 | Real GDP per capita US$ 1991 | Annual PGR* % 60-92 | Urban PGR % 60-92 | % 70-80 | % 80-92 | change | Rural Population % of Total 1960 | 1992 | Agriculture 1965 | Agriculture 90-92 | Industry 1965 | Industry 90-92 | Services 1965 | Services 90-92 |
|---|---|---|---|---|---|---|---|---|---|---|---|---|---|---|---|
| Angola | 9.9 | 1000 | 2.3 | 5.9 | . | 5.2 | -3.3 | 90 | 73 | 79 | 73 | 8 | 10 | 13 | 17 |
| Benin | 4.9 | 1500 | 2.5 | 7.4 | 8.5 | 8.8 | -1.2 | 91 | 60 | 83 | 70 | 5 | 7 | 12 | 23 |
| Botswana | 1.3 | 4690 | 3.2 | 13.5 | 10.0 | 8.7 | 2.3 | 98 | 73 | 88 | 28 | 4 | 11 | 8 | 61 |
| Burkina Faso | 9.5 | 666 | 2.4 | 4.6 | 6.4 | 5.1 | -2.6 | 95 | 83 | 90 | 87 | 3 | 4 | 7 | 9 |
| Burundi | 5.8 | 640 | 2.2 | 5.5 | 7.7 | 5.4 | -2.1 | 98 | 94 | 94 | 92 | 2 | 2 | 3 | 8 |
| Cameroon | 12.2 | 2400 | 2.6 | 6.5 | 7.5 | | | 86 | 58 | 87 | 79 | 4 | 7 | 9 | 14 |
| Cape Verde | 0.4 | 1360 | 2.1 | 4.1 | | 4.7 | 0.0 | 84 | 70 | | 31 | | 6 | | 63 |
| C.A.R. | 3.2 | 641 | 2.3 | 3.6 | 4.7 | 6.8 | -1.0 | 77 | 52 | 88 | 81 | 3 | 3 | 9 | 16 |
| Chad | 5.9 | 447 | 2.1 | 7.1 | 7.8 | | | 93 | 66 | 92 | 83 | 3 | 5 | 5 | 12 |
| Comoros | 0.6 | 469 | 3.2 | 6.8 | | 4.5 | 0.8 | 90 | 71 | | 83 | | 6 | | 11 |
| Congo | 2.4 | 2800 | 2.8 | 3.6 | 3.7 | 4.7 | -2.7 | 68 | 58 | 66 | 62 | 11 | 12 | 23 | 26 |
| Côte d'Ivoire | 12.9 | 1510 | 3.9 | 6.5 | 7.4 | | | 81 | 58 | 80 | 65 | 5 | 8 | 15 | 27 |
| Djibouti | 0.5 | 1000 | 5.7 | 7.3 | | 4.8 | 0.0 | 50 | 14 | | | | | | |
| Equatorial Guinea | 0.4 | 700 | 1.2 | 1.5 | | 5.8 | -2.5 | 75 | 71 | | 77 | | 2 | | 21 |
| Ethiopia | 53.1 | 370 | 2.5 | 4.8 | 4.8 | | | 94 | 87 | 86 | 88 | 5 | 2 | 9 | 10 |
| Gabon | 1.2 | 3498 | 3.0 | 6.3 | 8.3 | 4.3 | 1.4 | 83 | 53 | | 75 | | 11 | | 14 |
| Gambia | 0.9 | 763 | 3.0 | 5.2 | | 5.8 | 1.0 | 87 | 76 | | 84 | | 7 | | 9 |
| Ghana | 16.0 | 930 | 2.7 | 3.9 | 2.9 | 3.8 | -2.0 | 77 | 65 | 61 | 59 | 15 | 11 | 24 | 30 |
| Guinea | 6.1 | 500 | 2.1 | 5.3 | 4.8 | 7.7 | -0.8 | 90 | 73 | 87 | 78 | 6 | 1 | 7 | 21 |
| Guinea-Bissau | 1.0 | 747 | 2.0 | 3.2 | 5.8 | 6.7 | -0.2 | 86 | 80 | | 82 | | 4 | | 14 |
| Kenya | 25.3 | 1350 | 3.5 | 7.7 | 8.5 | 5.7 | 0.4 | 93 | 75 | 86 | 81 | 5 | 7 | 9 | 12 |
| Lesotho | 1.8 | 1500 | 2.4 | 8.6 | 6.9 | 6.1 | -1.4 | 97 | 79 | 91 | 23 | 3 | 33 | 6 | 44 |
| Liberia | 2.8 | 850 | 3.1 | 6.2 | | 5.2 | 0.4 | 81 | 53 | 79 | 75 | 10 | 9 | 11 | 16 |
| Madagascar | 12.9 | 710 | 2.8 | 5.6 | 5.3 | | | 89 | 75 | 85 | 81 | 4 | 6 | 11 | 13 |
| Malawi | 10.3 | 800 | 3.4 | 6.5 | 7.5 | | | 96 | 88 | 92 | 87 | 3 | 5 | 5 | 8 |
| Mali | 9.8 | 480 | 2.6 | 4.4 | 4.8 | | | 89 | 75 | 91 | 85 | 1 | 2 | 8 | 13 |
| Mauritania | 2.1 | 962 | 2.4 | 9.8 | 10.4 | 7.2 | -3.2 | 94 | 50 | 89 | 69 | 3 | 9 | 8 | 22 |
| Mozambique | 15.1 | 921 | 2.2 | 9.5 | 11.5 | 9.9 | -1.6 | 96 | 70 | 87 | 85 | 6 | 7 | 7 | 8 |

**Table 10.1 (Continued)**
Statistical indices of African de-agrarianization 1960–92

| Country | Population million 1992 | Real GDP per capita US$ 1991 | Annual PGR* % 60–92 | Urban PGR % 60–92 | Urban PGR % 70–80 | Urban PGR % 80–92 | Urban PGR change | Rural Population % of Total 1960 | Rural Population % of Total 1992 | Agriculture 1965 | Agriculture 90–92 | Industry 1965 | Industry 90–92 | Services 1965 | Services 90–92 |
|---|---|---|---|---|---|---|---|---|---|---|---|---|---|---|---|
| Namibia | 1.5 | 2381 | 2.8 | 4.8 | 4.9 | 5.1 | –0.2 | 85 | 71 | | 43 | | 22 | | 35 |
| Niger | 8.3 | 542 | 3.2 | 7.4 | 7.5 | 7.3 | –0.2 | 94 | 81 | 95 | 85 | 1 | 3 | 4 | 12 |
| Nigeria | 115.9 | 1360 | 2.7 | 6.3 | 6.1 | 5.7 | –0.4 | 86 | 63 | 72 | 48 | 10 | 7 | 18 | 45 |
| Rwanda | 7.5 | 680 | 3.2 | 7.4 | 7.5 | 3.8 | –3.7 | 98 | 94 | 95 | 90 | 2 | 2 | 3 | 8 |
| Sao Tomé | 0.1 | 600 | 2.1 | | | | | | 74 | | | | | | |
| Senegal | 7.8 | 1680 | 2.8 | 3.5 | 3.7 | 4.0 | 0.3 | 68 | 59 | 83 | 81 | 6 | 6 | 11 | 13 |
| Seychelles | 0.1 | 3683 | 1.7 | | | | | | | | | | | | |
| Sierra Leone | 4.4 | 1020 | 2.1 | 5.2 | 5.2 | 5.2 | 0.0 | 87 | 69 | 78 | 70 | 11 | 14 | 11 | 16 |
| Somalia | 9.3 | 759 | 2.8 | 5.8 | 3.8 | 4.0 | 0.2 | 83 | 65 | 81 | 76 | 6 | 8 | 13 | 16 |
| South Africa | 39.9 | 3885 | 2.6 | 3.2 | 2.8 | 2.8 | 0.0 | 53 | 50 | 32 | 13 | 30 | 25 | 38 | 62 |
| Sudan | 26.7 | 1162 | 2.8 | 5.4 | 5.0 | 4.1 | –0.9 | 90 | 77 | 81 | 72 | 5 | 5 | 14 | 23 |
| Swaziland | 0.8 | 2506 | 2.8 | 10.5 | | | | 96 | 72 | | 74 | | 9 | | 17 |
| Tanzania | 27.9 | 570 | 3.2 | 10.3 | 11.4 | 6.6 | –4.8 | 95 | 78 | 91 | 85 | 3 | 5 | 6 | 10 |
| Togo | 3.8 | 738 | 2.9 | 6.2 | 8.6 | 5.5 | –3.1 | 90 | 71 | 78 | 65 | 9 | 6 | 13 | 29 |
| Uganda | 18.7 | 1036 | 3.3 | 6.1 | 3.7 | 5.0 | 1.3 | 95 | 88 | 91 | 86 | 3 | 4 | 6 | 10 |
| Zaire | 40.0 | 469 | 3.0 | 4.8 | | | | 78 | 71 | 82 | 71 | 9 | 13 | 9 | 16 |
| Zambia | 8.6 | 1010 | 3.2 | 7.1 | 5.9 | 3.8 | –2.1 | 83 | 58 | 79 | 38 | 8 | 8 | 13 | 54 |
| Zimbabwe | 10.6 | 2160 | 3.2 | 5.9 | 5.8 | 5.9 | 0.1 | 87 | 70 | 79 | 71 | 8 | 8 | 13 | 21 |
| Sub-Saharan Africa | 560.2 | 1314.022 | 2.8 | 5.2 | 6.3 | 5.4 | –0.9 | 85 | 69 | 79 | 67 | 8 | 8 | 13 | 25 |
| Least Dev'd Countries | 540.0 | 237 | 2.5 | 5.3 | | | | 92 | 79 | 83 | 73 | 6 | 8 | 11 | 19 |
| Developing Countries | 4240.0 | 770 | 2.3 | 4.0 | 3.7 | 3.7 | 0.0 | 78 | 65 | 72 | 58 | 11 | 15 | 17 | 27 |
| Industrial Countries | 1210.0 | 17017 | 0.8 | 1.4 | | | | 39 | 27 | 22 | 9 | 37 | 33 | 41 | 58 |
| World | 5450.0 | 3836 | 1.8 | 2.9 | 2.6 | 2.8 | 0.2 | 66 | 56 | 57 | 43 | 19 | 21 | 24 | 36 |

Sources: UNDP, *Human Development Report 1994*
World Bank, *World Development Report 1994*

* PGR – population growth rate

per cent in 1992 for sub-Saharan Africa as a whole. Thus, a significant proportion of the African population no longer work primarily as rural farmers.

Over the last thirty years, African countries have been undergoing a process of what might be called 'de-agrarianization' involving the reorientation of income-earning, occupational activities and human settlement away from strictly agrarian patterns.[2] The tone of much development literature has changed over the past decade. In the context of economic crisis, expectations of development have been largely forsaken. Coping has become the key theme. More important, coping strategies have been disaggregated and are increasingly viewed from the perspective of the household or, at most, the village.

This chapter endeavours to examine some of the changes in rural-urban configurations and to explore avenues of material improvement in Africa. This requires devoting some attention to historical trends. The first section focuses on the way thinking and policy formulation concerning African rural labour have evolved over time. The second section considers the impact of structural adjustment, followed by a section overviewing patterns of economic differentiation arising from forms of control over land and capital during the last fifteen years. The final section poses the question of what feasible and effective development strategies could arise from the current situation. Rural public works and the role of the service sector, the forgotten sector in development equations, are highlighted. Where possible, individual countries' experiences will be cited for illustrative purposes.

## The Legacy of Rural Zoning

Sub-Saharan Africa's agrarian character is related to what can best be termed the zoning of rural areas. During the colonial period, this zoning was constituted by the convergence of racial, locational and occupational categories in colonies of white settlement in particular: Africans were delimited as a race, occupationally restricted to farming and migrant labour and locationally circumscribed in rural areas.[3] The struggle for national independence which in most countries began during the 1950s was, amongst other things, a struggle against racial discrimination and the socio-economic barriers which undermined Africans' participation in the non-agricultural sectors of the economy. In most countries, Africanization, a process whereby African nationals assumed positions in non-farming occupations, took place in the period immediately before and after independence.

In fact, rural zoning remained a central feature of post-independent government policy. The nationalist phase, spanning the 1950s through the 1980s, was characterized by policies which continued to delineate rural areas as zones of agricultural work versus urban areas as zones of industrial and service-sector development. Thus urban areas were seen as areas of economic growth and new opportunities for the expanding population who had received formal education in contrast to rural areas where old agrarian occupations prevailed. This occupational/locational dichotomy was implicit in the policies of African governments and foreign donors alike, marking the dividing line, and sometimes the battle front, between those who gave precedence to industrialization versus those who favoured concentration on agricultural investment.

---

[2] D.F. Bryceson, *De-Agrarianization and Rural Employment in Sub-Saharan Africa: Process and prospects* (Afrika-studiecentrum, Working Paper no. 19, Leiden, 1993).
[3] cf. the remarks made by Chaloka Beyani in Chapter 14 of the present volume on the colonial imposition of migration controls.

During the nationalist phase, the strong 'modernizing' post-colonial state, rather than market forces, was seen as the central motive force behind economic transformation. The omnipresence of the state tended to be irrespective of the political complexion of the country. A spectrum of states, ranging in character from the extreme left (e.g. Ethiopia's Marxist-Leninism) to Tanzania's 'African socialism', to Zambia's 'African humanism', and extending to the extreme right (the South African apartheid state), were all projected to their respective citizenries – and indeed, to the world – as agencies of economic transformation and modernization.

Most African governments saw rapid urbanization as a concomitant of modernization. Some, however, did attempt to curb urban migration and keep rural dwellers farming. In Tanzania and Ethiopia, large-scale villagization campaigns represented an effort to create more nucleated settlements. In Ethiopia, the rationale behind this was to facilitate the collectivization of peasant agricultural production,[4] whereas in Tanzania it was more a matter of streamlining the provisioning of social services like clinics and schools and the distribution of agricultural inputs to fewer but larger rural settlements.[5] In Tanzania, agricultural input supply and marketing services were provisioned by urban-headquartered parastatals. Such nationwide, centrally planned and executed distribution by quasi-government agencies ran into enormous logistical and financial tangles.[6] In South Africa, the pass laws denying Africans freedom of movement and settlement in urban areas accompanied a homelands policy aimed at deterring permanent settlement of those classified as Africans in metropolitan areas, and fostering instead semi-rural settlement.[7]

How successful were any of these policies in keeping rural dwellers on the farm? The differences in outcome are illuminating. In Tanzania, despite the promise of improved rural services, very high urban migration persisted during and after the villagization campaigns of the 1970s.[8] According to the *World Development Report* of 1994, Tanzania's urban migration rate was 11.4 per cent between 1970 and 1980.

By comparison, Ethiopia's urban growth rate, at 4.9 per cent per annum, was remarkably low and stayed stationary from the 1970s until the end of the Mengistu period in 1991. This was attributable to the high level of rural land scarcity and the uncertainty engendered by the land reform and collectivization policies of the government which predisposed people to stay in the rural areas and try to safeguard their access to land. Furthermore, it is possible that the upheaval caused by famine and war deterred people from migrating to urban areas.

The coercive force of the apartheid state kept urban migration in South Africa throughout the 1970s and 1980s exceptionally low by African standards at 2.8 per cent. However, this was accompanied by the undermining of African rural areas as agricultural producing zones. As Donaldson notes: 'South African influx control and under-investment in urban infrastructure and services, have created a vast rural and semi-rural

[4] C. Clapham, 'Revolutionary socialist development in Ethiopia', *African Affairs*, 86, 343 (1987), pp. 151–66; Dessalegn Rahmato, *Agrarian Reform in Ethiopia* (Red Sea Press, Trenton, NJ, 1984).

[5] D.F. Bryceson, *Food Insecurity and the Social Division of Labour in Tanzania* (Macmillan, Basingstoke, 1990).

[6] D.F. Bryceson, *Liberalizing Tanzania's Food Trade: Public and private faces of urban marketing policy* (James Currey, London, 1993).

[7] C.J. de Wet, 'Cultivation', in C.J. de Wet & S. Bekker (eds), *Rural Development in South Africa: a case study of the Amatola Basin in the Ciskei* (Pietermaritzburg, Shuter and Shooter (Pty) Ltd, 1985).

[8] D.F. Bryceson, 'Urban bias revisited: Tanzanian staple food pricing', in C. Hewitt de Alcantara (ed.), *Real Markets: Social and political issues of food policy reform* (Frank Cass, London, 1992), pp. 82–106.

population whose land claims are assertions of social and communal entitlements, and only secondarily or partially, agriculture'.[9]

South Africa's and Ethiopia's low rates of urban migration were exceptional. Overall, urban migration in sub-Saharan Africa was very high, averaging 6.3 per cent per annum during the 1970s, compared with other developing countries which averaged only 3.7 per cent (Table 10.1). Various Western critics associated these high rates of in-migration with 'urban bias'. Beginning with Arrighi,[10] followed by Bates[11] and the World Bank's Berg report,[12] African states were criticized for being over-centralized and over-extended into various realms of the economy. It was argued that African policy-makers had allowed the terms of trade between rural and urban areas to turn unfavourably against rural dwellers because the urban population exerted a much stronger political force. Furthermore, the self-interest of African politicians and policy-makers was perceived to be that of urban dwellers. The gap between rural and urban incomes was blamed for encouraging unsustainable rates of urban migration.

In pointing an accusatory finger at African policy-makers, Western critics of urban bias tended to ignore the historical development lessons of their own countries. The cost of urban infrastructure provisioning is extremely expensive in any state/market configuration, a fact that Arthur Lewis drew attention to when delineating the characteristics of debtor nations during the nineteenth century. The newly urbanizing countries of that time – Canada, the United States, Australia and Argentina – generally had urban migration rates of over 3 per cent per annum. The already urbanized 'creditor' nations, like Britain, Germany and France, had urban migration rates of less than 3 per cent.[13] More than a century later, in the 1980s, sub-Saharan Africa's 6.3 per cent urban growth rate was considered unprecedentedly high at a time when African governments, reeling under balance-of-payment crises, sought help from international agencies such as the International Monetary Fund and World Bank. But world optimism regarding African nations' development potential was quickly switching to pessimism. With the influence of monetarist philosophy and 'mono-economics',[14] sub-Saharan African countries came to be viewed as wayward rather than formative members of the world economy. Financial discipline was required by creditor institutions in the form of structural adjustment.

### Structural adjustment: continent-wide reform

During the 1980s, most African countries implemented structural adjustment programmes (SAPs) which first involved stabilization policies to bring foreign sector payments into balance. The second main aim of structural adjustment, the realignment of state and market forces, has displayed more inter-country variation. Toye's inventory

---

[9] A. Donaldson, 'Dependent Transkei: the economics of a labour reserve and a caretaker regime', *Journal of Contemporary African Studies*, 11, (1992), p. 134.

[10] G. Arrighi, 'International comparisons, labour aristocracies, and economic development in tropical Africa', in I. Rhodes (ed.), *Imperialism and Underdevelopment* (Monthly Review Press, New York, 1970).

[11] R.H. Bates, *Markets and States in Tropical Africa* (University of California Press, Berkeley, CA, 1981).

[12] World Bank, *Accelerated Development in Sub-Saharan Africa* (World Bank, Washington, DC., 1981).

[13] Annual urban growth rates were: Canada 3.9%; United States 3.7%; Australia 3.5%; and Argentina 5.3% in comparison with England 1.8%, Germany 2.5% and France 1.0%. W.A. Lewis, *The Evolution of the International Economic Order* (Princeton University Press, Princeton, NJ, 1978), p. 39.

[14] 'Mono-economics' is defined as the assumption that economic behaviour is intrinsically the same everywhere. J. Toye, 'Structural adjustment: context, assumptions, origin and diversity' in R. van der Hoeven & F. van der Kraaij (eds), *Structural Adjustment and Beyond in Sub-Saharan Africa* (Netherlands Ministry of Foreign Affairs, James Currey and Heinemann, The Hague, London and Portsmouth, NH, 1994), pp. 18–35.

**Table 10.2: Component coverage in SAP country packages 1980–86**

| Components | % of Country Packages |
|---|---|
| Export Incentives Improvement | 76 |
| Improvement of Financial Performance of Public Enterprises | 73 |
| Agricultural Pricing Reform | 73 |
| Budget or Tax System Reform | 70 |
| Revision of Industrial Incentives | 68 |
| Revision of Public Investment Priorities | 59 |
| Reform of Public Enterprise Efficiency | 57 |
| Import Quota Removal | 57 |
| Marketing Improvement and Other Support for Agriculture | 57 |

Source: Toye, 'Structural adjustment', pp. 29–30.

of SAPs in sub-Saharan Africa between 1980 and 1986 reveals that export promotion, agricultural pricing, and improving the financial performance of public enterprises were the policy areas that topped the list in the early stages (Table 10.2).

A general theme of structural adjustment policies has been the containment of the African state, seen to be incompetent at its best and predatory at its worst. Work demotivation, the stifling of enterprise, and corruption have all been attributed to the over-extended African state. Thus, SAPs aimed to create an 'innocuous state' by lifting state controls and interference in production.

There have been contradictory findings as to the degree of success of SAPs and widely differing assessments of their impact on different occupational groups and income strata.[15] What is abundantly clear, however, is that reduction in state control has had the effect of drastically reducing rural labour zoning. Market liberalization and economic crisis have combined to create a stimulus for people to pursue any combination of agricultural/non-agricultural activities regardless of rural or urban location. The rural-urban divide has become extremely hazy. Non-agricultural activities on the part of rural households have proliferated.[16] Conversely, urban food production has become commonplace, although it is small in absolute terms.[17] In most countries there are indications that urban migration, at least to the large primate centres, has tapered. For example, between 1967 and 1978 growth in Tanzania was concentrated in Dar es Salaam, the primate city, and the large regional towns. Between 1978 and 1988, the pattern was very different with a mushrooming of settlements within the range of 20–30,000 people.[18] Evidence from other countries displays a similar tendency.[19] It appears that only in countries like Ethiopia and South Africa, where urban migration rates were for so long forcibly depressed, is urban migration to primate cities currently increasing.

Change in the pattern and rate of urban growth can be directly related to the influence of the economic crisis and structural adjustment. By the mid-1990s, industrial pretentions

[15] J. Pronk & F. van der Kraaij, 'Epilogue', in van der Hoeven and van der Kraaij *Structural Adjustment*, pp. 186–94.

[16] This observation is the subject of a rapidly growing literature, including a number of publications by the International Food Policy Research Institute, Washington DC. It is the subject of an international research programme coordinated by the Afrika-studiecentrum, Leiden.

[17] C. Rakodi, 'Self-reliance or survival? Food production in African cities with particular reference to Lusaka', *African Urban Studies*, 21 (1985), pp. 53–64.

[18] Bryceson, 'Urban bias revisited'.

[19] e.g. G. Mainet, 'The emergence of intermediate and small towns in several countries of French-speaking tropical Africa', *African Urban Quarterly*, 6, 3/4, (1991), pp. 192–8.

had largely collapsed. The removal of subsidies to large numbers of parastatal industries, the foreclosure of banks on lending to indebted industries and the lack of private investors to step in and take over parastatal industries have contributed to a high rate of industrial lay-offs. Enforced redundancies in the civil service, where government is often the largest formal sector employer, have caused formal employment to contract rapidly.[20] Jamal estimates that informal-sector employment accounted for 60–66 per cent of the urban workforce at the end of the 1980s compared with the 1960s when the informal sector was virtually absent.[21]

### The impact of SAPs on agricultural earnings

In rural areas, structural adjustment policies, designed to eliminate 'urban bias', have aimed at invigorating African agriculture and providing a material boost to rural areas generally. The means to these ends was the reduction, if not the elimination, of state involvement in the rural productive and marketing infrastructure. Commodity markets were quickly liberalized. In food, notably grains like maize and rice, the immediate outcome of market liberalization was very much dependent on the weather. For example, Tanzania liberalized its grain markets between 1986 and 1990 during a period of good harvests. Private traders, with virtually no fixed costs, operating on extremely low margins, were able to supply the market. In contrast, Zambia's transition to private grain trading during 1991–92 engendered a high level of food insecurity among poor rural and urban households, because of its coincidence with drought.[22] Over the long run, the reliability and scope of privatized grain markets will be put to the test by the extremely wide year-to-year fluctuations of rain-fed food harvests in tropical Africa. Can they regularly supply adequate amounts of grain to the food-purchasing segments of the national population at affordable prices under these conditions?

Whether farmers have received higher prices for their food crops since the implementation of market liberalization is not always clear. Liberalized markets show considerable regional price variation reflecting transport and other transactional costs. As a result, food farmers in remote regions have sometimes experienced a substantial decline in price.[23] Conversely, there are better price incentives for farmers in areas with good transport connections to urban centres. Nonetheless, with the dominance of rainfed food production, the main determinant of food output is good rainfall rather than price. Only farmers producing on a large scale, capable of substantial capital investment, notably in irrigation and fertilizers, can consistently take advantage of better prices, boosting their economic position relative to others. For example, in Hausaland, it is the bigger entrepreneurial farmers who are benefitting from rising urban food prices precipitated by structural adjustment.[24] But such programmes can also serve to strengthen the

[20] V.P. Diejomaoh, 'Employment in Africa: trends and prospects', *African Development Perspectives Yearbook 1989*, (Schelzy & Jeep, Berlin, 1990), pp. 63–75.

[21] V. Jamal, 'Wages and implications for structural adjustment – how to survive in Africa?', *African Development Perspectives Yearbook 1990-1* (Lit Verlag, Münster & Hamburg, 1992), pp. 247–56; V. Jamal & J. Weeks, *Africa Misunderstood* (Macmillan, Basingstoke, 1993).

[22] J.M. Chizuni, 'Food policies and food security in Zambia'. Paper presented at the SIDA-sponsored Workshop on Alternative Food Policies, Jinja, Uganda, August 1993.

[23] e.g. K.M. Mtawali, 'Trade, price and market reform in Malawi: Current status, proposals and constraints', *Food Policy*, 18, 4 (1993), pp. 300–7. See also Chapter 8 by Jean-Paul Azam in the present volume.

[24] M.A. Iliya & K. Swindell, ' "Winners and losers": Household fortunes in the urban peripheries of Northwest Nigeria', paper presented at the De-agrarianization and Rural Employment Workshop, Leiden, May 1994.

**Table 10.3 World market trends in African agricultural commodities**

A Volume index of major agricultural exports, 1987 (1980 = 100)
(Major is defined as exports of over 30,000 tonnes.)

| Country | Coffee | Cocoa | Tea | Cotton | Tobacco | Sugar | Ground-nuts | Palm Oil | Rubber | Oilseeds |
|---|---|---|---|---|---|---|---|---|---|---|
| Angola | 23 | | | | | | | | | |
| Benin | | | | | | | | | | |
| Burkina Faso | | | | 175 | | | | | | |
| Cameroon | 54 | 126 | | | | | | | | |
| Chad | | | | 86 | | | | | | |
| Côte d'Ivoire | 78 | 161 | | 174 | | | | | | |
| Ethiopia | 96 | | | | | | | | | |
| Gambia | | | | | | | 52 | | | |
| Ghana | | 100 | | | | | 142 | | 109 | 152 |
| Kenya | 125 | | 179 | | | | | | | |
| Liberia | | | | | | | | | 109 | |
| Madagascar | 67 | | | | | | | | | |
| Mali | | | | 77 | | | | | | |
| Malawi | | | 107 | | 100 | 71 | | | | |
| Mauritius | | | | | | 106 | | | | |
| Nigeria | | 63 | | | | | | 88 | 320 | |
| Rwanda | 209 | | | | | | | | | |
| Senegal | | | | | | | 142 | | | |
| Sudan | | | | 132 | | | | | | 50 |
| Swaziland | | | | | | 145 | | | | |
| Tanzania | 109 | | 133 | | | | | | | |
| Uganda | 136 | | | | | | | | | |
| Zaire | | 134 | | | | | | | | |
| Zimbabwe | | | | 120 | 108 | 168 | | | | |
| **Average** | 100 | 117 | 143 | 128 | 104 | 123 | 112 | 88 | 179 | 101 |

B Average annual growth rate of real prices in world market

| | | | | | | | | | | |
|---|---|---|---|---|---|---|---|---|---|---|
| 1960–70 | 0.8 | 3.5 | −4.0 | 0.1 | 0.7 | −3.7 | 0.1 | −1.7 | −6.0 | n.a. |
| 1970–80 | 3.9 | 7.5 | −2.8 | −2.2 | −1.0 | −1.3 | −3.5 | −2.4 | 1.3 | n.a. |
| 1980–90 | −11.5 | −11.5 | −0.9 | −3.0 | | −8.4 | −7.3 | −4.7 | −2.9 | n.a. |

C World Bank 1988 forecasts of real commodity prices

| | | | | | | | | | | |
|---|---|---|---|---|---|---|---|---|---|---|
| 1970/1 | 85 | 54 | 114 | 100 | 79 | 40 | – | 38 | – | – |
| 1980/1 | 100 | 100 | 100 | 100 | 100 | 100 | – | 100 | 100 | – |
| 1990 | 58 | 120 | 73 | 75 | 73 | 50 | – | 44 | 61 | – |

*Sources:* Crop indices: World Bank, *Sub-Saharan Africa: From crisis to sustainable growth* (World Bank, Washington DC, 1989), pp. 246–8. Price changes: World Bank, *Accelerated Development in Sub-Saharan Africa* (World Bank, Washington DC, 1981) p. 157. World Bank, *Adjustment in Africa: Reforms, results and the road ahead* (Oxford University Press, New York, 1994) p. 77. World Bank, *Global Economic Prospects and the Developing Countries.* (World Bank, Washington DC, 1992), p. 63. Commodity forecasts: World Bank, *Trends and Prospects 1989* cited in M. Barratt Brown & P. Tiffen, *Short Changed: Africa and World trade* (Pluto Press; London, 1992), p. 172.

economically weak. There is evidence that liberalized food markets have sometimes given women farmer-traders entry where previously they had faced exclusion from male-dominated marketing cooperatives.[25]

Sarris and Shams' detailed analysis of the effects of structural adjustment on Ghanaian food farmers shows that the value of export crops rose relative to food crops.[26] Nonetheless, devaluations caused the price of consumer goods to rise even more steeply, with two implications: first, farmers' purchasing power decreased and, second, the cost of hired labour on farms increased. It seems likely that family labour has been increasingly substituted for hired labour. Furthermore, as a result of the elimination of input subsidies, farm production costs rose, causing even nominal returns per man-day in the production of maize, rice and cassava to decrease. In real terms, the decline was much larger.

The effect of SAPs on export crop production has been varied. Not surprisingly, annual crops like cotton have shown the most positive response, compared with tree crops like cocoa and coffee which take years to mature after planting (Table 10.3). SAPs aimed to provide farmers with higher real prices by increasing the proportion of the world market price that they get by eliminating the margins of marketing boards and parastatals. The fact remains that most of the major African agricultural export crops face stagnant or declining real price levels in the world market.[27] This must be seen in the wider context of a long-term decline in African terms of trade as agricultural exports depreciate in value relative to industrial imports (Table 10.3).

The incentive for African farmers to produce more export crops is seriously dampened by the configuration of world market prices. Devaluations and other structural adjustment measures aimed at increasing the influence of the market merely reinforce this fact. Even ardent promoters of African export-crop expansion, such as Elliot Berg,[28] concede the 'fallacy of composition' dilemma. As producers of commodities with low demand elasticities, African countries which respond to the general call to raise their traditional export production can be faced with the disappointing result of succeeding in producing higher volumes which fetch lower prices in the world market for key commodities like cocoa and coffee.[29]

In the face of these difficulties, the World Bank and various donors have advocated diversification into 'non-traditional' agricultural exports such as horticultural products and spices. Some countries, notably Kenya and Zimbabwe, have made substantial inroads into horticultural exports, but these tend to be in areas with a tradition of large-scale, commercial farming.[30] The productive and marketing infrastructure for these non-traditional exports can be quite demanding; special cultivation techniques, high packaging standards, and good transport infrastructure, including air freight, are required. Not least is the need for effective agricultural extension services to introduce farmers to new cultivation techniques. Consequently, diversification attempts in some countries have not

---

[25] Bryceson, *Liberalizing Tanzania's Food Trade*, pp. 118–50.

[26] A. Sarris & H. Shams, *Ghana under Structural Adjustment: the impact on agriculture and the rural poor* (New York University Press, New York, 1991), p. 179.

[27] R.C. Duncan, 'Agricultural export prospects for sub-Saharan Africa', *Development Policy Review*, 11, 1, (1993), pp. 31–45; J. Houtkamp & H.L. van der Laan, *Commodity Auctions in Tropical Africa* (Afrika-studiecentrum, Report 54, Leiden, 1993); A. Bigsten & S. Kayizzi-Mugerula, 'Rural sector responses to economic crisis in Uganda', *Journal of International Development*, 7, 2 (1995), pp. 181–209.

[28] E. Berg, 'Reappraising export prospects and regional trade arrangements', in D. Rimmer (ed.), *Action in Africa* (James Currey, London, 1993), pp. 59–61.

[29] Recent rises in the world price of coffee, which have brought considerable benefit to some African farmers, are unlikely to be sustained.

[30] T. Dijkstra & T.D. Magori, *Horticultural Production and Marketing in Kenya* (Afrika-studiecentrum, Leiden, 1994).

met with much success[31] and may carry environmental risks. For example, intensive carnation production in Kenya represents the introduction into the tropics of a temperate plant which, due to its lack of natural immunity, normally necessitates the heavy application of agro-chemicals. Their residues drain into Lake Naivasha. If concentrations of agricultural pollutants build up they could jeopardize the rich fauna of that lake, one of Kenya's tourist attractions. If ecological damage were to proceed unchecked, the economic costs of luxury export crops of exotic origin, measured in foreign-exchange earnings, could outweigh the benefits.[32]

Overall, economic crisis and cutbacks implemented as a result of structural adjustment have undermined most countries' cadre of government agricultural extension agents. Case-study findings reveal that removal of subsidies on crop inputs, especially fertilizer, has been counter-productive.[33] In turn, there has been a noted reluctance for the private sector to ferry fertilizers and various other inputs to rural areas on a regular and geographically comprehensive basis.[34] Thus, the impact of structural adjustment on smallholders' crop production is debatable. Evidence from various countries suggests that it has not provided the strong producer incentives originally projected. But to focus solely on rural households' agricultural performance would be to miss the most striking feature of the response to structural adjustment, namely, the proliferation and intensification of non-agricultural activities in rural areas.

### Rural non-agricultural endeavours

For decades, non-agricultural income diversification has been a feature of households in sub-Saharan Africa, especially in drought-prone areas, and has served to mitigate the high risk connected with climatic uncertainty. The growing prevalence of non-agricultural income diversification, beginning in the crisis years of the 1970s and accelerating under SAPs, has a similar function. It is clearly a response to economic uncertainty in the first instance, increasingly mixed with some economic opportunity as market liberalization opens up pockets of lucrative enterprise for those with favourable asset-endowments.

The growth of income diversification is widely recognized, but its actual operation and contribution to rural household livelihoods is still under-investigated. Part of the problem for economists is that the proliferation of erratic income streams associated with non-agricultural income diversification makes accurate modelling of rural household productive behaviour extremely difficult. Other more qualitative data collection techniques are required, although macro and meso-level generalizations on the basis of in-depth case-study findings can only be done with extreme care using a wide cross-section of studies.

Nonetheless, it is apparent that there are patterns of non-agricultural income diversification practised by rural households that can usefully be distinguished, namely: (i) rural wage labour or trading activities of select members of the household during the off-agricultural season, (ii) part-time non-agricultural work by select members within villages, and (iii) full-time non-agricultural work of specific household members within

[31] K.S. Mbatia, 'Constraints to the growth of non-traditional exports: incentive schemes', *Tanzanian Economic Trends*, 5, 3/4, (1992/93), pp. 52–63.

[32] P. Denny, 'Africa', in M. Finlayson & M. Moser (eds), *Wetlands* (Facts on File, Oxford, 1991), p. 141.

[33] P. Mosley, 'Decomposing the effects of structural adjustment: the case of sub-Saharan Africa', in Van der Hoeven and Van der Kraaij, *Structural Adjustment and Beyond*, pp. 70–98; D. Booth, 'Timing and sequencing of agricultural policy reform, Tanzania', *Development Policy Review*, 9, 4, (1991), pp. 353–80.

[34] Sarris & Shams, *Ghana under Structural Adjustment*, pp. 207–8.

the village or nearby town who continue to have residential rights within the household in terms of claims on household resources. From the perspective of the household, all the activities of a 'diversified occupational portfolio' spread risks and/or optimize returns over a wider range of economic activities.

Despite growing numbers of households with diversified occupational portfolios, the array of non-agricultural activities in African villages is often 'unimpressive',[35] being dominated by low-income activities like mat-making and beer-brewing. Nevertheless, the significance of non-agricultural rural employment derives from the fact that it now accounts for a substantial proportion of total household labour time and is making a vital contribution to household disposable income in periods of low and uncertain income. Furthermore, field studies suggest that it enables households to make capital investments in agriculture, notably the purchase of agricultural inputs.[36]

Most non-agricultural activities face operational constraints due to market inadequacies, such as lack of rural purchasing power and poor transport infrastructure, which limit the geographical range of clientele they serve. For those who attempt trading over a wide geographical area, physical security can be problematic, given the lack of credit facilities. Government policies regarding trading activities may be ambiguous, making traders vulnerable to interference or to extortionate practices by officials purportedly enforcing controls on trade. The lack of technical and accountancy skills often poses an obstacle to achieving a viable enterprise with a reliable income flow.

The emerging profile of non-agricultural activities has bifurcated into that of small-scale, self-employed activities, on the one hand, and waged employment, primarily in public works programmes sponsored by the government and/or donor agencies, on the other. This bifurcation has several policy implications. Because the bias in the development literature pertaining to non-agricultural activities is weighted towards small-scale industries, the relative absence of growth in firm size has been viewed with concern. It is felt that such activities merely amount to individual or household survival rather than commercial success. On the other hand, there are those who advocate non-agricultural activities as a means of poverty alleviation and see household livelihood as an end in itself.

From the perspective of households with diversified occupational portfolios, the phenomenon is an extension of a risk-minimization strategy hitherto practised primarily in agricultural endeavours, such as crop inter-planting, the cultivation of several fields spread over different micro-environments, and cropping in more than one agricultural season during the year. It would be a mistake at this point to see households' income diversification as a step on the way to industrialization. Such activities are not in conformity with a model in which non-agrarian enterprises in rural areas mark the emergence of greater labour specialization. This becomes clear when considering the nature of markets currently existing in rural Africa.

---

[35] Final assessment by the Income Diversification Committee Report in D.F. Bryceson & C. van der Laan, *De-agrarianization in Africa: Proceedings of the 'De-agrarianization and Rural Employment' workshop held at the Afrika-studiecentrum, Leiden, May 1994* (Afrika-studiecentrum, Leiden, 1994), p. 89.

[36] H. Moore & M. Vaughan, *Cutting Down Trees: Gender, nutrition and agricultural change in the Northern Province of Zambia, 1890–1990* (James Currey, London, 1994), pp. 226–31.

## Land, Labour and Capital Markets in Formation

Market exchange is not a universal phenomenon. Commodity markets for agricultural produce exist, but they have tended to be a thin veneer in local rural economies primarily characterized by various forms of non-market exchange based on patron-client relations and the rights and duties of lineage members.[37] Thus, the implementation of structural adjustment, aimed at replacing the state with the market, has first to establish or nurture market relations. In many places markets in land, labour and capital have barely surfaced and in other places the conditions are ripe for their development. While it is dangerous to generalize, it is worth observing that, in comparison with the past, the balance of supply and demand between land and labour has been edging towards market formation. The imposition of structural adjustment has simply hastened the process.

### Labour

For decades, it was accepted that the limiting factor of production in sub-Saharan African agriculture was labour, not land.[38] The land resources of the so-called 'under-populated' continent were bountiful when compared with South Asia or Latin America. Now, the cumulative effect of steady population growth over two generations and the reduction in urban migration has caused many areas to experience rural surplus labour conditions. Rwanda, a country with recorded rural person-land ratios of 5.5 adults per hectare in 1986, is a clear example. According to a survey by the International Food Policy Research Institute, a 10 per cent increase in the person-land ratio resulted in a 3.6 per cent decline in labour productivity.[39] Terms like 'under-employment' or 'disguised unemployment' no longer apply only to urban Africa.

The 'surplus' characteristics of rural labour are most painfully revealed in areas where civil war has been experienced. After the cessation of violence, refugees and ex-soldiers attempting to re-establish themselves in their home areas find it difficult to achieve a viable agrarian livelihood with the physical resources at hand. In Rwanda, part of the reason for the continuing tension between rival groups is that they are making claims on the same village land.

In some areas, structural adjustment appears to have exacerbated the problem of rural surplus labour. During the 1970s, many African countries sought to achieve universal primary education and often had low-fee or even no-fee primary school systems. Under structural adjustment, cutbacks in education expenditure and the imposition of higher fees on parents have led to the curtailment of enrolments. In some countries this has resulted in the drop-out of girl students whose parents feel female education is unnecessary or damaging to future marriage prospects.[40] In other countries, more boys than girls have been dropping out to get involved in petty trade, a phenomenon that

[37] Bryceson, *Food Insecurity*, pp. 61–3; S. Berry, *No Condition is Permanent* (University of Wisconsin Press, Madison, WI, 1993).

[38] E. Boserup, *The Conditions of Agricultural Growth: the economics of agrarian change under population pressure* (Aldine Publishing Company, New York, 1965): idem, *Economic and Demographic Relationships in Development* (Johns Hopkins University Press, Baltimore, MD, 1990), pp. 209–69.

[39] J. von Braun, H. de Haan & J. Blanken, *Commercialization of Agriculture under Population Pressure: Effects on production, consumption and nutrition in Rwanda* (IFPRI Research Report No. 85, International Food Policy Research Institute, Washington DC, 1991), p. 12.

[40] M. Touré, S. Ouattara & E. Annan-Yao, 'Population dynamics and development strategies in the Ivory Coast', in M. Touré & T.O. Fadayomi (eds), *Migrations, Development and Urbanization Policies in Sub-Saharan Africa* (Codesria Book Series, Dakar, 1992), p. 31.

started during the crisis years of the 1980s and continues under conditions of structural adjustment.[41]

### The contraction of land availability

Land scarcity is the natural converse of surplus labour. The build-up of population pressure in highland areas and other ecological zones favourable to agriculture is nothing new. In East Africa, a crisis point was reached with respect to the Kenyan highlands already in the early 1950s, marked by the Mau Mau rebellion. Problems associated with population pressure areas have proliferated and now include virtually all highland zones of East and Central Africa. Signs of agricultural involution are now quite common in these areas, despite their continued classification in development plans as high potential agricultural land.[42]

At present the incidence of land shortage is spreading outside climatically favourable areas to others with lower population-carrying capacities. Many semi-arid regions are registering population densities which, at prevailing levels of technology, are seriously over-taxing the resource base.[43] Over-grazing and soil erosion are common.

Land scarcity has contributed to growing wealth differentials in rural Africa.[44] This is expressed in the form of income stratification and emerging occupational divisions amongst farmers within villages. For example, survey data from Kano State, Nigeria, show that with an increasing concentration of land ownership in the hands of large-scale and better-off medium-scale farmers, there has been a rising share of agricultural incomes among large-scale farmers (16 per cent in 1974 and 53 per cent in 1992) and a declining share of agriculture in total incomes among small-scale farmers (47 per cent in 1974 and 33 per cent in 1992).[45]

The landless tend to be doubly disadvantaged, with restricted access to capital as well as land. In Ethiopia, where plough agriculture prevails, this combined handicap effectively prevents landless households from engaging in sharecropping and land rental, since they do not have oxen or cash to enable them to work the land.[46]

Rural wealth differentiation is marked between villages and agro-ecological zones within the same country. The increased mobility associated with market trade has made this differentiation more apparent and has the potential to fuel ethnic resentment. These feelings can rebound on the problem of land availability. As rural land becomes scarcer and assumes market value, it becomes attractive to outside buyers. This is true whether or not a country has officially sanctioned freehold tenure. Nowhere can this be more aptly demonstrated than in the Kenyan highlands. The impoverishment of various strata of rural dwellers has opened up the market to outside, often to urban-based purchasers.[47] So, too, ethnic groups who have long experienced land scarcity in their home areas, such

[41] M. Mbilinyi & P. Mbughuni (eds), *Education in Tanzania with a Gender Perspective* (SIDA, Stockholm, 1991).
[42] e.g. J.K. van Donge, 'Agricultural decline in Tanzania: the case of the Uluguru Mountains', *African Affairs*, 91, 362 (1992), pp. 73–94.
[43] e.g. L.M. Kisovi, 'Population pressure and human carrying capacity in Kitui District Kenya', *Eastern and Southern Africa Geographical Journal*, 4, 1, (1993).
[44] D. Siddle & K. Swindell, *Rural Change in Tropical Africa* (Basil Blackwell, Oxford, 1990), p. 86; C. Mung'ong'o, *Social Processes and Ecology in the Kondoa Irangi Hills, Central Tanzania* (Arash Trysk & Förlag, Stockholm, 1995).
[45] K. Meagher & A.R. Mustafa, 'De-Agrarianization in rural Hausaland, Nigeria: flexibility or fragility?' Paper presented at the De-agrarianization and Rural Employment Workshop, Leiden, May 1994, p. 10.
[46] Yohannes Habtu, 'Landless and rural labour markets: a study of households in Northern Shewa Region of Ethiopia'. Paper presented at the De-agrarianization and Rural Employment Workshop, Leiden, May 1994.
[47] Personal communication from Dick Foeken, Afrika-studiecentrum, Leiden.

as the Kikuyu people, have purchased freehold land in other less densely populated non-Kikuyu areas. Over the years, land scarcity has become a feature of these areas as well. As the concurrent process of wealth differentiation unfolds, local resentment of the 'outsiders' can reach explosive levels. Disputes over who is entitled to use the land – the official title holder or the original people occupying the land – carry the risk of violence. The two sides, using the non-intersecting legal frameworks of statutory and customary law, cannot be reconciled. 'Ethnic cleansing' has been the unfortunate outcome of such encounters on some recent occasions.[48]

But the most widespread incidence of rural land grab in sub-Saharan Africa has been an internal affair, within villages and within rural households. Concentration of rural land in the hands of 'outsiders' is, despite media attention and policy concern, relatively minor compared with the concentration of land control and usage in the hands of local men at the expense of local women and male youth.

Although relatively undocumented, there is a growing awareness that African youth, notably young men within the marriageable ages of 18 to 30, have a severe land-access problem. In the Ethiopian data cited above, the majority of the landless were young men. Traditionally, in many parts of rural Africa, older men monopolized land, women and cattle. Young men were subject to bride-price systems requiring them to accumulate sufficient wealth before getting married and setting up their own households. The migrant labour economies that were established in many parts of Africa capitalized on this pattern, affording men a way of accumulating capital independent of their elders' control.

In the first decades after independence, urban migration fulfilled the same function. Now, however, external job opportunities have contracted. The bright lights of urban capitals no longer beckon, and disillusionment with their economic prospects leads some young men to seek excitement and lucrative earnings through the barrel of the gun.[49] Numerous civil war hot spots and the general post-Cold War availability of guns in a radius around these areas has made this possibility a reality for tens of thousands of young men in rural Africa.

Young men's current restricted land availability and consequent limited agricultural prospects constitute an old dilemma with a new twist. Previously they had little choice but to conform to local societal dictates and were eventually rewarded with the productive resources and social status that their societies offered. Now, as village agricultural resource availability contracts, many circumvent the norms of their villages and indeed the norms of the world community to seize economic resources and power violently. Old and new circumstances blend to produce a travesty of youthful initiative.

Women's declining land availability is also an outcome of the clash between old and new values. However, in this case they have very little room for manoeuvre and the denial of land access to them could have even more serious implications for African agricultural production and rural welfare, given their central role in food production and agriculture generally.[50] Under customary law, in many societies women's usufruct

---

[48] M. Rutten, 'The process of individualization of landownership among the Maasai pastoralists of Kajiado District, Kenya' Paper presented at a seminar on the Marginalisation of Pastoral Societies, Afrika-studiecentrum, Leiden, April 1995.

[49] C. & D. Newbury, 'Rwanda: the politics of turmoil, *Africa Notes* (Cornell University), (October 1994), pp 1–2; P. Richards, 'Sierra Leone and Liberia: a crisis of youth?', in O.W. Furley (ed.), *Conflict in Africa* (Tauris Academic Press, London, 1995), pp. 134–70.

[50] D.F. Bryceson (ed.), *Women Wielding the Hoe: Lessons for feminist theory and development practice from rural Africa* (Berg Publishers, Oxford, 1995).

rights to land have been very strong, whereas their inheritance rights have tended to be weak. In a situation of land abundance, these circumstances did not impinge on women's agricultural pursuits. The problem arises, however, as land becomes scarcer and external influences such as policies to promote more cash cropping cause a re-allocation of land resources in the community.

The detrimental effect of donor agencies' intervention is well-documented. Here and there throughout rural Africa, women's usufruct rights have been neglected in irrigation projects and other land investment projects when men, as the main cash-crop producers, assert their land inheritance rights at the expense of female usufruct rights.[51] As a consequence of structural adjustment, the problem is no longer isolated to specific project sites. The priority currently placed on cash cropping poses a continent-wide threat to women's usufruct land rights.

In areas where patrilineal land inheritance is combined with land scarcity, women are on the defensive. Mersmann documents how women's food-crop fields have been pushed further and further up the mountain slopes in northeastern Tanzania.[52] Increasingly women have been forced to give up their fields and seek employment either as casual labour on neighbours' fields or as workers in nearby tea plantations.[53] In the Northwest Province of Cameroon, pressure on available land is said to be 'driving women from the more sheltered valleys to farm on higher slopes' in competition with men's cash cropping.[54]

Male monopolization of land resources hints at the possibility of class divisions within the countryside being drawn on gender lines. This stark outcome is certainly feasible, given the existing split between male cash cropping and female food farming, and the high incidence of separate rather than joint purses between male and female adult members of rural households. The emergence of a female rural proletariat, devoid of the land resources requisite for provisioning themselves and their dependants, is already evident in southern Africa, where different historical circumstances, namely the male labour migration system, have created the same effect.[55]

The urgency of land-tenure reform is clear. Most African countries are now faced with an overlap of customary and statutory laws that are manipulated by the socially powerful against the weak.[56] Several countries are in the process of reviewing their land laws. The debate over the direction of reform tends to centre on the advisability or otherwise of unleashing market forces and sanctioning freehold. Many authors recommend avoidance of this step, citing countries where freehold has caused marked rural wealth differentiation.[57] On the other hand, it is quite clear that customary forms of land

[51] J. Dey, 'Gambian women: unequal partners in rice development projects?', in N. Nelson (ed.), *African Women in the Development Process* (Frank Cass, London, 1981), pp. 109–22; D. Brautigan, 'Land rights and agricultural development in West Africa: a case study of two Chinese projects', *Journal of Developing Areas*, 27, 1, (1992/93), pp. 21–32.

[52] C. Mersmann, 'The impact of indigenous knowledge systems on changing patterns in land endowment: the case of Mbaramo village in the Usambara Mountains, Tanzania'. Paper presented at the 'Changing Rural Structures in Tanzania' Symposium at the University of Bayreuth, Germany, June 1994.

[53] J. Sender & S. Smith, *Poverty, Class and Gender in Rural Africa* (Routledge, London, 1990).

[54] E.M. Chilver, 'Women cultivators, cows and cash crops in Cameroon', in S. Ardener (ed.), *Persons and Powers of Women in Diverse Cultures* (Berg Publishers, Oxford, 1992).

[55] B. O'Laughlin, 'The myth of the African family in the world of development', in Bryceson, *Women Wielding the Hoe*, pp. 63–91.

[56] P. Shipton, 'Debts and trespasses: land, mortgages, and the ancestors in Western Kenya', *Africa*, 62, 3 (1992), pp. 357–388; M. Goheen, 'Chiefs, sub-chiefs and local control: negotiations over land, struggles over meaning', *Africa*, 62, 3 (1992), pp. 389–412.

[57] L.K. Agbosu, 'Land registration in Ghana: past, present and the future', *Journal of African Law*, 43, 2 (1990), pp. 104–27.

tenure based largely on community sanctions are not only imprecise but provide a useful smokescreen for 'big men' to aggrandize their land holdings at the expense of everyone else. Women in patrilineal societies are particularly at the mercy of the failure of customary land law to recognize them as legitimate heirs.

As land scarcity worsens, a market in land will emerge, whether or not it is officially sanctioned. Land grabbing will take place whether the prevailing land law legitimizes freehold or customary practices; the appropriators' rationales are infinitely flexible. Thus, the essential policy issue is not freehold versus customary tenure, but rather how social checks and balances can be built into rural areas such that those actually cultivating retain their functional hold on the land.

### Bridging capital: networks of people and resources

Capital formation in most rural households of sub-Saharan Africa is still extremely limited. To a Western observer, residential buildings, farm implements and livestock would appear to be the sum total of most rural households' fixed capital. Cattle and wives have been the traditional forms of capital accumulation on the part of male heads of households and remain one of the most telling indicators of rural wealth.

With stimulus to market expansion and the diversification of rural income-earning into more non-agricultural activities, fixed and recurrent capital investment becomes more critical to rural household participation in the market. Already there are indications that those in a position to invest – be it in land, labour or capital – are benefitting relative to others.[58]

Previously the basis for accumulation was typically a monopoly position held by someone who could straddle the state and the market, using tenure of a bureaucratic office to gain privileged access to state-held resources and market information. Such monopolists controlled scarce resources and the means of improved production and consumption which made them attractive patrons for a peasant clientele. Usually, the patrons straddled different locations with an urban as well as rural basis of operation. The means for improved production and enhanced living standards that the monopolists channelled to clients often originated in the industrial nations of the world.[59] Thus, the monopolist patron was the link in a chain that extended from the local agrarian economy through state and market channels to the international level of the world market. The social relations between the producers and the monopolists were largely characterized by non-market personalized exchanges in which the client assumed a dependent status that alleviated his material insecurity, while the monopolist patron assumed a position of power and control.

Now, as African state resources contract, control of the market is becoming relatively more important in the acquisition and maintenance of power. There are still scarce resources and goods and services that rural producers need to attain improved production and a higher standard of living. The market is becoming the chief means of delivery of these goods and services in rural areas. To the extent that the goods and services are imported from the industrial world, then their distribution over the length and breadth of continental Africa is bound to be extremely patchy. In this context, the monopolists of today and tomorrow are those who can bridge physical distances, in other words, those who can monopolize long-distance means of transport.

[58] Iliya & Swindell, 'Winner and losers'; D. Booth, 'Timing and sequencing in agricultural reform: Tanzania', *Development Policy Review*, 9, 4 (1991), pp. 353–80.
[59] Bryceson, *Food Insecurity*, pp. 61–3.

## The Role of Service-Sector Development

A sober assessment of sub-Saharan African economic performance suggests that neither industry nor agriculture can be the 'primary source of growth'[60] in the foreseeable future, since Africa lacks competitiveness in both of these sectors. The service sector is the only area where African producers have a clear advantage vis-à-vis international producers by virtue of their location and the immediacy of service provisioning.

Agricultural export or industrial strategies will have limited effectiveness until strides have been made in the development of rural services. It is appropriate, in these circumstances, to discuss the use of surplus agricultural labour to provide vital non-agricultural infrastructure. As one study has put it, 'Spatial, time series and consumption data uniformly point not to manufacturing, but rather to commerce and services as key growth sectors over the course of Africa's rural structural transformation'.[61]

Services are defined here as the value-added production of non-agricultural goods and market provisioning of needs supplied by both public and private economic activity. In the private sector, this refers to goods and services which meet an individualized (as opposed to industrial mass product) demand involving customized supply which is largely contingent on a specific delivery location and timing. Public-sector services embrace administrative, transport and energy provisioning for goods and service exchange flows. Thus the service sector is generally two-tiered, with private activities functioning in the context of the public domain. The service sector is closely associated with agriculture and industry, but its special characteristic is its delivery of goods and services tailored to customers' needs.

### Rural transport services

The deficiencies of rural transport in Africa are frequently cited as a prime reason for the poor performance of agriculture.[62] Africa's transport problem is usually attributed to a shortage of physical infrastructure, notably roads, whereas less attention is devoted to the paucity of transport services for both goods and passenger movement. Accordingly, we shall examine the role of services in general, including their contribution to agricultural production, their employment potential, and their potential to undermine the advantageous position and power of monopolists of long-distance transport, who can currently take advantage of the rural populace's poor access to transport and communications.

The implicit thrust of the rural transport strategy advocated by African governments and donors to date has been efficient long-distance transport for exports. Thus, a priority has been the provision of conventional publicly constructed infrastructure, with motorized transport supplied by the private sector. In fact, actual performance of the private vehicle service sector has been dismal, as signified by the very low levels of ownership and a per capita decline in the number of motor vehicles in the 1980s to just below 7 per 1000 population.[63] At the end of 1988, only about 1 per cent of households in

[60] World Bank, *Sub-Saharan Africa: From crisis to sustainable growth* (World Bank, Washington DC, 1989), pp. 89–107.
[61] S. Haggblade, P. Hazell & J. Brown, 'Farm-nonfarm linkages in rural sub-Saharan Africa', *World Development*, 17, 8 (1989), pp. 1173–1201.
[62] J. Mellor & C. Delgado, *Food Production in Sub-Saharan Africa* (Food Policy Statement No. 7, IFPRI, Washington DC, 1987).
[63] J. Howe, 'Enhancing non-motorised transport use in Africa: Changing the policy climate' Paper presented to Transportation Research Board 74th Annual Meeting, Washington, DC, January 1995.

sub-Saharan Africa had access to a private motor vehicle. The figure varies between countries and between rural and urban areas, but it is evidently insufficient to address the travel needs of the mass of the population.

Detailed studies during the 1980s reveal the implications of these low levels of vehicle access at rural household level. In Tanzania, 90 per cent of all trips, 80 per cent of time spent on transport, 95 per cent of the total weight of goods and 80 per cent of load carrying effort was transport within and around the village and almost entirely on foot.[64] Ghanaian study findings were similar. Long-distance travel accounted for less than 1 per cent of total trips.[65] Rural household-level transport in Africa consists overwhelmingly of women's head-loading and walking. Village studies in East and West Africa have recorded men spending about 25 to 33 per cent of the time and effort women spend travelling and performing only about a tenth of the load-carrying.[66] The gross inefficiency of women's transport activities has to be set alongside the fact that they are usually their families' chief food producers. Given the tendency for women's working day to intensify, it seems unlikely that food-crop productivity can be increased unless greater attention is devoted to the issue of more efficient short-distance transport.[67] Thus, what is perhaps of greatest concern in the field of rural transport is the neglect of efficient short-distance transport improvements which could have immediate positive effects on agricultural productivity.

The neglect of short-distance transport facilities in Africa stands in contrast to Asia where a variety of, often non-motorized, means of transport enhances human efforts. This includes such things as bicycles and bicycle-drawn carts, animal-drawn sledges and carts, handcarts, wheelbarrows and simple rope or cableways for mountainous terrain. In Bangladesh such non-motorized transport is the backbone of the country's transport system, and is likely to remain so for the foreseeable future, with a static carrying capacity and output (tonne-kms) about twice that of the mechanized sector. Non-motorized transport accounts for nearly 94 per cent of all commercially operated vehicles, 75 per cent of the value added and 80 per cent of the employment in the transport sector.[68] This demonstrates that labour-intensive service-sector activities can have an important role to play in the alleviation of rural unemployment and poverty.

As for long-distance transport, continental capacity for goods movement by road has at best stagnated. In 1981 Africa received more than 31,000 new trucks of 16 or more tonnes capacity. In 1990 the continent received only 6,500 units with a near continuous decline in the intervening period.[69] It is thus surprising that in the effort to renew sub-Saharan Africa's deteriorated road infrastructure the issue of how the vehicle stock is going to be replenished is rarely raised. There has been a surge in vehicle imports in a number of countries following market liberalization. However, the volumes appear to be small and it is too soon to judge whether this will reverse the downward trend in vehicle stocks. For most countries the effects of the protracted foreign-

[64] I. Barwell, J. Howe & P. Zille, *Household Time Use and Agricultural Productivity in Sub-Saharan Africa* (I.T. Transport Ltd., London, November 1987).

[65] J. Howe & I. Barwell, *Study of Potential for IMT: Executive Summary and Main Report (Ghana)* (I.T. Transport Consultancy commissioned by World Bank, Washington, DC, June 1987).

[66] D.F. Bryceson & J.D.G.F. Howe, 'Rural household transport in Africa: Reducing the burden on women?', *World Development*, 21, 11 (1993), pp. 1715–28.

[67] D.F. Bryceson, 'Easing rural women's working day in sub-Saharan Africa', *Development Policy Review*, 12, 1 (1994), pp. 59–68.

[68] E.G. Jansen, A.J. Dolman, A.M. Jerve & N. Rahman, *The Country Boats of Bangladesh : Social and economic development and decision-making in inland water transport* (The University Press, Dhaka, 1989).

[69] Anon., 'Trucks for developing countries', *Development Journal Issues*, 3 (1991).

exchange crisis beginning in the 1970s are a blow from which they have still not recovered.

Road transport in Africa is very high-cost by international standards. A study of long-distance freight transport in Cameroon, Côte d'Ivoire and Mali showed that costs were several times as expensive as in Pakistan.[70] The research suggests that a halving of Africa's freight transport costs could be achieved, even with the present road system, chiefly through human capital investment. Raising levels of mechanical skill and giving drivers more responsibility, as well as adopting cheaper and more standardized vehicles, could bring about substantial improvement.

The difficulty of sub-Saharan Africa's competitiveness in agricultural commodity export is intimately related to the paucity of rural transport services. A substantial per centage of the f.o.b. price of agricultural commodities from Africa's ports is taken up in transport costs. African agricultural exports have to compete with products from Asia and Latin America, continents which on average have superior transport service infrastructure.

### Public works and human capital investment

Infrastructure investment is expensive, but costs can be defrayed by using labour-intensive methods which draw on sub-Saharan Africa's growing supply of under-employed rural labour. Labour-intensive public works can provide physical infrastructure such as roads, housing, sanitation, electricity, etc. while offering occupational skills training and mass employment of a short to medium-term nature. This not only holds the promise of improving the infrastructure, but also constitutes an investment in human capital.

For the past twenty-five years, labour-intensive public works have in fact been widely used as instruments of development policy, but have nearly always had to serve two purposes: relief and development. The former has an immediacy and political imperative that characteristically militates against the success of the latter. Labour-intensive public works have been highly successful in promoting relief from drought, famine or other natural disasters, but in doing so have generally contributed little to the development of sustainable infrastructure.[71] It is difficult to combine the relief and development objectives, since their operational requirements are diametrically opposed. Relief operations have to be executed quickly to address people's acute needs for food, shelter, or income: concern for the amount or longevity of any 'products' that result are necessarily second-order considerations. In contrast, the development of useful and sustainable infrastructure is a slow process of planning, design, training, implementation and maintenance.

The development of efficient labour-based methods was not undertaken in earnest until the early 1970s. Initial research by the World Bank[72] and the ILO's World

---

[70] The rates for the three African countries were found to be comparable to rates for international traffic between Zambia, Zimbabwe and neighbouring countries. Similarly, the low rates found in Pakistan were also found to exist for long-distance traffic in Vietnam and other Asian countries including India. J. Hine & C. Rizet, 'Halving Africa's freight transport costs: Could it be done?' (International Symposium on Transport and Communications in Africa, Brussels, November 1991).

[71] P. Terhal, 'Some aspects of rural public works in underdeveloped countries: a literature survey'. (Discussion Paper no. 26, Centre for Development Planning, Erasmus University, Rotterdam, February 1975); J. von Braun, T. Teklu & P. Webb, 'Labor-intensive public works for food security: Experience in Africa', (IFPRI Working Papers no. 6, Washington, DC, July 1991); M. Bezuneh, B. Deaton & G. Norton, 'Farm level impacts of food-for-work in a semi-arid region of Kenya', *Eastern Africa Economic Review*, 5, 1 (1989), pp. 1–8.

[72] World Bank, *Study of the Substitution of Labour and Equipment in Civil Construction* (World Bank Staff Working Paper no. 172, Washington, DC, 1974).

Employment Programme[73] focused on Asian countries, although the implementation of subsequent projects and programmes was concentrated in Africa.[74] Labour-intensive road construction projects in Botswana, Kenya, Lesotho and Malawi have been widely recognized as efficient. They have demonstrated that well organized, labour-intensive public works can produce roads to the equivalent standard achieved by equipment, at cheaper financial and economic costs, while creating five to seven times more employment than by equipment-intensive methods.[75] The absolute level of employment creation can be considerable. For example, the number of people employed in 1990 on the programme in Botswana amounted to 19 per cent of the total number of government employees in the country, including teachers.

As part of its reconstruction effort, South Africa has made a substantial commitment to the promotion of labour-based public works. Starting in 1991, the African National Congress began formulating a major programme of labour-intensive works in an effort to combat the country's worsening employment situation. In June 1993 this resulted in a formal agreement between the unions and representatives of all employers in the civil engineering industry which is now enshrined in the government's Reconstruction and Development Programme.[76] Industry has agreed to maximize the use of labour-intensive methods of construction in public works with due regard to economic efficiency. In turn the trade unions have agreed to allow the linking of payment to productive output. The expectation is that within three years about 50 per cent of all state expenditure on construction will be spent on projects with some labour-intensive component. South Africa's civil engineering sector has moved quickly to establish the viability of labour-intensive methods in a wide range of activities including housing, water supply, sanitation and drainage, and roads. The experience that has been gained has valuable lessons for the spread of both urban and rural public works in Africa more generally.

These programmes have revealed how public works ought to be conducted if their primary developmental objectives – significant and sustainable employment creation, infrastructure, and benefits to the poor – are to be attained. Four main elements have been identified as necessary for success: (i) adoption of a long-term national perspective in which a programme is developed; (ii) attention to technical, institutional, administrative, organizational and socio-economic detail during the preparatory phase and throughout the programme; (iii) institution-building at community, regional and national levels; and (iv) extensive training at site, multi-site and national levels.[77]

To succeed they need large numbers of trained people at all levels. Experience shows that programme expansion should only proceed at the rate at which the training programme can produce skilled site supervisors and managers. Short-term objectives, typical of relief projects, do not allow sufficient time for the necessary training programmes to be implemented and for sustainable institutions to develop.

At least three general trends could be said to argue in favour of labour-intensive public

---

[73] D. Lal, *Men or Machines: a study of labour-capital substitution in road construction in the Philippines* (ILO, Geneva, 1978); G.A. Edmonds & J.D.F.G. Howe, *Roads and Resources* (Intermediate Technology Publications, London, 1980).
[74] J.J. de Veen, *The Rural Access Roads Programme: Appropriate technology in Kenya* (ILO, Geneva, 1980); S. Hagen & C. Relf, *The District Road Improvement and Maintenance Programme: Malawi* (ILO/WEP, Geneva, 1988). Descriptions of other pilot projects are to be found in the ILO's Construction Technology Programme report series.
[75] R.T. McCutcheon, 'Labour-intensive road construction and maintenance in Africa: an introduction', *The Civil Engineer in South Africa*, 32, 11 (1990).
[76] 'The Framework Agreement for Public Works Projects using Labour-Intensive Construction Systems'.
[77] McCutcheon, 'Labour-intensive road construction'.

works as development programmes. First, the changing relationship between capital and labour favours labour-intensive investment. As Toye has noted, 'If a pervasive impact of adjustment policies is a reduction in the real wage, it is plausible to argue that those whose sole or main asset is their own labour will be made worse-off unless this is accompanied by an expansion of the demand for labour. . . . Without a strong up-swing in labour-intensive employment, therefore, a worsening of the inequality of income distribution is likely.'[78] A second factor is increasing food insecurity, which makes employment-focused interventions preferable to non-sustainable food subsidies. Third, rapidly deteriorating infrastructure requires repair, which by its nature is labour-intensive. By contrast, a fourth trend, namely the erosion of institutional capacity due to fiscal constraints and other factors, is often regarded as a factor militating against the establishment of labour-intensive public works.[79]

To date all the successful programmes in Africa have evolved over a period of five to seven years with special emphasis on institutional capacity-building. Programme experience strongly suggests that for efficient performance public works should be executed with significant, if not dominant, private-sector involvement, although government ministries have an important role to play in their instigation.

Labour-intensive public works projects have too often been identified with the state or associated with coerced labour, likened to the colonial government's use of tax defaulters for road building and maintenance. This is an antiquated view which fails to recognize the combined impact of market liberalization and rural labour-supply conditions now prevalent in Africa. The relative roles of the state and the market in any public works project will depend on local circumstances.[80] The existence of private building contractors is definitely a bonus, making it possible for labour-based public works to be established on a commercial basis from the outset. Conversely, the existence of public works can play a useful rule in setting a floor to the rural wage level in the local private sector by boosting the opportunity costs of the labour of the poorest in the community.[81]

Although labour-based systems may take years to become fully effective, some of the social benefits of labour-intensive public works are reaped relatively quickly. In many cases, they provide employment to women of marginal economic standing in their communities who face very constrained livelihood prospects. As a stop-gap measure the job opportunity is highly appreciated, even though stable employment and more remunerative earnings from labour-intensive projects are not easily achieved.[82] Environmentally, there is evidence that the use of labour-intensive methods is less damaging than when the same operations are done by equipment because of the greater precision and sensitivity that are possible.[83] This advantage is even more marked for remedial operations which are the major requirement for Africa's deteriorated infrastructure.

Despite the documented success of some labour-intensive public works projects, much of the investment in infrastructure continues to emphasize capital-intensive technologies.

[78] Toye, 'Structural adjustment', p. 33.

[79] Von Braun et al., Commercialization of Agriculture under Population Pressure.

[80] For examples see World Bank, World Development Report 1994: Infrastructure for development (Oxford University Press, New York, 1994), pp. 52–73.

[81] M. Kevane, 'Village labor markets in Sheikan District, Sudan', World Development, 22, 6 (1994), pp. 839–57.

[82] D.F. Bryceson & J.D.G.F. Howe, 'Women and labour-based road works in sub-Saharan Africa', in B. Johannessen (ed.), Labour-Based Technology: a review of current practice (CTP 133, ILO, Geneva, 1993), pp. 140–53.

[83] S. McCormick, 'Environmental assessment of the feeder road program in Ghana' (Associates in Rural Development, Inc., Burlington, Vermont, 1990).

There are complex reasons for this situation, but planners' and engineers' prejudice against the whole notion of labour-intensive projects is undoubtedly one of the most significant.[84] Labour-based methods are not only an economically efficient way to build physical infrastructure, they also have immediate and longer-lasting social benefits in terms of job expansion and enhancement of occupational skills. The market alone is unlikely to respond sufficiently to such long-term developmental needs. Thus, the state has a limited role to play in labour-based rural infrastructure building, providing openings for market expansion in a rural Africa which is, in any case, being profoundly altered by changing land supply and labour markets.

## Conclusion

Structural adjustment programmes, based on neo-liberal theories of economic growth, have so far not brought about the African continent's recovery to pre-crisis levels of material welfare and may, in the course of pursuing economic goals, contribute to social and political destabilization. As an antidote, there is need for proactive national development strategies with realistic assumptions and aims in order to avoid the social fragmentation and economic anarchy already evident in many African countries, such as Rwanda and Zaïre. The issue is investment in basic economic building blocks now rather than disaster relief in a few years' time.

The welfare of the African rural population is increasingly being determined by market forces. After two and a half decades of decline, African agriculture has a considerable amount of catching up to do to regain its earlier share in world agricultural export markets. Agricultural productivity is not merely a matter of increased availability of fertilizers and improved seeds. This chapter advocates service-sector primacy, involving the promotion of labour-based public works and the proliferation of labour-absorbing rural services. Much of the success of African agriculture depends on rural service-sector expansion.

In any event if current demographic trends continue, Africa in the twenty-first century will be largely non-agrarian and will need a good geographical distribution of occupational skills, productive infrastructure and services to afford its people viable means of gaining their livelihood and an improved standard of living in an atmosphere of peace rather than physical strife. Labour-based investment to broaden and deepen sub-Saharan Africa's rural service sector is economically vital and politically critical to the continent's future.

[84] J. Howe & H. Bantje, *Technology Choice in Civil Engineering Practice: Experience in the road sector* (ILO, Geneva, 1995).

# III
# *Africa in the World*

ELEVEN

# The Crisis of the State

### TIÉBILÉ DRAMÉ

The last decade of the twentieth century will go down in history as one of upheaval in sub-Saharan Africa. It will probably be remembered for the political, institutional and economic disruptions that have altered the face of the continent immeasurably since the advent of independence. On the one hand, it has witnessed the end of colonialism, with the abolition of apartheid and the eclipse of the single-party system and of overtly authoritarian and brutal regimes. On the other hand, it will be remembered for the armed conflicts, massacres, migrations, epidemics and uprisings whose repercussions will continue to be felt into the next century.

African states like Liberia and Somalia have quite simply ceased to exist as politically organized entities. Others like Sudan, Angola, Mozambique and Sierra Leone have lost control of some of their territory in recent years during more or less protracted periods of one-party rule. Grave dangers await countries like Nigeria, Zaïre or Burundi. In roughly fifteen sub-Saharan countries, rebel groups are defying the central authorities, or are seeking a degree of autonomy for the areas they control. While peace has been restored to countries like Mozambique in part due to the action of the international community, and even though Angola is trying to escape from the nightmare of war, other countries are less fortunate. Their daily reality is one of despair, with no genuine prospect of ending the suffering of their people.

The number of Africans becoming refugees from war or persecution on the grounds of race, ethnic origin, religion and so on, is 7,450,100 according to the United Nations High Commissioner for Refugees. The number of internally displaced persons, in other words people who do not cross their countries' borders but are nevertheless forced to leave their homes because of war and intolerance, is just as high. The 23 million refugees and displaced persons around the world come from ten main countries, eight of which are African. The situation is so serious that some journalists are already prophesying 'the death throes of Africa' or predicting that the continent has reached the point of no return on the road to chaos and anarchy.[1]

Without reverting to apocalyptic visions, it would be fair to say that Africa is in the midst of a multi-dimensional crisis. Of all the crises it is undergoing – political, economic, social, cultural and ecological – the crisis that is affecting the state is by far the most threatening for the future, because it is likely to undermine the foundations of authority inherent in any human organization.

No one nowadays would seriously dispute the existence of a crisis of confidence between the state and society in Africa. This crisis lay dormant for decades before erupting following the deepening of the international economic crisis which has reawakened internal contradictions within African society. Nowhere is the lack of understanding between the state and society as pronounced as in Africa. It seems to me that this misunderstanding is the cause of the crisis of the state, which some believe is irreversible. Stability, peace and social and economic development will all depend on how this misunderstanding is resolved by the people of Africa.

The state as it exists in Africa today is a legacy of colonization. The colonial state was above all a military state. Colonization was often imposed by force of arms, or through intimidation based on the threat of force. The colonial order established by conquest was typically a military order, which coerced the colonized peoples into a state of submission. The conquerors dismantled pre-colonial systems of government. When they tried to introduce measures such as indirect rule in order to strengthen their authority, they embedded societies in dual authoritarian structures. As a result, traditional chiefs became more despotic.[2]

Because one of the main objects of conquest was the control of primary resources, the colonial state was organized in such a way as to ensure the conditions required for economic exploitation of the colonies. A bureaucracy modelled on military lines was installed to collect levies and taxes and to organize forced labour whenever it was necessary to construct the infrastructure required for colonial exploitation. Colonial power was absolute, elitist and rigorously centralized. It remained so for decades, even after the military had been replaced by civilian administrations.

During World War II the colonized peoples contributed to the victory over fascism and in the euphoria surrounding the end of the war, the democratic rights recognized in Europe were extended to the colonies. The freedoms of expression, association and assembly that were now enjoyed and exercised to the full, created the conditions for an easing of the colonial regime, leading to independence.

Before handing over power, administrators concentrated on preparing the change-over in many African countries in such a way as to install governments favourable to colonial interests. Although some regimes undeniably had the advantage of popular support, many were hardly representative and had been imposed through various manoeuvres by the colonial administration (such as elimination of nationalist leaders held to be unsympathetic towards colonial interests, gerrymandering and electoral frauds,

---

[1] Robert D. Kaplan, 'The coming anarchy', *The Atlantic Monthly*, February 1994, pp. 44–76; Thomas W. Lippman, 'Africa in agony', *Washington Post*, 4 September 1994.

[2] Dele Olowu, 'Au delà de la faillite de l'Etat centralisé en Afrique', Paper delivered at a conference on 'Quelques aspects de la décentralisation en Afrique de l'Ouest', organized by the Friedrich Ebert Foundation, Germany, 24–25 May 1994, Abidjan.

administrative and police harassment). The vague desire to create independent parties and nationalist leaders conflicted with the declared hostility of the ex-colonial powers.

Later, as a consequence of the East-West conflict, the state became harsher due to the establishment of strong military regimes that increasingly violated human rights, suspended basic democratic freedoms, and accelerated the exploitation of national resources. The arrival of the army on the African political scene generally resulted in illiberalism and political and economic repression. In our opinion, one of the characteristics of post-colonial administration has been the perpetuation of the colonial state, despite the efforts to Africanize the bureaucracy which had started during the last years of colonialism. The structures and *modus operandi* were neither Africanized nor democratized.[3]

In certain countries like Congo-Léopoldville (present-day Zaïre), Africanization was not well planned, following the hurried departure of the Belgian forces after the declaration of independence. The colonizers clearly intended to sabotage the first steps of the young Congolese state by fair means or foul, including the assassination of nationalist leaders, with a view to controlling the immense mineral riches of the country. Overnight and without any preparation, African cadres, only some of whom had received a rough and ready training, were put in control of the state apparatus. The subsequent excesses were almost inevitable. African politicians took over from white administrators without considering how to integrate the objective historical conditions of Africa into the foundations of a new state.

Where there were attempts to challenge these post-colonial influences, as in Guinea-Conakry under President Ahmed Sékou Touré, the *pouvoirs révolutionnaires locaux* (local revolutionary forces, PRL) showed themselves to be the tools of a new bureaucracy, through which the centralism of the one-party state stifled all democratic expression and popular initiative. Generally, the powers of agents of the state, the security forces, forest rangers, governors and mayors, remained unlimited in the rural areas of Africa. Until the omnipotence of the state was challenged by popular opposition movements in the late 1980s, it was not uncommon to see representatives of state authority beating citizens or subjecting them to all sorts of harassment, especially in rural areas. Like the colonial state, the post-colonial state remains alien to the overwhelming majority of African populations. Almost everywhere the language of government has remained the language of the colonizers. The fact that the literacy rate in Africa is still very low and that international organizations have concluded that some countries are even 'de-educating' people, gives some indication of the extent of the gulf separating governments and their citizens. In *Les soleils des indépendances*, the novelist Ahmadou Kourouma gives a fine description of the tribulations of an ordinary African trapped in the maze of African government.[4]

It is no exaggeration to say that the average African identifies neither with the judicial system nor with the other modern institutions inherited from colonialism. It is as if the state and the social and cultural environment in which most of the population exist are incompatible; there is a fundamental misconception on which are grafted all the other components which lead to the rejection of the state and to open antagonism from society.[5]

---

[3] Olowu, 'Au delà de la faillite de l'Etat'.

[4] Ahmadou Kourouma, *Les soleils des indépendances* (Le Seuil, Paris, 1970).

[5] The relation between the state and popular action has been the subject of prolonged debate. See Jean-François Bayart, Achille Mbembe, Comi Toulabor, *Le politique par le bas en Afrique noire: contributions à une problématique de la démocratisation* (Karthala, Paris, 1992).

The initial misunderstanding which prevailed between the state and society in Africa is evident in the way public authority is viewed in contemporary African societies. These societies are riddled with corruption from top to bottom, so much so that the popular perception of the state and its relationship with society has been affected. In general, the average African, especially the town-dweller, admires the outward signs of social success to some extent. In fact, those who use their positions within the state apparatus to become rich tend to be admired and envied,[6] and are criticized when they fail to distribute their gains to their families, entourage and networks. People who have access to high-ranking state functions are expected to enrich themselves; if they fail to do so, they become the object of sarcasm, criticism, and pressure from the people around them.

Corruption has caused so much damage that the popular perception in some African countries is that what belongs to the state or public authority belongs to no one. Public goods belong to the public: therefore one can help oneself to them as much as one's position permits, providing that others can profit as well. This phenomenon has been observed and described by J.-F. Bayart in a study of the state in Africa, sub-titled *La politique du ventre* ('the politics of the belly').[7] Academic writers on Africa have not sufficiently emphasized the role of the multinational companies of the ex-colonial powers in the spread of corruption in African state organizations. If one is to believe certain authors who have taken an interest in the subject, the phenomenon and the mechanisms of corruption are virtually institutionalized in certain Western countries, especially when it comes to the preparation and signing of major contracts.[8] It is not our intention here to blame the West for all that is bad in Africa, but merely to state all the implications of a phenomenon which is devastating African societies.

## The Rejection of the State

As the heir of the centralism of colonial power, the African state has for a long time monopolized the key positions and roles in economic activity and public life. In order to consolidate its base in society, the central state – the sole collector of levies, taxes and other dues paid by the population and foreign companies – has devoted itself to the redistribution of the national wealth, particularly to the benefit of the bureaucracy. In some countries, the state and the enterprises it controls are the main employers. This has led to the development of middle classes tied to the state sector or extensions of the state, which significantly influences current developments in Africa.

A degree of social peace prevailed so long as the middle classes were among the beneficiaries of the redistribution of national wealth through the welfare state. However, the rift which already existed between the state and society began to deepen when the standard of living of the middle classes began to deteriorate as they grew in number. Austerity measures and the reduction of state activity and of its social budgets (health and education), imposed in the wake of advice from the IMF and World Bank, also contributed to this development.

Rural populations and underprivileged urban strata may have become resigned to the failure and negligence of the elite. However, the middle classes, better educated and more

---

[6] This observation does not apply to politically conscious groups among the intelligentsia, the middle classes and the classes which have a different concept of 'success'.

[7] Jean-François Bayart, *L'Etat en Afrique : la politique du ventre* (Fayard, Paris, 1989).

[8] F.-X. Verschave & A.-S. Boisgallais, *L'aide publique au développement* (Syros, Paris, 1994).

aware of international economic relations and of how the ruling classes were going about lining their pockets, refused to pay for the 'mistakes' committed by others. Confrontation became inevitable. Unlike the silent majority who opposed the actions of the state mechanically and without much hope of success, the urban middle classes rejected the fate which had been thrust upon them. They vehemently condemned what was politely called 'illicit gain' (i.e. the corruption of the elite). This denunciation was echoed, especially by the underprivileged urban strata who led a miserable existence alongside the luxury of the elites.

Not only was the African state condemned for its economic failings, it was equally opposed in the political field as well. At the end of the 1980s, the single-party system ruled as absolute master from the Atlantic to the Indian Ocean, with the exception of a few countries like the Gambia, Senegal and Botswana. Worse still, in several countries military dictatorships had replaced civil regimes, suspending the constitutions and outlawing all political activity. Opponents or even people who simply objected were hunted down, arrested and detained, tortured and often murdered. In these very recent times some African states did not even nominally resemble constitutional states. The student leader Abdoul Karim Camara, known as 'Cabral', was murdered in 1980 in a military camp in Mali. In Benin, a student, Rémy-Glelé Akpopo, died under torture in a police station in 1988. I am convinced that had Nelson Mandela been born in Uganda or Central Africa, he would probably not have emerged alive from his twenty-seven years of imprisonment. It is enough to recall the numerous members of African opposition movements who reputedly 'committed suicide' in prison. The first secretary-general of the Organization of African Unity, Diallo Telli, died of hunger and thirst in an African prison in 1977.[9] Ex-President Modibo Keïta of Mali died in 1977 in circumstances that have remained unexplained, in a cell in a military camp.

The African state, which has come to grief economically, in a number of countries organized a system of brutal repression, in contempt of basic human rights and human dignity. It has thus been rejected by the overwhelming majority of African people who not only do not identify with it, but have become victims of the policies which it has implemented.

## *War as a form of opposition to the state*

In several African countries, more or less organized armed groups are in open conflict with central government and are calling for a distribution of power more favourable to the people in whose name they are considered to be fighting. Some of these conflicts, such as that in South Sudan, have been raging for over twenty years; others, like those in Liberia and Sierra Leone and the Tuareg rebellions in the Sahara, are more recent. In varying degrees, all have caused indescribable human suffering. One of the results is that Africa has become the foremost world producer of refugees and internally displaced people. These conflicts raise questions about good governance and about the capacity of the African state to govern the people living within its territory effectively and equitably. They constitute a violent form of rejection of the state by sections of the population. They are most frequently caused by the curtailment, the inadequacy or simply the non-existence of dialogue between the political actors, between rulers and ruled. Each time the scope for dialogue is restricted or disappears, factional political manouevring[10]

---

[9] André Lewin, *Diallo Telli : le tragique destin d'un grand Africain* (JAPRESS, Paris, 1990).
[10] The term applied by Jean-François Bayart, *L'Etat en Afrique.*

regresses into armed conflict. In this respect, armed conflicts raise the question of democracy in African societies and of the authoritarianism of African states.

The armed struggle for power by groups of citizens has brought about the disintegration of the state in Liberia and Somalia and threatens its survival in Sierra Leone. It considerably weakens the central authority in many countries. The loss of the state monopoly of violence has revealed how weak the structure of the state in Africa is. In a country like Liberia, the guerrilla warfare of the National Patriotic Front of Liberia (NPFL) provoked the rapid collapse of Samuel Doe's government and delivered the population into the hands of warlords who indulge in merciless combat. In Liberia, as elsewhere, war seems to have become a kind of economic and political organization. The fight against a dictator, slogans about democracy, nationalism and revolution are often a façade or a front for less acceptable activities. It becomes, according to Claude Meillassoux, 'a sordid affair, using arms as a means of doing business'.[11] The mineral wealth of Liberia or of countries like Angola, coveted by big multinational corporations, has certainly fuelled the wars which have cost tens of thousands of civilian lives.

The civil wars in West Africa have resulted in a proliferation of arms which has alarmed the United Nations to such an extent that the Secretary-General has designated a special representative to study ways of limiting the traffic of arms in the region. The war in Liberia, which seriously threatens Sierra Leone, is certainly at the heart of the arms trade sustaining other conflicts in the West African region. Liberia is a clear illustration of the fact that civil wars are often the extreme manifestation of the market economy and the lawless competition in which arms-traders and dealers in precious stones or in drugs confront each other.[12]

### Democratization

At the beginning of the 1990s the African state found itself confronted with opposition movements in various countries. These movements, which expressed the desire of the urban classes for social justice and freedom, have led progressively to the establishment of political pluralism, initially in the francophone countries, later in the English- and Portuguese-speaking countries. Because they began in countries where there was strong French influence, these movements have been styled 'Paristroika' by some French and African analysts.[13] This implies that the democratization of Africa was somehow a French initiative. This approach, which is resented by some Africans as an expropriation of their history, neither takes into account France's almost constant efforts to help maintain stability and the status quo in Africa, nor the objective reality of the African democratic movement. In Benin, where the democratic movement first emerged, it seems that, in order to resolve the social and political crisis, France tolerated at most a separation between the party and the state and 'the holding of a congress of the *single* Party[14] which will have to determine a new modus operandi whose structures can accommodate all the political feelings of the country'.[15]

---

[11] Claude Meillassoux, 'Poissons á brûler' (unpublished manuscript, 1990).

[12] ibid.

[13] Referring to the perestroika of Mikhail Gorbachev which sounded the death-knell for the monolithic political system of the former Soviet empire.

[14] Our italics.

[15] This quotation is taken from a memorandum drafted by the director of the president's office for the attention of President Mathieu Kérékou. Dated 7 December 1989, this document summarized a conversation during the course of which the French ambassador had made known the suggestions of the French authorities for the resolution of the political crisis in Benin. The note was published in 1990 in the international press.

It is worthwhile to recall here that the national conference in Benin, which put an end to the single-party system, met in February 1990, while the speech at La Baule, in which President Mitterrand invited his African peers to make efforts to liberalize their regimes, was delivered only in June 1990. The speech at Chaillot, delivered by the French Head of State in November 1991, advised Africans to move towards democracy at their own speed, and was widely interpreted as an encouragement to African leaders who were resisting the process of democratization. It would therefore be an exaggeration to say that France gave orders for the establishment of movements of opposition to African political regimes. These movements, which put forward economic and cultural claims and inaugurated an era of open crisis of state authority, are just as much the product of the political, economic and cultural environment as of the new international climate resulting from the disappearance of the Soviet Union.

The political and institutional changes occurring in Africa in recent years have taken place in an international context characterized by the end of the Cold War and the democratic revolutions in Eastern Europe. The demise of the Soviet bloc has created a new set of international rules. Africa is no longer a pawn in the rivalry between the superpowers, and it has seen its strategic importance decline along with the diplomatic interest of the great powers. The end of the Cold War has also limited the options for international manoeuvring by African states. However, it would be wrong to conclude that the end of the Cold War has put an end to inter-power rivalry in Africa. While Russia, facing countless difficulties within its frontiers and on its borders, has neither the resources nor the ambitions of the former USSR, the Western powers are still engaged in a struggle to preserve or extend their spheres of influence on the African continent. To all intents and purposes, the end of the Cold War has not resulted in any appreciable reduction of foreign troops stationed in Africa, nor have any foreign military bases been dismantled. For example, an estimated ten thousand French troops are stationed on the continent, in accordance with treaties of defence or cooperation.[16] The Soviet threat, which has disappeared for good, can no longer be used to justify this presence.

The end of East-West rivalry has allowed a degree of clarification of international relations and has revealed the ever increasing role of the Bretton Woods institutions in African politics and economics. Following the economic and financial failure of African states, the IMF and the World Bank have intervened and put into operation programmes of structural adjustment, based on criteria of profitability and aimed ultimately at re-establishing the financial equilibrium lost as a result of mismanagement. These programmes have considerably reduced the autonomy of decision-making by African leaders, as the international institutions now successfully use their veto to influence government projects, such as the refusal to allow the opening of an embassy or the insistence on the closure of an enterprise deemed unprofitable.

The economic crisis surrounding the debate on the African continent has provoked both a withdrawal of foreign companies which have relocated to areas more favourable for business and profit, and a repositioning around economically or linguistically promising centres like Nigeria, Côte d'Ivoire, Kenya and South Africa.

---

[16] A.-S. Boisgallais, 'Présence militaire française en Afrique: dérives' in '4ème "Dossier noir" de la politique africaine de la France' (mimeo, Coalition pour ramener à la raison démocratique la politique africaine de la France, Paris, 1994).

## The devaluation of the Organization of African Unity

The inauguration in 1963 of the OAU aroused great expectations among African nations. Its founders wanted to put aside their differences and complete decolonization, fight against apartheid, lay the foundations of African unity and solidarity, and assert the presence of Africa on the international scene. However, the African leaders had difficulty in speaking with one voice and the OAU soon became paralysed because of differences between its member states concerning strategy, tactics and the means by which to attain the objectives set out in the Charter adopted in Addis Ababa. Neither Africa nor its organizations were immune to the effects of the Cold War. Both became host to rivalries between the great powers, and the conferences of ministers or heads of state very often reflected the divisions between the two blocs. Moreover, the African states tended to adopt a position in international situations congruent with their external alliances, to the detriment of African solidarity. As a result a number of resolutions passed by the OAU have remained mere empty words. The political will of the member states has been lacking. The OAU has been unable to quench Africa's thirst for affirmation in the political arena. The organization has thus lost all credibility in the eyes of Africans and of the rest of the world. The grave economic and financial difficulties plaguing Africa and the end of the East-West conflict have further discredited the OAU. The continent is in the midst of a multi-dimensional crisis, but the OAU, which is, when all is said and done, only the sum of Africa's ambitions and resources, is powerless to react adequately. The spectacle of Somalian delegates coming to blows in Africa Hall in Addis Ababa at a meeting of foreign ministers in February 1992 is a sign of the times.

In the new international order resulting from the disappearance of the Soviet bloc, states in crisis and powerless organizations count for little. Because international relations are not democratic, African states are in a position of subservient compliance vis-à-vis the big powers. The voting system used in certain international organizations resembles a property-based vote, in that the allotment of voting rights is proportional to the contributions paid by the member states. African countries find themselves diminished in the international arena and in the eyes of their populations.

Six years after the initial appearance of democratic demands, what is the state of democracy in Africa? The political and institutional landscape of the continent has most certainly been thrown into upheaval. Multi-party elections have been held in most countries. Parliaments where majority and opposition exist side by side, private FM radio stations, a press which is dynamic despite a high level of illiteracy, are from now on a part of the African scene. Despite this indisputable progress, many obstacles stand in the way of the democratization of African societies. State institutions are monopolized by the parties in power, whether they are the old single parties or the old opposition parties who have been voted into office. The emergence of a non-partisan administration is thus purely hypothetical. Public radio and television remain essentially controlled just as in the old days of the single-party system. The judiciary rarely shows signs of real independence. The old authoritarian habits still persist in public life.

Beyond the general liberalization of political life and formal and visible signs of democracy, opposition movements had a variety of fates in store for the former ruling class. Some presidents lost power as a result of national conferences (Benin, Congo), revolution (Mali), or electoral defeat (Zambia, Cape Verde, Central African Republic, Malawi). Others were destabilized but have managed to resist the wind of change and have adapted to the new political context, retaining power (through elections) and control of the political game (Burkina Faso, Gabon, Kenya, Mauritania, etc.). This preservation of power by the old ruling class may be explained by the following factors:

- an ability to anticipate events which has allowed them to retain the initiative (declaration of multi-party systems, timing of elections) and avoid the damage which proved fatal to President Moussa Traoré in Mali;
- the control exercised through the state apparatus over rural populations (the majority of whom are far removed from the democratic process) and opposition movements, in contrast to the urban classes;
- control over the organization of elections;
- effective control exercised over the military and security forces to ensure their loyalty. Although certain regimes have been permanently weakened by the installation of multi-party rule, others seem to have been strengthened by the legitimacy acquired through the polls.

The military and the security forces have played a key role in the political evolution of African countries. At a time when African states found themselves confronted by opposition movements, the attitude of the military and security forces varied from country to country, and from one period to another within one country. In Togo, Zaïre and Nigeria, the armed forces impeded the process of democratization by intervening in the political arena. In Mali, after brutally suppressing the popular movement opposing the regime of General Moussa Traoré, the army turned against the dictator, arrested him, and encouraged the transition to democracy. In some other countries the army has tried to remain above political factions and to play the role of arbitrator. In South Africa, Benin, Congo and Niger, armies have generally supported the process of transition from the outset.

## Conclusion

The process of democratization has generally weakened African states, whose authority has been severely tested by the wave of opposition which spread over Africa in the late 1980s. The first targets of demonstrations in African towns were the symbols of the state: public buildings and vehicles.

The crisis of confidence between society and the state has intensified dramatically as a result of the democratic movements. The failure and incapacity of states have been repeatedly emphasized by the opposition. Attempts to crush or stifle popular movements by repression (in the cases of Mali and Togo) have not improved the standing of the state. The military and security forces, instruments of repression, have fallen further into disrepute. The fall or the liberalization of authoritarian regimes has led the average African to defy the state. The army and the police no longer inspire the same respect or fear as before. The agents of the state no longer have the same authority.

In several African countries, citizens have refused or are refusing to pay duties and taxes and even attack representatives of the state who try to force them to fulfil their civic duties. The 'sacred' aspect of the state seems to have disappeared as democratization has taken over.

The situation certainly varies from country to country. The state looks weaker in the countries which have seen changes in its higher echelons and where the old parties have been defeated (Congo, Mali, Niger). The state seems less weakened where the old single parties have remained in power (Kenya, Togo, Mauritania). Despite the renewal of the political class and the change of leadership in some African countries – even if one-party regimes have disappeared and been replaced by multi-party systems – African society is still a long way from trusting the state. The democratic movements have even accelerated the loss of confidence, and weakened the state further. It seems that what was considered to be the crisis of the one-party state was in fact the crisis of the contemporary African state in general, the organization which sanctions the rule of bureaucracy over the vast majority of the population, especially in the rural areas.

Since colonization, the gulf separating state and society has not ceased to widen. Essentially, neither decolonization nor political pluralism has resolved the problem of democratization and the redistribution of power in Africa. A reform of the structures of power will have to take into account the objective historical conditions in Africa and will have to base itself on the principle of devolution of responsibility to the grassroots communities and their institutions.

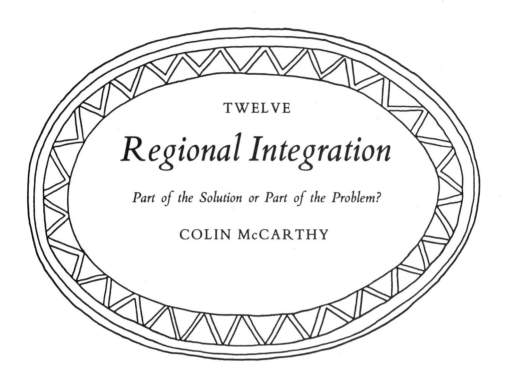

TWELVE

# Regional Integration

*Part of the Solution or Part of the Problem?*

COLIN McCARTHY

Lack of economic growth and development in Africa has taken a heavy toll in human misery.[2] The external environment has been hostile, but it is increasingly realized that mistaken economic policies have made the economic position of most African countries worse than it need have been. Formal exercises in regional integration, intended to play a prominent role in reversing the marginalization of African economies, are one of the policy stances that can be questioned.

The story told here will not differ much from the rather pessimistic one encountered in most analyses of integration in the developing world, notably in Africa where gains have been modest compared with the resources used in promoting integration.[3] However, there are cogent reasons why a re-assessment of regional integration in Africa is opportune. Apart from the fact that hope exists, at least in policy-making circles, for the contribution which integration can make towards economic development, major developments have recently taken place which will reinforce the attention given to regional integration. The most prominent event has been the transition to an inclusive democracy in South Africa, Africa's largest and most sophisticated economy. While the major economies of north, west, and east Africa – Algeria, Nigeria and Kenya – remain

[1] I am grateful to Douglas Rimmer and Daniel Bach for comments on an earlier draft of this chapter. Normal caveats apply as to my responsiblity for the final product.
[2] For an analysis of national economic policies, see Chapter 6 by Janine Aron in this volume.
[3] John Ravenhill, 'Overcoming constraints to regional cooperation in Africa: Coordination rather than integration', in World Bank, *The Long-Term Perspective Study of Sub-Saharan Africa*, Vol. 4 (World Bank, Washington DC, 1990), p. 81.

bogged down in autocratic governance, southern Africa can look forward to the closer integration of the dominant economy of the sub-continent into the economic and political structures of the region.[4] Also of considerable importance is the widespread implementation of structural adjustment programmes, which are bound to have an effect on regional integration.

## Regionalism in the Global Economy

During the post-World War II period, regional integration has been an important part of international trade relations and policy worldwide. Two waves of emphasis are discernible. The first started with the establishment in 1957 of the forerunner of the European Union and, in the developing world, the adoption in Latin America of regional integration as the means to effect inward-looking growth through import-substituting industrialization. The latter strategy was actively promoted by the UN Economic Commission for Latin America as an important instrument in creating a larger protected market in a scenario which saw little hope in focusing the outward-looking industrial growth of developing countries on the markets of the industrialized world.

The growth during the 1960s and 1970s of multilateralism in lowering barriers to trade under the auspices of the General Agreement on Tariffs and Trade (GATT) contributed to a decline in the importance attached to regionalism. However, a second wave in regional integration started during roughly the latter half of the 1980s. The origin of the 'new regionalism', as the second wave is sometimes called, might be found in the protractedness of, and slow progress made in, the Uruguay Round of GATT negotiations, the prospect of a European single market in 1992, and the conversion of the United States to regionalism with its concomitant negotiations of the North American Free Trade Agreement and the Enterprise for the Americas Initiative.[5] In Latin America some old integration arrangements were revived, sometimes in the wake of political change (the Central American Common Market and the Andean Pact), and new ones, such as MERCOSUR, created. In Asia, the ASEAN proceeded further in economic cooperation by starting to shift its focus from investment coordination to market integration.

An element of the new regionalism is the hypothesis of a triad of trading blocs developing – Europe, the Americas, and East Asia – which could pose a threat to multilateralism and to the trade position of those countries and regions without natural links with any of the major blocs. Although the possibility of an inward-looking and protectionist approach in the trading blocs is foreseen by some observers, a characteristic of the new regionalism is the widespread emphasis on outward orientation rather than on import substitution within the regional market. Other characteristics are the importance attached to the harmonization of macro-economic policies and to regional labour and capital flows.

Trade data show that the first wave of regionalism did not put a stop to global integration. Intra-regional trade had grown, but the propensity for regions to trade a portion of their gross domestic product with other regions had also increased; intra-regional trade and the formation of integration arrangements had not taken place at the cost of extra-

---

[4] The demise of apartheid and South Africa's acceptance in the community of nations mean that, henceforth, scholars will have to include South Africa in analyses of sub-Saharan Africa. Also, the spurious exclusion of the Southern African Customs Union (SACU), perhaps the oldest functioning customs union in the world, from comparative reviews of integration arrangements will presumably now come to an end. ◆

[5] Jaime de Melo & Arvind Panagariya, *The New Regionalism in Trade Policy* (World Bank, Washington, DC & Centre for Economic Policy Research, London, 1992), pp. 1–2.

regional trade.[6] At this stage it is not clear, however, what the influence of the second wave of regionalism, with its proliferation of integration arrangements and the extension and deepening of existing arrangements, will be on trade flows and global trade liberalization during the 1990s.

In Africa, the desirability of regional integration, although it did not achieve what it set out to do, has remained more prominent and more strongly asserted in policy pronouncements than in any other developing area. Consequently, a separate, second, wave is not so clearly discernible. However, the signing in 1991 by the African Heads of State of the Abuja Treaty on the establishment of a Pan-African Economic Community by the year 2025 could be regarded as having initiated a second wave, with a number of developments on the integration front during the 1990s. These will be discussed below. Because of the prominence given to regional integration, Africa – sub-Saharan Africa in particular – has the largest number of regional integration arrangements in the world. Unfortunately, many of these are ineffective or dormant.[7] An important arrangement with a significant potential, the East African Community, broke up in 1977.[8]

## Characteristics of Regional Integration in Africa

Regional integration in Africa has a number of characteristics which explain the rationale and proliferation of integration arrangements, the nature or pattern of integration exercises, and the lack of significant success. Some of these, it may be noted, are unique, but others are common to the experience in the developing world, Latin America in particular.

### Integration models

A feature that should be noted at the start concerns the model of trade integration adopted. In the literature, integration is differentiated from regional cooperation. Cooperation refers to any joint activity across national frontiers for the purpose of cooperation in economic matters, from running a joint regional airline or coordinated rail system to the joint management of river basins. Integration arrangements take on a narrower meaning. They aim to expand intra-regional trade through the lowering or removal of barriers to trade in goods and services.

In the conventional linear model integration is described in terms of a progressive lowering of trade barriers and the creation of a single market among a number of countries. It starts with preferential trading arrangements where countries share preferential access to their markets, mostly in the form of lower rates of tariffs on imports. However, the first proper step in the process of integration is the creation of a free trade area, which means that barriers to trade among participating countries are removed while each member state still maintains its own restrictions vis-à-vis non-participating economies. The next step produces the prototype of integration, namely the customs union, where

---

[6] Kym Anderson & Hege Norheim, 'History, geography and regional economic integration', in Kym Anderson & Richard Blackhurst (eds), *Regional Integration and the Global Trading System* (Harvester Wheatsheaf, New York, 1993), pp. 45–6.

[7] Augusto de la Torre & Margaret R. Kelly, *Regional Trade Arrangements* (International Monetary Fund, Washington, DC, 1992), p. 25.

[8] Regional cooperation is currently being revived in East Africa, albeit at a lower level of integration than the earlier East African Community.

free trade among members is combined with a common external barrier to trade. Tariffs on imports and other restrictions on free trade are thus shared by all members towards non-members. A common market is the next step and develops when capital and labour join goods and non-factor services in a free flow among member states. When common fiscal and monetary policies (the latter implying a single central bank) are added to the common market, the most advanced form of economic integration, namely an economic union, arises.

If the post-war experience with integration in North America and Europe is anything to go by, market integration is a process that moves at a tempered pace over a long period. The North American Free Trade Agreement (NAFTA), which as a free trade area is a less-intensive form of market integration, was ratified in 1993 after decades of incremental integration arrangements between Canada and the United States and Mexico and the United States. In Europe, not even the considerable force of the geo-political considerations generated by the Cold War and the need for economic recovery – with integration meant to speed-up post-war recovery and the creation of European unity against the Soviet Union – could prevent the incremental development of a common market from being spread over four decades.

In Africa, the goal of integration has been ambitious, with the common market the typical arrangement aimed for.[9] However, the experience has been that this goal remained elusive and over-ambitious, with very few arrangements having achieved their integration targets within the timetables adopted. In the case of the Economic Community of West African States (ECOWAS), for example, negligible progress has been made, since its inception in 1975, towards a free flow of trade and a common external tariff (that is, a customs union) by the original target date of 1990. Only the Southern African Customs Union (SACU) and the Economic and Customs Union of Central Africa (best known by its French acronym, UDEAC) have common external tariffs. In the case of SACU this is a historical legacy which has determined that the South African tariff applies as the common external tariff.

## The rationale of integration

A characteristic of African economies, with important implications for regional integration, is their small size and low levels of average income. It is sobering to note that South Africa's GDP of $103,651 million in 1992 – which is approximately three times larger than that of Algeria (the second largest economy in Africa) and three and a half times larger than the Nigerian GDP (the second largest economy in sub-Saharan Africa) – is slightly smaller than the Norwegian GDP of $112,906 million.[10] In other words, Africa's largest economy by far is approximately the same size, when measured in terms of GDP, as that of a small European economy.

This observation leads to two perspectives on integration, one pointing to the rationale for integration among developing countries, and the other, in a somewhat paradoxical sense, to the problem of creating viable integration organizations in Africa.

The role of regional integration as an instrument of development has been alluded to earlier with reference to the Latin American experience. Proponents of development-oriented market integration regard industrialization as the engine of economic

[9] Omotunde E.G. Johnson, 'Economic integration in Africa: Enhancing prospects for success', *The Journal of Modern African Studies*, 29 (1991), p. 3.
[10] World Bank, *World Development Report 1994* (Oxford University Press, New York, 1994), pp. 166–7.

development. For them the principal goal of integration and growth in intra-regional trade is economic development and structural change through industrial growth; as one writer expressed it: 'Integration in many developing areas of the world is . . . a paradigm for industrialization'.[11] But growth in manufactured output requires more than action on the supply side of the equation, such as investment in productive capacity. It requires markets for the growth in output. In fact, it can be argued that while high investment ratios are associated with economic growth, viable and growing markets are prime determinants of investment. Investment does not take place in a vacuum, but is initiated by a desire to create capacity to produce for an identified market.

If it is believed that developing countries will find it difficult, if not impossible, to gain access to the markets of the industrialized world with manufactured exports, import substitution suggests itself as the only viable demand source of manufacturing growth, at least during the initial stages of industrialization. However, the small size of most developing economies, notably those in Africa, restricts the ability of these countries to benefit from lower unit costs (derived from economies of scale) and viable import-substituting opportunities; hence the argument that African countries should attempt to create customs unions or common markets. This will enable manufacturers to produce at lower unit costs for a larger protected market.

Regional integration in this way becomes an inward-looking instrument of industrial development, diverting trade from cheaper sources in the rest of the world to higher-cost producers within the union. Aligned to this argument for protection, but viewed from the opposite end of the spectrum, is the view that the larger protected market could serve as a training ground within which long-protected domestic industries can cut their competitive teeth in the larger regional market before being exposed to the harsh conditions of the global market-place. In contrast to the first interpretation, which sees regional integration as a means to effect import-substituting industrialization, the second approach views the larger protected market as the incubator that will assist manufacturing to become fully export-oriented.

In Africa, however, the smallness of the economies leads to a second perspective: when combined into a larger market behind a common external barrier, the larger, combined market remains small by world standards, and further constrained by high costs of transport and communication. At $80,000 million the GDP (1989) of the sixteen-member ECOWAS, with a population of 180 million and poor infrastructure, is smaller than that of Denmark with its GDP of $90,000 million, population of 5.1 million, and integrated, comparatively low-cost transport and communication services. The 20-member Preferential Trade Area for Eastern and Southern Africa with a GDP of $70,000 million and a population of 192 million has an even smaller market than ECOWAS. While the sum of the markets is much larger than the individual markets of the participating economies, thus raising the potential for inward-looking industrial growth to a level which is not possible in the individual states, the combined market is still not large enough to reach high levels of industrial development through import substitution. Of course, even this is hypothetical since the creation of these single markets remains a goal which for most integration arrangements in Africa is not likely to be achieved in the foreseeable future.

Nevertheless, the small size of African economies and the observation that over the long run the prices of many primary commodities tend to decline in relation to those of manufactures have converted a number of African leaders and the UN Economic

[11] Lyn K. Mytelka, 'The salience of gains in Third World integrative systems', *World Politics*, 25 (1973), p. 240.

Commission for Africa (ECA) to economic integration as the road to development. But development-oriented market integration, based as it is on the goal of creating a larger market for import-substituting growth, is inherently out of touch with the need to establish producers who are competitive in international markets. Regional trade liberalization is not a substitute for an outward-looking development strategy, and, as Douglas Rimmer has reminded us in reaction to Africa's regional integration, a better economic future for Africa will require that trade opportunities be exploited worldwide rather than within any particular geographical area.[12] The current emphasis on market integration as a means to enable development towards competitive entry into the world market – observed, for example, in Latin America where MERCOSUR has this as its ultimate goal – is largely absent or down-played in Africa. Nevertheless, the economic restructuring programmes adopted in many African countries have international competitiveness as their long-term objective, which means that national development strategies are out of kilter with the philosophy of the integration arrangements within which these countries find themselves.

However, sight should not be lost of the fact that integration is often prompted by political factors. The European Union, after all, originally started through concern for security in the face of the Cold War threat. In Africa, also, political considerations have motivated economic integration. African unity, the formation of regional political structures in a process of post-colonial consolidation, and the creation of regional blocs for effective use in international political fora, underlie much of the thinking of the proponents of integration in Africa. Okolo is very explicit in this regard when he describes the political goal of ECOWAS as 'the need to have an institutionalized instrument to maximize the bargaining position of the smaller and weaker West African states vis-a-vis the bigger and more powerful industrialized nations of the world and, particularly, to extricate the region's economy from western neocolonial control'.[13] Elsewhere, explicit security factors have laid the foundations for regional cooperation. The Southern African Development Coordination Conference (SADCC) is an example of an organization that developed largely on the basis of security considerations, namely, as noted below, the desire to become less dependent on apartheid South Africa in a period of strong regional economic and military confrontation. In North Africa, the establishment of the Arab Maghreb Union (AMU) in 1989 was to a large extent driven by the politico-economic consideration of creating a body which could bargain collectively with the European Community (as it was then called) with which 70 per cent of the AMU countries' trade takes place. Furthermore, the founding of AMU followed the major rapprochement in 1988 between Algeria and Morocco who both saw the new arrangement as a framework within which the long dispute over the Western Sahara could be resolved. These considerations prompted Robert Mortimer to refer to AMU as 'more a diplomatic than an economic construct'.[14]

*Integration arrangements*

Current African integration arrangements can be divided into two broad groups: those that fit into the Lagos Plan of Action adopted in April 1980, and those that were either

---

[12] Douglas Rimmer, 'Africa's economic future', *African Affairs*, 88 (1989), p. 182.

[13] Julius Emeka Okolo, 'The development and structure of ECOWAS', in J.E. Okolo & Stephen Wright (eds), *West African Regional Cooperation and Development* (Westview Press, Boulder, CO, 1990), p. 25.

[14] Robert Mortimer, 'Regionalism and geopolitics in the Maghreb', *Middle East Report*, September–October 1993, p. 18.

in existence or came about outside the Lagos Plan. The more prominent integration schemes are discussed briefly in this section.

The Lagos Plan was launched as a special initiative of the Heads of States and Governments of the OAU and actively promoted by the ECA. It created a unifying framework for the creation of, in the words of Omotunde Johnson, 'regional unions [as] a centrepiece in the grand strategy for Africa in the pursuit of development'.[15] The ECA has sponsored three regional arrangements aimed at the creation of separate but convergent and over-arching integration arrangements in three sub-Saharan sub-regions: West Africa, East and Southern Africa, and Central Africa. West Africa would be served by the Economic Community of West African States (ECOWAS), which pre-dates the Lagos Plan, having been established in 1975 mainly through the initiative of Nigeria in an effort to counter French influence in the region and to enhance its own. In 1981, the Preferential Trade Area (PTA) was established, coming into operation in 1984, to cover East and Southern Africa. In 1993 a new treaty established the Common Market for Eastern and Southern Africa (COMESA) which replaced the PTA. For Central Africa the treaty of the Economic Community of Central African States (ECCAS) was approved in 1983 but its operation is still under negotiation. Together with the AMU in North Africa, these arrangements have been expected to bring about an all-Africa common market by the year 2025.

The Lagos Plan of Action was followed up in 1991 by the Abuja Treaty, re-affirming the commitment of the OAU's Heads of State to an integrated African economy.

In the second group of integration arrangements there are two important ones which are associated with the CFA zone (discussed below): within the ambit of ECOWAS, the West African Economic and Monetary Union (the French acronym is UEMOA) whose members – Benin, Burkino Faso, Côte d'Ivoire, Mali, Niger and Togo – share a common central bank (*Banque centrale des Etats de l'Afrique de l'ouest*), and in central Africa the Economic and Monetary Union of Central Africa (the French acronym being CEMAC) – Cameroon, Central African Republic, Congo, Gabon, Chad, and Equatorial Guinea – with its central bank, the *Banque centrale des Etats de l'Afrique centrale*. The UEMOA treaty was adopted in 1994 as part of a re-alignment of integration arrangements among francophone states and transformed the West African Monetary Union (French acronym UMOA) which had co-existed with a prominent West African francophone integration arrangement, the Economic Community of West Africa (best known by the French acronym CEAO). The latter – a revival of the former Customs Union of West African States (UDEAO) – was established in 1973 through French initiative to serve as a countervailing power to Nigeria's influence and dominance in West Africa. The establishment of CEAO at the time added an important element to a large number of cooperation and integration arrangements which francophone states in West Africa carried over into the post-colonial era, in contrast with former British colonies which mostly at or shortly after independence severed the regional links that existed in colonial times.[16] In francophone Central Africa the demise of CEAO was paralleled by the abolition of UDEAC subsequent to the establishment of CEMAC.

Within the geographic area of COMESA there are the Southern African Customs Union (SACU), with its associated monetary union (the CMA, discussed below), and the Southern African Development Community (SADC). SACU – with South Africa, Botswana, Lesotho, Namibia, and Swaziland as members – is a well-established customs

---

[15] Johnson, 'Economic integration', p. 2.
[16] See Daniel Bach, 'Francophone regional organizations and ECOWAS', in Okolo & Wright, p. 53.

union that currently operates in terms of an agreement concluded in 1969, but as an operating union goes as far back as 1910. SADC started out as the Southern African Development Coordination Conference (SADCC), which was established as a nine-member organization (Angola, Botswana, Lesotho, Malawi, Mozambique, Swaziland, Tanzania, Zambia, and Zimbabwe) in 1980. The principal aim of SADCC was to reduce the dependence of the region on the outside world, especially South Africa, and to promote and coordinate regional cooperation in development projects. The 1990s introduced the imminent demise of apartheid in South Africa and with this the very existence of SADCC came into question. In August 1992 the Treaty of Windhoek was accepted and SADC was launched.[17] Whereas SADCC was structured on the basis of regional cooperation with a concentration on infrastructural development, SADC, like COMESA, has an integration agenda, albeit more of an enabling nature without a fixed framework of target dates towards the establishment of a common market. South Africa became the eleventh member of SADC in November 1994, Namibia having joined at independence in 1990.

As noted earlier, monetary integration becomes part of the process of trade integration when participating countries move towards the common market model (which has a free flow of capital between countries) and finally an economic union when fiscal and monetary harmonization takes place. In Africa, monetary and trade integration have been moving on two tracks in prominent cases. The most eminent example is the francophone African monetary union, known as the CFA (*Communauté financière africaine*) zone. The members of this union, with the exception of ex-Spanish Equatorial Guinea, share a common colonial history and bond with France as their former colonial power and owe the monetary union to this link. The thirteen members of the CFA zone do not as a group belong to an over-arching trade integration arrangement but are linked into different arrangements. For example, the seven countries of the CFA zone that form the UEMOA do not share their membership of ECOWAS with the other six members of the CFA zone.

In Southern Africa the four-member Common Monetary Area (CMA) is closely paralleled by the five-member SACU, with the CMA consisting of the SACU members with the exception of Botswana. The South African rand is the anchor currency of the CMA in a way which effectively integrates the capital and money markets of Lesotho, Namibia and Swaziland into the South African financial system. An interesting feature of the CMA is that it operates in terms of the Multilateral Monetary Agreement (MMA) of 1992, supported by bilateral agreements between South Africa and its partners, designed to meet the requirements of each of the partners within the broader ambit of the MMA. The Botswana pula is convertible, which means that SACU operates with convertible currencies and therefore at a level of integration which does not exist elsewhere in southern Africa.

From the foregoing it is clear that African integration arrangements are characterized by overlapping membership. In Southern Africa, for example, Lesotho and Swaziland are members of SACU, CMA, SADC, and COMESA. In West Africa, Benin, Burkina Faso, Côte d'Ivoire, Mali, Niger, Senegal and Togo are members of UEMOA and of ECOWAS. Mauritania is a member of both ECOWAS and AMU. Overlapping membership as such should not be considered a problem. However, it will be seen below that complications and inconsistencies arise when countries belong to different integration arrangements with similar agendas and objectives.

---

[17] The pronounciation of the acronym as 'Sadec' was maintained.

## Intra-Regional Trade

By its very nature, progress in regional integration will be reflected in increases in the share of intra-regional trade in total foreign trade.[18] From a continental perspective Africa's trade, as is well-known, has never been characterized by a high degree of recorded intra-regional trade. The continent's intra-regional trade as a share of total foreign trade has always been low (6 per cent in 1990) compared with Western Europe (72 per cent), Eastern Europe (46 per cent), Asia (48 per cent) and North America (31 per cent). If an interpretation of long-term data is to be trusted, it might also be noted that Africa is the only region which has experienced a consistent decline in this share, from 10 per cent in 1928, to 6 per cent in 1979 and 1990.[19]

It follows as a matter of composition that the continental situation will also be reflected in Africa's regional arrangements. These arrangements have the lowest levels of recorded intra-regional trade of all integration exercises, with shares of intra-regional exports typically below 5 per cent.[20] The exception was CEAO, the only arrangement with a share of intra-regional trade above 10 per cent (11.3 per cent in 1990).[21] The CEAO was noted for its currency convertibility, capital mobility and, unlike the UDEAC that also shared this feature but found itself on the opposite side of the spectrum of success, for its significant labour mobility, a pragmatic product-by-product approach to intra-regional trade liberalization, and a compensation system that addressed the issue of the distribution of integration gains. In general, however, African arrangements have shared the experience of most arrangements in the developing world of not having a consistent and large increase in the share of intra-regional trade. But these low shares hide the fact that for some of the participating countries intra-regional trade is significant. This applies especially in the case of land-locked states. Nevertheless, the conclusion remains valid that regional integration exercises have not proved successful in achieving their basic aim, namely an increase in intra-regional trade.

The reasons for this lack of performance can be discussed at length but noting the probable causes in broad outline will suffice for our purposes.[22] The first is rather obvious. The conclusion of integration agreements is only the first step; these agreements have to be implemented and in Africa the degree of implementation of trade liberalization within the regions has generally been low. Two prominent African arrangements, ECOWAS and UDEAC, have been noted for their 'almost complete non-implementation of intra-area liberalization'.[23] The ECOWAS protocol on labour mobility signed in

---

[18] It must be emphasized that the growth in intra-regional trade does not necessarily reflect an increase in the economic welfare of the societies concerned. An increase in trade among countries participating in a regional arrangement with a common external tariff may lead to higher prices if goods previously imported from low-cost producers outside the common market are replaced with the goods of high-cost, protected sources located within the customs union. This is known as trade diversion, which contrasts with welfare-enhancing trade creation. The latter occurs when the goods of high-cost domestic producers are replaced with lower-cost goods from a producer from within the union who, prior to union, had been protected by the domestic tariff.

[19] Anderson & Blackhurst, *Regional Integration*, p. 29.

[20] De la Torre & Kelly, *Regional Trade Arrangements*, p. 31.

[21] ibid., p. 30.

[22] A more extensive discussion of constraints on intra-regional trade in Africa may be found in the following sources: World Bank, *Intra-Regional Trade in Sub-Saharan Africa*, Report No. 7685-AFR (document for internal use), pp. 56–73; for a Southern African perspective, Gavin Maasdorp & Alan Whiteside, *Rethinking Economic Cooperation in Southern Africa: Trade and investment* (Konrad-Adenauer-Stiftung, Johannesburg, 1993), pp. 17–23; and for a West African perspective, Elliot Berg, 'Strategies for West African economic integration: Issues and approaches' mimeo, 1992, pp. 6–8.

[23] De la Torre & Kelly, *Regional Trade Arrangements*, p. 32.

1979 has still not been implemented. In COMESA, the commendable Clearing House, established in 1984 to facilitate the settlement of claims arising from transactions among member countries, has not had the positive impact on intra-regional trade hoped for. Increased trade can take place only in an environment of trade liberalization, but intra-COMESA trade does not receive preferential treatment in the allocation of import licences, in spite of a PTA recommendation to this effect in 1991.

Non-implementation of course begs the question of why this is so. It is not easy to provide a succinct answer to this question since the problem has many facets, many of them inter-related. A fair approximation would be to emphasize the lack of political ability and will to carry through integration programmes in the face of the loss of sovereignty which this causes and uncertainty over the distribution of the gains and losses of integration.

Firstly, it must be borne in mind that regional integration, particularly the ambitious programmes adopted in Africa, inevitably implies a willingness to sacrifice some control over economic policies that directly affect the populations of the participating countries. Installing a common external tariff and regional free trade, coordinating macro-economic policies (monetary, fiscal and exchange-rate policies), harmonizing industrial development policies (which might even ambitiously include a regional plan for the location of industry), and promoting intra-regional labour and capital mobility are all required to give effect to the intended programmes. But these entail a sacrifice of national sovereignty and, presumably, the creation of a supra-national regional authority with real powers. Many political leaders find it difficult to accept this, especially in the African setting where political and government institutions still lack maturity and skill, political life is strongly influenced by personalities and ethnic diversity, and the fragile economic environment encourages a short-term horizon in policy formulation. Also, it can be hypothesized that a sacrifice of sovereignty requires, somewhat paradoxically, a strong state and confident national governance. It is difficult to envisage the successful integration of weak states; the creation of integration arrangements cannot serve as a substitute for poor or weak national governance. Finally, in respect of political will, it is also difficult to integrate and sacrifice sovereignty if the member states are divided on major political and ideological issues.

Many African integration arrangements do not meet these requirements. In West Africa, for example, integration is hampered by the existence of weak states. In the case of the AMU the members have been distracted in their efforts to construct an economic union by issues such as the problem of Western Sahara, the Islamist movement in Algeria and the breakdown of the rapprochement between Algeria and Morocco – the two largest economies in the AMU.[24] As might be expected, African integration arrangements are not characterized by strong supra-national bodies. Integration institutions are virtually all inter-governmental. This allows governments the opportunity to avoid a loss of sovereignty through unilateral decisions on the application of regional agreements.

Secondly, political will is affected by expectations of gains and losses from integration and regional interests tend to be accorded priority if they promote national interests. Countries will participate actively in regional integration exercises if they believe that they will benefit. Moreover, a belief exists that integration should lead to balanced growth within the region. However, if left to the operation of the market, cumulative forces driven by economies of scale will, within a single market, cause development and growth to gravitate towards the more developed participating countries, thus causing

[24] Mortimer, 'Regionalism and geopolitics', p. 16.

inequality in the distribution of the costs and benefits of integration. These forces, differences in perceptions of benefits and in the time scale within which the benefits are expected to materialize, and political expediency in the face of pressure group activity, explain why the unequal distribution of costs and benefits is claimed to be the most important reason for the major conflicts experienced by developing countries participating in integration schemes.[25]

Africa has been no exception in this regard. For ECOWAS the polarization impact on the dominant economy, Nigeria, is an important explanation of the lack of progress, while similar conditions contributed to the break-up of one of Africa's potentially most promising integration arrangements, the East African Community. At the other end of the spectrum, as noted earlier, the CEAO seems to have done better than most regional schemes because two more prosperous members, Côte d'Ivoire and Senegal, have been willing to shoulder a larger compensating burden. SACU, in turn, can credit its longevity as a customs union of unequal partners to compensatory payments which South Africa makes to the smaller members of the union.

But even a fair degree of political commitment will not succeed in promoting intra-regional trade if the underlying economic structures of participating countries are not conducive to this. The general pattern for the member countries of African integration schemes is to have open economies (foreign trade as a percentage of GDP is high) with a large exposure to trade in primary commodity exports and manufactured imports with industrialized countries, and little trade among themselves. Diversity in size and level of economic development is a characteristic of most arrangements and industrial sectors exist that do not compete with one another. The economies are not complementary but mostly supplementary with many producing the same range of primary commodities, leaving little room for trade among themselves or for the static benefit of trade creation which might be found when countries with significant and competitive industrial sectors integrate their markets. Most of these economies also lack the capacity to develop complementary industrial sectors; consequently, a sound base for growth in intra-regional trade through inter-industry trade does not exist. All in all, these characteristics limit the scope for potential gains through intra-regional trade.

## Success Stories?

Amid the general perception of a lack of progress with regional integration there are two cases which might indicate that integration can have some measure of success in Africa.

The first is the franc zone which, certainly until the early 1980s, 'appeared like [an island] of economic rationality and modest development in a continent of egregious economic failure and mismanagement'.[26] It will be argued below that this bright light may be dimming. The second hopeful situation is found in Southern Africa where the existence of an established customs union in the form of SACU, the establishment of

---

[25] See, for example, Bela Balassa & Ard Stoutjesdijk, 'Economic integration among developing countries', *Journal of Common Market Studies*, 14 (1975), p. 43; Rafael Vargas-Hidalgo, 'The crisis of the Andean Pact: Lessons for integration among developing countries', *Journal of Common Market Studies*, 17 (1979), p. 213; and Constantine Vaitsos, 'Crisis in regional economic cooperation (integration) among developing countries: a survey', *World Development*, 6 (1978), pp. 719–48.

[26] Nicolas van de Walle, 'The decline of the franc zone: monetary politics in francophone Africa', *African Affairs*, 90 (1991), p. 383.

SADC, the democratic transition in South Africa and its even closer integration into the economy of the region hold out a potential for progress with possible repercussions beyond the region.

### The CFA zone

The death on 7 December 1993 of Félix Houphouët-Boigny, president of Côte d'Ivoire, and the devaluation of the CFA franc in January 1994 reverberated throughout the whole of francophone Africa. It would be mischievous to link the devaluation of the CFA franc to the death of Houphouët-Boigny, the doyen of francophone Africa and the arch-advocate of the maintenance of the reigning fixed exchange rates between the CFA and French francs. But both events, future developments might show, were of fundamental importance for the CFA zone and its continued existence.

The CFA zone, although not a formal scheme in trade integration, is a high-profile integration arrangement. It is in the first place a monetary union, characterized by a fixed exchange rate between the CFA franc and the French franc. Pegging to a single currency is not unusual in the developing world. It is, for example, also found in the CMA where the currencies of Lesotho, Swaziland and Namibia are effectively pegged to, and convertible at par into, South African rand, and further afield in Latin America where a notable feature of recent economic reform in Argentina has been the pegging of the Argentine peso to the US dollar at parity. However, the major difference is that whereas the United States does not guarantee the convertibility of the peso, the convertibility of the CFA franc is guaranteed by France.

The CFA zone has always been more than a mere monetary union. In the non-economic sphere the special influence of France in the political and social affairs of the francophone countries is important. In the economic field the special relationship of France with the members of the CFA zone is epitomized by the French support which enabled the members of the zone to postpone the policy adjustments which other African countries had to undertake at an earlier stage.

The French connection and the way in which the CFA zone operated have long been regarded as setting the zone members apart from other African countries as far as higher economic growth and stability are concerned. Simultaneously they served as evidence of the advantages to be had from monetary integration. However, empirical research does not support these suppositions fully. During 1975–85 average annual GDP growth of 4.6 per cent in the CFA countries was found to be significantly higher than the 1.4 per cent of non-CFA African economies.[27] But external shocks and inadequate policy adjustments, accentuated by the accumulated effect of the postponement of adjustment of the CFA economies to live within their means, led to mounting difficulties after 1985. The zone's terms of trade deteriorated by about 50 per cent because of the drop in the market prices of major exports. The nominal appreciation of the French franc against the currencies of the zone's major trading partners further weakened the international competitive position of the zone countries. The end result was a deterioration of average annual GDP growth of the CFA zone to 0.1 per cent during 1986–93. This was considerably lower than the growth of 2.5 per cent in other African economies. Budget and current account deficits were also much larger in the CFA zone than elsewhere. On the positive side, however, inflation has consistently remained lower in the CFA

---

[27] These and other figures in this paragraph are derived from Jean A.P. Clement, 'Striving for stability: CFA franc realignment', *Finance & Development*, 31 (1994), p. 12.

zone, but particularly so during 1986-93 when average zone inflation was 1.1 per cent compared with 22 per cent in the non-CFA countries.

In a comprehensive econometric analysis of economic growth and its causes during the period 1970–89 Assane and Pourgerami compared the economic performance of the CFA zone with that of other non-zone sub-Saharan African countries. They were 'unable to find evidence to support the growth-enhancing effects of . . . CFA membership, as it has been suggested by previous studies'.[28] Again, the up-side of the story is that the analysis found benefits of zone membership on the inflation front. The sacrifice of monetary independence therefore appears to produce the advantage of price stability, while it does not necessarily follow that economic growth will benefit.

Two over-riding factors will have an important bearing on the future performance and operation of the CFA zone. The first is the major measures adopted in January 1994, including a 50 per cent devaluation of the CFA franc (the Comorian franc was devalued by 33 per cent). The devaluation was preceded by the abolition on 2 August 1993 – quietly in the middle of a European currency crisis – of the convertibility of CFA banknotes outside the CFA zone. A month later this was followed by the ending of the convertibility between the notes of the two CFA central banks. Although convertibility through banks has not been affected, the ending of banknote convertibility contradicted the very essence of the franc zone concept and represented a clear pointer that the devaluation was in the offing.

The devaluation was accompanied by the adoption of a comprehensive adjustment programme, including drastic fiscal, wage, monetary, and structural measures which varied according to the circumstances of the individual countries. Of particular importance for integration in Africa was the resolution of the CFA countries to strengthen the foundations of their economic integration. To give effect to this the members of the West African Monetary Union adopted a treaty to establish the West African Economic and Monetary Union referred to earlier.

By and large the measures adopted represented a belated reaction to developments which had earlier forced other African countries to adjust. The devaluation in particular was seen by many as a potentially fatal blow to the survival of the CFA zone. Essentially it represented a victory for the technocrats in Paris; henceforth the French Treasury would no longer finance African budget deficits. This represented a major defeat for the view that economic considerations were not always of over-riding importance in evaluating the CFA zone and for the decision on whether to devalue or not. Houphouët-Boigny, for example, is reported to have been implacably opposed to devaluation because he feared the psychological and political consequences of the parity change. He was concerned about the engagement of France in the zone and in this respect the CFA zone with its fixities was viewed as one of the manifestations of France's commitment to Africa.[29]

More than a year has gone by since the devaluation. While the jury is still out on its outcome, the preliminary indications provide mixed signals. The pessimists about the political outcome have been proved wrong; in spite of life in the towns having become more expensive, no government has fallen. In the economic sphere good rains and an improvement in world commodity prices have helped to improve economic growth modestly. The expectations are that growth will improve further during 1995, but in

---

[28] Djeto Assane & Abbas Pourgerami, 'Monetary co-operation and economic growth in Africa: Comparative evidence from the CFA zone countries', *Journal of Development Studies*, 30 (1994), p. 437.
[29] See Kaye Whiteman, 'France and Africa: the end of an era', *Africa Report*, March–April 1994, p. 14.

this respect the optimism is much greater for the western than for the central sub-region.[30] Most governments succeeded in containing wage pressure, thus preventing a strong upsurge in inflation. The liquidity of the banking system has increased, mainly because of the return of flight capital. Tourism is growing, and the producers of soft commodities, also boosted by increases in international prices, have benefitted. However, outside tourism there is little interest in service industries, while manufacturing remains in the doldrums. Domestic and foreign investment in manufacturing and hence in the diversification of the francophone economies remain absent.

The special relationship with France remains the unique feature, but whether this can transform the CFA zone into something substantively different from other African countries remains to be seen. Even more crucial is continued French participation. Should France withdraw – which appears quite possible – the decline of the CFA zone will be inevitable. Bearing in mind that '[T]he zone was created not because of inter-African relations but because of the relations between a non-African leader (France) and a zone which embodied social relations and inequalities, both internal and external',[31] the withdrawal of the 'non-African leader' would bring the zone to an end, at least in its present form. After all, a zone essentially 'conceived in a colonial situation and aimed at avoiding serious disruption in the post-colonial development of existing structures'[32] represents an element of incongruity in the integration scene more than three decades into the post-colonial era. France, it should be noted, has enabled an inherently unsustainable integration arrangement to survive, one which puts the cart before the horse in having monetary integration without trade integration.

Finally, a complication that will increasingly feature in the development of the CFA zone and other integration schemes in Africa is the overlapping membership of organizations. In the case of the zone, relations between ECOWAS and its CFA members are of particular importance since there is uncertainty as to the implications of some of the Lagos Plan proposals for the other arrangements operating within the ambit of the over-arching institutions of the Lagos Plan framework. Of particular importance is the challenge which the UEMOA poses for ECOWAS, a challenge which cannot be divorced from the cohesive nature of UEMOA and its origin (CEAO) as an organization to counter the dominant position of Nigeria within ECOWAS.[33] Furthermore, the co-existence of an area with advanced currency convertibilty on the one hand and cases of severe inconvertibility on the other, will make it very difficult to create a common market.

## Southern Africa

Problems posed by overlapping membership also exist in southern Africa with its four integration arrangements: COMESA – a Lagos Plan initiative – and SADC, SACU and CMA. The crucial development here is prospective changes in the accommodation in the region of Africa's industrially most advanced economy and a global trading nation of some note. In the Southern Africa region, South Africa's manufacturing sector, which is nearly seven times larger than that of Nigeria (in terms of value added), produces five

[30] Jean-François Bayart, 'Réflexions sur la politique africaine de la France', *Politique africaine*, 58 (1995), p. 42.

[31] Jean Coussy, 'The franc zone: Original logic, subsequent evolution and present crisis', in Anthony Kirk-Greene & Daniel Bach (eds), *State and Society in Francophone Africa since Independence* (Macmillan, Basingstoke, 1995), p. 176.

[32] ibid., p. 166.

[33] Daniel C. Bach, 'The politics of west African economic co-operation: CEAO and ECOWAS', *The Journal of Modern African Studies*, 21 (1983), p. 621.

times more than the combined total of the other SADC members. In 1988 South Africa exported $5,583 million worth of manufactured goods. This was almost twice the value of manufactures exported by the rest of sub-Saharan Africa.[34]

South Africa's most intensive involvement in the region remains its membership of SACU and its particular position as the dominant economy within it. This customs union, noted for its longevity in a world in which successful integration arrangements are scarce, in many respects represents a legacy of Southern Africa's colonial past and has been regarded by some observers as an instrument used by apartheid South Africa to maintain its hegemonic position in the region and the dependency of the smaller members. However, it is difficult to deny that SACU has worked and that the member states would wish it to continue. Although all members have expressed strong views on the perceived shortcomings of the Customs Union Agreement and the way in which it operates, it is clear that the major thrust of the current renegotiation of the Agreement is to maintain and improve SACU.

SACU's longevity can be explained with reference to the problems experienced with regional integration in the developing world. The compensatory payments made to Botswana, Lesotho, Namibia and Swaziland (BLNS) have already been referred to. They compensate BLNS for the disadvantages of being in a customs union with a much larger country, including inequality in the distribution of costs and benefits. The system is based on the distribution of customs and excise revenue through a formula which leaves South Africa with what remains in the revenue pool after enhanced allocations have been made to the BLNS countries. A stabilization factor guarantees the BLNS countries a revenue rate of between a minimum of 17 and a maximum of 23 per cent. For BLNS the advantages of receiving these payments as recurrent revenue are clear and are preferred to the vagaries of assistance and funding from a special regional development fund, a mechanism used by other integration arrangements such as ECOWAS.

Another reason for SACU's longevity is that the arrangement was originally established in 1910 as an effective customs union, a system of free trade behind a common external tariff. That the tariff has always been determined by South Africa under policies designed to suit its own development objectives has had important implications for the industrial development of the smaller states and is bound to be one of the main issues in the current round of negotiations. However, if the situation of a received common external tariff, with certain disadvantages compensated for through revenue transfers, is compared with the complex procedures which ECOWAS will have to go through eventually to reach such a situation,[35] the constraints and pitfalls of the latter route and the benefits of a received common external tariff become clear.

But perhaps the most important reason for SACU's longevity may be found in the willingness of the smaller member countries to sacrifice sovereignty in monetary and fiscal policy to South Africa, primarily in exchange for the compensatory fiscal transfers discussed above. Relegating the affairs of SACU to South Africa effectively served as a substitute for the supra-national body which would have been required to act in the common interests of the customs union. This characteristic of SACU is frequently described as a lack of democracy in its operations, a perceived problem which is to be addressed in the current renegotiation of the Customs Union Agreement. Ironically, the democratization of SACU could, in the absence of consensus among the member states

---

[34] African Development Bank, *Economic Integration in Southern Africa* (Abidjan, 1993), p. 249.

[35] For an account of the ECOWAS position see Okolo, 'Development and structure of ECOWAS', pp. 32–5.

on development issues and the establishment of a strong and effective supra-national body, contribute to the regression of SACU.

Different views exist on the impact which the new South Africa could have in the region. One prospect is that it could serve as an engine of regional growth that could pull the region to higher levels of growth and development through trade, investment and development assistance. Another view is that South Africa's closer integration into the region will be accompanied by strong polarization effects, with industries in the smaller economies unable to survive or prosper in the face of South African competition.

A scenario which places an emphasis on a locomotive role for South Africa is somewhat unrealistic. Since the mid-1970s the South African economy has experienced a consistent decline in growth from 5.1 per cent per year during 1965–70 to 1.6 per cent during 1985–90, thus leading to negative growth in per capita income during the 1980s. This declining growth performance has been coupled with a sharp decline in job creation. During the 1960s more than 80 per cent of the annual growth in the labour force found employment in the modern sector of the economy; this ratio fell sharply to 26 per cent during 1980–85 and to 14.6 per cent during the subsequent five years. Since mid-1994 clear signs of an up-swing in the economy have appeared and current forecasts indicate 3 per cent growth for 1995. But it is too early to judge whether this represents a turn-around in the long-term growth trend of the South African economy, or merely a cyclical up-swing around a downward trend line.

However, the fact remains that the South African economy is powerful by African standards, but it has been ailing and it is difficult to see it in the position of regional growth engine. To this must be added the large welfare gap which exists between the white population and the newly enfranchized black population. The bridging of this gap is the first priority of the Government of National Unity. In view of the tight fiscal position, coupled with the government's declared commitment to fiscal discipline, expectations are that domestic poverty will come before regional needs in the allocation of scarce resources.[36]

Nevertheless, South Africa will exert a strong influence as a regional economic power, even if the region is not given priority. South Africa has close links with the region through trade, infrastructure, and capital and labour flows. These and the size of the economy would, in a normalized political situation, cause even moderate growth in South Africa to have a substantial impact on the neighbouring countries. For example, if moderate growth could be accompanied by a 50 per cent increase in South African imports from Zimbabwe, the latter's commensurate export growth would, in terms of the 1990 trade figures, equal 4 per cent of its GDP. It might also be expected that the large and growing inflow of migrants who see South Africa as a haven of wealth, coupled with the political sensitivity of a new democratic government to reacting strongly to illegal migration, will prompt the government to emphasize regional development to contain at source the migration to South Africa. This, however, could at best have an influence only in the long run.

South Africa's competitive position and trade situation within the region are characterized by a mercantilist pattern of one-way trade which cannot form the basis for region-wide economic growth and development. With the exception of Zimbabwe, with which South Africa has significant two-way trade, trade between South Africa and

---

[36] The new government, in the reported words of Nelson Mandela, 'entertain[s] no illusion of becoming the regional benefactor because such capacity we do not possess.' 'Presidents set common market goal', *Business Day*, 10 June 1994.

the rest of the region is overwhelmingly in South Africa's favour. In 1992, South Africa exported goods to SADCC to the value of $6,090 million while importing to the value of only $899 million, 60 per cent of which came from SACU members and 29 per cent from Zimbabwe. The ratios between South African exports and imports, all in South Africa's favour, are 8.3 for SACU members, 6.8 for SADC as a whole and 2 for Zimbabwe.

These one-sided trade flows are explained by the comparative size and diversified nature of the South African economy. While tariff and non-tariff barriers to trade are a constraint on access to the South African market, the main problem is the capacity to produce goods which can be exported to the South African market. Enhancing market access can be an important factor in creating more export opportunities for a country like Zimbabwe, which has industries such as clothing, textiles and footwear that can compete with those in South Africa. But in most countries in the region the over-riding problem is the absence of industries that can produce goods for the South African market. This problem is associated with the absence of a dynamic private sector and entrepreneurial class, which is the price to be paid in Africa for the emphasis on parastatal development, the deprivation of the private sector, and resentment of big business, which usually – since big business is frequently foreign-owned – translates into resentment of foreign firms. Unfortunately, the important role of a dynamic and market-driven private sector in the creation of a capacity to produce tradeable goods competitively is not always sufficiently recognized. In a recent African Development Bank study on regional integration in southern Africa the important chapter on the manufacturing sector revealed a strong preference for dirigism in an otherwise market-friendly report.[37]

However, organized business could itself play an important role in supporting regional development. The Eastern and Southern African Business Organization (ESABO), established in August 1994 to replace the failed PTA- and SADC-affiliated business organizations, intends to represent business on matters of regional cooperation within the area of the PTA and promote trade and cross-border investment for the direct benefit of its members. Since the origin of many barriers to trade can be traced to vested domestic interests, often located in private business interests, an active regional body within which business can liaise should be a helpful instrument in breaking down trade barriers.

In addition to addressing tariff and non-tariff barriers to growth in intra-regional trade, the situation in Southern Africa illustrates the need for a sharp focus on appropriate economic development strategies in general, an issue which, as will be argued below, should be addressed within the wider context of regional economic cooperation. In Southern Africa growth in two-way trade will require at least two developments. The first is the acceptance of a broader view of the range of products that should be traded to include not only manufactured goods, but also agricultural produce, minerals, and those products which are usually defined as non-tradeables, namely, electricity, water, and financial and commercial services (tourism included). This change in emphasis will increase the scope for mutually beneficial trade. An example of what can be achieved in this regard is the Lesotho Highlands Water Project which will effectively bring about the importation of water to supplement the water supply of South Africa's industrial heart (the Pretoria/Witwatersrand/Vereeniging area – Gauteng province) while substituting hydro-electric power generated in Lesotho for power currently being imported from South Africa.

Clearly, the capacity to produce tradeable goods will also benefit from intra-regional

[37] African Development Bank, *Economic Integration in Southern Africa.*

factor flows. In Southern Africa, the whole region could benefit from South African investment. South Africa has a large and sophisticated private sector, including an ultra-modern financial services industry, whose active involvement through joint ventures and on its own could make a difference in the economies of the region. Bearing in mind that by African standards South Africa is a high-wage economy, South African labour-intensive industries would benefit from the lower wages that apply in the neighbouring economies. The pre-condition for such investment would be an investment-friendly and outward-looking policy environment in the host economies.

But complementary to intra-regional capital flows, the literature on integration also emphasizes the need for intra-regional labour mobility to effect balanced growth. Although wages in South Africa are comparatively high, these wage levels exist in a labour market characterized by growing structural unemployment, powerful trade unions, and a large gap between the average income of skilled, mainly white workers and unskilled and semi-skilled, mainly black workers. Given these circumstances, it is unlikely that South Africa will agree to a free flow of labour in the region. The experience of ECOWAS with the free movement of people, in particular the reaction during the early 1980s of the more developed Nigeria and Ghana to the large inflow of foreign work seekers (Ghana closed its border in September 1982 and Nigeria expelled illegal aliens in 1983 and 1985), will be remembered by the South African authorities.

The free movement of labour in Southern Africa, and presumably also large-scale cross-border investment by South African firms seeking the benefits of lower-cost labour, refer-red to in the preceding paragraph, are likely to be very sensitive issues in South Africa, requiring delicate handling and careful footwork in a country which is still in the process of economic and political transition.

## Overlapping Membership

Two issues discussed within the context of Southern African integration apply across the board in Africa: the appropriateness of formal market integration arrangements and the problem of overlapping membership of regional integration agreements.

As far as the latter is concerned, it is obvious that if overlapping membership occurs in arrangements with more or less the same objectives and expected development path, conflicting interests will develop and progress with integration will suffer. Should overlapping membership occur among arrangements at different levels of integration, problems need not arise. In this case tiers of integration suggest themselves with all the fashionable terms that go with it: multiple speed, variable geometry or concentric circles. In Southern Africa, this would mean that SACU, which in tandem with the CMA is an advanced integration exercise, could co-exist with SADC or COMESA. One commen-tator has suggested, for example, that integration could deepen within SACU to a com-mon market or even an economic union, at least between some of its members (that is, variable geometry within SACU), with SACU forming an association agreement with the remaining SADC countries or the southern countries of COMESA along the lines of the EU/EFTA agreement for the European Economic Area.[38] Variable tiers of integration can also provide for the expansion of existing arrangements. In a consultative document prepared for its annual meeting in January 1995, SADC proposed, together

---

[38] Gavin Maasdorp, 'Models of co-operation in Southern Africa', in Minnie Venter (ed.), *Prospects for Progress: Critical choices for Southern Africa* (Maskew Miller Longman, Cape Town, 1994), p. 26.

with free labour and capital mobility, the expansion of SACU by drawing in the other SADC countries to create a common market in the region. Widening SACU within the framework of the current SACU Agreement (which is being re-negotiated) is easier said than done. But the principle remains valid: variable geometry can also be used in expanding membership at different levels of integration.

It is difficult to envisage how SADC and COMESA, given their convergence to both sectoral cooperation and trade integration, can live and prosper with the overlapping membership of the Southern African countries. Restructuring seems inevitable if institutional rivalry between COMESA and SADC and malaise in integration are to be contained.

Variable geometry and the flexibility in institutional development which this allows are also relevant elsewhere in Africa. In West Africa they could form the basis for the co-existence of ECOWAS and UMOA. A guiding principle in this regard should be that organizations that have proved their value and have been operating efficiently should be built on in widening the scope for regional integration. SACU and the CMA are examples of such arrangements.

## Is Market Integration Appropriate?

The discussion thus far leads to a final question of whether the model of market integration is the most appropriate means to effect development and growth in a regional setting.

While recognizing current integration arrangements in Africa as a *fait accompli*, we should note that experience in Africa and elsewhere in the developing world reveals that market integration is not effective. By and large, diversifying industrial growth, the final goal of the development-oriented market integration model, has not materialized.

An important reason for this failure has already been discussed: the model demands unrealistic levels of political commitment and of technical and administrative expertise which are not available in developing regions.[39] Where the creation and strengthening of a national identity are strong, as in many African countries, governments are naturally loath to sacrifice national sovereignty. Furthermore, the asymmetry in the size and levels of development of the participating economies leads to polarized development; consequently, the distribution of the costs and benefits of integration becomes the focal point of the integration exercise.

Also, one must take cognizance of the fact that the underlying philosophy of development-oriented market integration runs counter to an approach which emphasizes the reduction and rationalization of protection. Sustainable growth and development will in the long run demand competitiveness in world markets – the rationale for the inclusion of trade regime reform in structural adjustment programmes. Policies aimed at the creation, eventually, of a protective common external tariff represent movement in the opposite direction.

Function-based cooperation – broadly defined as cooperation between independent countries or agencies on identified projects or schemes – could be a more appropriate means to address Africa's problems. This approach to regional affairs, which these days

[39] Tom Ostergaard, 'Classical models of regional integration: What relevance for Southern Africa?', in Bertil Odén (ed.), *Southern Africa after Apartheid: Regional integration and external resources* (Nordiska Afrikainstitutet, Uppsala, 1993), p. 35.

features prominently in the literature, could take the form of sectoral development (for example, project cooperation in sectors such as transport and communications, water and electricity) or thematic cooperation (for example, a regional programme on food security or cross-border investment). The advantages of this approach are its flexibility and pragmatism in circumventing the problems posed by nationalism and equity in the distribution of costs and benefits. It is also better suited to deal with the many fiscal, physical and technical barriers to trade that cannot be addressed by trade policy.

Since specific tasks are addressed, issues are depoliticized and thus present less of a challenge to existing power structures. In time a culture of regional cooperation is created, thus laying the foundation for market integration and the acceptance of the loss in sovereignty this will entail. Greater integration becomes a minimalist approach, in contrast to the present maximalist approach adopted in Africa. Incremental steps are taken that do not make unrealistic demands on the institutional, technical and political capacities of African states. Its targeted nature also serves as a practical means of including and thereby neutralizing the demands of domestic interest groups and is suited to the creation of the infrastructure and production capacity necessary for a successful entry into world markets.

No doubt critics of regional cooperation could point to the relative lack of success achieved by SADCC in this regard. This can be countered by arguing that SADCC has achieved some success, and also that the limited extent of the achievements can be ascribed to the way in which SADC(C) has been operating. Furthermore, with South Africa in the fold, more progress may be expected. Considering the number of successful exercises in functional cooperation between apartheid South Africa and its neighbours, notably in the field of transport and energy, it would require little imagination to envisage what could be possible in the post-apartheid era.

## Conclusion

Economic growth and development is a complex process in which a large number of causal factors play a complementary role in creating and distributing wealth and income. It is becoming increasingly clear that the quality of governance is a crucial determinant. One of the features of good governance is the use of appropriate economic policies. The central argument of this chapter is that the acceptance of over-ambitious integration schemes in Africa has not been good policy. The story told is not new, but the lack of originality does not make the message less relevant.

Africa needs rapid economic growth and development. Although the logic of regional integration as a means to foster growth and development is clear, the conditions for success do not exist. Consequently, integration arrangements by and large have not produced the desired outcome. A fundamental condition for success falls outside the realm of economics, namely, the existence of mature institutions within a strong state. Unless this condition is met, the political will and ability to sacrifice national sovereignty for the sake of the development of the region will not exist. Regionalism will only prosper if the constituent states are strong, confidently and well governed, and among themselves undivided on the major issues concerning development and economic and political systems. To the extent that these conditions are not met in large parts of Africa, it would seem in order to argue that political growth and development will have to precede economic growth through development-oriented integration.

Does this mean that economic integration should be ignored in the foreseeable future?

Certainly not. An appreciation of the importance attached to visions of African common markets means that *Realpolitik* alone would exclude such a possibility. However, the political and economic realities of Africa caution against ambitious integration arrangements. In reviewing the African experience and the process and impact of market integration it would seem that the more appropriate approach would rather be to focus on regional cooperation in a continuous process which has integration as its ultimate aim. This does not imply that the current arrangements, based on the model of market integration, should be abandoned. They could provide the basis for building a regional identity and a framework and enabling environment for economic and political cooperation while goals of integration and the creation of a common external tariff are shifted to a back-burner, the heat of which can be turned up when the circumstances for integration are more favourable.

But even if regional integration could in the end succeed as a formal exercise, sustainable growth will require competitiveness in world markets. In this respect the emphasis in the second wave of regionalism on an outward-looking approach cannot be ignored. In my view, the theory underlying the outward-looking approach to regional integration is somewhat vague, especially if one should venture beyond the incubator argument (discussed earlier) for creating common markets. However, to argue that growth in intra-regional trade is a prerequisite for, or could make an important contribution to, growth in extra-regional trade, would seem to place an even greater emphasis on the conditions for successful integration discussed in this chapter.

Finally, this chapter has addressed regional integration only within Africa. A feature of the new regionalism is the widening of integration to incorporate developed and developing countries. In the western hemisphere NAFTA and the Enterprise for the Americas Initiative are examples of this. In Africa, little has developed, outside Lomé, in this regard. However, the potential for AMU members to link into Europe exists, and in South Africa the possibilities of cooperation and eventually integration of the Indian Ocean rim countries are being disussed. For South Africa the latter could prove fruitful, with significant gains to be had from closer links with larger and competitive economies.

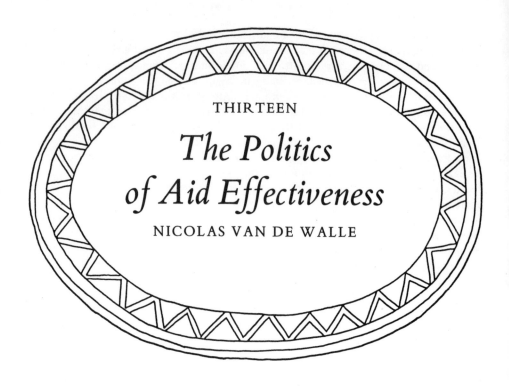

THIRTEEN

# The Politics
# of Aid Effectiveness

NICOLAS VAN DE WALLE

Aid to Africa is at a crossroads in 1995. The end of the Cold War and economic recession
have led Western donors to reconsider their past levels of support to developing countries
in general, and overall aid levels are on a downward path as a result. In much of the
Third World, the decline of public assistance has been more than compensated by significant increases in private capital inflows, and commercial relations with the West are
replacing the old aid relationships. With the exception of South Africa, however, private
capital has continued to avoid sub-Saharan Africa, leaving the continent ever more dependent on public aid flows. As the West reconsiders its relationship with Africa, aid – one
of the central pillars of that relationship – is undergoing a reappraisal, which is bound
to have significant implications for the continent.

It is widely recognized that the old geo-political rationales for aid undermined its
economic effectiveness. Aid was often granted to African governments for reasons that
had little to do with the quality of their developmental efforts. While the end of the
Cold War has lessened the perceived strategic justification for aid, it does provide an
opportunity to rationalize aid and make it more effective in developmental terms.
However, the recent geo-political changes have coincided with growing 'aid fatigue' in
the West. Several decades after the end of colonialism, aid has lost much of its lustre,
particularly in Africa south of the Sahara. As other regions of the Third World have
enjoyed successful economic growth, Western public opinion has grown more impatient

[1] I wish to acknowledge useful comments on an earlier draft by Stephen Ellis and Catherine Gwin, and the research
assistance of Liz Garland.

with Africa's economic shortcomings. The negative image of Africa in the media – of human misery, government corruption, and ethnic fanaticism – has encouraged a growing popular perception that Africans have only themselves to blame for their predicament and that, as a result, aid will not help.

Old academic criticisms about aid effectiveness have gained new currency to reinforce these popular ideas, with a growing number of studies doubting that foreign aid is an appropriate vehicle to promote economic development and poverty alleviation. As a result, the old political constituencies for aid to Africa are weakening and are increasingly unable to defend the budgetary allocations of the past, notably as aid previously earmarked for the region is re-allocated to the states of the old Eastern bloc.

At the same time that the West appears to be reconsidering its commitments in Africa, the continent is threatened with growing instability. Several states have already collapsed, ceding the way to the pretensions of rival warlords over devastated economies. Ethnic conflict, mismanagement and economic crisis threaten the foundations of other states. How is this growing instability related to the evolving nature of economic relations between Africa and the West? What role could any amount of aid play in preventing future tragedies such as the ones that unfolded in Somalia and Rwanda in 1993–4?

The time appears ripe for an assessment of aid in Africa. Given Africa's dismal economic record over the last twenty years, it is fairly clear that aid has not lived up to its early, perhaps naive, promise of promoting rapid economic development and poverty alleviation. This chapter asks what factors have hampered the effectiveness of aid, and what can be done to improve its economic impact in the future. In addition, however, it assesses the broader political and ideological impact of aid in Africa. It will argue that aid has been the primary instrument of the West's relationship with Africa, that simultaneously stabilized the continent but failed to encourage the emergence of strong states there.

Following OECD usage of the term, this chapter defines aid as 'official development assistance', or any form of Western government-financed grant to African nations, running the gamut from technical assistance projects to structural adjustment lending, programme assistance and food aid. In the brief space allotted, it necessarily paints with a broad brush, making only occasional distinctions between the effectiveness and impact of these different kinds of aid. The chapter is divided into three sections. The first section describes the evolution of aid flows to Africa and the reasons for their decline in the last couple of years after a long period of rapid increases. The second section assesses the impact of aid to the continent. Past studies have focused on the economic impact of aid, but I argue that a broader definition of impact is appropriate and suggest that aid has had a powerful non-economic impact in Africa, despite its economic deficiencies. A final section surveys different propositions to reform aid and puts forward some practical suggestions.

## A Crisis in Foreign Aid?

Economic aid to Africa from bilateral and multilateral sources underwent a remarkable growth during the 1970s and 1980s. Overall official development assistance (ODA) to the entire Third World grew steadily during this period, at over 4 per cent annually in real terms during the 1970s and 2.7 per cent during the 1980s.[2] As a result, ODA

[2] Virtually all the data in this section are based on the various annual reports of the OECD Development Assistance Committee, *Development Co-operation: Efforts and policies of the members of the Development Assistance Committee* (OECD, Paris).

233

Table 13.1 Net disbursements of ODA from all sources combined (current US$m.)

| | 1975 | 1980 | 1985 | 1986 | 1987 | 1988 | 1989 | 1990 | 1991 | 1992 | 1993 |
|---|---|---|---|---|---|---|---|---|---|---|---|
| North of Sahara[a] | 3088.1 | 2709.1 | 2880.5 | 2448 | 2665.6 | 2465.6 | 2477.5 | 7181 | 6986.3 | 5427.6 | 3713.3 |
| South of Sahara[b] | 3687.9 | 8076.6 | 9041.9 | 10910.9 | 12666.7 | 14444.9 | 15363.1 | 17891.2 | 17650 | 19120.7 | 17400.2 |
| Africa Total | 6824.4 | 10957.3 | 12311.6 | 13742.1 | 15786.1 | 17275.7 | 18380.4 | 25563.3 | 25168.5 | 25068 | 21522.3 |
| of which: | | | | | | | | | | | |
| % from DAC donors | 42.8 | 62.3 | 65.5 | 67.9 | 67.7 | 69.4 | 66.1 | 32.4 | 66.3 | 65.2 | 62.8 |
| % multilateral | 18 | 25.1 | 26.4 | 27.4 | 28.5 | 29.3 | 32.9 | 25.5 | 29.4 | 32.6 | 34.9 |
| Total All LDCs[c] | 19307.9 | 33780 | 32260.2 | 37813.9 | 41674.2 | 44959.2 | 46810.5 | 57995.9 | 61826.4 | 61429 | 56566 |
| New Independent States[c] | | | | | | | | | 1996.7 | 3213.9 | 3094.7 |
| Central and Eastern European Countries[d] | | | | | | | | 1727.8 | 4710.2 | 2986.4 | 2350.1 |
| Total NIS/CEEC | | | | | | | | 1727.8 | 6707 | 6200.3 | 5444.8 |
| Total ODA | 19307.9 | 33780 | 32260.2 | 37813.9 | 41674.2 | 44959.2 | 46810.5 | 59723.7 | 68533.4 | 67629.3 | 62134.2 |
| of which: | | | | | | | | | | | |
| % from DAC donors | 50.7 | 51.2 | 65.7 | 66.7 | 69.3 | 71.1 | 70.3 | 67 | 70.6 | 71.1 | 70.7 |
| % multilateral | 19.9 | 23.1 | 25.1 | 23.1 | 23.7 | 24.7 | 26.5 | 23.3 | 26 | 27.2 | 27.8 |
| deflators[e] | | 55.71 | 53.46 | 66.55 | 76.69 | 82.5 | 81.77 | 91.16 | 94.33 | 100 | 98.01 |
| % Total ODA to Africa | 35.3 | 32.4 | 38.2 | 36.3 | 37.9 | 38.4 | 39.3 | 42.8 | 36.7 | 37.1 | 34.6 |

Sources: OECD, Geographical Distribution of Financial Flows to Developing Countries (1978/81, 1983/86, 1988/91, 1989/92, 1989/93).

Notes:

a) North of Sahara includes Algeria, Egypt, Libya, Morocco, Tunisia, and unallocated.

b) South of Sahara includes Namibia, starting in 1985, and South African black communities, starting in 1993.

c) New Independent States include Bealarus, Moldova, Russia, Ukraine, and unallocated.

d) CEECs include Bulgaria, Czech Republic, Estonia, Hungary, Latvia, Lithuania, Poland, Romania, Slovak Republic, and unallocated.

e) Deflators taken from OECD DAC Report 1994, reflecting price and exchange-rate changes for all DAC countries.

went from 4.6 billion current US dollars in 1960 to $33.8 billion in 1980 and a peak of $61.8 billion in 1992 (see Table 13.1). In sub-Saharan Africa, ODA increased even faster, reaching $19.1 billion in 1992. As a result, the share of total ODA going to sub-Saharan Africa increased sharply, from 24 per cent in 1980 to 31 per cent in 1990. In that year North Africa received another 12 per cent, so that as a whole the continent received more than 4 out of every 10 dollars of overall ODA.

The growth in total ODA slowed down in 1990-92 to some 2 per cent, in part because of a steep decline in Organization of Petroleum-Exporting Countries (OPEC) and Soviet economic bloc (COMECON) assistance. Nonetheless, up to 1993, it seemed that ODA to the developing world might escape the recession in the West unscathed, despite the much remarked upon need to 'rethink' North-South relations following the end of the Cold War. That has changed in the last two years, however. The OECD estimated that total ODA declined in 1993 by some 7 per cent in nominal terms and is forecasting another decline in 1994. The decline in aid was particularly striking in the United States, its total ODA declining by some $2 billion to $9.7 billion, a 19 per cent reduction in real terms. American ODA now stood at some 0.15 per cent of GDP, the lowest level since 1945. But it should be said that aid declined in all the major donors with the exception of Japan, and that only three minor OECD donors actually increased their contribution in nominal terms (Luxembourg, Ireland and New Zealand).

Aid to Africa has followed this downward trend, albeit in the context of distinct sub-regional dynamics. Aid levels continued to increase in sub-Saharan Africa in 1992, before slightly declining in 1993. What may be a sharper long-term decline has so far been disguised by new donor commitments to Namibia and South Africa, up from no aid as recently as 1985 rising quickly to $166 million and $193 million respectively in 1993, as well as large relief efforts in war-torn countries like Somalia ($881 million) and Mozambique (an astounding $1.16 billion). In addition, the continued commitment to focus aid on the least developed states, many of which are in Africa, has so far protected the continent from sharper cuts.

On the other hand, sub-Saharan Africa has been excluded from the dramatic increase in aggregate private capital flows to the developing world, which has more than compensated for the decline in public sector financial flows. Private flows include direct investment, international bank lending and bond lending, as well as grants by non-governmental organizations (NGOs). These almost doubled in the early 1990s, reaching some $93.9 billion in 1993. With the exception of NGO grants, sub-Saharan Africa has not benefited from these private capital flows: indeed, net foreign direct investment to the region was actually negative in 1991–2.

In North Africa, the trend is somewhat different. Aid levels have been in sharp decline since they peaked in 1990, although they remain higher than during most of the 1980s. On the other hand, Maghreb states like Morocco or Egypt have managed to attract significant private capital and are less dependent on public flows.

Given these trends, it appears likely that past increases of ODA to Africa will not be sustained in the coming years, even if the continent is spared an actual decrease in nominal terms. Growing fiscal pressures brought on in part by the early 1990s recession in the OECD economies have pushed governments to squeeze aid budgets. In some countries, those levels may well return to their former growth path when the economy picks up. But there is a more profound crisis in aid that goes beyond the business cycle, and governments have begun to reassess the role of aid to the Third World in general. With the end of the Cold War, the standard geo-political justifications for aid no longer carry much weight in debates within countries like the United States or the United Kingdom.

For their part, Eastern bloc countries have terminated what were once significant aid efforts, under pressures brought on by their own transitions to market economies. Indeed, in a stunning reversal, by 1993 these former donors received just under 9 per cent of total ODA for their own development.

This attitudinal shift is particularly striking in the United States, in part because there has never been widespread support for aid among the American public. The Clinton Administration had already cut aid substantially and decided to close 21 overseas USAID missions, including 9 in Africa. The Republican victory at the polls in November 1994 presaged further cuts in the bilateral aid programme and the possibility of a sharp reduction in the American contribution to multilateral aid institutions such as the World Bank. Much of the public's opposition to aid appears to be bred of popular misinformation and ignorance. A recent poll revealed, for example, that a majority of Americans believed aid to be the biggest item in the federal budget, accounting for some 15 per cent of all outlays. In fact, of course, USAID spending accounted for some one-half of one per cent of the US budget in 1994.[3]

Popular disaffection with aid is not unique to the United States, although it is more pronounced there. With the possible exception of the Scandinavian countries, popular support for aid has begun to slip in all developed countries. A 1992 poll in Canada revealed a sharp drop in support, with 58 per cent of the respondents agreeing with the proposition, 'as a country, we spend too much time and money on the world's problems, and not enough on problems at home'.[4] In countries like France, Belgium and particularly the United Kingdom, the sense of obligation brought on by the colonial experience has receded, decreasing support for aid. Even in France, where political and cultural links with the ex-colonies in Africa had been the most assiduously maintained, the 1990s has witnessed the resurgence of *Cartieriste* opposition to aid, and perhaps the beginning of a long-term disengagement.

The end of the Cold War has also resulted in a reassessment by policy elites of the justification for aid as an instrument of foreign policy. The end of superpower competition in the Third World is widely viewed as attenuating the need to cultivate allies there with economic and military support. Moreover, as overall aid budgets shrink, sub-Saharan Africa is likely to suffer relative to other regions of the Third World, as both commercial and geo-political concerns will lead decision-makers to favour other regions. The growing emphasis on mercantile considerations is particularly unlikely to favour the small and largely stagnant economies of sub-Saharan Africa, relative to the more dynamic economies of Asia and Latin America.

In the United States, the new congressional Republican foreign policy leadership publicly targeted sub-Saharan Africa for aid cuts in early 1995 with the argument that there are no significant American security interests in the region.[5] Similarly, the January 1994 devaluation of the CFA franc may well have been a watershed event in French-African relations, reflecting a growing impatience on the part of a new generation of state technocrats with the performance of governments in the franc zone, and the

---

[3] See the Center for the Study of Policy Attitudes, 'Americans and foreign aid: A study of American public attitudes. A summary of findings', (School of Public Affairs, University of Maryland. 23 January 1995). In 1993, the per capita tax burden for ODA was about $40 for the United States, compared with more than $270 paid by citizens in some of the northern European states with the highest ODA/GNP ratios.

[4] Maureen O'Neil & Roy Culpeper, 'Development co-operation in Canada', in Adrian Hewitt (ed.), *Crisis or Transition in Foreign Aid?* (Overseas Development Institute, London, 1994), pp. 8–9.

[5] See 'Wrong about Africa', *The Washington Post*, 3 January 1995.

beginning of a re-orientation of French foreign policy towards other, more dynamic economies in the Third World.

It should be noted that North Africa and the Middle East have been viewed somewhat differently in these foreign policy debates, thanks to the combination of their proximity to Europe, the presence of oil in the region and the perceived threat of fundamentalist Islam. In the United States, for instance, Egypt has so far been explicitly spared from the current rounds of budgetary cuts, despite criticism of the Mubarak regime's misuse of aid funds, while France has taken care to maintain a high level of assistance to the Maghreb in recent years, largely out of a concern for the stability of the region in the wake of events in Algeria. While the vast mineral wealth in Southern Africa may serve to maintain some Western interest in the continent's southern tip, and while Nigeria's oil reserves might have a similar impact, overall the end of the Cold War has dramatically reduced sub-Saharan Africa's leverage vis-à-vis the West.

## Assessing Aid Effectiveness

Political opposition to aid in the donor countries is fostered by growing doubts regarding its ability to promote economic development. These doubts are particularly strong with regard to sub-Saharan Africa, the region where aid is viewed as most clearly having failed to bring about economic development. Thus, critics point to the fact that Africa has received more aid than other regions of the Third World and yet has had a much worse economic record. That much is undeniable: during the period 1980–88, Africa received an average of $21.85 per capita in aid, compared with 50 cents in all other developing countries. Aid as a percentage of per capita income, or of gross domestic investment and of imports, similarly shows markedly larger aid flows to sub-Saharan Africa.[6] Despite this significantly higher level of aid, GDP grew by 1.8 per cent a year in Africa south of the Sahara compared with 3.1 per cent in all low- and middle-income developing countries between 1980 and 1992.

Has aid to Africa been ineffectual then? In fact, an answer to this question is complicated by several methodological difficulties. First, there is the issue of the counterfactual, in other words, how the region's countries would have performed in the absence of aid. It is impossible to establish with certainty whether economic growth would not have been even worse without foreign aid. Certainly, it can plausibly be asserted that aid has significantly increased aggregate demand in resource-poor countries like Senegal or Malawi, where it is typically the biggest employer and purchaser of goods and services other than the government.

It is probably true, moreover, that the correlation between aid and growth is lower than it might otherwise be because the criterion for its allocation has not always been the growth potential of the recipient. Throughout the Cold War period, donors' objectives were often political rather than economic; as is discussed at greater length below, Third World states have been supported for geo-strategic reasons, regardless of their economic policies. Evaluating the economic effectiveness of aid in such circumstances is beset with intractable difficulties. Moreover, even when donors have been more altruistic, aid has often been allocated according to recipient needs rather than economic potential. For instance, when aid has responded to drought, it may have averted famine and had

---

[6] Tony Killick, 'The developmental effectiveness of aid to Africa', in I. Husain & J. Underwood (eds), *African External Finance in the 1990s* (World Bank, Washington, DC, 1991), p. 87.

a significant impact on people's welfare, without, however, promoting the kind of economic growth countries with more abundant natural resource endowments are capable of achieving. Given that successful countries, such as those in East Asia, have grown their way out of eligibility for concessional capital flows, it makes sense to expect that the less successful countries would receive a growing share of aid over time. In sum, a number of problems complicate the estimation of a plausible counterfactual.

The fungibility of aid poses a second difficulty. Does aid alter government spending patterns, and to what extent does aid free up resources for governments to spend on activities in other areas that the donors may actually oppose? If aid is highly fungible, it makes little sense to evaluate individual donor projects, and attention should be focused instead on overall investment patterns, over which the donors and their assistance may have had little effective control. While most aid specialists recognize the existence of this phenomenon, there is little agreement on the extent of aid fungibility.

Third, it is sometimes argued that economic growth is the wrong yardstick by which to assess aid effectiveness. Aid can have other legitimate objectives that may not be fully compatible with economic growth, such as poverty alleviation or improved welfare. Aid, for example, is often given much of the credit for the victories over endemic diseases such as smallpox, now completely eradicated, or yaws, onchocerciasis and trypanosomiasis, the incidence of which have all declined significantly in Africa and elsewhere. Similarly, a number of signal improvements in health and education in Africa can be at least in part credited to aid efforts. Infant mortality rates in Africa declined from 140 per thousand in 1970 to 99 in 1992. The adult literacy rate went from 16 per cent in 1960 to 50 per cent in 1990.

These are real achievements, which improve the quality of life, yet they may not be fully reflected in higher economic growth rates, at least in the short term. Unfortunately, it is no easier to determine precisely how much credit aid can claim for this progress. Nor is it clear that aid to Africa has been any more successful at reaching these kinds of objectives than the more conventional economic indicators of effectiveness; a number of recent economic studies have cast doubts on the more general proposition that aid has promoted welfare-enhancing or poverty-alleviation measures effectively, suggesting instead that it has actually favoured the consumption of the better off.[7]

In sum, the macro-economic impact of aid is difficult to establish with precision. These caveats aside, however, the evidence does still suggest that aid to Africa has been significantly less effective than elsewhere in the Third World. Thus, a number of studies have demonstrated that aid has had a much weaker impact on such economic and social indicators as economic growth, savings rate, investment, but also infant mortality or literacy in Africa than elsewhere.[8] These macro-level studies are largely corroborated by project-level evaluations, which have consistently suggested that the average rate of return on individual projects has been lower in Africa than elsewhere.[9] The empirical evidence does lead one to the conclusion that aid has not been an effective instrument of economic development in Africa in the period since independence. Such a general assessment should

[7] e.g. P. Boone, *Politics and the Effectiveness of Foreign Aid* (Centre for Economic Performance, London School of Economics, Working Paper No. 1267, 1994).

[8] e.g. Robert Cassen et al., *Does Aid Work?* (Oxford University Press, Oxford, 1986); Anne Krueger, Constantine Michalopoulos, & Vernon Ruttan, *Aid and Development* (Johns Hopkins University Press, Baltimore, MD, 1989); Paul Mosley, *Overseas Aid: Its defence and reform* (Wheatsheaf Books, Brighton, UK, 1987).

[9] e.g. Uma Lele (ed.), *Aid to African Agriculture: Lessons from two decades of donor experience* (World Bank, Washington, DC, 1990); World Bank, *Sub-Saharan Africa: From crisis to sustainable growth* (World Bank, Washington DC, 1989).

not be taken to suggest that some aid has not been highly effective, or that some governments in Africa have not made good use of aid. In every country in Africa there are examples of aid projects that have had a lasting and positive impact on the welfare of target populations, and for every nation that has squandered large aid volumes with impunity, there are economies like those of Tunisia or Botswana, in which aid has probably contributed to solid economic growth performances.

Why, then, has aid to Africa not been more effective? A standard list of proximate causes has emerged in the aid literature to explain deficiencies in effectiveness, that usually distinguishes between factors related to donor agency policies and practices, and factors within the recipient countries themselves.

### Donor country agencies

Several deficiencies within the donor agencies themselves are often held to be responsible for the low effectiveness of aid. First, donor-agency choices are often accused of being driven by internal political or bureaucratic objectives and constraints, rather than the needs of the recipient countries. For example, domestic political pressures have helped perpetuate the practice of procurement-tying, in other words the obligation to procure aid equipment, expertise and services in the donor country. This practice results in non-competitive pricing of donor goods and services, thus squandering resources and undermining effectiveness. It also probably contributes to other problems, such as the excessive use of imported equipment and the reliance on inappropriate technologies, or to the proliferation of often incompatible national standards and technologies in the recipient country.

Again in response to bureaucratic pressures, agency staff are often accused of putting undue stress on starting new projects rather than managing and improving old ones. Prestige and promotions accrue to staff who launch promising big new activities rather than to those who spend time on the more mundane tasks of everyday management. There is similarly said to be a common bias for spending: as J.D. Naudet puts it, 'a bad project is better than none at all'.[10] As a result, aid programmes are characterized by an excessive number of projects, on the one hand, and inadequate monitoring, adaptation and evaluation of on-going projects, on the other. The excessive number of projects in the field is often remarked upon by studies of aid effectiveness. One study estimates the number of projects in Kenya in the mid-1980s at some 600, from some 60 donors, and 614 projects from 69 donors in Zambia.[11]

These problems are all the more pernicious because of the absence of effective coordination between donors. Individual donor programmes are often formulated and implemented without taking much account of the activities of other donors, resulting in costly duplication and conflicting objectives. The absence of coordination imposes added administrative burdens on recipient governments, and thus probably affects project quality. Local civil servants have to manage or at least oversee this multitude of projects, and the proliferation of procurement requirements, project visits, expert missions, evaluations reports and training workshops that result tax their limited capacities. The Cassen

---

[10] J.D. Naudet, 'Development aid to West Africa', in *External Finance for Development in West Africa: Trends in resource transfers and discussion of official development aid, 1960–1990* (West Africa Long Term Perspective Study, Working paper no. 6, OECD/CILSS, Paris), p. 105.
[11] Roger Riddell, *Foreign Aid Reconsidered* (James Currey for ODI, London, 1987), p. 210.

report on aid provides the notorious example of the 350 different expert missions that allegedly visited Burkina Faso in one year alone in the early 1980s.[12]

The donors have long officially advocated greater coordination, and a number of mechanisms have been developed in recent years to ensure communication between both donor headquarters and field missions. At the national level, the UNDP Round Tables or the World Bank-led Consultative Group processes have helped get donors and government together to discuss development strategy and to attempt to rationalize the process, but there remain powerful forces militating against effective coordination. Coordination is extremely time-consuming and administratively complex. It typically requires that donors adapt their own procedures and management approach to the requirements of other complex organizations, which implies a loss of discretion and compromises for each individual donor, often in contradiction with the powerful administrative forces described above. As for the recipient government, which after all should be coordinating aid efforts as an integral part of its own policy-making processes, the absence of donor coordination has the advantage of allowing the administration to play one donor off against another, as when a project proposal that has been refused by one donor can be shopped around to others. As a result, there has been little improvement in donor coordination in recent years, despite general agreement on its importance.

These managerial weaknesses are probably symptomatic of more profound causes of low aid effectiveness. First, much donor aid has been motivated by political and commercial rather than economic objectives. Throughout the Cold War, for example, the United States viewed its foreign assistance programme as an instrument to achieve various American strategic and political objectives, as much as one to assist the economic development of the recipient country. In the case of a country like South Korea, these two objectives proved largely compatible. But where they conflicted, short-term strategic interests often predominated and undermined the aid's economic effectiveness. That the four leading African recipients of American aid during the 1980s were Zaïre, Somalia, Liberia and Sudan, offers eloquent evidence that developmental efficiency was not the dominant motive for American aid during this period. Indeed, the premium put on political stability by American diplomacy in the region sustained particularly venal regimes in power with economic assistance long after they had proved their developmental incompetence beyond a reasonable doubt. The best example of this logic is probably Mobutu's Zaïre, a particularly inept and brutal regime which received over US$1 billion in American assistance between 1962 and 1990 essentially because of its perceived usefulness to American intelligence operations in Central and Southern Africa.

Other donors have rarely invested Africa with the same geo-strategic importance, but many have used aid to pursue non-developmental objectives. France, for example, has long viewed Africa as an arena in which to project its own power, while the Scandinavian countries lavished aid on Tanzania and Zambia during the 1970s and early 1980s out of ideological sympathy for the socialist regimes there, despite their disastrous economic records.[13] The significant aid flows to the Southern African Development Coordination Conference (SADCC) countries in Southern Africa were dictated first and foremost by the desire to lessen the region's dependence on South Africa, for instance, rather than with a view to economic growth alone, which would have sought to integrate the region's economies better.

[12] Cassen, *Does Aid Work?*, p. 223.

[13] See e.g. the particularly damning retrospective report by the Swedish government of its own aid programme in Zambia: the Secretariat for Analysis of Swedish Development Assistance, *Evaluation of Swedish Development Cooperation with Zambia* (Ministry of Foreign Affairs, Stockholm, August 1994).

Commercial reasons have played a significant role for some donors. Maintaining French influence and commercial dominance in its ex-colonies has been a significant motivation for French aid, for example, but all donors have at one point or another sought to use their aid programmes to promote their exports or national companies. This is, of course, the primary motivation for the tying of aid to related procurement. It is also a major motivation for food aid, which has been extended to African states even when it clearly had a negative impact on local food production.

These non-economic motivations for aid have served to help block reform of aid to improve its effectiveness, often despite the sincere convictions of most practitioners in the aid agencies themselves. There is no real political constituency for reform of aid within the donor countries, at least not one powerful enough to counter the foreign-policy and commercial interests that are well served by current programmes. This partly explains why attempts to reform aid practices have not had much impact. The aid agencies have engaged in an enormous amount of learning about the advantages and disadvantages of different aid modalities and have proposed – in a long list of reports – a variety of reforms based on many of the criticisms described in this essay. Yet aid has proved resistant to change because of the combination of bureaucratic pressures for the status quo, on the one hand, and little interest in reform on the part of the domestic overseers of aid.

Nor, perhaps even more importantly, has there been a vocal constituency for reform within Africa. Governments in the region have at times disputed sectoral aid allocations or criticized specific aid modalities – for example, the reliance on long-term foreign expertise has increasingly come under fire – and they have fought against donor conditionalities. But on the whole, governments have been remarkably passive about aid effectiveness, an issue to which we now turn.

## Recipients

Two sets of factors within recipient countries are generally held to undermine aid effectiveness. The first is the policy context within which aid is given. There is now considerable evidence to suggest that inappropriate economic policies that distort incentives, undermine investment or create uncertainty have had a devastating impact on the effectiveness of aid in a number of African economies.[14] This suggests a positive link between the health of the real economy and aid effectiveness; a policy environment which discourages productive activity and investment will undermine aid effectiveness as well. For example, an agricultural intensification project is unlikely to reach its objectives if the economic climate discourages rural investment, perhaps because of a high rate of inflation or because of low agricultural producer prices. It was indeed the widespread perception that many African governments were pursuing disastrously wrong-headed economic policies that led Western donors to begin to push for policy reform during the 1980s.

Second, the limited effectiveness of aid in Africa is often blamed on the low administrative capacity of governments in the region. Various shortages of skilled staff within the administration, high rates of turnover, the weakness of manpower planning, corruption, low morale and absenteeism all undermine the ability of governments to design, implement, monitor and evaluate aid programmes. Administrations with low capacity are unable to solve complex problems within the project environment, they do

---

[14] This is the theme, for example, of Krueger, Michalopoulos & Ruttan, *Aid and Development.*

not plan well or adapt to change quickly. Enhancing administrative capacity has proved to be slow and uneven across the continent, despite the emphasis donors and governments have put on training. For instance, a study of Kenya estimates at 5,000 the number of Kenyans receiving university level training in the West in the late 1980s, a number that is probably matched by other countries in the region.[15] Yet the same study suggests that the Kenyan state's capacity has improved little in recent years, and notes that very few of these Kenyans will ever return to work for the state, in large part because the salaries they can expect there are no more than one-fifth of those prevailing in similar positions in the Kenyan private sector.

This anecdote illustrates well how the economic policy environment interacts with administrative lacunae to lower aid effectiveness: poor economic performance caused in part by past policy mistakes results in budgetary difficulties, leading governments to cut the real salaries of civil servants and undermining their ability to retain qualified staff, which in turn adversely affects the quality of public-sector management. These two factors similarly combine to exacerbate a problem which continues to haunt aid projects in Africa: the systematic inability to budget properly for recurrent costs; project equipment does not get serviced, for example, or vehicles remain in the garage for lack of gasoline or spare parts, roads and bridges get inadequate maintenance, and so on. All too often, projects are not sustained after the end of donor funding, because the government has not budgeted for the necessary expenditures.

So far, we have discussed the proximate managerial factors that account for low aid effectiveness. To understand why these weaknesses have persisted so long, however, we need to turn our attention to a number of more profound socio-political characteristics of recipient governments. First, low state capacity in Africa is directly related to the non-developmental nature of the states in the region. The states that emerged in the years following independence were for the most part poor, weakly institutionalized and lacking in popular legitimacy. Executive leaders quickly found it convenient to resort to extensive patronage, clientelism and rent-seeking to consolidate and then maintain power. Rather than try to develop lean and effective state bureaucracies with a small cadre of skilled and well remunerated civil servants, most African governments preferred to allow the emergence of a vast ill-trained and poorly paid public bureaucracy. Kenya's civil service thus increased from a few thousand at independence to 268,669 persons in 1990, a rate of expansion matched if not exceeded by most of the regimes in the region.

Economic development requires certain public institutions, such as effective and secure property rights backed by an effective judicial system, accountable and predictable systems of authority, and the provision of basic public goods. Yet, because of the way in which they have exercised power, African states have proved unable or unwilling to promote these kinds of institutions. In sum, the institutions necessary for economic growth were sacrificed on behalf of those necessary for political stability. Over time, for example, increased administrative capacity within the state apparatus was undermined by many African rulers because it was not compatible with the rent-seeking and patronage practices they viewed as essential for political stability. Similarly, they adopted economic policies that made little sense from an economic point of view, but were politically perfectly rational.[16] Of course, the degree to which these practices dominated the administrative

---

[15] John M. Cohen, 'Foreign advisors and capacity building: the case of Kenya', *Public Administration and Development*, 12 (1992), p. 500.
[16] See Robert Bates, *Markets and States in Tropical Africa: The political basis of agricultural policies* (University of California Press, Berkeley, CA, 1981).

apparatus and undermined aid effectiveness varied across African states, but in most of them one can notice their impact.

It is important to realize the extent to which foreign aid became a key element of this political economy and contributed to its stability. On the whole, donors did not contest or try to undermine the manner in which power was exercised. Until the 1980s, the donors condoned policies that were often counterproductive in economic terms. In Tanzania, for instance, Collier argues persuasively that aid resources and advice played a key role in sustaining the disastrous agricultural and industrial policies on which the government embarked in the 1970s.[17] The sheer size of aid relative to the economy – by the late 1980s it reached 10 per cent of GDP in many countries – probably lessened the motivation of some governments to try to improve their economic governance or pursue politically difficult economic reform, given their expectations that donor finance flows would continue at present levels.

Even after they began to question the economic policies being implemented, most donors continued to limit scrupulously their involvement with the non-economic functions of government, not least out of respect for the government's sovereignty. Until the late 1980s and the emergence of donor interest in governance issues, donors remained remarkably inattentive to government habits that were patently undermining the development process. Indeed, various donor practices have often sustained them; for example, extensive reliance on expatriate experts and independent project authorities has undermined capacity-building in ministries and allowed many to drift along as little more than patronage machines. In the late 1980s, as many as 100,000 foreign experts worked in the public sectors of sub-Saharan Africa alone, accounting for over a third of ODA to the region.[18] Officials in government ministries have often not felt accountable for the deficiencies of the services they are meant to deliver because they know that donors will at least in part compensate and meet needs as they arise. Over time, the population's expectations are shifted away from the government and to the donor projects and the informal sector, which further relieves the government of pressure to improve performance.

Aid resources have too often been obligingly provided to the government to be used at its political discretion – from project benefits such as roads or water wells, to fellowships to study abroad or 'sitting fees' to attend meetings, or even project equipment such as cars, which governments can dole out to reward supporters. The government of Botswana has tried to integrate foreign aid into its national development planning exercises. Donor projects are carefully scrutinized and shaped to conform to targets and objectives set by the government, to ensure their sustainability after the end of donor support, even when this scrutiny has slowed down project implementation and questioned donor priorities and procedures. This cautious development planning has almost certainly contributed to Botswana's enviable economic record, even if one allows for the country's important mineral resources.[19] Few other African governments have demonstrated similar discipline, however, preferring to maximize the short-term flow of donor resources. For governments whose inability to promote a coherent development strategy has contributed to a stagnant economy, donor resources have been too attractive to scrutinize.

---

[17] Paul Collier, 'Aid and economic performance in Tanzania', in Lele, *Aid to African Agriculture*, pp. 151–71.

[18] Cited in Cohen, 'Foreign advisors', p. 493.

[19] On Botswana, see Stephen John Stedman (ed.), *Botswana: The political economy of democratic development* (Lynne Rienner Publishers, Boulder, CO, 1993); and Louis Picard, *The Politics of Development in Botswana: a model for success?* (Lynne Rienner Publishers, Boulder, CO, 1985).

## The Impact of Aid

It is perhaps useful at this point to make a distinction between the impact and the effectiveness of aid. In the aid literature, effectiveness is usually meant in the economic sense of an appropriate ratio of cost to benefits. A project or an aid programme is effective when that ratio is higher than it would have been in a plausible alternative project. The opportunity cost of the project is typically estimated in the context of the cost of capital. In theory, effectiveness need not be assessed in a totally economistic manner; a huge cost-benefit literature has developed ingenious ways to attach a value to all sorts of non-economic goods in order to include them in the project evaluation. In practice, nonetheless, the literature on effectiveness has assessed aid to Africa in pretty narrowly economic terms. The literature typically asks whether aid has promoted economic growth, or whether it has promoted high levels of savings, investment, physical capital or even human capital.

On the other hand, it rarely makes a serious assessment of the impact of aid on the recipient country. By impact, I mean the broader sociological, political and economic effects of aid: has aid had an effect on urbanization, for example, or on the status of women? Has it helped promote stable states, or has it undermined political stability? Impact questions may be just as important as effectiveness ones. Indeed, given the weight of aid relative to the local economy, it would be remarkable if aid had not had a substantial impact on the economy even when its economic effectiveness had proved extremely limited. Given space limitations, this essay can not do full justice to this complex topic, but will limit itself to a handful of observations on the economic, political and ideological impacts of aid.

First, what can we say about the economic impact of aid? As we have seen, aid has not been effective at promoting economic development. On the other hand, aid has almost certainly abetted the central tendencies in the long-term evolution of these economies. For example, aid almost certainly contributed to the extremely rapid urbanization which is one of the most striking features of contemporary Africa. As Paul Collier has argued, the macro-economic effect of aid is to lower the shadow price of foreign exchange, favouring the net consumers of tradeables in the cities to the disadvantage of the net producers of tradeables in the countryside.[20] In that sense, aid probably has enhanced the impact of governments' urban bias policies, abetting the rapid growth in the urban population and the growing disparity between urban and rural purchasing power.

Aid, similarly, has had an important impact on growing social inequalities. This proposition is admittedly more speculative, as there has been remarkably little research on the topic, but it is corroborated by anecdotal and indirect evidence. Because aid spending has favoured urban over rural populations and the public rather than the private sector, it is likely that it has had on balance a regressive impact on the distribution of income and assets. Aid monies have been overwhelmingly spent in the capital – if they are spent at all in the country – and the goods and services financed by aid disproportionately benefit the better-off. There is much evidence that public expenditures have not been progressive in most African countries, favouring instead the emergence of a largely urban and public-sector middle class.[21] There is some evidence that aid has favoured this class

---

[20] Collier, 'Aid and economic performance', p. 167.

[21] e.g. Ravi Kanbur, 'Poverty and the social dimensions of adjustment in the Côte d'Ivoire', (SDA Working Paper no. 2, World Bank, Washington DC, 1990).

as well; in the education sector, for example, aid has concentrated its efforts almost entirely on the secondary and tertiary level, rather than primary education, which has received only 0.4 per cent of total ODA, according to one recent study.[22]

This may change as poverty alleviation has once again become a rallying cry of donors in recent years, and it is possible that economic reforms may have a dampening effect on inequalities in some countries, notably by altering the terms of trade between the urban and rural economies.[23] Nonetheless, poverty alleviation programmes continue to represent a small percentage of overall aid spending. Moreover, when aid has consciously aimed to benefit the more disadvantaged segments of society, projects have not necessarily reached their target. Thus, a project may be directed at rural poverty alleviation, but its experts and most of the project staff will lodge in the capital, where most of the procurement will take place; and the project trains college graduates abroad who will eventually either leave the project or sit in a ministry in the capital. If the project is ineffective, then its net impact will almost certainly be to increase inequalities.

Second, aid has had a powerful political impact in Africa. Has aid helped create stronger states? It seems clear that aid has been a critical component of the international community's efforts to legitimate, support and maintain viable states in Africa following decolonization. Starting from a notoriously low level of basic state capacity at independence, perhaps best symbolized by the eight college graduates in Zaïre at the end of the colonial era, foreign aid has propped up these states in all sorts of fundamental ways, from training and equipment for the police and military to emergency food aid during droughts and technical assistance to the ministry of finance's tax collection efforts. In the countries racked by political instability and leadership turnovers, aid provided much needed continuity. In others, it helped states undertake all the basic functions of government with minimal effectiveness. Early on, the donors decided that they would channel all of their assistance through state institutions, thus promoting the ascendancy of the state vis-à-vis civil society, which the state was in any event typically trying to eliminate or emasculate. The donor discovery of civil society in the 1980s has in this sense been something of a cultural revolution, but one that came too late to prevent the state's almost uncontested ascendancy.

More recent financial support from the international financial institutions (IFI) and donor groups like the Paris Club has also helped maintain the stability of essentially bankrupt states. Whatever one thinks of the price paid by states and their citizens for coming to terms with their Western creditors, there can be little doubt that 'the ritual dances of the debt game', with its repeated stabilization loans, debt rescheduling and debt forgiveness exercises, have improved the prospects for state elites to survive debilitating economic crises. Because few of these countries can attract significant private capital, the continued net positive flows of public capital have been critical to political stability: in countries like Togo, Cameroon, Kenya or Senegal, overall international debts have more than doubled in the last decade and the economy has continued to stagnate, yet the same political elite has remained safely ensconced. On the other hand, the withdrawal of aid has been a watershed event in the collapse of Liberia, and in the erosion of the state in Sudan or Zaïre.

At the same time, as we argued above, aid is partly to blame for the 'anti-

---

[22] OECD-CILSS, *External Finance for Development in West Africa*, p. 116.

[23] e.g. David Sahn (ed.), *Adjusting to Policy Failure in African Economies* (Cornell University Press, Ithaca, NY, 1994); and Alex Duncan & John Howell (eds), *Structural Adjustment and the African Farmer* (James Currey, London and Heinemann, Portsmouth NH, 1992).

developmental' state that has emerged during the same period. The paradox is only apparent: aid has played a significant role in ensuring the political stability of the region, without at the same time building effective states. The weakest states in the region have survived thanks to this external support without undergoing real institutionalization. Somewhat more speculatively, donor support has shaped state-society relations in ways that weaken state legitimacy in the long run. On the one hand, governments have been able to substitute donor support for the support of their citizens. Large infusions of aid have resulted in lower rates of fiscal extraction in Africa than anywhere else in the developing world; governments did not need to tax their citizens and could allow a sizeable proportion of revenue to disappear in corruption, knowing that aid would compensate. As Janine Aron shows in her contribution to this volume, a third of the states in Africa have central revenues equivalent to less than 12 per cent of GDP, an amount that allows them barely to cover their wage bill and interest payments. Because they relied on outsiders to balance their budgets, states were freed from the need to gain legitimacy with their citizens, to whom in any event they were not accountable.

Given these phenomena, governments have had little incentive to improve the effectiveness of aid. For one thing, aid flows were not conditional on effectiveness: the Zaïres of the continent have not been punished for their egregious misbehaviour nor the Botswanas rewarded for their relatively good performance. For another, even when it has not been effective, aid has provided all sorts of discretionary resources with which to maintain the support of various political constituencies. Not willing to look a gift horse in the mouth, governments have exerted little effort to manage aid, despite its obvious economic importance. In the immediate period after independence, under the impetus of the dominant development ideologies of the day and helped by donor assistance, governments made an effort to integrate foreign aid into a national development planning process. Often unrealistic, inflexible and incompatible with the donors' own planning exercises, five-year plans soon passed out of fashion, leaving donors almost entirely free to devise the orientation and modalities of aid. Few governments invested in efforts to monitor projects or evaluate their impact, granting the donors enormous latitude. Instead, many governments became adept at catering to donor concerns and fashions, as evidenced in recent years by the proliferation of new ministries for the environment, or for women or – with seemingly little sense of irony – for privatization. These institutions exist almost entirely for the donor projects that they come to house and service.

## Improving Aid Effectiveness: Some Modest Proposals

There is today much agreement in the donor community that a key to effective aid and the renewal of economic growth in Africa is the development of a sense of ownership among Africans regarding the development process. By this is usually meant the need for greater indigenous commitment to the viable economic policies and programmes that are needed, a recognition that outsiders have driven the development process in the past. Put into the language of this essay, it requires developmental states. How do developmental states emerge? How could aid help promote them? This essay cannot do justice to this hugely complex topic, but I conclude by criticizing two ideas sometimes put forward as panaceas, and then offer several more modest suggestions.

First, proposals are sometimes made for large increases in aid flows to Africa. Thus, the United Nations' Economic Commission for Africa has made a number of proposals calling for both major debt forgiveness and a massive infusion of new aid into Africa, modelled on the Marshall Plan, the financial aid given to Western Europe by the USA after World War II.[24] Forgiving debt that is in any event often not being serviced is not necessarily all that onerous for Western governments, and they will probably continue to undertake unilateral forgiveness on a piecemeal basis. Indeed, some $11.5 billion of bilateral debt was written off between 1982 and 1992 by OECD governments, most of it benefitting Africa. Nonetheless, if the description of the political climate presented above is accurate, a sizeable increase in overall net aid flows must be considered highly unlikely for the foreseeable future. Is it in any event desirable? Aid levels are already extremely high in most African states, accounting for 12.6 per cent of sub-Saharan Africa's overall GNP, with highs of over 90 per cent in countries like Tanzania or Mozambique; there is no reason to believe that increasing these levels further would improve governmental performance. On the contrary, our analysis suggests that even the current aid levels have induced a dependency that is unhealthy for the governments in the region. A large infusion of extra aid might provide some temporary relief for cash-strapped governments in the midst of major economic crises, but the relief would be short-lived unless the root causes of the current crisis were addressed. In addition, moreover, the capacity of most states to manage aid is limited and seems already excessively taxed by current flows. In sum, even if there may be a case for increasing aid to individual states under certain circumstances, there is little reason to believe that a significant increase in aid flows would provide lasting benefits to African states.

A second general solution that is sometimes offered to Africa's current woes is for a significant expansion of donor conditionality. There have been growing calls in the donor community to impose tougher conditions on assistance to African governments; how effective is political and/or economic conditionality likely to be? As Africa's economic crisis has grown, states in the region have become more dependent on aid than ever before, providing donors with much greater leverage than in the past. It has been very tempting for donors to impose various kinds of conditionality on Africans. Donors have always to a certain extent attached conditions to their aid. But the 1980s witnessed a sharp increase both in the number of conditions and in their scope, under the impulsion of the IFI-led 'dialogue' with African governments on economic policy reform. Policy conditionality soon proved relatively toothless: studies suggest that governments have complied with as few as half of the conditions that have accompanied stabilization and structural adjustment loans,[25] for example. However, adjustment programmes have only extremely rarely been terminated; governments have become masters at giving the donors the impression that they are complying just enough with policy conditions to ensure the continuing flow of aid. Sometimes, they have miscalculated and aid has been temporarily suspended, but in general the donors lack the inclination to monitor compliance carefully and are easily satisfied with any evidence of progress, however limited.

Nonetheless, the trend has been towards continuing to expand conditionality, first from narrowly defined macro-economic indicators to ever more specific sectoral and sub-sectoral policies, to non-economic issues; since the current democratization wave hit Africa in 1990, some donors have toyed with explicit political conditionality, linking

---

[24] e.g. Economic Commission for Africa, *The African Alternative Framework to Structural Adjustment Programmes for Socio-Economic Recovery and Transformation* (E/ECA/CM.15/6/Rev. 3, Addis Ababa, 1989); or, more recently, Adebayo Adedeji, 'An alternative for Africa', *Journal of Democracy*, 5, 4 (October 1994), pp. 119-32.
[25] The most complete of these studies is Paul Mosley *et al.*, *Aid and Power: The World Bank and policy-based lending* (2 vols., Routledge, London, 1991).

aid to political liberalization and democratization. Thus, for example, in 1992 the donors withheld some aid from Kenya to encourage the Moi regime to undertake some measures of political liberalization. Such actions are based on the recognition that, in the words of the World Bank, Africa's economic problems are due to a 'crisis of governance',[26] and that real progress on the economic front was not likely in the absence of fundamental changes in the way African nations were governed.

This argument is convincing, but there is little reason to believe that political conditionality will prove any more effective than economic policy conditionality has these last few years. Indeed, compliance with political conditions is likely to be even more difficult to monitor than economic conditions. In a dozen or so countries in the region, effective opposition movements combined with donor pressure to impose a real alternation of power on governments. Elsewhere, in the absence of strong domestic pressures, ruling elites responded to external pressures with limited political liberalization that did not threaten their hold on power. Opposition parties and a free press are now tolerated but it is difficult to discern significant changes in the manner in which power is wielded. Once again, governments in Cameroon or Kenya and Togo have proved masters at doing just enough to placate the donors.

That is why the extension of conditionality to the political realm is not likely to be effective. Does that mean that conditionality should be further relaxed, if not eliminated? I do not think so. There is no justification for granting money to governments that are not serious about development. Instead, both political and economic conditionality should be simplified as much as is practically possible and limited to a small number of unambiguous rules and targets, to facilitate the monitoring of compliance. Conditions should reflect the broad consensus within the development community regarding what is appropriate policy practice to promote development. Governments that fail to meet these criteria should not receive aid, which should be reduced and re-directed to non-governmental actors and humanitarian goals. The savings could be channelled to reward the governments that do comply and make significant progress on economic and political reform. There is a need to rectify the present situation where there is too little difference in aid flows between good and bad performers to provide effective incentives for good behaviour.

Ultimately, nonetheless, the primary objective of aid should be the long-term development of effective states in Africa. It is a cliché in development circles to argue that aid can only play a marginal role in the development process, but it is a truth that few in Africa and in the development community have fully assimilated. Their proponents have sometimes presented increasing donor conditionality and/or aid flows as 'magic bullets' that could offer quick solutions to Africa's economic dilemmas. Yet, no amount of aid can substitute for a governmental will and commitment to the development process. Where these are missing, short-term solutions such as creating independent project units outside of the ministries, long-term resident experts, detailed conditionality and/or ever more intrusive donor oversight and control will be ineffectual palliatives. Nor will increasing aid levels or more generous debt forgiveness prove to offer more than temporary respite, if governments are not able to attract private investment and promote sustainable economic policies.

To contribute to the slow and arduous process of nurturing developmental states, donors can, nonetheless, pursue at least four interrelated strategies through their aid to Africa. First and foremost, the importance of sound, sustainable and predictable

---

[26] World Bank, *Sub-Saharan Africa: From crisis to sustainable growth*, p. 60.

macro-economic policies to long-term economic success cannot be overstated. There remain significant areas of disagreement among experts regarding the exact sectoral policies that African governments should pursue to promote industry, say, or agriculture, but there is now extremely widespread professional agreement on what constitutes the desirable macro-economic environment that government policy should seek to promote. This is an environment of low inflation, realistic exchange rates and relative prices that more or less reflect actual scarcities. Experience suggests that it is a *sine qua non* of long-term private investment, without which there can be no appreciable economic growth; it is also almost certainly a prerequisite for effective state governance, as we have witnessed in the recent past the devastating impact of economic instability on state capacities. In sum, donors should endeavour to promote this environment by emphasizing macro-policy dialogue with African governments and continuing to support ongoing stabilization efforts.

Second, donor assistance should promote, or at least not undermine, the emergence of more accountable and transparent governments. On the one hand, this implies financial and technical support for non-governmental actors in civil society or for public institutions that promote accountability, such as the judiciary, the legislature and independent media. These institutions can in the long run discipline governments and improve their performance much better than donor conditionality, and they are requisites for democratic governance. A lively press and legislature will promote public debate about development policy, a key for policy learning and the construction of a national consensus regarding economic priorities. It also implies donor intransigence about government corruption and the enforcement of property rights, an issue regarding which donors remain too indulgent.

On the other hand, it is also important for the donors themselves to practise greater transparency in their own programmes. The project cycle and the macro-economic policy dialogue should be opened to more public scrutiny in the recipient countries than is typically the case today. Far from being laggards in the area of governance, the donors themselves should systematically set an example of transparency and accountability.

Third, donors should emphasise civil service reform, in most states in the region the first step for building effective states. This means at the most banal level the downsizing of the civil service, often by up to 50 per cent, combined with a dramatic improvement in the conditions of service for the remaining staff. It must be recognized that such measures will be costly and politically difficult, but development requires states with the capability to devise and implement policies with at least a minimum level of efficacy, which most African bureaucracies lack today. It also means empowering the senior, most competent members of the civil service and granting them a much larger role in the making of development policy. Donors should be much more passive in the design and implementation of policy, which should be the responsibility of the civil service and local expertise. Governments should be allowed to experiment with policy and learn from mistakes, the only way in which consensus about and ownership over policy can be built.

Fourth, and related to this latter proposition, donors should concentrate their efforts on improving indigenous technical capacity. Measures must be taken to reverse the current exodus from Africa of many of the continent's most talented minds. This implies supporting the rehabilitation of Africa's decaying universities and research institutes, in particular those in the development field. The creation of the African Economic Research Consortium in Nairobi is the kind of experience which should be replicated and extended. It also implies encouraging the repatriation of African experts to these institutions, notably by hiring their services in the field, particularly for routine project monitoring and evaluation.

## Conclusion

Aid to Africa can be made more effective. For too long, aid to Africa has been motivated by factors other than Africa's economic development. As a result, significant amounts of aid from the West did not prevent economic stagnation in large parts of the continent. Indeed, we have argued that, in some respects, aid contributed to that stagnation by supporting weak and corruption-riddled states. Today, Africa's growing geo-strategic marginalization threatens to lower the generous aid levels of the past, but it also provides an opportunity to rationalize the remaining aid in a way that will enhance its effectiveness. As aid flows decline in quantity in the years to come, the challenge will be to increase its quality, in particular to help promote effective states in Africa. Only if aid meets this challenge will it provide a lasting contribution to Africa's economic renewal in the twenty-first century.

FOURTEEN

# Some Legal Aspects
# of Migration

CHALOKA BEYANI

The United Nations Conference on Population and Development which was held in Cairo in 1994 noted that there are more than 125 million international migrants in the world, including refugees. So far as migration and development are concerned, the Conference recognized that:

> International economic, political and cultural interrelations play an important role in the flow of people between countries, whether they are developing, developed or economies in transition. In its diverse types, international migration is linked to such interrelations and both affects and is affected by the development process. International economic imbalances, poverty and environmental degradation, combined with the absence of peace and security, human rights violations and the varying degrees of development of judicial and democratic institutions are all factors affecting international migration.[1]

The purpose of this chapter is to examine the problem of migration from an international legal perspective within this context. A particular objective is to link migration patterns in Africa to economic and political pressures at national and international levels.

First, there will be a brief historical profile of migratory movements in Africa which will consider pressures behind the phenomenon of migration, both internal and external. The second part of the chapter will deal with basic aspects of international law concerning migration. Of particular importance are the standards relating to international migration in general, and refugees and migrant workers. Regional responses to migration are also

---

[1] United Nations, *Cairo Declaration on Population and Development* (Advance and unedited version, 19 September 1994), p. 67.

discussed in this context. There will then follow a discussion of migration in relation to regional economic arrangements under the European Union and the Economic Community of West African States. The fourth and final part of the chapter considers the formative policies on migration and development as set by the Cairo Conference.

## A Brief Historical Profile of Migration in Africa

Africa has a history of general population movements which predates the establishment of the modern state on the continent. Among the factors associated with these historical migratory movements are ethnic conflict and access to economic resources such as water, grazing pastures, and fertile land for farming. Historically, many ethnic conflicts were connected with access to economic resources and control over them, and the pattern of migration was closely linked to the dominant economic activity of specific groups. Thus, for example, the famous wars waged by Shaka the Zulu king against the Ngoni, the Lozi and the Ndebele in the early nineteenth century may be seen as the result of tensions resulting from territorial claims over resources. In their defeat, the Ngoni settled partly in Zambia and partly in Malawi, and the Lozi in western Zambia, while the Ndebele settled in what is now Zimbabwe.

Similar patterns of migration could be found in West and North Africa prior to the establishment of the modern state. By virtue of its proximity to Europe, the rest of Africa and the Middle East, Morocco has had a history as a crossroads for migratory flows since antiquity, and its present population is a mixture of peoples of Berber and Arab origin.[2] Groups with a nomadic way of life, such as the Masai in East Africa, inhabited wide tracts of land which suited their migratory lifestyle, revolving around their herds.

The modern African state is the product of boundaries drawn by the colonial powers as a means of exercising control over people and resources. These frontiers paid little regard to ethnic configurations. Certain forms of traditional migration have been constrained by territorial frontiers which delineate the physical existence of the state and set territorial limits to the power, or authority, exercised by it over its population and property. There are a few instances in which states, such as Libya and Chad, are bound by mutual agreement to grant trans-frontier freedom of movement to nomadic groups that traditionally trade and maintain traditional caravan links.[3] But most population groups are no longer able to migrate, in the historical sense, into open space, or into space inhabited by others, across such frontiers in search of better resources and welfare.

The appearance of the modern state denotes, as an aspect of its control over territory, regulatory measures with regard to migration within and from outside it. In Africa, states generally regulate internal migration by a variety of means which include identity cards, registration, travel permits, internal passports or other documents. Similar requirements are to be found in some European states in correlation with controlling and monitoring the presence of foreigners.[4]

---

[2] Abdulla Berranda, 'Migration, structural change and economic development in Morocco', in OECD, *Migration and Development: New partnerships for co-operation* (Organization for Economic Cooperation and Development, Paris, 1994), p. 267.

[3] See *Case Concerning the Territorial Dispute (Libya v Chad)*, International Court of Justice Reports (1994), p. 26, para. 53.

[4] French legislation in 1888 and 1889 provided for strict rules for the registration of all resident foreigners as a way of monitoring their presence. A further example is the Aliens Acts 1793 to 1914 in the United Kingdom. See further, Haycraft, 'Aliens legislation and the prerogative of the Crown', *Law Quarterly Reviews*, 13 (1897), p. 172; and James Fawcett, *Application of the European Convention on Human Rights* (2nd edn., Clarendon Press, Oxford, 1987), p. 71.

Registration of persons within states spread to Africa during the colonial period as a way of controlling rural-urban migration.[5] After independence, many African states continued the system of national registration in order to identify and control nationals, but a few others, such as Tanzania under its socialization policy of *ujamaa*, and Sudan, retained the system of rigid controls of movement between regions within the country as part of development planning and the control of internal migration.

The system of registration as a device to monitor the presence and identity of persons is permissible provided that it is neither discriminatory nor a condition for the lawful exercise of freedom of movement and residence within the state.[6] However, in reality many countries in Africa abuse its application by using it to place rigid constraints on the freedom of movement and residence of nationals as a way of controlling internal migration and the activities of nationals. Thus roadblocks are a common feature in very many African countries.[7] The legality of such controls remains open to question, although there are arguments in favour in the context of development planning.[8]

Whatever the legality of the issues involved, it is clear that the regulatory capacity of many African states over internal migration, as in other areas of public life, is weak. Moreover, such control is probably undesirable in the face of a combination of several factors which lead to such migration. A study published by the International Organization for Migration in 1995 noted the obvious ones:

> War, ethnic and religious conflicts, natural disasters, tribal hostilities and persecution are some additional causes of both individual and group mass migration, as is progressive ecological deterioration, which renders land uninhabitable for human beings, as a result of soil erosion, deforestation, flooding, desertification, air pollution and chemical soil destruction.[9]

In addition to these, there are problems of poverty, economic retrogression and the crisis of statehood which cause significant migratory trends. It is impossible in the face of these factors to justify or impose crude methods of controlling internal movement since migration within the state becomes a way of avoiding their consequences as well as a means of searching for alternative livelihoods.

## International Migration

The problems noted above are as much a cause of international migration as they are of internal migration. In approaching the issue of international migration, however, it is important to note that different categories of migrants are involved. Apart from ordinary international movement, the categories of migrants which have given rise to specific international responses are those of refugees, migrant workers, and undocumented migrants. While refugees and migrant workers have a specific legal status,

---

[5] S.16, Native Registration Ordinance, Cap 169 of the Laws of Northern Rhodesia, and Government Notice No. 337.

[6] Fawcett, *Application of the European Convention on Human Rights*, p. 71.

[7] Chaloka Beyani, *Restrictions on Internal Freedom of Movement and Residence in International Law* (D.Phil thesis, Oxford 1992, to be published by Clarendon Press, Oxford).

[8] Rosalyn Higgins, 'Liberty of movement within the territory of a state: the contribution of the Committee on Human Rights', in Y. Dinstein (ed.) & M. Tabory (ass. ed.), *International Law at a Time of Perplexity* (Nijhoff, Dordrecht, 1989), p. 326.

[9] International Organization for Migration, *International Migration Pressures. Challenges, policy response and operational measures: An outline of the main features* (IOM, Geneva, 1995), p. 14.

undocumented migrants have none, and their plight has only recently begun to receive collective international attention as shown below.

## Ordinary migration

So far as ordinary or orderly international movement is generally concerned, states have a wide discretion regarding the admission into their territory of foreign nationals.[10] For example, in entertaining an application concerning a refusal by Germany of the entry of a foreign national, the European Commission of Human Rights determined that no right to residence in a country of which the applicant was not a national was guaranteed under the European Convention on Human Rights 1950.[11]

Nevertheless certain obligations pertaining to human rights operate to restrain the discretion exercised by states over the entry of non-nationals. The Covenant on Civil and Political Rights 1966 recognizes the right of every person, regardless of nationality, to leave any country, including their own, and the right to return to their own country.[12] The right to leave one's own country implies a right of entry to another state, but the extent to which this has fettered the discretion exercised by states in controlling immigration is minimal. The Covenant expresses only a stronger commitment to states of origin not to deprive nationals arbitrarily of the right to enter their own state.

Significantly, and perhaps in recognition of the latitude enjoyed by states in this respect, the right to leave and to return is subject to restrictions in the public interest.[13] To be lawful or valid such restrictions must, of course, be justified in the public interest, but there may be a presumption of legality which operates in favour of restrictions which give effect to the discretion of states in issuing entry visas as a form of immigration control. Conditions on which visas are issued underlie the discretion enjoyed by states and such conditions vary considerably between countries.

Since 1987 immigration control in a number of European countries is reinforced by punitive sanctions against carriers or airlines which carry persons without visas to their territories. Thus Belgium, Denmark, the former Federal Republic of Germany and the United Kingdom have enacted legislation to fine carriers which bring in passengers without valid entry visas or travel documents or with forged travel documents.[14] The world's airlines have effectively become immigration control posts so that measures aimed at restricting migration extend to the means of travel.

However, there is a certain arbitrary, if not discriminatory, pattern to the control of migration. In general, persons from Africa, Asia, Latin America, and more recently, the former communist countries of Eastern Europe, face stiff conditions of entry into Europe and North America. Strict immigration controls with respect to these parts of the world stem partly from concerns about political and economic instability which give rise to migration, and partly from xenophobic concerns bordering on racism or discrimination based on colour, race, origin, language, or religion.

---

[10] See the authoritative work of Guy Goodwin-Gill, *International Law and the Movement of Persons Between States* (Clarendon Press, Oxford, 1978).

[11] Admissibility of Application No. 2951/66. See Council of Europe, *Digest of Strasbourg Case Law Relating to the European Convention on Human Rights*, 5 (1985), pp. 877–8.

[12] Article 12(2)(4), Covenant on Civil and Political Rights 1966; Hurst Hannum, *The Right to Leave and Return in International Law and Practice* (Nijhoff, Dordrecht, 1987).

[13] Article 12(3) lists the protection of national security, public order (order public), public health or morals or the rights and freedoms of others.

[14] Antonio Cruz, 'Carrier sanctions in four European Community States: Incompatibilities between international civil aviation and human rights obligations', *Journal of Refugee Studies*, 4, 1 (1991), p. 63.

Ironically, this is the one area in which human rights standards in international law have made vital inroads into the discretion of states to regulate freely the entry of non-nationals. Application of the principle of non-discrimination as contained in human rights instruments, both of general and regional application, forbids unjustified differential treatment on grounds frequently specified in such instruments. Among the grounds on which such discrimination is commonly forbidden are colour, race, origin, sex, language, or religion, but the principle of non-discrimination itself applies to all the rights protected under a human rights treaty.[15]

In a case brought before the European Court[16] by Asian women whose husbands were refused entry into the United Kingdom, the Court admonished that even if the right of a foreigner to enter as such is not protected by the European Convention on Human Rights, immigration controls had to be exercised consistently with the obligations of the Convention. The Court found that the exclusion of the men in question was unlawful because it discriminated against the women concerned on grounds of sex.

The decision of the Court in this case has to be appreciated in the light of the fact that women placed in similar circumstances were allowed to join their husbands. It rejected the argument by the United Kingdom that this difference of treatment, i.e. the exclusion of men but not of women, was necessary for the protection of the domestic labour market. Although, in the opinion of the Court, the latter was a reasonable objective, it did not justify separate treatment between women and men. Conclusions to be drawn from this case are as follows:

1. Policies underlying control of immigration must be consistent with obligations towards human rights, particularly the principle of non-discrimination.
2. Where non-discrimination is violated under immigration controls, refusal to grant entry may be unlawful, and policies underlying immigration controls, such as protection of the domestic labour market, must yield to the principle of non-discrimination.
3. Policies underlying immigration controls must be reasonable and applied even-handedly in the sense of non-discrimination in order to be legally justified.

### Refugees

The specific legal status accorded to refugees as persons who no longer enjoy the protection of their country of origin entails different treatment from that of ordinary migrants when it comes to entry and staying in host states. This status derives chiefly from the standards enshrined in the United Nations Convention Relating to the Status of Refugees 1951.[17] By providing a basis for the entry of refugees in states which are parties to it, the Convention highlights the spirit of the right to seek and enjoy asylum under the Universal Declaration of Human Rights 1948, and also the African Charter of Human and Peoples' Rights 1985.

---

[15] Cf. the effect of the decision of the European Court of Human Rights in the *Belgian Linguistics* Case, *European Court of Human Rights Reports*, Series A (1968), p. 34.

[16] *Abdul Aziz*, 7 *ECHR Reports* (1985), vol. 7, p. 495.

[17] The Convention was adopted by the United Nations Conference on the Status of Refugees and Stateless Persons, held at Geneva 2-25 July 1951. It entered into force on 22 April 1954. The text is available in the *United Nations Treaty Series* No. 2545, p. 137; UNHCR, *Collection of International Instruments Concerning Refugees*, (2nd edn, Geneva), p. 10; Ian Brownlie, *Basic Documents on Human Rights*, (3rd edn, Clarendon Press, Oxford, 1992), p. 64.

The requirements for refugee status are set out in the definition of a refugee. For its part, the UN Convention[18] defines a refugee as any person who,

> owing to a well-founded fear of being persecuted for reasons of race, religion, nationality, member-
> ship of a particular social group or political opinion and is outside the country of his nationality
> is unable or owing to such fear, is unwilling to avail himself of the protection of that country;
> or who, not having a nationality and being outside the country of his former habitual residence. . . .
> is unable or, owing to such fear is unwilling to return to it.

The essence of this definition recognizes the necessity for the protection of individual persons whose safety, lives and fundamental freedoms and rights are at risk in their state of origin. States Parties to the Convention assume the responsibility to provide such protection in accordance with the criteria carried in this definition. The underlying premise of this criterion is the loss or lack of protection in the country of origin. A loss or lack of protection may be determined by establishing a 'well founded fear of persecution' on the grounds specified in the definition, including unwillingness on the part of the claimant to return to the country of origin.[19]

A major aspect of persecution involves the violation of human rights in countries of origin, for the flight of refugees from their countries of origin is the clearest indication of any such human rights violation. Although the concept of persecution appears open-ended, the 'persecution-based criterion' of the UN Convention is narrow in character and its effect is to allow the entry of refugees on an individual basis.

The individualized response to refugee outflows under the UN Convention was determined to be unsuitable in Africa in the face of mass movements of refugees. Hence in addition to the UN Convention, there are specific regional standards for the protection of refugees in Africa under the Convention Governing the Specific Aspects of Refugee Problems in Africa (OAU Convention) of 1969.[20] The adoption of the African Convention was prompted by a specific concern about large flows of refugees whose flight was related to Africa's colonial occupation and wars of national liberation rather than persecution on an individual basis.[21]

This concern led to the formulation of a definition of refugees which reflected the special character of the African refugee phenomenon. Under the African Convention,[22] the term refugee also applies

> to every person who, owing to external aggression, occupation, foreign domination or events
> seriously disturbing internal order in either part or the whole of his country of origin or nationality,

[18] See Article 1(2) of the Convention Relating to the Status of Refugees 1951 and the Protocol Relating to the Status of Refugees 1967. Before this Protocol was concluded, the definition of refugees in the 1951 Convention had a limited geographical and date application to events which occurred in Europe before 1 July 1951. The effect of the Protocol was to remove these limitations by omitting the words 'As a result of events occurring before 1 July 1951' and 'as a result of such events'.

[19] Atle Grahl-Madsen, *The Status of Refugees in International Law*, Vol. 1 (Nijhoff, Leiden, 1966), p. 173, See further, pp. 176, 188–189. Guy Goodwin-Gill, 'Transnational legal problems of refugees', *Michigan Yearbook of International Legal Studies* (1982), p. 299; idem, *The Refugee in International Law* (Clarendon Press, Oxford, 1982).

[20] For analysis, see Joe Oloka-Onyango, 'Human Rights, the OAU Convention and the refugee crisis in Africa: Forty years after Geneva', *International Journal of Refugee Law*, 3 (1991), pp. 453–60. Officially, the status of the African Convention is that of an effective regional complement to the Convention Relating to the Status of Refugees. It must therefore be read and applied in conjunction with the latter, and its content must be viewed further in relation to human rights instruments, particularly the African Charter on Human and Peoples' Rights 1985 which, as noted earlier, embodies the right to seek and enjoy asylum.

[21] U.N. Doc. MHCR/175/66. After the Kampala Draft Convention 1964, the Organization of African Unity Conference on Legal, Economic, and Social Aspects of African Refugee Problems which was held in Addis Ababa in 1967 recommended adopting a definition based upon the specific aspects of the situation of refugees in Africa.

[22] Article 1(2) of the OAU Convention of 1969 concerning the Specific Aspects of the Refugee Problem in Africa.

is compelled to leave the habitual place of residence in order to seek refuge in another place outside of the country of origin or nationality.

The criteria on which refugee status may be granted under this definition are self-evident in the broad grounds listed in the definition. In practice, this definition enables the admission of refugees to host countries on a *prima facie* group basis, having regard to the events which cause flight in the country of origin. This process of group eligibility obviates the necessity for admitting refugees on an individual basis and, in any case, the processing of individual claims would be overwhelmed in the face of large numbers of refugees.

However, the massive presence of refugees in host countries in Africa has stretched their capacity to breaking point. At the time of the adoption of the Convention, it was thought that group eligibility would be mitigated by 'burden sharing' and the temporary character of the refugee problem in Africa.[23] With time, the problem of refugees in Africa has proved not to be temporary and burden sharing on the basis of African solidarity and international cooperation has not been effective, except in an *ad hoc* manner in the most serious cases of massive refugee flows. As a consequence, many refugees in host countries are placed in camps in rural areas on arid land, living in poor and squalid conditions adverse to human dignity. Of the one million or so refugees who fled Rwanda to Zaïre in 1994, many died of disease, exhaustion, and hunger.

The problem of refugees in Africa is compounded by the fact that donor fatigue has clearly set in, and the liberal open-door policy to refugees within Africa is beginning to shut. Tanzania denied entry to refugees from Burundi in April 1995 and in the same month Kenya asked the United Nations to repatriate Somali and other refugees from its territory. For many years Tanzania had followed a liberal policy towards refugees and it has been host to many refugees in East Africa.

Europe's response has been harder. The 1990 Schengen Agreement on the Gradual Abolition of Checks at the common borders of some European states,[24] namely Belgium, France, Federal Republic of Germany, Luxembourg, and the Netherlands, in order to facilitate the free movement of persons and goods, contains measures to prevent illegal immigration.[25] Other measures include the detention of asylum seekers in the United Kingdom, the categorization of certain countries, such as Zaïre, as safe areas of origin from which no persons may be admitted as refugees, readmission agreements concerning the return of nationals staying illegally,[26] and the non-admission of asylum seekers who enter prospective countries of asylum by travelling via other safe countries.

## Migrant Workers

Recognition of the role played by migrant workers in development has contributed to the development of standards for their entry into other countries at international and national levels. Recently, in 1990, the United Nations adopted an International Convention on the Protection of the Rights of Migrant Workers and their Families. Under the Convention, the term 'migrant worker' refers to a person who is to be engaged, is engaged or has been engaged in a remunerated activity in a state of which he or she is not a national. The Convention also establishes the category of documented migrant

---

[23] Articles II(4) and V.

[24] See (1991) p. 68.

[25] Council of Europe, *Activities of the Council of Europe in the Migration Field* (Strasbourg, 1993) *International Legal Materials*, vol. 30., p. 45.

[26] UNHCR, *Readmission Agreements, 'Protection Elsewhere' and Asylum Policy* (Geneva, 1994).

workers in a regular situation if they are authorized to enter, to stay and to engage in a remunerated activity in the state of employment. By contrast, migrant workers who do not comply with these conditions are considered as non-documented.[27] The extent to which this Convention will facilitate the migration of workers and their families is unclear and it is probably too early to tell. As at December 1994, the Migrant Workers Convention had been ratified only by Egypt and Morocco, while only Chile, Mexico, and the Philippines had indicated a willingness to assume its obligations formally.

Migration of labour is, however, considerably regulated in regional economic organizations. The major examples are the treaty on European Union read in conjunction with the Treaty of Rome which established the European Community (EC), and the Treaty of the Economic Community of West African States 1975 (ECOWAS), and the treaty establishing the *Communuaté économique de l'Afrique de l'ouest* (CEAO) concluded on 27 October 1978.

Surprisingly, the Southern African Development Community (SADC) has no treaty provisions on the movement within the territories of its member states, since such movement is an important aspect of the movement of goods and services. It would have been preferable to deal with the issue of migration in a regional context in Southern Africa, particularly in the light of increasing migration to South Africa. Unilateral measures on the part of Southern African states to regulate migration are likely to fail and may also be inward-looking. Zimbabwe, in May 1995, waived visa fees for South African nationals wishing to visit it in order to attract capital, investment and tourism. But the gesture in unlikely to be reciprocated, given that many Zimbabwean nationals are flocking to South Africa in search of a better life.

The European Union has a well established legal regime with an elaborate functional structure under which rules governing the movement and residence of migrant workers have been systematically developed. The Treaty of Rome originally set out the freedom of movement of migrant workers which is now enjoyed within the European Union. The scope of this freedom entails the right to:[28]

(a) accept offers of employment actually made;
(b) move freely within the territory of a member state for this purpose;
(c) stay in a member state for the purpose of employment in accordance with the provisions governing the employment of nationals of that state as laid down by law, regulation or administrative action;
(d) remain in the territory of a member state after having been employed in that state, subject to conditions which shall be embodied in implementing regulations to be drawn up by the Commission.

Free movement under this provision may be exercised only by persons who are actually engaged, or who seriously wish to be engaged, in employment in the territory of a member state.[29] The essential characteristic of the term 'employment' is the provision of services by employed persons for, and under the direction of, another in return for

---

[27] See Article 5 of this Convention.
[28] Article 48(3) of the Treaty of Rome.
[29] *Kempf v Staatssecretaris van Justitie*, 3 June 1986, *Official Journal* (1986), C188/3.

remuneration.[30] Part-time employees are included in this category, although persons in public employment are excluded.[31]

The model originally set by the Treaty of Rome regarding the free movement of persons within the European Community has been adopted by ECOWAS and CEAO in West Africa.[32] The preamble to the ECOWAS treaty recognizes the need for the removal of obstacles to the free movement of goods, capital and persons. For this purpose, the preamble lists the abolition of obstacles to free movement of persons between member states as central to the activities of the Community. Art. 27 of the Treaty of ECOWAS provides for the free movement of persons within the Community. It grants Community citizenship status to citizens of member states, and obliges the latter to undertake to abolish obstacles to the free movement and residence of Community citizens within the Community. But questions of exempting Community citizens from holding visitors' visas and residence permits, and of allowing them to work in the territories of member states, were left open to be negotiated in separate agreements between member states.

A protocol concluded on 29 May 1979 amplified the provisions of Art.27. It set out three phases of five years each in which the principle of free movement of migrant workers was to be realized progressively beginning from June 1980. Respectively, the phases were aimed at achieving the guaranteed right of entry of Community citizens without the requirement for visas; securing the right of residence within the territories of member states; and conferring the right of establishment. The protocol carries a general provision reserving the right of member states to refuse admission to any citizen who, according to local law, comes within the category of an inadmissible immigrant.

The reference to local law left a loophole potentially exploitable by member states in furtherance of their individual interests. Each member state retained a discretion unfettered by the treaty unilaterally to exclude or restrict entry, movement and residence, or to expel migrant workers in accordance with its domestic law, without external Community supervision. Consequently, when the second phase under the Protocol began on 4 June 1985, Nigeria declared that it would unilaterally impose conditions regarding the implementation of this phase. Conditions set by Nigeria allowed unrestricted entry into its territory only to persons belonging to certain professions, including engineers, surveyors, teachers and bilingual secretaries. These were to be permitted to reside in Nigeria provided that they secured employment within a limited period of six months.

Difficulties of this kind were avoided by CEAO. Arrangements for free travel under the treaty establishing this Community closely resemble those of the European Community. Article 29 of the treaty makes the usual linkage between the free movement of persons and that of services, goods, and capital within the Community. The treaty deals with the right to enter and settle in the territories of member states and the grounds on which it may be restricted. Subject to public interest, nationals of member states may enter the territory of any other member state without restriction and may travel and remain there and leave such territory simply on production of a valid national passport. Formal requirements for visas are dispensed with, and provisions prohibiting

---

[30] Case 149/79, *Commission v Belgium* (1980), *European Court Reports*, p. 3881.

[31] Provisions on free movement within the European Community have been augmented by subsidiary legislation. Council Directive 68/360 obliges member states to grant the right of residence in their territory to workers who are able to produce a valid identity card or passport. Council Directive 73/48 makes provision for abolishing restrictions on the movement of nationals of member states when they desire to go to other member states for purposes of providing or receiving services.

[32] *United Nations Treaty Series*, vol. 595, p. 287.

discrimination against nationals of member states[33] strengthen free migration within the Community.

## Formative Policies on Migration and Development

The UN Conference on Population and Development held in Cairo in 1994 recognized the role played by migration in the process of development. Chapter X of the document produced by the Conference addressed the issue of international migration. From the point of view of the Conference, three things stood out:

(a) International migration policies need to take into account the economic constraints of the host country, the impact of migration on the host country and its effects on countries of origin.

(b) The long-term manageability of international migration hinges on making the option to stay in one's country a viable one for all people, and sustainable economic growth with equity and development strategies consistent with this aim are a necessary means to this end.

(c) International migration also has the potential of facilitating the transfer of skills and contributing to cultural enrichment.

On the basis of these and other considerations, the international objectives which have been set in the context of migration include: addressing the root causes of migration, especially poverty; encouraging more cooperation and dialogue between countries of origin and countries of destination in order to maximize the benefits of migration and to increase the likelihood that migration will have positive consequences for the development of both sending and receiving countries; and facilitating the process of returning migrants.

Though the objectives are laudable it remains to be seen how far states and the United Nations are willing to implement them. Both documented and undocumented migrants are the subject of specific attention, and the primary target in relation to the former is to provide long-term residence, integration, and protection of human rights, including family reunification and non-discrimination. In relation to the latter, the balance lies between reducing undocumented migrants and providing a humane response to them which avoids xenophobia and safeguards their human rights.

However, in examining the question of refugees, the Conference may be criticized for lumping them with undocumented migrants. Nevertheless, impressive commitments were made towards addressing the root causes of forced migration and providing protection to refugees and displaced persons in accordance with international law and human rights.

---

[33] Arts. 2 and 3 of the Treaty of the CEAO.

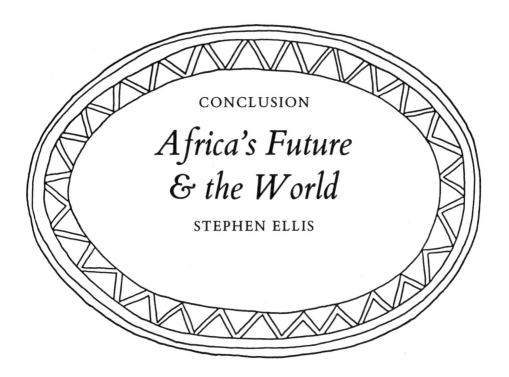

CONCLUSION

# Africa's Future & the World

STEPHEN ELLIS

Each contributor to this volume was asked to write an essay on an agreed subject of general importance for recent social, economic and political developments in Africa, drawing examples as far as possible from the whole of the continent, even if it was necessary to restrict certain discussions to particular countries or regions. The resulting essays have been grouped in three parts, whose main themes represent a progression in scale from individual men and women to factors which play out at the international level. The present chapter aims to discuss each of these three themes in turn, drawing on the information and the conclusions of the contributors to the volume, in order to highlight some key elements which may be a feature of debates on Africa as a whole, and its place in the world, in the next few years.[1]

## States and Citizens

Concerning the first theme of the book, the relationship between people and the states which govern them, there seems to be widespread consensus among the contributors to the present book, and indeed elsewhere, that many African states are in deep crisis. This may amount to a major historical shift, as important in its way as the imperial

---

[1] Even more than is habitual, it should be emphasized that this concluding chapter reflects my own opinions alone, notwithstanding the valuable advice I have received from other contributors to this project, named in the introduction, and especially from Janine Aron.

partition of Africa, the struggle for independence, or some of the other major markers of Africa's history described in the opening essay by Toyin Falola.

It is generally agreed that the one-party states which, with only a few exceptions,[2] governed much of Africa from the 1960s to the early 1990s, not only deprived Africans of civil liberties, but also impeded the economic development which was one of their main justifications, or at the very least failed to deliver it. Only a small number of African countries, such as Botswana and Mauritius, can be regarded as real exceptions to this generalization on the relative lack of sustained high rates of economic growth in Africa. It is interesting, but by no means conclusive, that these two are also among the handful of countries which maintained multi-party political systems from the time of independence.

The extraordinary wave of popular opposition which swept the continent in the late 1980s and early 1990s indicated that many Africans held their governments responsible for their worsening economic circumstances, as people tend to do all over the world. In 1989, the World Bank published a report which suggested that a fundamental impediment to economic development lay in the nature of the governments which had the task of designing and implementing policy in Africa, or in what the report's authors called 'governance.'[3] This report was particularly significant because of the enormous influence wielded in Africa by the World Bank and its sister institution, the International Monetary Fund (IMF), since the early 1980s.

These days, the North Atlantic version of multi-party democracy is generally regarded by influential commentators and opinion-makers as being the only inherently fair system of government. This can be debated. It is also sometimes said to be the only system of government which can assure prosperity or economic development. The latter assertion is clearly untrue, as there are plenty of examples both in the contemporary world and in the past of tyrannies or oligarchies which have governed stable and economically prosperous societies. It is relevant to note, for example, that some of the newly industrialized economies of South-East Asia emerged under highly authoritarian and undemocratic political systems. Quite why this has not been possible under the single-party governments of most of Africa is a subject we shall examine in due course. It is clearly related to the observation made by a number of authors in the present volume that the state in many African countries has become the principal means for individuals to acquire wealth. Toyin Falola goes so far as to say that 'power has been used primarily to steal from the state'[4] in modern times, an assertion which seems undeniably true in regard to many African countries. Before considering to what extent democracy and other recent changes may have modified this state of affairs, we shall first consider what light the essays in the present collection throw on the question of governance in general.

### Governance

Several authors in the present collection, explicitly or implicitly, advance suggestions as to why Africa is governed the way it is. Broadly speaking, we may divide these explanations into two types, one relating to the machinery of government, the other relating to political culture. Government and politics are of course intimately connected, but it is useful for analytical puposes to discuss them separately.

[2] For a synthesis, see Rob Buijtenhuijs & Elly Rijnierse, *Democratization in Sub-Saharan Africa, 1989–1992: an overview of the literature* (Research Reports 51, Afrika-studiecentrum, Leiden, 1993).
[3] World Bank, *Sub-Saharan Africa: From crisis to sustainable growth* (World Bank, Washington DC, 1989).
[4] Above, p. 13.

Regarding the form of government, at least five authors point to the legacy of the colonial administrations which are the immediate forebears of modern African states. In the late nineteenth century, foreigners partitioned Africa, acquired political power over territories they had designated, and used it to establish authoritarian administrations which attempted to reorganize certain aspects of society in the interests of the colonial powers or of local settlers of non-African origin, or according to the colonizers' own view of morality. The result was a legacy of authoritarian government which was inherited by African states at independence, notwithstanding the introduction of political parties and elections in most places on the eve of independence and the more or less liberal constitutions with which they were endowed. There are important exceptions to this generalization on the nature of colonial administration, such as Ethiopia, and there are countries like Egypt or regions like Northern Nigeria which were governed by indigenous administrations under imperial control. But this hardly alters the fact that, since the state machinery had authoritarian and undemocratic qualities built into it by colonial rule, it is not surprising that it retained much of this character when it was taken over by Africans at the time of independence. Moreover, even after independence, former colonial powers or other international actors intervened directly and indirectly to influence the course of events in their own interest, showing little compunction in supporting dictatorships, as Tiébilé Dramé reminds us.

These administrations were taken over at independence by nationalist elites[5] which had emerged during the colonial period. It was generally the 'modern' elites, educated in the Western manner, who were the most prominent nationalists rather than traditional leaders such as chiefs or sultans, and who were most successful in mobilizing political followings on the eve of independence. Both Toyin Falola and Solofo Randrianja show that the crucial period in the formation of Africa's modern political elites was the mid- to late colonial era, which in most of Africa meant from the 1930s to the 1950s or 1960s. Colonial administrations required Africans to produce primary commodities for the metropolitan economies, drawing large numbers of people, including peasant farmers, into a rigorously centralized system of regulation and taxation (what Janine Aron calls 'a small but interventionist state'). At the same time, Africans who had access to European education in particular were able to articulate nationalist ideologies, accepted as universally valid after 1945, to press for an end to colonial rule.

Only after independence was there a change in the nature of nationalism and the use to which it was put. Having been a movement to claim national freedom, it became an ideology to defend national sovereignty, now firmly in the hands of entrenched elites, against real or imaginary threats. Nationalist movements lost their democratic aspect. Nationalist politicians and holders of public office tended to use government to their own personal or factional advantage. The nationalist ideology, and the policies articulated by that ideology such as economic development and nation-building by means of the one-party state, became increasingly hollow, while the real substance of politics passed elsewhere.

The Africans who were drawn into the colonial economy and into nationalist politics in the mid-twentieth century were also the heirs of the older heritage of pre-colonial history. This leads to our second point concerning, not government as such, but the style of politics which has become an important part of Africa's governance. Like all human societies, the pre-colonial societies of Africa described by Toyin Falola

---

[5] Elites are defined as groups of people who are able to act, singly or in concert, so as to affect national outcomes substantially and regularly.

encapsulated degrees of social and economic inequality based ultimately on the particular arrangements which people made for securing access to resources or the production of wealth. The specific forms of these arrangements, and the degree of inequality between elites and others, varied from place to place and time to time, although no doubt the degrees of inequality were far less than those which were to develop during the twentieth century. For example, from the sixteenth century onwards the slave trade encouraged the formation of states in many places based on predation, and this has certainly had a long-term effect on the way in which Africa developed, or failed to develop, economically, and in the suspicion of central power held by peasant communities in various parts of the continent.

These historical factors help to explain why the political and managerial elites which took control of Africa at independence were authoritarian in their mode of operation and interventionist in their thinking. They do not in themselves, however, explain why most modern African governments have been unable to implement policies which have encouraged economic growth since, as we have mentioned, there are many examples of authoritarian governments elsewhere in the world which have been able to do precisely that. An investigation of this problem requires further consideration of the actual substance of politics, the way in which elites articulate with the populace. Here, elements which might be labelled political become inter-twined with broader social factors.

### Political and social relations

All political relationships can be said to rest on the combination of three elements: first, the exchange of wealth in the form of taxation or tribute from below and redistribution of benefits from above; second, coercion; third, the way in which this system is represented to those who take part in it, which we could call ideology. All parts of modern Africa have inherited from their past, to some degree or other, a tradition in which political relations – which always imply the exchange of wealth – are embedded in social relations. Solofo Randrianja describes how, in pre-colonial times, ruling groups asserted their power over small groups of people, overwhelmingly agriculturalists, whose allegiance to the ruling dynasty was expressed, among other ways, in the form of ethnic identities. The latter were, so to speak, negotiated between rulers and ruled. It was largely through such socially-mediated relationships between rulers and ruled, implying the formation of identities that were both social and political, that politics was conducted and governments kept under constitutional check.

This legacy continues to have an important influence. Those in power exert their authority not only through the formal, Western-originated organs of state which they have inherited from their colonial past, but also through the socially-based networks by which they build constituencies. As with all politics, African politics is dominated by groups of people competing or combining to advance their interests. These interests are both individual and collective. The largesse which patrons distribute, and which is the oil of political relationships in such a system, may often have been acquired indirectly or directly from tenure of public office. In extreme cases this may be through simple plunder, embezzlement or theft, or it might come, for example, from a politician associating himself (rarely herself) with various economic lobbies. The latter may include traders who make their money from large-scale smuggling. Historically, the main source of taxable wealth in many parts of Africa has been that generated by interaction between an African country and the outside world, in the form of taxes or rents on foreign trade or foreign contacts generally.

Patrons have to redistribute some of this wealth in order to secure political allegiances. Ordinary people – those who cannot be considered to belong to any elite – use such relationships as a way of safeguarding themselves against the harsher aspects of authoritarian governments and even of turning them to advantage.[6] If African elites were to cease to redistribute wealth, the short-term effect on society would be – and sometimes is – grave, and coercion and violence might ensue. Changes in the means which patrons use both to acquire and to redistribute wealth can have an unsettling effect on the people lower down the social scale who depend on their links with the powerful for survival. Such measures as the creation of new political parties, the privatization of state assets and liberalization of the economy generally, become key sites in the struggles to advance factional interest, and this has a bearing not only on the elites themselves, but also on their constituents. It is by no means a foregone conclusion that multi-party politics and liberal economics will help to create the conditions of more active citizenship or more widespread prosperity, or narrow the gap of inequality which separates elites and wider populations, since, whatever the technical merits of such measures, their outcome is the result of factional struggle in which people participate with regard to their own perceived self-interest. The internal coherence of African elites and their relationship with the mass of the population are the most important issues at stake in the processes of democratization and structural adjustment currently at the forefront of public life in Africa.

Political patrons are under enormous pressure from their constituents to amass resources in money or other assets which they are then expected to redistribute, if not formally, such as through provision of health-care facilities, education, and so on, then through relations of clientelism. Holders of public office or other rich or powerful people in Africa who refuse to redistribute wealth through social channels – which often means, in managerial terms, tolerating or practising nepotism and corruption[7] – risk a range of serious social sanctions including hostility from members of their own family, as Tiébilé Dramé describes, and even, in some countries south of the Sahara, allegations of witchcraft, that is to say, of fomenting disorder by a deliberate disruption of proper social relations.[8] In a multi-party system, politicians who neglect their constituents are also likely to receive few votes. One of the main difficulties facing a politician is to procure sufficient funds to satisfy a mass of supplicants who will, whatever their previous protestations of loyalty, adopt a new patron without hesitation if the substance of the relationship ceases to be satisfactory. A political patron in Africa, like a congressman in the USA, searches ceaselessly for money to secure his tenure of office.

This observation on the nature of patron-client relations helps to illuminate why African governments adopted in the past such policies as massive state employment, systems of import licensing, consumer subsidies and so on, closely associated with the one-party state, which have proved to be economically unsustainable in recent decades. During the first years of independence, such policies were both justifiable in terms of the then current theories of state-led development and nation-building and also redistributed wealth and opportunities for advancement to the populace. It is true that

---

[6] J.-F. Bayart, A. Mbembe & C. Toulabor, *Le politique par le bas en Afrique noire* (Karthala, Paris, 1992); cf. James C. Scott, *Weapons of the Weak: Everyday forms of peasant resistance* (Yale University Press, New Haven, CT, 1985).
[7] Corruption is a notoriously difficult term to define. See Arnold Heidenheimer, Michael Johnston & Victor Levine (eds), *Political Corruption: a handbook* (Transaction Publishers, New Brunswick, NJ, 1989), pp. 3–68; on Africa, Robert Williams, *Political Corruption in Africa* (Gower Publishing, Aldershot, UK, 1987), pp. 12–20.
[8] cf. Peter Geschiere, *Sorcellerie et État : la viande des autres* (Karthala, Paris, 1995).

in the first years after independence in Africa, the people who had taken over responsibility for national affairs in such a short space of time lacked experience of government and had little technical expertise. It is also true that some of the best-educated Africans today choose to live overseas, thus depriving the continent of their talents. This, however, hardly changes the essentially political logic of redistributive practices. Political elites have an intimate knowledge of the constituencies which they are held to represent and which, if they are in office, they govern. Given the fact that many political elites have been in uninterrupted power for decades, they must also have a shrewd idea of the likely effects of given policies. In these circumstances, the use in so much of the recent literature on Africa of such value-laden terms as 'good governance' or 'appropriate policies', while understandable as a conveniently short description, risks being misleading. Governance or policies can be good, bad or middling, but the standard by which they are judged is the benefit they may bring to specific groups of people. The reform measures proposed in much of the literature on governance may be good for a nation as a whole, but they may not be in the interests of specific factions which have access to power, and their followers who are mobilized in vertically-constructed systems of patronage and redistribution which are the real substance of political relationships.

Not all African states operate equally in this way. In some, like Ethiopia, traditions of relatively 'neutral' bureaucratic administration are more entrenched than in others. Not all Africans desire this state of affairs. Politicians who are out of power, like all politicians, want to attain power. If they succeed, they may be content to maintain the system they have inherited. Intellectual critics and democratic activists who can see the shortcomings of this system have difficulty in attaining power precisely because of their lack of resources with which to mobilize support. Reformers may genuinely aim to make governments more representative of the public as a whole and to encourage sustainable economic growth, but they have little influence as long as they are not in power.

## Democracy, reform and society

Reformers both inside and outside Africa have tended to advance suggestions for action in three related spheres, intended collectively to rectify the shortcomings of current systems of governance. These three spheres of reform are in regard to democracy, economic reform, and the development of civil society. We shall discuss briefly the extent to which these three elements have altered the relationship between citizens (whether real or putative) and states in this section. It should be noted that these factors are also relevant to the discussion of specific policies and formal institutions in part two of the present essay.

There is no doubt that democracy has led to a real extension of citizenship in some cases, most notably those of South Africa and Namibia, where millions of people were deprived of their aspirations to citizenship under apartheid. However, in a number of countries, the transition from single-party to multi-party states has enabled previously faltering dictatorships to prolong their tenure of power (Cameroon, Gabon, Guinea, Kenya, Togo, Zaïre and others). In these cases, multi-party activity has given a new form to factional politics, as Solofo Randrianja shows in more detail in the case of Madagascar, without generally altering the substance of political relations built on clientelism. Congo, the Central African Republic, Equatorial Guinea, Tanzania and others could be added to this example, not to mention Rwanda, Burundi and Chad. In other cases, incoming governments are too weak to hold out much prospect of reviving their countries' fortunes (Benin, Mali, Niger, Zambia). Incumbents may reject the results of elections, as in Algeria and Nigeria, or take measurs to rig the elections (Cameroon), or the losers may reject the results, as in Angola. Political patrons starved of funds are liable to adopt increasingly desperate measures to maintain their supply of wealth for personal consumption and for redistribution. This appears to have happened in a significant number of African countries including some of the most important, such as Nigeria, Kenya and Zaïre. The genocide in Rwanda in 1994 is perhaps the most notorious example of a specific faction of the national political elite going to the extreme limit – the organization of mass violence – in order to retain power at all costs.

Senior government officials and political patrons starved of funds from dwindling state resources may even condone smuggling or other forms of economic crime, or even major fraud. It has become relatively common to find that unofficial militias or even ordinary criminal gangs actually enjoy protection from the police (themselves an important element in clientelist systems) or from politicians whose official duty is to uphold public order. Such cases have become quite common from Algeria to South Africa and from Guinea to Madagascar. Ali El-Kenz describes graphically how a state which has lost its monopoly of legitimate violence and its powers of patronage may split into baronies or 'mafias', in which rival political patrons and chiefs of the security forces build personal militias and may even use these for the conduct of criminal activity. This may or may not accompany an appeal to ethnic identity in the competition for national power. Politicians may become technical counterfeiters of their own currency, like the Kenyan government which, in order to finance its election campaign, printed vast quantities of genuine banknotes which it failed to register at the central bank, thus corrupting its own money supply.

The latter example illustrates how economic reforms intended to produce sustainable economic growth may also be thwarted by entrenched interests. In part, this is precisely because these same structural economic reforms can all too easily favour elites rather than broader populations. Elites are able to control the pace and nature of privatization, for example, and of reform generally.[9] They are well-placed to turn the process to their advantage, not least because the wealthiest people are wealthy precisely because they prospered under the old single-party system, as did those foreign interests well-entrenched locally. Here, as Tiébilé Dramé points out, we should not underestimate the role played by large companies with headquarters in the developed world in advancing their own interests. Elites with vested interests in the tenure of power at the national level can also manipulate emerging markets through land speculation, for example. Hence, even in a reforming economy with a shrunken state, tenure of political office may continue to be of crucial importance for groups who aspire, if not to formal tenure of public office, then to economic prosperity and the influence it can bring. Nevertheless, Botswana, Egypt, Mauritius, Morocco, South Africa, Tunisia and perhaps others can be considered actual or at least potential 'developmental' states, meaning that they have found systems of government which seem able to produce a reasonable degree of consistent economic growth.

It was perhaps to be expected that African elites would struggle to maintain their positions and privileges in changing circumstances, since this is no more than what elites do all over the world. Whereas policies which favoured factions rather than the public as a whole could be implemented, under single-party regimes, without formal public

---

[9] For examples of liberal economic reform leading to the creation of new monopolies or oligopolies in the rice trade, see Béatrice Hibou, 'Économie politique de la protection en Afrique', (2 vols, doctoral thesis, École des Hautes Études en Sciences Sociales, Paris, 1995), pp. 99–164.

scrutiny or discussion, they are now subject to debate in a free press and in national assemblies. This has certainly changed the tenor of debate and has generally undermined the fear or respect owed to governments, as Tiébilé Dramé also maintains, but political patrons are still able to manipulate events through their command of resources, through new techniques of political mobilization such as an enhanced appeal to ethnicity, through coercion or violence, and through straightforward bribery. It is worth making the point that systems of clientelism, even under single-party regimes, were never absolutely lacking in transparency, as is sometimes said, since such systems have always been quite clear to those who participate in clientelist networks, that is to say the mass of people, in the sense that the bargains that are made and the relationships they foster are a matter of public knowledge and discussion, sometimes in formal assemblies, more often on the street-corner and, now, in the press.[10] The people who read the newspapers and vote in the elections are, by and large, also the people who constitute the system and perpetuate it by a thousand actions and inactions.

Hence civil society, generally defined as associations of citizens who come together for purposes other than politics, continues to be closely connected to politics by unofficial means, due to the vertical solidarities which link patrons and clients in fields even outside the ambit of the state. In practice, aid-donors tend to consider as civil society in Africa institutions of Western form, such as formal non-governmental organizations, formal private-sector firms, trade unions and so on, many of which are effectively controlled by members of the same elite, or sometimes by the same individuals, who were previously the pillars of one-party states. In such cases, those concerned with the effectiveness of governance in Africa are likely to find exactly the same characteristics reproduced in what they consider institutions of civil society as they earlier saw in formal institutions of state. Nevertheless, there are clearly cases, such as South Africa, where trade unions and a myriad of civil associations have proved their capacity to bring about major changes in government policy from a position of autonomy. In Africa generally, there appears to be a multiplication, including at the lower levels of society, of groups of people brought together for cultural, economic or similar purposes, many of which represent a genuine manifestation of civil society. In the present collection, for example, Ernest Aryeetey discusses the informal savings clubs which are so prominent in all parts of Africa and which are often very effective in mobilizing resources among their members. We shall return to this discussion in the second part of the paper in considering how these may be linked to national institutions.

In rural areas particularly, a vital component of civil society is the small-scale kinship-based communities which are described by Solofo Randrianja. As he points out, these are also building-blocks of clientelist systems, which are increasingly taking the form of large-scale ethnic constructions vying for national power, which he terms 'ethno-nationalisms'. It would seem that analysts might wish to extend the use of the term 'civil society' so as to take account of the manner in which associational life outside the ambit of the state is nevertheless bound to holders of public office through patron-client systems. An accurate model of civil-state relations in Africa would regard certain institutions standing formally outside the state as in fact being substantially controlled by state actors, either directly or indirectly. Conversely, as Solofo Randrianja suggests, ethnic groups considered as cultural creations, when they have not been politicized, are a vital component of civil society although often having no formal or legal existence.

---

[10] Stephen Ellis, 'Tuning in to pavement radio', *African Affairs*, 88, 352 (1989), pp. 321–30.

### The moral foundations of political and social order

The crisis of African states, then, takes a curiously ambivalent form. On the one hand, one-party states grew remote from their citizens through the practice of authoritarian and undemocratic government, increasing the tendency for office-holders to use state assets for factional or personal purposes. On the other hand, the pre-colonial legacy of African politics binds together patrons and clients in essentially personal and social (and not just bureaucratic) vertical solidarities.

This phenomenon aids our understanding of the breakdown of control of the young, illustrated in the essay by Ali El-Kenz, himself an Algerian, in many parts of Africa. There are unprecedented numbers of young people in Africa as a result of the high birth rates of recent decades. In the past, young people were kept under social control by their elders by a complex of social, moral and economic sanctions, even in North Africa with its long tradition of bureaucratic states. The rapid erosion of traditional values in big cities in particular puts the young out of the control of the older generation; at the same time, states having to adjust to difficult economic circumstances have little to offer the young. During the three decades or more of independence the young in particular learned through state education and the rhetoric of state-led development and nationalism that they could expect jobs and social security from a munificent state. This expectation is now exposed as hollow in the face of economic stagnation and budget cuts. As Ali El-Kenz points out, there are millions of youngsters in Africa in just the same situation as Ibo, the adolescent rioter from Dakar, or Boualem, the young insurgent from Algiers, whom he describes.

In previous decades, not only were the young less numerous and under more effective social control than today, but the new independent states were able to bring them under effective political control as well. The 'founding fathers' of African independence, Houphouët-Boigny, Kenyatta, Nasser, Bourguiba and many others, sat atop a pyramid of political and social relationships secure in their pre-eminence and were able to provide a fair degree of stability, predictability and economic growth. This was accompanied by important personality cults which represented the president as 'the father of the nation', a far from meaningless representation. No doubt these founding fathers sincerely believed that the economic progress which they delivered, the schools and hospitals which they built, the modernity which they offered in their paternal manner, amounted to an authentic and sustainable model of development. An important part of the model was a welfare state which would assume many of the functions of older social networks which people looked to it in times of need, and even, as Lilia Labidi mentions, a reorientation of male-female relationships within the family on the Western model of romantic love. The latter implied an abandonment of polygamy, for example, and of the systems of social solidarity which are the traditional mainstays of village life. Such values came to be seen after independence as old-fashioned and non-progressive, and in any case they were difficult to sustain for the millions of people who moved from the villages to the cities. In short, there was a period when the rural young remained under the control of their elders, themselves subsumed in nation-wide patronage and political systems, while the young who developed radically different social ambitions through education and city-life could be accommodated in government employment and systems of state welfare generally. This break between old and new systems of values and even social relationships, the subject of hundreds of novels and films, is referred to by Lilia Labidi as an 'epistemological' rupture.

At bottom, these relationships repose on morality. Our preceding observation of the fact that systems of political mediation and economic distribution based on social relations have always been at the heart of the relationship between rulers and ruled in Africa, particularly outside the countries most influenced by bureaucratic states of European origin such as Algeria and South Africa, emphatically does not mean that African politics have always been corrupt. The legitimacy or otherwise of the system depends crucially on the moral and legal ties which constrain political relations and bind societies together.

These moral values are vested in the symbols which bind together complex imagined communities such as nations. But nationalism as a political mobilizing force has declined in Africa to a considerable degree, with few exceptions, and with the qualification that it remains a powerful cultural factor, fully expressed for example in the massive popularity of national football teams. Nationalism remains a powerful cultural factor in cities especially, where ethnicity is diluted. It is not that people have ceased to think of themselves as Kenyan, Nigerian or Algerian; it is that they can only with difficulty be persuaded to support a given person or party on that basis, since they have learned to distrust the political leader who claims to represent the whole nation, other than, for example, in newly liberated South Africa and Namibia. Here we may note that, in succession to the political language which has been used since independence (that is, the Western-originated language of modernization, development and nation-building), the two symbolic systems most clearly emerging are those of ethnicity and religion, which are discussed at length by Solofo Randrianja and Mohamed Tozy respectively.

Far from representing mini-nations as has often been erroneously supposed, ethnic groups in Africa can be located on a scale of size, somewhere between small kinship-based groups whose existence is dependent on the daily necessity of their members to cooperate and live together, and larger groups which are created or used by political entrepreneurs for purposes of mobilization. Contrary to a valuable insight which has now been over-used, this does not mean that ethnic identities are manufactured by politicians and servants of power only.[11] Danger arises when ethnic or quasi-ethnic communities are politicized, and turned into instruments for the attainment of national power by elites. That way lie Rwanda and Burundi.

The use of religion to attain political power can also be highly dangerous, as Algeria demonstrates, although this example should not blind us to the fact that the real roots of the conflict in Algeria are less religious than social and economic, as demonstrated by the example of Boualem, the young Algerian drawn into terrorism, described by Ali El-Kenz.[12] And this is naturally the case, since systems of symbols, like all systems of communication, can be used to convey all sorts of messages. But the religious revival sweeping Africa, not only in Muslim circles but also in Christian ones and others, is more than anything else a formidable means of building, or rebuilding, moral communities which have rules of conduct backed by the most powerful sanction of all: the will of God. This is all the more significant in view of the fact noted by Toyin Falola in his introductory essay that religion was a mainstay of governance in pre-colonial Africa, and it is deeply rooted.

Governments may make reasoned attempts to co-opt grassroots movements in society or to negotiate power-sharing with them. Mohamed Tozy demonstrates that it was the governments themselves in some countries of North Africa which, during the 1980s, invited clerics to enter the political arena, as they sensed themselves to be in need of

---

[11] Eric Hobsbawm & Terence Ranger (eds), *The Invention of Tradition* (Cambridge University Press, Cambridge, 1983).

[12] cf. Luis Martinez, 'L'enivrement de la violence : "djihad" dans la banlieue d'Alger', in Rémy Leveau (ed.), *L'Algérie dans la guerre* (Editions Complexe, Brussels, 1995), pp. 39–70.

an infusion of popular legitimation. This opened the doors to a struggle for control of the interpretation of the sacred texts of Islam. Muslim activists in Morocco and Egypt, often young, and quite often with university-level technical qualifications, are now making deliberate attempts to win over others in their society through the provision of services in health, education and welfare generally, as well as through preaching and the formation of prayer-groups. Although this implies the adaptation of state power to socially based movements, it is by no means a uniformly benign process since it is on the fringes of such social movements that there may exist groups using violence in the name of Islam. Broadly similar developments can be seen in many African countries of mostly Christian persuasion also.

A basic question posed by the Islamic renewal in particular is the place which it threatens to assign, in some variants, to women. One of the most often noted aspects of the Islamic renewal movements (generally referred to in the West as 'fundamentalism' in spite of their innovatory nature) is the bleak prospects they appear to offer to women, particularly in North Africa. In the case of Tunisia, for example, at least two generations of women have been emancipated from a place behind the closed doors of the house by state-sponsored education, birth control, and state welfare systems generally. Mohamed Tozy argues that some movements of Islamic renewal, such as in Morocco, in fact attract significant support from young educated women, precisely because such movements offer them legitimate use of public space in their role as Islamic militants. In the case of Egypt, however, as Lilia Labidi states, it is from Islamists that there is the most resistance to a new legal code governing the rights of women in marriage. In fact the violence and intolerance associated with some groups calling themselves Islamic in Algeria and Egypt in particular are clearly a general menace to the present order. Whether new forms of Islam have the potential to be creative of new rights of citizenship for women especially remains to be seen. In countries where a religious renewal is overwhelmingly Christian, it is also unclear whether this can lead to the creation of a status of citizenship among the many, or merely among the few, and there are Christian movements which have also made use of violence, in Uganda for example. Here too the question of gender is relevant, for Christianity was presented by missionaries in Africa as a peculiarly male-dominated religion, run by male priests and church officials. In some cases it deprived women of important roles in older religious systems.[13] In other cases, such as south-central Cameroon,[14] it was able to offer new types of expression which were perceived by women as forms of emancipation.

It is striking that these new religious movements, Christian, Muslim and other, tend to grow in cities rather than in villages, among the young rather than the old, among the partly or even highly educated rather than the illiterate. In short, they are not archaic, but modern. Ethnicity and religion are likely to be the languages of politics in Africa, and no doubt in some other parts of the world as well, for the foreseeable future. From a political point of view, the key question will be to what extent the rights of citizens are entrenched in the debates which emerge in these symbolic languages. A number of experiments are clearly taking place already in these respects. Ethiopia is experimenting with an ethnically based constitution which, to an outsider, looks hazardous. But perhaps it looks different to those who live in Ethiopia. The government of Ethiopia must receive full credit for having ended the wars which ravaged the country for three decades and

---

[13] Hugo Hinfelaar, *Bemba-speaking Women of Zambia in a Century of Religious Change (1892–1992)* (E.J. Brill, Leiden, 1994).
[14] Personal communication by Jean-François Bayart.

for accepting the independence of Eritrea. The theocracy proposed by the government of Sudan, or the atrocities committed in the name of Islam in Algeria and Egypt, are distinctly unwholesome, to say the least, since they lead directly to misery, violence and exclusion. But it would be wrong to suppose that all attempts to build political institutions from the symbolism of a popularly accepted religion must look like these. One of the most attractive aspects of religious renewal movements is that they can offer workable social institutions to the frustrated and the poor, and especially to those in cities, including such things as education and health care, as Lilia Labidi and Mohamed Tozy both show. The beneficiaries of social work organized by religious activists are people who are often the victims of recent economic and social changes and who have lost access to the welfare state held up as a model since independence.

The formation of new moral communities expressed in ethnicity and religion is already having an impact on national politics. A vital determinant of Africa's destiny in the years ahead will be the way in which these social movements and the moral codes they represent translate into new formal expressions of the relationship between governors and governed. This is already the case, for example, with calls for the establishment of *shari'a* law in countries with large Muslim populations. At present, in a number of African states the formal rules of public life are clearly regarded with widespread scepticism, notwithstanding the recent incidence of liberal constitutions and a free press.[15] Institutions have a vital role to play in channelling social movements into politically and economically productive spheres and in extending real rights of citizenship. Consequently, we shall turn to consider the second main theme of the essays presented here, that of institutions and policies.

## Institutions and Policies

In recent years, there has been a lively debate among scholars from different disciplines on the question of public institutions in various parts of the world, which has prompted inquiries into the theories of endogenous growth discussed by Janine Aron. Some influential writers on political science have enriched this debate with their perception that public institutions can generate economic growth only when they are suffused with a suitable civic culture on the part of the populace.[16] There is an emerging consensus that what really produces economic growth is not only a specific set of policies, but a winning combination of embedded civic culture and clusters of public institutions which encourage growth by providing a framework conducive to the building of confidence and trust. Business confidence is clearly a key factor governing investment decisions. When citizens have the habit of trusting one another in the context of the social and cultural institutions which they create (sports clubs, religious groups, business enterprises and so on), government institutions are far more likely to design and implement policies responsive to the needs of the societies they govern. To cite an example from outside Africa, the spectacular business success of the Emilia-Romagna region in northern Italy, which in less than a century has become one of the most successful economic regions in the world, is largely based on networks of small family-based companies operating

[15] See, for example the Centre for Law and Research International (CLARION), 'The anatomy of corruption: Legal, political and socio-economic perspectives' (Research monograph No. 7, mimeo, Nairobi, 1994). Report written for the Royal Danish Embassy, Nairobi.
[16] Robert Putnam, *Making Democracy Work: Civic traditions in modern Italy* (Princeton University Press, Princeton, NJ, 1993).

within a tradition of entrenched civic culture, in spite of the notorious corruption of Italy's central government.[17] The fact that there are many examples in Africa of societies with similar traditions of economic dynamism and civic culture, such as in parts of western Cameroon and eastern Nigeria,[18] makes it quite realistic to suppose that these could become leaders in modern business if they were not constrained by rivals who have control of the apparatus of state power. It is this observation which leads from the preceding discussion of history, governance and society to consideration of the forms public institutions may take in Africa.

### Economic activity and state revenue

It could be said that any state endures only by extracting money and resources from those over whom it has power or influence, and by using this revenue to perform certain tasks or services, including the maintenance of a system of justice. A well-regulated state, which can hope to survive or to reproduce itself, does not rob its own citizens and levies only such taxes as it is able to negotiate politically. It is telling, in this light, that state revenue in sub-Saharan Africa is on average only 18 per cent of Gross Domestic Product, with some states having less than 12 per cent, according to figures quoted by both Janine Aron and Ernest Aryeetey. This is too low for a modern state to carry out its basic functions. African states clearly need to improve the level of revenue derived from formal taxation. The immediate obstacle in doing this is the inefficiency of the departments of state responsible for revenue collection, but ultimately it is connected to the question of civil society. Citizens who associate with one another for non-political, including economic, purposes, have a vested interest in being free from arbitrary interference and arbitrary taxation, thus providing a check on power. By the same token, a government can negotiate payment of taxes and various other obligations with citizens. The greater the legimacy of the government, the better it is able to negotiate such bargains with even powerful groups within society. It is precisely these elements of negotiation and checks and balances, of predictability and rules, which are necessary for investment, stability and long-term prosperity. Here too, however, history casts a long shadow. In her summary of the macro-economic history of sub-Saharan Africa, Janine Aron illustrates the phenomenon which she calls path dependence or hysteresis in African economies, where initial conditions strongly constrain the eventual economic outcomes, while the impact of shocks and policy changes on economic capacity and institutions is not temporary but persistent, rather like a metal which is permanently reshaped when it has been heated.

Janine Aron maintains that, notwithstanding the implementation of multi-party politics in Africa in recent years, an independent judiciary and further substantial constitutional change, with a bill of rights, are necessary in many countries to reduce the overwhelming concentration of power in presidential or ministerial hands. Although constitutional changes alone will not solve Africa's problems, changes which make holders of public office accountable to their citizens through formal channels are first steps towards increasing the credibility of African governments domestically and internationally. But effective changes in existing institutions, which avoid sudden and dangerous ruptures, have to be negotiated over considerable periods of time and have to accompany

[17] ibid., pp. 152–85.
[18] Tom Forrest, *The Advance of African Capital: the growth of Nigerian private enterprise* (Edinburgh University Press, Edinburgh, 1994); Jean-Pierre Warnier, *L'esprit d'entreprise au Cameroun* (Karthala, Paris, 1993).

the development of the moral bonds which bind societies together. To decree decentralization, democracy or other institutional reform, even with the best of intentions, is unlikely to lead to any positive outcome unless it is accompanied by shifts of this nature over substantial periods of time. Such a process, if it is not to result in destructive instability, requires creative political leadership. It also requires a degree of patience and understanding on the part of Africa's international partners. As Ernest Aryeetey demonstrates, liberal economic reforms enacted in sub-Saharan Africa, intended to bring economic activity within formal structures, have actually led to an increase in informal-sector economic activity. The latter is generally highly fragmented and makes state revenue collection and productive investment more difficult.

A real advance of democracy, or at least accountability, in such conditions can come about only when power is effectively devolved to a level below that of the national elite, not merely in the form of administrative decentralization, but in real rights of power-sharing, including decision-making and control of funds by small communities. This may even imply recognition of the right for provinces to secede, as in Ethiopia. Devolution of government accompanied by the devolution of rights to raise taxation may help to produce a greater harmony between institutions, between the working of the real economy and the notions of civic virtue or public morality which tend to be more locally than nationally rooted. This is no easy task, since devolution of power or power-sharing implies risks of secession and conflict.

It is striking how frequently one finds juxtaposed in Africa public institutions which hardly function and are seen as the epitome of governance conducted for factional interest, and arrangements based on small communities which work remarkably well. A good example of the latter is the well-known local savings clubs which are also to be found in many other parts of the world and which we have referred to as examples of effective institutions of civil society.[19] Ernest Aryeetey, in his analysis of the informal and formal sectors, identifies a number of specific factors, notably in the case of Ghana but also in the light of case-studies of Malawi, Tanzania and elsewhere, which actually led to a growth of commerce and services in the informal sector rather than in the formal sector, the intended beneficiary of the structural reforms of the 1980s. In part this outcome is due to the sequencing of reforms, but in part it is simply the legacy of the distrust of government caused by previous decades in which businesspeople came to regard public policy as unpredictable. The success of informal-sector financing is usually related to the fact that savings clubs and unofficial moneylenders are able to identify clients or members whom they know personally rather than using bureaucratic methods of identification. That such institutions are able to flourish is due to their being operated by a group of people who share some form of moral community.

It is when one considers Africa's economies over a relatively long period, as Janine Aron does, that the reasons for the economic failure of the last two decades become clearer. African nationalism thrived, and African countries achieved independence, in the long economic boom which began in 1945. What brought this to an end, in Africa, was a combination of several factors including a loss of efficiency in the means of production and distribution and a consequent loss of international competitiveness as the newly constituted nationalist elites rapidly became a *nomenklatura* and consolidated their own factional interests. This then combined with profound changes in the world economic system in the 1970s, notably the delinking of the dollar from the gold standard, the

---

[19] For a brief discussion of such credit associations and their relation to economic development, see Putnam, *Making Democracy Work*, pp. 167–71.

rise in oil prices and, later, a fall in commodity prices. The historian Eric Hobsbawm is surely correct in regarding this as a more significant sequence of events in world history even than that of the revolutionary year of 1989.[20] In Africa, high recurrent expenditure in the face of undiversified export bases meant that both policies and the institutions which designed and implemented them became unsuccessful. Until this happened, African systems of governance appear to have delivered prosperity to a reasonable degree, which reinforces the point that it is not a particular policy or institution alone which produces economic growth, but its adaptability to the overall context in which it exists. Governments have choices available in their distribution of revenue. Lilia Labidi quotes Tunisia as an example of a government which prefers to invest in welfare spending rather than defence, and shows how it has received popular recognition for this, including in electoral success.

At the time when these seismic changes were taking place, mainstream international opinion failed to register the full implications of the end of the great economic boom of 1945–73. African governments behaved as though commodity prices would soon revive, after they had fallen in the wake of oil price rises, and tried to borrow their way through a temporary depression, encouraged by the World Bank which saw its role as that of a redistributor of petro-dollars to the Third World. But African economies did not have the capacity or the flexibility to use these loans for productive purposes, and money was often wasted on consumption, creating a debt problem in the process. Only a small number of countries have been able to use either borrowing or export receipts to set up a significant manufacturing or value-adding sector. As late as the 1980s, the World Bank was still basing its calculations on a revival of commodity prices which has not materialized in most cases.

Only after the boom ended did it become apparent that the economic advances made by many African countries after independence had been largely the result of highly specific conditions. Few countries had succeeded in locating or building a productive apparatus which could supersede the economic system inherited from colonialism. In the most extreme cases it appeared that the state had been used as little more than a source of plunder by the elite who operated it and who redistributed a share of the booty to their clients and subjects, as kings and patrons have done for centuries, in Africa and elsewhere. This commonly took the form under one-party states of the provision of commercial opportunities to favoured political supporters, subsidized parastatals with privileged access to credit, and so on.

The economic challenge facing Africa today is to locate or develop new forms of production which can be taxed in such a way as to provide a stable revenue for the state: in the short term, this requires a diversification in exports which can be sold for foreign exchange and a move away from commodities subject to price fluctuations and mineral resources which are finite. The foreign exchange earned from exports is necessary, in import-dependent African economies, for investment in transport infrastructure and manufacturing, for example. Janine Aron points out that a climate of stability fostered by public institutions which enhance both domestic and international confidence can improve the security even of individual households. This will then encourage the mobilization of domestic savings for investment. This, however, takes time, and in the meantime African states are likely to be highly dependent on foreign aid or loans to make up for the foreign-exchange shortfall. If Africans collectively are unable to achhieve this diversification of their economic base, there is a high risk that some sections of the

---

[20] Eric Hobsbawm, *Age of Extremes: the short twentieth century, 1914–1991* (Michael Joseph, London, 1994).

population will engage in violent protest or, even worse, that certain segments of national elites and their followers will maintain their income by predation based on violence, as happens in such unfortunate countries as Liberia and Angola.

### Harnessing civic virtue

The key to attracting both foreign and domestic investment lies in formal institutions, often at the national level. State institutions which are seen to be independent of political interference, such as an independent judiciary and effective oversight bodies, combined with a bill of rights, may help to generate confidence locally and internationally. Improved institutions of credit can provide a link between the fragmented systems of saving described by Ernest Aryeetey so as to mobilize them for investment. As we have seen, the interface between public and private sectors, and formal and informal or even legal and illegal, is an area in which political entrepreneurs operate for factional gain. To generate confidence, it is necessary to submit these same spheres to the control of institutions which are seen to enforce predictable rules.

In this regard, Jean-Paul Azam provides concrete examples of how public institutions can be effective, and his survey of the effects of reform on agricultural production and marketing systems implies that reformers may need to take a more nuanced view of situations in which state institutions, rather than being almost invariably baleful as they were sometimes seen by liberal reformers in the 1980s, can play a positive role in economic reform. He demonstrates the effectiveness of some policies or institutions which were not generally favoured in the first round of structural adjustment reforms, such as marketing boards, or even, in the case of Morocco, minimum wage legislation. A similar argument could be made with regard to manufacturing activity. The lowering of tariff barriers and the application of high interest rates caused havoc in Africa's industries, in the analysis offered by Lindani Ndlovu. He cites a survey of British investors to demonstrate that structural adjustment policies actually drove out some foreign private investment. Africa's fragile industrial capacity could, in some cases at least, play a significant role in the development of future exports. In South Africa, Zimbabwe, West Africa and elsewhere, Lindani Ndlovu cites examples of industries which are able to produce goods which can compete on world markets. Industries in these places and elsewhere have the potential to develop in fields such as textiles, shoes or finished leather goods, where local supplies of raw materials could supply processing industries.[21] They can certainly do so only with public institutions which are effective. Moreover, inasmuch as such industrial development requires protection rather than a completely free market, states will need to persuade donors and lenders that such measures are not enacted in order to restore or perpetuate a practice of 'rent-seeking' but are motivated by a genuinely national economic strategy.

Here, aid donors and lenders may be required to re-examine their attitudes to markets and to government intervention and to pay further regard to the social aspects of government. Not only health and education, but high levels of state employment play a prominent role in the maintenance of political stability, and the maintenance of effective security forces is necessary for public order. It would be irresponsible to ignore these factors in the single-minded pursuit of reform according to text-book theories only. Consensus is necessary between aid donors and lenders and African states on these matters.

---

[21] T. Biggs, G. Moody & J.-M. van Leeuwen, *Africa Can Compete! Export opportunities and challenges for garments and home products in the U.S. market* (World Bank Discussion Paper 242, Washington, DC, 1994).

The way in which the relationship between productive economic activity, state revenue, social justice and public order evolves will depend largely on changes at the lower levels of society. Deborah Fahy Bryceson and John Howe, citing cases from East Africa but also from other parts of the continent, show how structural adjustment has given a considerable impetus to fundamental changes in spheres of life which had previously been relatively impervious to market forces, such as rural labour and land, or even inter-personal relations within families. The emergence of land markets may be acting against the interests of rural women in particular, since they are not well positioned to defend land usufruct rights. Women are, in many cultures, the main producers of food crops. The creation of markets in land and labour, in circumstances of rapid population growth, is leading to rising rural unemployment and a process which Deborah Fahy Bryceson and John Howe call 'de-agrarianization', or the disaggregation of agrarian economies without any countervailing increase in urban or industrial employment. It can also lead to a risk of environmental degradation as rural communities come under both economic and population pressure to produce on marginal lands, or to apply capital-intensive farming measures to fragile soils and eco-systems. These authors cite cases in which the application of market mechanisms in spheres of life previously dominated by social networks of obligation and exchange is leading to a monetization of personal relations. However, this clearly varies from place to place, since Ernest Aryeetey identifies a contrary trend in Northern Ghana, where saving is increasingly demonetized.

## The role of the Bretton Woods institutions

Powerful foreign influences, including aid donors and the Bretton Woods institutions, have recognized that public institutions, national, regional or local, are likely to be sites – or battlegrounds – for the infusion and transmission of new forms or methods of governance.

The Bretton Woods institutions, often called the international financial institutions, began work in Africa in earnest some 15 years ago when they were approached for loans by governments which had, in effect, gone bankrupt. Such governments had been living beyond their means and, above all, had over-taxed, or created other disincentives to, various types of production especially in the context of a long-term fall in commodity prices. Officials of the international financial institutions concluded that Africa's poor economic performance could be improved by the application of policies which they judged to be technically correct. Their belief was that a liberal macro-economic policy and measures encouraging the development of free markets in goods and services would tend to produce greater economic growth. Only later, and after the first round of results fell short of expectations, did officials of these institutions come to the further conclusion that the crux of the problem was less the policies than the institutions which administer them.[22] Since then, the international financial institutions have been leaning towards the reorganization of public institutions in African countries when they are called upon to intervene by giving loans.

We have suggested that there is indeed a problem posed by public institutions in Africa, but that the solution is not to restrict the role of the state across the board, since some state institutions have demonstrated that they can play a useful role in economic life and since, in any event, liberal reforms in some cases risk causing political

---

[22] World Bank, *Sub-Saharan Africa: From crisis to sustainable growth.*

turbulence which is certainly not conducive to investment or economic growth. Several authors in the present collection make suggestions as to which policies might be implemented in the future and how public institutions might be made more useful. All suggest that combinations of public and private-sector activity (and even activities involving both formal and informal sectors) need to be combined in specific contexts, as may be inferred from all the chapters in the second part of the present collection. This could apply to such institutions as marketing boards and such policies as the use of tariffs to protect nascent industries, and even minimum wage legislation. Deborah Fahy Bryceson and John Howe suggest investment in human capital in the context of infrastructure projects, which tend to be used in any case in the course of relief operations when aid agencies intervene in the aftermath of catastrophes natural or man-made. Janine Aron proposes that aid donors may consider motivating, through substantial debt relief, effective constitutional reform enacted by African governments. She maintains that effective constitutional reform, voluntarily enacted if possible, will signal a lasting credibility and commitment on the part of governments to maintaining consistent macro-policy and transparent and accountable institutions. These would effectively tie future governments if the relevant institutions or measures could be overturned only by referendum or an independent court. She sees constitutional reform as the root of the problem of oversight of government in Africa. Only if voluntary adoption failed to materialize would donors consider stimulating such reform through debt relief.

In retrospect, the earlier policies of the Bretton Woods institutions, in the form of stabilization and structural adjustment, can be seen to have been short-term in orientation. Longer-term gradual change is costly, while the World Bank's internal structure was more geared towards lending and less towards the results of lending. Officials of these organizations tended to believe in the early 1980s that macro-policies, 'getting prices right', were a sufficient remedy, and to neglect the institutional and social aspects of reform. It is also apparent that, in the 1980s at least, the Bretton Woods institutions were motivated by an ideological belief in the virtue of markets and in a view of states which saw them as incompetent at best, and destructive at worst. Their reforms were applied with a speed which risked destabilizing the societies they were meant to help.

World Bank and IMF officials have not explicitly recognized earlier mistakes in the application of measures of stabilization and structural adjustment and continue to argue, in public at least, that governments which apply the correct measures single-mindedly reap positive results in the form of higher economic growth.[23] In gradually moving towards a belief in the need for institutional reform, officials of these institutions continue to use a series of classical concepts which tend to come in the form of rather rigid distinctions between opposing categories: state and society; formal and informal; economics and politics. While these distinctions are helpful up to a point, they are not always adapted to a reality which is far more fluid, in which state apparatuses are in some respects the captive of societies, where leading politicians and businesspeople work in both formal and informal or even legal and illegal sectors simultaneously, and where economic patterns are the product of a myriad of political actions.[24]

[23] World Bank, *Adjustment in Africa: Reforms, results and the road ahead* (Washington DC, 1994). For a critique, see Nguyura Lipumba, *Africa Beyond Adjustment* (Policy Essay No. 15, Overseas Development Council, Washington DC, 1994), and references therein. A good background essay is John Toye, 'Structural adjustment: Context, assumptions, origin and diversity', in Rolph van der Hoeven & Fred van der Kraaij (eds), *Structural Adjustment and Beyond* (Netherlands Ministry of Foreign Affairs, James Currey and Heinemann, The Hague, London and Portsmouth, NH, 1994), pp. 18–35. .

[24] Thomas M. Callaghy & John Ravenhill, (eds.), *Hemmed In: Responses to Africa's economic decline* (Columbia University Press, New York, 1993).

The ultimate goal of recent economic reforms is to attract private investment to Africa. South Africa, Egypt, Tunisia, Morocco, Mauritius, Botswana and other countries do attract significant private investment. However, it is noteworthy that even the countries most committed to World Bank/IMF reforms, such as Ghana, have not proved very attractive to private investors other than in very particular sectors, such as gold-mining in the Ghanaian case. Previous decades of wrong policies and unpredictable shifts have left a legacy of distrust which discourages private investment.

While some African countries have the potential to develop exports for world markets in both agricultural products (described by Jean-Paul Azam) and industrial products based on local agriculture or other resources (described by Lindani Ndlovu), there are major reasons why some areas of the continent cannot realistically be expected to become exporters of agricultural or other local products for world markets. Some countries have a combination of poor soils and erratic rainfall which makes them zones of chronic low productivity. In the past and even now, farmers in such areas have responded to a difficult environment by migrating either regularly or occasionally, and by mixing agricultural work with other types of activity, such as trading, small-scale manufacture or wage labour. In the dry savannah belt which extends from the Sahel through Chad as far as Somalia it is difficult to imagine any widespread intensive agriculture of a type which has the potential to compete on world markets. Elsewhere there exist zones of first-rate agricultural land and plentiful water, like the Kenyan highlands or the Nile Valley. It is precisely because of their agricultural potential that these places are densely populated and, often, the scene of intense political competition to control their valuable resources. In such places intensive agricultural production for export is feasible in the right political environment. Each country needs to be viewed with an eye to its particular aptitudes, traditions and physical environment. On the other hand, even environmentally poor zones can produce for local or regional markets. For example, beef produced from cattle in Mali could supply the cities of Côte d'Ivoire, were it not displaced by subsidized beef exports from the European Union. Exports from North Africa depend crucially on access to European markets. Donor countries and governments must clearly address the opening of their own markets and their own trade policies if they are to contribute effectively to a revival of prosperity in Africa and the diversification of its export base.

In the meantime, some of the most enterprising and successful businessmen and businesswomen in Africa continue to see the main opening for making money in trade, sometimes in combination with industrial and agricultural production. If Ghana has become a nation of traders, as Ernest Aryeetey reports, the same is true of other parts of the continent where people buy and sell almost anything to survive. Much trade of this sort adds no value to a product and can hardly be seen as the leading edge of economic recovery. Many Senegalese, from a highly commercial culture but a mostly dry country, emigrate in search of work and to trade. Senegalese traders are to be found in central Africa, and, these days, throughout Europe, on the East Coast of the USA, and in East Asia. Senegalese trading syndicates are generally not structured in the formal Western manner but may be made up of members of an extended family or adepts of a single *marabout* or holy man. Powerful *marabouts* are also wealthy businessmen. Family firms have also proved themselves well adapted to business in some other cultures, and in certain respects are more flexible than more structured companies. In cases where individuals or family firms make significant profits in a branch of activity, it is instructive to look at where they invest their profits. More research is needed on this subject, not least because significant aspects of the African trading economy go unrecorded in either national accounts or World Bank figures.[25] Spheres in which African businesspeople show the most enterprise and have been the most successful in international markets include the re-export of manufactured goods from South-East Asia to North America. It has to be said that Nigerian middlemen have been conspicuously successful in the international heroin trade.[26] These all demonstrate the dynamism of at least some African businesspeople. No doubt some countries, given a more predictable business climate and confidence in public institutions, could attract investment in productive activity rather than trading or services.

## Africa in the World

We have suggested that African countries need to diversify their export base and to attract investment both from without and within, and that neither of these is likely to occur without their developing dependable public institutions. No matter what stimulation is offered from outside, this can only happen through internal action. Africa's international partners are looking anxiously, and often impatiently, for signs of such a development and may find encouragement in, for example, the democratization of South Africa, the revival of Uganda, the emancipation of women in Tunisia, and the sheer doggedness of the government of Ghana. Peace has come to Namibia, Ethiopia, Mozambique and Eritrea, and even Angola may be edging towards an end to armed conflict. However, the international community will need to continue to provide aid and loans for countries making such transitions until such time as they can diversify their export base. And here, as we have suggested, trade policy on the part of developed countries has a key role to play.

Meanwhile, it is quite feasible, although perhaps distasteful to contemplate, that groups in Africa with a history of involvement in such ventures as the pre-colonial slave trade may re-emerge in the major global smuggling trades of today. In view of the acute financial problems faced by African governments, it is perhaps not surprising to find evidence of officials in several countries colluding in such activities as illegal currency dealing or the laundering of money from the highly lucrative international drug trade.[27] Smuggling, after all, is one of the world's most profitable businesses. Nigeria, in addition to being a major base of narcotics smuggling, is a major oil smuggler. It is not fanciful to suppose that the accumulated expertise acquired over long periods in such activities can be used on a global scale in the future, quite possibly using the facilities afforded by the institutions of national sovereignty such as central banks, diplomatic passports and national legislation in such matters as offshore banking. Liberal investment codes facilitate the investment of funds of dubious origin in businesses such as hotels and casinos.

In fact the smuggling of products which are not themselves harmful, such as agricultural produce, oil, diamonds, consumer goods and so on, is already a main source

[25] Stephen Ellis & Janet MacGaffey, 'Research on sub-Saharan Africa's unrecorded international trade: some methodological and conceptual problems', *African Studies Review* and *Cahiers d'études africaines* (forthcoming).

[26] United States Department of State, Bureau for International Narcotics and Law Enforcement Affairs, *International Narcotics Control Strategy Report, March 1995* (Washington DC), pp. 435–8; Observatoire géopolitique des drogues, *État des drogues, drogue des États* (Hachette, Paris, 1994), esp. pp. 68–78.

[27] cf. Peter Truell & Larry Gurwin, *False Profits: the inside story of BCCI, the world's most corrupt financial empire* (Houghton Mifflin, Boston & New York, 1992), esp. pp. 161–3. In 1994, the press in Madagascar reported President Zafy as publicly suggesting the use of funds from such sources. There is evidence of central banks in several African countries being used for the laundering of criminal funds.

of income for many traders in Africa. While a considerable quantity of such smuggling is carried out by small-scale operators and farmers at the lower reaches of the informal economy, who understandably see nothing immoral in trading with relatives from whom they are separated by international borders,[28] operators who wish to work on a large scale without fear of arrest need to secure political protection, further entrenching the systems of patronage described in the first part of this essay. Hence not only does the outside world have a role to play in helping Africa's economic recovery, but it risks feeling the effects of an extension of the systems of informal trade and rent-seeking to the international level in the new context of globalized markets and money flows.

## The African state system and the question of frontiers

The system of political economy which exists in much of Africa is one of the main reasons why the frontiers of African countries assume such importance. They impose political constraints which can impede regional trade but which also provide situations from which those in positions of power can derive benefit, formally in the form of taxes on trade, or illegally in the form of rents from smuggling. Particularly sensitive, for example, are the borders between the French-speaking countries of West Africa with their 'hard' CFA franc, pegged to the French franc, and the floating or 'soft' currencies of the English-speaking countries of the region, and notably of the West African giant, Nigeria. Small states such as the Gambia and Benin owe their economic existence largely to their role as smuggling entrepots.[29] The significance of this aspect of African frontiers is enhanced by the fact that in many cases, as is well known, they cut across ethnic groups and long-standing systems of commercial exchange. In North Africa, Algeria and Morocco, and Libya and Chad, have had long-standing disputes over their borders.

Africa's national boundaries are still by and large the ones created in 1884–5 by the colonial powers and preserved tenaciously by modern African states. However, this state system is now under great pressure from a combination of factors, including massive population movements and trade liberalization. In many cases these pressures imply an erosion of the colonial boundaries and tend to emphasize the continuing importance of older commercial and political boundaries which are invisible on maps of Africa but which are the product of the continent's human and physical geography.

Tiébilé Dramé lists a number of examples of states which have come near to total collapse. Liberia and Somalia are examples of states which have effectively ceased to exist as organizations for the regulation of government. In several other cases – Sierra Leone, Sudan, Chad, Zaïre, Rwanda, Burundi – the crucial definition of the modern state seems to be in question, namely Weber's contention that the state is that organization which maintains a monopoly of legitimate violence in a defined territory. Where there is an advanced erosion of institutions of government, the result can be a frightening impulsion towards combinations of violence and long-distance trade in the form of raiding and predation. In Liberia for example, this takes the form of war-bands exporting diamonds, timber and other products across international borders and buying weapons in return, a process in which the country's international frontiers continue to play an important role in spite of the virtual absence of a functioning state. European, Middle Eastern and

---

[28] cf. Janet MacGaffey, *The Real Economy of Zaïre* (James Currey, London, and University of Pennsylvania Press, Philadelphia, PA, 1991), and other works by the same author.

[29] John O. Igue & Bio G. Soule, *L'État entrepôt au Bénin : commerce informel ou solution à la crise?* (Karthala, Paris, 1992).

Asian economic interests participate in this system.[30] Aid agencies which intervene to provide relief become sucked into the resultant *logique de guerre* by providing resources to be fought over.

A crucial field for the regulation and management of such pressures lies in emerging patterns of regional economic cooperation, the subject of much new thinking in recent years. Colin McCarthy describes how earlier economic integration schemes generally did not meet with success. Some were simply too ambitious in scope, while others have foundered on the interests vested in Africa's frontiers which were threatened by such measures as customs unions. He sees little prospect of instant solutions through yet more cooperation or integration arrangements. The most promising perspective, he suggests, probably lies in the field of piecemeal and gradual regional economic cooperation. However, progress remains dependent on a number of important qualifications, including the proviso that progress can come about only with the existence of strong (or, at least, effective) states, and that it will in any event require competitiveness in world markets.

Much of the new thinking on the widening of regional cooperation described by Colin McCarthy proposes the incorporation of both developed and developing economies, as in the North American Free Trade Area (NAFTA) or the Enterprise for the Americas Initiative. There has been little movement in Africa in this respect, other than through the Lomé agreement with the European Union, although Colin McCarthy sees potential for North African countries to link with the European Union and for South Africa to extend its relations to the countries of the Indian Ocean rim. Arrangements of this sort clearly require partnership between African and non-African actors and imply the opening of markets in the North, especially Europe, to exports from Africa. The Bretton Woods institutions also have an essential role to play in the encouragement of regional economic cooperation, a subject which received little attention in earlier structural adjustment programmes. Particularly important is France, which has such a long relationship with Africa. Colin McCarthy questions the future of the CFA franc zone, notwithstanding its past achievements. If, as many commentators believe,[31] part or all of the French-supported CFA currency zone is dismantled at some time in the quite near future, the consequences will certainly be of sufficient importance to require international attention. The major problems lie with the Central African CFA zone, where the possibilities sometimes debated include that of oil-rich Gabon leaving the CFA area in order to develop its own currency, which would probably do irreparable damage to the whole Central African zone. Such a measure would certainly destabilize existing frontiers. It would probably enhance the regional economic and political influence of Nigeria and Sudan, for example, and seriously threaten the fragile coherence of Chad and the Central African Republic.

## The role of the wider world

Several African states both inside and outside the CFA zone are largely dependent on foreign aid for their finances, as Nicolas van de Walle demonstrates, and their continued existence in their present form therefore depends to a large extent on the policies which international aid donors adopt in the future. It is by no means certain that aid will continue at present levels, particularly if Western governments and Western publics see

---

[30] William Reno, 'Foreign firms and the financing of Charles Taylor's NPFL', *Liberian Studies Journal*, XVIII, ii (1993), pp. 175–87.
[31] See Mitterand, a special number of *Politique africaine*, 58 (1995).

little interest in it, or at least unless they see it serving some effective purpose. In the past, aid was allocated in large part for political and strategic reasons, as official aid from the USA and some European powers tended to go in the first instance to Cold War allies. Although the Cold War has ended, this has not altogether eliminated political factors from the allocation of funds which are ostensibly intended for economic development. There are relatively new international actors in Africa, such as Iran or Japan, in whom some of Africa's older partners may see allies or enemies and whose presence may produce new political imperatives. Old-established communities of Lebanese, Indian and Pakistani traders have important political connections with their countries of origin. Some commentators see evidence of aid being channelled for geo-political reasons, as during the Cold War, but this time to governments claiming to be in the forefront of resistance to international Islamic fundamentalism.[32] Africans themselves will need to produce evidence of why aid needs to be continued. It should be noted that there exists in the West a body of opinion suggesting that aid is not in the long-term interest of African economies since it does not actually assist sustainable economic growth but only a variety of distortions. These and other factors have already contributed to the recent decline in foreign aid to most of Africa identified by Nicolas van de Walle. A network such as the Global Coalition for Africa provides a forum where the interested parties can deliberate on these matters.

The fact that Africans continue to travel and migrate on a large scale, as they always have done, is a vital factor in all of these equations. Chaloka Beyani examines critically the legislation governing such movements. Large numbers of people move regularly from city to country and vice versa, or are absent from their homes for long periods as labour migrants. This often involves crossing national frontiers, and even continental ones. Political strife has led millions of Africans to flee across borders as refugees, and millions more to find refuge as displaced persons within their own country: according to figures quoted by Tiébilé Dramé, there are over seven million refugees in Africa and the same number of internally displaced people. Whether they are voluntary or involuntary migrants, the numbers who are able to find employment and enjoy full civic rights in their new places of residence are small. Generally speaking, it is those with qualifications who find it easiest to prosper. An engineer or a doctor, for example, may find it relatively easy to migrate to the developed world: there are said to be some 100,000 highly qualified Africans who form part of the 'brain drain' and are living permanently in the industrialized world. Similarly, many seek to migrate from tropical Africa to South Africa. It is the poorer and less qualified people who are unwelcome in the developed world, which has its own unemployment problems to consider, and who are a burden on host countries inside Africa. All too often they are forced to live in demoralizing camps or reception centres in enforced idleness, dependent on international charity. Having crossed an international border, these people lose such rights of citizenship as they had in their country of origin. Chaloka Beyani's brief review of the relevant legislation reveals how little such refugees are actually protected.

Undoubtedly the most distressing and serious example of this at present is to be found in the Great Lakes region of Africa, where millions of people are moving between Rwanda, Burundi, Uganda, Tanzania and Zaïre as a result of economic hardship and political violence. So great is the need to protect these refugees that there is some talk in international diplomatic circles of creating a Hutu 'homeland' or protected zone,

---

[32] Roland Marchal, 'Le sud-Soudan à l'aube d'un nouveau drame humanitaire', *Bulletin du Centre d'Analyse et de prévision*, 61 (Ministry of Foreign Affairs, Paris, 1994–5), esp. pp. 115–16.

presumably like that designated in Iraq for the Kurds. Given the history of Rwanda and Burundi and the trauma of recent events, there appears no realistic hope that the refugees now in Zaïre, Tanzania and elsewhere will voluntarily return to Rwanda to be reintegrated into anything resembling a nation-state. It is more likely that they will remain outside Rwanda's frontiers and that some at least will use force to try to create a home either by fighting to retake control of Rwanda or by carving out for themselves a territory somewhere else. It could well be that no long-term solution to the upheavals in this area is possible without some fundamental adjustment to the state system of the region, possibly implying an imaginative redefinition of citizenship rights. The crisis in the Great Lakes region generally poses the most serious threat to Africa's state system certainly since the Biafran war of 1967–70 and perhaps even before that, especially as there are signs of countries both in the immediate region and elsewhere in Africa closing their borders to refugees, as Kenya has threatened to do with refugees from Somalia.

In spite of these pressures to create new political entities, no fundamental adjustment of Africa's state system seems likely. To support this point, it is sufficient simply to examine the possible mechanisms by which a change to Africa's recognized frontiers could come about. The OAU has made it an article of faith to protect existing frontiers and has been conspicuous by its failure to take effective action on Rwanda. Regional organizations have failed to find satisfactory solutions to the near-collapse of some states, such as the Economic Community of West African States (ECOWAS) in the case of Liberia. Both the OAU and ECOWAS are dominated explicitly by elites which have a vested interest in the existing state system and existing borders. The United Nations, for its part, is founded on the principle that it is an organization of sovereign states: it has no power to impose fundamental changes of this sort and, moreover, its earlier interventions in Somalia and Rwanda have clearly exposed many of the difficulties it faces in African crises. It is hard to see from what other quarter changes in international legislation could come if Burundian and Rwandan refugees were to be incorporated satisfactorily in some state or other. Non-state actors are not empowered to take decisions on matters of international law, although they can lobby their own governments.

International peace-keeping poses formidable logistical and financial problems in every continent and in any case can only provide a short-term solution to profound problems of this type.[33] No developed country seems willing to commit its own forces on a large scale to Africa for long periods, other than France, whose forces have helped guarantee the integrity of Chad for well over a decade. We have already noted the likelihood that France may reduce its commitment to Africa in the next few years. The French role in Rwanda in 1994, moreover, provoked severe criticism from within and outside France,[34] and the whole experience is hardly likely to encourage either the offer or the acceptance of French military intervention in situations of conflict in the future. Among the suggestions currently under international discussion is the establishment of an African intervention force. Some African armies, such as those of Ghana and Senegal, have long experience of international peace-keeping and acquired a good reputation for their role in Liberia, for example. Nevertheless there would be formidable financial problems, while African military contingents operating in their own region are as likely to become parties to conflict as they are to be peace-keepers, as the Nigerian role in Liberia has shown.

---

[33] Winrich Kühne, *Fragmenting States and the Need for Enlarged Peacekeeping* (Stiftung Wissenschaft und Politik, Ebenhausen, 1994).

[34] e.g. François-Xavier Verschave, *Complicité de génocide? La politique de la France au Rwanda* (La découverte, Paris, 1994).

Despite the deep crisis of the African state system, then, the present system is likely to endure for the foreseeable future if only because there is no obvious means of changing it. Meanwhile such factors as Africa's continuing high birth rate suggest that the continent's economic problems are likely to remain acute. One of the effects of colonization was, as one of Africa's most distinguished historians has pointed out, 'the establishment of some forty-eight new states [south of the Sahara] . . . in place of the existing innumerable lineage and clan groups, city-states, kingdoms, and empires without any fixed boundaries.'[35] The large-scale political units created by colonialism are likely to remain in some shape or form, not least because of the massive cities which have grown up in recent decades – Lagos, Kinshasa, Nairobi, Johannesburg-Pretoria, Cairo and other megalopolises with millions of inhabitants. These are permanent features of Africa and it is certain that they will remain centres of trade and commerce of various sorts. They are also formidable centres of political power. Whatever their system of government or the quality of governance, these great concentrations of population are likely to exercise sufficient political muscle to command the attention of aid donors and other international actors. The weaker states and the more remote areas, unable to foster much economic activity and quite possibly prey to insecurity, may continue to lose population to the great metropoles. These nodes of power are likely to become even more important. Moreover, if donors were to adopt a more strict conditionality, and to reward reforming states while refusing aid to non-reformers, it is likely to increase the preponderance of a handful of centres whose power and influence extend deep into political and commercial hinterlands, irrespective of formal frontiers.[36] Finally, it should be noted that even the increase of ethnicity as a political factor is not actually leading to pressures towards secession, but is chiefly a form of political mobilization used in contests for national power. Eritrea remains the only example of a successful secession. We may see the development of centres of power in the major cities which continue to be players on the international stage, while they simultaneously benefit from instability elsewhere in the continent and from forms of smuggling and predation which they are able to disavow on the grounds that these are occurring outside their frontiers, thus reproducing on an international level the straddling of formal/informal, legal/illegal positions. In which case, the sovereign institutions and the respect for international norms of legality and morality of those states which had a commanding position in such a system would be no more than facades.

In addition to Janine Aron's observations on the role aid donors and lenders could play in recognizing effective constitutional reform, Nicolas van de Walle specifically addresses the role of donors. His suggestions go broadly in the same sense as those of Janine Aron. He is sceptical about both the desirability and the likelihood of a 'Marshall Plan' for Africa, but does agree with the necessity for debt relief. Debt forgiveness in the case of the smaller African debtors would have little or no effect on world capital markets or on the creditworthiness of the international financial institutions.[37] He suggests giving no aid to states which show no interest in effective reform of their constitutions and their systems of governance, and giving aid only to the non-government sector

[35] A. Adu Boahen, *African Perspectives on Colonialism* (Johns Hopkins University Press, Baltimore and James Currey, London 1987), p. 95.

[36] For some penetrating ideas on the concepts of shifting frontiers, see André du Toit, *Understanding South African Political Violence: a new problematic?* (Discussion Paper 43, United Nations Research Institute for Social Development, Geneva, 1993).

[37] Percy Mistry, *Multilateral Debt: an emerging crisis?* (Fondad, The Hague, 1994); World Bank, *Reducing the Debt Burden of Poor Countries: a framework for action* (World Bank, Washington DC, 1994); Non-Aligned Group, *The Continuing Debt Crisis of the Developing Countries* (Non-Aligned Movement, no place given, 1994).

in such cases. He recommends continuing dialogue on macro-policy issues, and particular support for institutions, whether inside or outside government, which can aid the development of real constraints on arbitrary government, such as an independent judiciary. He also recommends aid to civil service reform and to centres able to develop the formulation of policy.

In any event, as Nicolas van de Walle also points out, policy conditionality has been relatively ineffective, and it is universally agreed that aid can play only a limited role in the best of circumstances. It is certainly within the power of Africans (not just, and not even primarily, governments, but also associations within society) to create more stable and effective states by encouraging the spread of citizenship and real power-sharing. And Africans alone can do this.

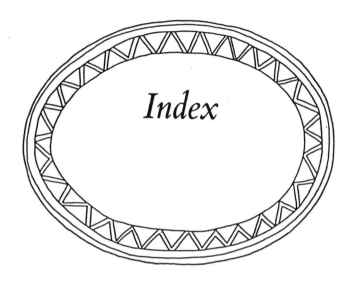

# Index